]   l

Theatre and Performance

Themes in Theatre
Collective Approaches to Theatre and Performance

2

Intermediality in Theatre and Performance

Edited by
Freda Chapple &
Chiel Kattenbelt

IFTR/FIRT
Theatre and Intermediality Working Group

Rodopi

Amsterdam - New York, NY 2006

Official Publication of the International Federation for Theatre Research/
Publication officielle de la Fédération Internationale pour la Recherche
Théâtrale

Layout: Ed Smet
Cover design: Pier Post

The paper on which this book is printed meets the requirements of "ISO
9706:1994, Information and documentation - Paper for documents -
Requirements for permanence".

Third edition: 2007
Second edition: 2006
ISBN: 978-90-420-1629-3
©Editions Rodopi B.V., Amsterdam - New York, NY 2006
Printed in the Netherlands

Contents

List of illustrations — page 7

Key Issues in Intermediality in theatre and performance — page 11
Freda Chapple and Chiel Kattenbelt

Section One: Performing intermediality — page 27

Theatre as the art of the performer and the stage of intermediality — page 29
Chiel Kattenbelt

The actor as intermedialist: remediation, appropriation, adaptation — page 41
Ralf Remshardt

Mise en scène, hypermediacy and the sensorium — page 55
Andy Lavender

Swann's way: video and theatre as an intermedial stage
for the representation of time — page 67
Sigrid Merx

Digital opera: intermediality, remediation and education — page 81
Freda Chapple

Section Two: Intermedial perceptions — page 101

Aesthetic art to aisthetic act: theatre, media, intermedial performance — page 103
Peter M. Boenisch

Audio theatre: the mediatization of theatrical space — page 117
Christopher B. Balme

Of other bodies: the intermedial gaze in theatre — page 125
Meike Wagner

New small screen spaces: a performative phenomenon? — page 137
Robin Nelson

Mediation unfinished: choreographing intermediality in contemporary
dance performance — page 151
Peter M. Boenisch

Section Three: From adaptation to intermediality — page 167

Theoretical approaches to theatre and film adaptation: a history — page 169
Thomas Kuchenbuch

The staging of writing: intermediality and the avant-garde — page 181
Klemens Gruber

Shadow of the Vampire: double takes on *Nosferatu* — page 195
Johan Callens

Modularity as a guiding principle of theatrical intermediality.
Me-Dea-Ex: an actual-virtual digital theatre project — page 207
Hadassa Shani

Hamlet and the virtual stage: Herbert Fritsch's project *hamlet_X* — page 223
Birgit Wiens

References — page 237

Indices — page 255

Notes on the contributors — page 263

List of Illustrations

Front cover –Proust 2: *Albertine's Way*, ro theater performance directed by Guy Cassiers (May 2003). Photo by Jaap Ruurs.

Figure 1 — page 21
Theatre as word, image and sound Freda Chapple and Chiel Kattenbelt
Figure 2 — page 21
Theatre and performance Freda Chapple and Chiel Kattenbelt
Figure 3 — page 23
Theatre, performance and technology: Live and mediatized / analogue and digital Freda Chapple and Chiel Kattenbelt
Figure 4 — page 24
Intermediality in theatre and performance Freda Chapple and Chiel Kattenbelt
Figure 5 — page 33
Theatre as the art of the performer Chiel Kattenbelt
Figure 6 — page 43
Joseph Jefferson III in his *Rip van Winkle* series (dir. W.L.K. Dickson, 1896), British Film Institute
Figure 7 — page 48
Sarah Bernhardt performing her death scene in *Les Amours de la Reine Elisabeth* (dir. Louis Mercanton, 1912), British Film Institute
Figure 8 — page 50
Eleonora Duse in *Cenere*, (dir. Febo Mari, 1916) British Film Institute
Figure 9 — page 57
Actual-fictional presence: *Jet Lag*: 'Part One: Roger Dearborn', presented by The Builders Association in collaboration with Diller + Scofidio. Photo by Tina Barney.
Figure 10 — page 60
The virtually distorted body: *D.A.V.E.*, presented by Klaus Obermaier and Chris Haring. Photo by Felix Noebauer.
Figure 11 — page 61
Multimedia *mise en scène: The Elephant Vanishes*, presented by Complicite in association with Setagaya Public Theatre. Photo by Joan Marcus.
Figure 12 — page 68
Proust 1: Swann's way: An example of the combination of the body of the actor and a video projection of his face in one stage image. Photo by Jaap Ruurs.
Figure 13 — page 68
Proust 1: Swann's way: The narrator Proust recalls his childhood. Memories of his parents appear as video images on the projection screen. Photo by Jaap Ruurs.
Figure 14 — page 73
Proust 1: Swann's way: The relationship of the young Marcel Proust with his parents is expressed in the play through the scale of the human body and the scale of the video projection. Photo by Jaap Ruurs
Figure 15 — page 74
Proust 1: Swann's way: An image of Odette, the mother of Gilberte, whose appearance mesmerises the young Marcel Proust. Photo by Jaap Ruurs.

Figure 16 — page 75

Proust 1: Swann's way: The salon of Madame Verdurin. The actors present themselves directly towards the video camera and the microphone. Photo by Jaap Ruurs.

Figure 17 — page 76

Proust 1: Swann's way: An example of text projection. The text says 'knocking on a door'. The action of the actor is replaced by the words, which have become an image. Photo by Jaap Ruurs.

Figure 18 — page 84

A moment of *immediacy* for Jennifer Westwood as Ladybird Begbick. *The Rise and Fall of the City of Mahagonny*, University of Sheffield 1999, Department of Music, Conductor Peter Hill, Director Freda Chapple. Photo by Ian M Spooner

Figure 19 — page 85

Hypermediacy in music, song, dance and *mise-en-scène*. *The Rise and Fall of the City of Mahagonny* University of Sheffield 1999, Department of Music, Conductor Peter Hill, Director Freda Chapple. Photo by Ian M Spooner.

Figure 20 — page 87

Remediation: The proletarian hero, sung by Martin Hindmarsh *The Rise and Fall of the City of Mahagonny* University of Sheffield 1999, Department of Music, Conductor Peter Hill, Director, Freda Chapple. Photo by Ian M Spooner.

Figures 21 and 22 — page 88

Competing ideologies *The Rise and Fall of the City of Mahagonny* University of Sheffield 1999, Department of Music, Conductor Peter Hill, Director, Freda Chapple. Photo by Ian M Spooner.

Figure 23 — page 93

Remediating operatic space. *The Forest Murmurs: adventures in the German Romantic Imagination*. Opera North, 2001, Conductor, Steven Sloane, Director, scenic design and original film, Tim Hopkins, Dramaturg, Meredith Oakes. Photo Stephen Vaughan.

Figure 24 — page 95

Lyric digital opera *The Forest Murmurs: adventures in the German Romantic Imagination*. Opera North, 2001, Conductor, Steven Sloane, Director, scenic design and original film, Tim Hopkins, Dramaturg, Meredith Oakes. Photo Stephen Vaughan.

Figure 25 — page 95

Framing the staging of the orchestra. *The Forest Murmurs: adventures in the German Romantic Imagination*. Opera North, 2001, Conductor, Steven Sloane, Director, scenic design and original film, Tim Hopkins, Dramaturg, Meredith Oakes. Photo Stephen Vaughan.

Figure 26 — page 96

Epic digital opera. *The Forest Murmurs: adventures in the German Romantic Imagination*. Opera North, 2001, Conductor, Steven Sloane, Director, scenic design and original film, Tim Hopkins, Dramaturg, Meredith Oakes. Photo Stephen Vaughan.

Figure 27 — page 98

Remediating the opera experience: digital opera *The Forest Murmurs: adventures in the German Romantic Imagination*. Opera North, 2001, Conductor, Steven Sloane, Director, scenic design and original film, Tim Hopkins, Dramaturg, Meredith Oakes. Photo Stephen Vaughan.

Figure 28 — page 125

Family Album, video print from *Máquina Hamlet*, El Périferico de Objectos, 1997

Figure 29 — page 134

Dismemberment of the writer, video print from *Máquina Hamlet*, El Périferico de Objectos, 1997

Figure 30 — page 154

Demediating the performer's body: Xavier Le Roy performs his *Self Unfinished* (1998). Photo by Katrin Schoof.

Figure 31 — page 157

Erasing the fixed perspective: The Merce Cunningham Dance Company, performing *Split Sides* (2004). Photo by Tony Dougherty.

Figure 32 — page 160

Transcoding movements: Christine Bürkle, Dana Caspersen, Helen Pickett, and Jacopo Godani (left to right) in front of the TV screen showing movie clips, in William Forsythe's *ALIE/NA(C)TION* (1993). Photo by Dominik Mentzos.

Figure 33 — page 164

Listening to the bodies as they write the dance: Sophie Lavigne, Guy Trifiro, Tanya White, and Mark Eden-Towie in Lynda Gaudreau's *Encyclopœdia: Document 3* (2002). Photo by Georg Anderhub.

Figure 34 — page 184

Man Ray, *La Ville*, 1931.

Man Ray, Köln: Könemann 1997, p. 76.

Figure 35 — page 185

Bragaglia, *Dattilografia*, 1911.

Anton Giulio Bragaglia, *Fotodinamismo futurista*, Torino: Einaudi 1970, fig. 13.

Figure 36 — page 185

Balla, Sketch for Macchina tipografica, 1914.

Photo: Museo Teatrale alla Scala, Mailand

Giovanni Lista, *Lo spettacolo futurista*, Firenze: Cantini, no year.

Figure 37 — page 186

Gerald Murphy, *Within the Quota*, Choreography by Jean Börlin, Paris 1923.

Photo: Atelier Sully.

Nancy Van Norman Baer, *Paris Modern. The Swedish Ballet 1920 - 1925*, San Francisco: Fine Arts Museums of San Francisco 1995, p. 121.

Figure 38 — page 187

Liubov Popova, *The Magnanimous Cuckold*, Moscow 1922.

Les voies de la création théatrale 7: Mises en scène années 20 et 30, Paris: CNRS 1979, p. 18.

Figure 39 — page 187

Ljubov Popova, Slogan for Meyerhold's *The Earth in Turmoil*, Moscow 1923.

Die Russische Avantgarde: Sammlung Costakis, ed. Angelica Zander Rudenstine, München: Haus der Kunst 1996, nr. 900.

Figure 40 — page 189

Aleksandr Rodchenko, Intertitle for Dziga Vertovs *Kinopravda*.

Von der Malerei zum Design. Russische konstruktivistische Kunst der Zwanziger Jahre, From Painting to Design: Russian Constructivist Art of the Twenties, Köln: Gmurzynska 1981, p.39.

Figure 41 — page 190

Dziga Vertov, *Man with the Movie Camera*, 1929.

Figure 42 and 43 — page 191
Subterranean Homesick Blues, 1965

Figure 44 — page 192
Desire which rules the world / Clinton, Starr, Ovid and Marcel Proust
News & Stories, dctp, Düsseldorf.

Figure 45 — page 192
It's all about a cultural organ
News & Stories, dctp, Düsseldorf.

Figure 46 — page 192
Prof. Detlef B. Linke, M.D., on the character of human brains and the metaphysics of the moving image.
News & Stories, dctp, Düsseldorf.

Figure 47 — page 212
Khaula Elhaj-Dibsi (Medea) on her wheelchair, with its control panel.

Figure 48 — page 212
Medea and spectators during a performance, the set is controlled through the screens with the projector lights dominating.

Figure 49 — page 227
hamlet_X, scene from the short film *The Crown*, featuring Martin Wuttke and Margarita Broich. © Volksbuehne am Rosa-Luxemburg-Platz Berlin

Figure 50 — page 228
hamlet_X screenshot from *Fight* – an inter-active online game.
© Volksbuehne am Rosa-Luxemburg-Platz Berlin

Figure 51 — page 228
hamlet_X screenshot from *Bloodhead: To be or not to be* – an interactive online game.
© Volksbuehne am Rosa-Luxemburg-Platz Berlin

Figure 52 — page 230
Photo from the *hamlet_X* night at the Prater, June 21, 2003 showing a user joining 'the chat'.
Photo K. Krottenthaler © Volksbuehne am Rosa-Luxemburg-Platz Berlin

Figure 53 — page 232
Photo of Prater exterior/Kastanienallee Berlin. Photo K. Krottenthaler © Volksbuehne am Rosa-Luxemburg-Platz Berlin

KEY ISSUES IN INTERMEDIALITY
IN THEATRE AND PERFORMANCE

Freda Chapple and Chiel Kattenbelt

Every good book needs a reason for writing – otherwise one should properly remain silent. This book is no exception to that rule. Our focus and central concern is *Theatre and Performance in the age of the Intermedial*. All the authors in this book approach the subject of intermediality from the perspective of theatre, and all the individual chapters in the book address the central research question: *What is Intermediality in theatre and performance?* The book is the result of a collective effort by the members of the Theatre and Intermediality Research Working Group within the International Federation for Theatre Research.[1] We have worked together for several years and have come to some conclusions about the nature of intermediality in theatre and performance that we would like to share. This is the reason for writing. We have some things to say that we hope the reader will find of interest, which may be at times provocative and at other times reassuringly familiar. As with all good books, we hope to take you into another reality – the reality of intellectual space and of the imagination. As with theatre, whether performing or observing, reality changes as we experience it and this is a central idea of our book: intermediality leads us into an arena and mental space that may best be described as *in-between realities*.

What is intermediality?

Intermediality is a dominant trend in the arts and media of the twentieth century (Albersmeier and Roloff 1989). In looking to define intermediality, our starting point is that a significant feature of contemporary theatre is the incorporation of digital technology into theatre practice, and the presence of other media within theatre productions. In turn, film, television and digital media reference theatre in a variety of ways. Therefore, a first assumption is that intermediality is associated with the blurring of generic boundaries, crossover and hybrid performances, intertextuality, intermediality, hypermediality and a self-conscious reflexivity that displays the devices of performance in performance. From here we can see that there is a need to assess how the incorporation of digital technologies and the presence of other media within the theatrical and performance space is creating new modes of representation; new dramaturgical strategies; new ways of structuring and staging words, images and sounds; new ways of positioning bodies in time and space; new ways of creating temporal and spatial interrelations. These new modes of representation are leading to new perceptions about theatre and performance and to generating new cultural, social and psychological meanings in performance. However, despite the apparent 'newness' of contemporary intermediality it is important to recognise the decisive role played by the historical avant-garde in establishing the necessary conditions for intermediality. This is pertinent insofar as intermediality is associated historically with the exchangeability of expressive means and aesthetic conventions between different art and media forms. The historical avant-garde achieved this through a playful staging of signs, which provided an aspect of *performativity* and a self-criticism of the arts and media (Bürger 1974).

In looking to identify and define the essence of intermediality in theatre and performance, we present a variety of interpretative strategies into research on theatre, performance and intermediality. Informed directly by theatre practice we place theatre and performance at the heart of the intermediality and 'new' media debate. Locating theatre and performance as the focal point from which we survey, receive and re-engage with the media of film, television and the digital technologies foregrounds the performance process as integral to the intermedial exchange. Although at first sight, intermediality might appear to be a technologically driven phenomenon it actually operates, at times, without any technology being present. Intermediality is about changes in theatre practice and thus about changing perceptions of performance, which become visible through the process of staging. We locate intermediality at a meeting point in-between the performers, the observers, and the confluence of media involved in a performance at a particular moment in time. The intermedial inhabits a space in-between the different realities that the performance creates and thus it becomes, at the minimum, a tripartite phenomenon. Intermediality is a powerful and potentially radical force, which operates in-between performer and audience; in-between theatre, performance and other media; and in-between realities – with theatre providing a staging space for the performance of intermediality. In addition, intermediality is positioned in-between several *conceptual frameworks* and *artistic/philosophical movements*. We see intermediality as part of a wider movement in which all postmodern arts and media are involved. Therefore, intermedial performance incorporates some, but not all of the features of postmodernism. Similarly, research into intermedial performances draws on some key areas of, but not the whole of contemporary theories about *performance, perception and media*. As the name of the research working group implies, intermedial researchers inhabit the *space of the in-between*. We put forward the proposition that intermediality in theatre and performance is about the process of how something that appears fixed becomes different, and our conceptual framework reflects the processes of change.

Our thesis is that the intermedial is a space where the boundaries soften – and we are in-between and within a mixing of spaces, media and realities. Thus, intermediality becomes a process of transformation of thoughts and processes where something different is formed through performance. In our concept of intermediality, we draw on the history of ideas to locate intermediality as a re-perception of the whole, which is re-constructed through performance.

Mapping the intermedial discourse

Intermediality is not a new concept and therefore it has a history. Different discourses about the relationships between the arts and media have taken place throughout the whole twentieth century. Of particular interest to film and literature scholars have been the 'classical film theories', which now might best be described as the 'pre-intermediality' debate, which ranged from *The Photoplay* (1916) by Hugo Münsterberg to *The Imaginary Signifier* (1977) by Christian Metz. In that debate it becomes clear how comparisons of film with theatre and the other arts played a significant role in defining the specificity of film and vice versa. In particular, how the French and Russian aesthetic film debates of the 1920s, helped to 'legitimise' film as a new art form, with its own 'material' principles of representation, construction and style.

The late 1980s onwards saw several collective editions published on intermediality written by art and media scholars working at the 'borderlines' of art (literature, visual arts, performing arts and music) and media studies. Led by Jürgen Müller, Joachim Paech, Franz Josef Albersmeier, Jörg Helbig and Karl Prümm this intermedial discourse is mainly a German debate with a focus on the inter-relationships and crossover movements between the arts and media. Christopher Balme and Jens Schröter have looked at the extensive debate and identified some trends in the different understandings of intermediality in the German discourse. In *Einführung in die Theaterwissenschaft* (second edition) Balme distinguishes three different understandings of intermediality. The first refers to the *transposition of subject matter* from one medium to another medium. The second is intermediality as a *specific form of intertextuality* and the third refers to intermediality as the *re-creation of aesthetic conventions* of one particular medium within a different medium (Balme 2001: 154-156). In his online article *Intermedialität*[2], Schröter distinguishes four types of discourses on intermediality. The first is *synthetic intermediality*, which refers to the fusion of different arts and media into new art or media forms. The second, based on the assumption that methods and modes of representation (aesthetic conventions) operate in several media is *formal and trans-medial intermediality*. The third is *transformational intermediality*, which refers to the representation of one medium in another medium. Here the reference becomes operative at the intermedial, as opposed to intertextual level. Transformational representations always have ontological implications because they assume an awareness of the ontology of the medium. Indeed, the reverse of transformational intermediality is *ontological intermediality*, which is the fourth type that Schröter distinguishes. This is where a medium defines its own ontology through relating itself to another medium, and raises the issue that it is not possible to define the specificity of a medium in isolation except through comparison with another medium. In this book, Thomas Kuchenbuch considers some of these debates in his chapter *Theoretical approaches to theatre and film adaptation: a history*. However, Klemens Gruber, in *The staging of writing: intermediality and the avant-garde* and Johan Callens in *Shadow of the vampire: double takes on Nosferatu* engage, in different ways, with the German discourse as points of reference from which they then move on to make their own contribution to our understanding of intermediality in theatre and performance. However, looking from an international and interdisciplinary perspective, there are some recent publications that individually draw on historical and cultural understandings of media relationships; the technical language of new media; and philosophical frameworks, which together form important *compass points* on our intermedial map.[3]

Remediation by Jay David Bolter and Richard Grusin (1999) is probably one of the most well known recent books on media relationships. It is set in a historical framework and explores the relationship of literature and art to the digital media in the context of visual culture. Although they argue that *remediation* existed as artistic practice as far back as the Renaissance, Bolter and Grusin regard it "as a defining characteristic of the new digital media" (1999: 45). They distinguish different forms of remediation, ranging from digitizing older media objects (photographs, paintings, printed literary texts) to absorbing an older medium entirely (ibid., 45-49). They suggest that remediation may operate also in different directions: new media may literally adopt and improve the methods of representation of previous media, but they can also change the methods of representation of the older media (for example, extending film and television through digital technology). The key concepts in *Remediation* are *immediacy, hypermediacy* and *transparency*. Immediacy or *transparent immediacy* aims at making the viewers forget the presence of the medium, so that they feel that they have direct access to the object. *Transparency* means that the viewer is no longer aware of the medium because the medium has – so to say – wiped out its traces. The opposite of immediacy is *hypermediacy*, which aims to remind the viewer of the medium by drawing attention to itself in a very deliberate way. According to Bolter and Grusin, immediacy and hypermediacy are two sides of the same coin, and operate, often simultaneously, to evoke an authentic *real* experience.

While we like the model, particularly the emphasis on *remediating realities* evoked by different media, what we notice is that Bolter and Grusin do not pay any attention to theatre – there is only a small reference to the corporeality of performance art as opposed to virtual reality. Thus, in our book, we address the omission with some enthusiasm, and we provide some of the missing elements. Several authors take up the immediacy/hypermediacy/remediation model and apply them to theatre and performance. Peter Boenisch explores remediation extensively as part of his chapter *Aesthetic art to aisthetic act: theatre, media, intermedial performance*, and it is reviewed by Thomas Kuchenbuch at the end of his historical overview. In *Mise en scène, hypermediacy and the sensorium* Andy Lavender uses the model to discuss *mise en scène* and the production of pleasure in contemporary mixed media theatre productions. Ralf Remshardt engages with remediation in his exploration of actors operating in silent cinema in *The actor as intermedialist: remediation, appropriation, adaptation*, and Freda Chapple discusses remediation as part of her exploration of contemporary opera in *Digital opera: intermediality, remediation and education*. However, Robin Nelson, working from the perspective of television and performance, uses the model to identify that these features situate the television viewer as both 'inside' and 'outside' the televisual experience, which leads the viewer to become involved in different acts of perception.

Thus, media theory, theories of perception and performance theory integrate to highlight the place that intermediality plays in the analysis of theatre and performance.

In *Liveness: performance in a mediatized culture* by Philip Auslander (1999) media theory and performance theory are at the centre of the book. This time theatre is included in the matrix but is not, we would argue, the focus of the debate. Indeed, theatre plays a relatively minor part in the book as a whole, apart from being seen as the traditionally accepted holder of the concept of *live performance*. However, there is an important section on the relationship of television to theatre, where the argument and literature explored is that early television modelled itself on theatre, as opposed to film, because both early television and theatre were acknowledged as *live media*. Auslander tells us that in this section, he employed the Bolter and Grusin model and his use of language reflects this:

> Vardac shows how film remediated theatre by adopting the narrative structures and visual strategies of nineteenth century melodrama. Whereas film could only remediate the theatre at these structural levels, television could remediate theatre at the ontological level through its claim to immediacy. It is also significant in this context that television not only remediates live performance, it remediates film in a way that film has never remediated television (Auslander 1999: 13).

As visual culture is the focus of *remediation*, so *mediatized culture* is the focus of the Auslander book, within which he sets theatre in opposition to and within the larger context of mass culture, and he remediates the *live/mediatized binary model* into *liveness*. He is quite clear that his target is the binary model of *live/mediatized*, which he wants to open up through "a critique of it by employing its terminology" (ibid., 3) because he finds the model reductive in today's cultural context, where there are many clear examples of the incursion of other media into theatre performances and vice versa. Auslander refers to Wurzler's definition as a summary of the live/mediatized debate:

> As socially and historically produced, the categories of the live and recorded are defined in a mutually exclusive relationship, in that the notion of the live is premised on the absence of recording and the defining factor of the recorded is the absence of the live (Wurtzler 1992: 89, cited in Auslander 1999: 3).

From this Auslander says that "a common assumption is that the live event is 'real' and that mediatized events are secondary and somehow artificial reproductions of the real" and that this kind of thinking "persists not only in culture at large but even in contemporary performance studies" (ibid., 3).

Working from a performance studies approach and including theatre, television, the performance event, popular culture and the giving of evidence in the American legal system within its remit, Auslander puts forward the proposition that theatre must recognise that it is only one element amongst many operating in a mediatized cultural system. In this system, financial and market dominance of the mass media denote success, and this position is set against those who are convinced of the special cultural and political significance of the live performance because of its authenticity and subversiveness. For those who regard the live performance as a refuge, in which it is still possible to offer some resistance to a cultural economy based in mediatization and reproduction (Fischer-Lichte 2001, 12, Peggy Phelan 1993) Auslander has little truck. Thus, he raises the spectre that an all-embracing mediatization and reproduction has the *live performance* in its grasp. He argues that this includes not only large-scale events like sporting events and Broadway shows, which are, moreover, produced for television, but also small-scale theatre performances which would be guided increasingly by models of television and other mediatized cultural formats. A point of difference (but still a connecting point) for us is Auslander's use of the term *mediatized*, which he acknowledges he borrowed from Baudrillard and employs:

> somewhat loosely, to indicate that a particular cultural object is a product of the mass media or of media technology. "Mediatized performance" is performance that is circulated on television, as audio or video recordings, and in other forms in technologies of reproduction. Baudrillard's own definition is more expansive: "What is mediatized is not what comes off the daily press, out of the tube or on the radio: it is what is reinterpreted by the sign form, articulated into models and administered by the code" (1981: 175-6, cited in Auslander: 5).

As will become clear, this book prefers the Baudrillard model, which is not to deny the cultural and economic factors in the Auslander debate but rather to ground it, if one can say that of Baudrillard's *simulacrum*, differently.

The third connecting point with Auslander is that of definition of *live performance*, which he argues was invented only in order to define theatre in response to the arrival of film and then again with the arrival of television, video and the digital media. The Greeks, he suggests, did not go to see 'live theatre' but to the theatre and he has a point here. He claims, we have no reason to disbelieve him, that theatre and performance is important to him, and that live performance (not theatre) remains powerful. To demonstrate how firmly ingrained the power of the live voice is in contemporary culture generally, he cites a student essay on internet romance as his conclusion to chapter two:

> [I] have a constant low-grade fear of the telephone, and I often call people with the intention of getting their answering machines. There is something about the live voice that I have come to find unnervingly organic, as volatile as live television (Daum 1997: 80 cited in Auslander: 60).

However, rather than taking the route of the Auslander conclusion on the student comments, which relate to the cultural power and prestige of owning videos of stage performances of what were once films, this book is more likely to give a cheer that the live voice can still provoke emotion – even one of fear. That the student seems confused between the 'live' of television and the (not actually live but mediatized) voice on the telephone, confirms the need for an approach that includes understanding of the materiality of media and their codes. Mediality and perception are linked inextricably to each other (Fischer–Lichte 2001, 13–14) and – as will be argued in several contributions to this book – it is important to distinguish performances according to their materiality and mediality because these two aspects are, in the end and in many ways, decisive for how performances are perceived.

Auslander's contribution is an important point of reference, not least because of the matrix of media/performance theory within the cultural studies paradigm. The *live performance* must be central to any book that is examining intermediality in theatre and performance, which is why it is explored first in Chiel Kattenbelt's chapter *Theatre as the art of the performer and the stage of intermediality*. However, our position is different to that of Auslander, in that our research indicates a sharper focus on the perception of the audience is required also. This we explore through Peter Boenisch in *Aesthetic art to aisthetic act: theatre, media, intermedial performance;* and *Mediation unfinished: choreographing intermediality in contemporary dance performance;* Meike Wagner in *Of other bodies: the intermedial gaze in theatre;* Robin Nelson *New small screen spaces: a performative phenomenon?* and Christopher Balme in *Audio theatre: the mediatization of theatrical space.*

The structure and language of the digital media, which we believe is so important to contemporary theatre and performance in the age of the intermedial is the clear focus of *The Language of New Media* (2001) by Lev Manovich[4], who is a computer programmer and designer, new media artist, animator and theorist. The research centre *mediawork*[5] to which Manovich has contributed concentrates on the relationship between visual arts, music, science and technology.

Manovich characterises the two principles of digital media as *numerical representation* and *modular structure*: from these two principles flow *automation, variability* and *transcoding*. Digital coding (the numerical representation of a new media object) has two separate elements: it is represented mathematically and is subject to *algorithmic manipulation*. Thus, it becomes *programmable* (Manovich: 27). Created on the computer, a new media object originates in mathematical form, but if it is converted from old media, for example, a photograph that is scanned into a computer, then the process of conversion is called *digitization*. This is a two-step process: first the image is sampled and then it is quantified (ibid., 28). Crucially, the process of digitization turns old media from continuous linear data into discrete data units. What is important about this is that each unit must be separate from other units – actually as well as conceptually – there must be a gap *in-between the units* even if that gap is not perceptible to the human eye. Manovich goes on to explain:

> [...] a new media object has the same modular structure throughout. Media elements, be they images, sounds, shapes, or behaviors, are represented as collections of discrete samples (pixels, polygons, voxels, characters, scripts). These elements are assembled into larger-scale objects but continue to maintain their separate identities. The objects themselves can be combined into even larger objects - again, without losing their independence. (Ibid., 30)

It is because of the modular structure of digital media objects that they can easily be changed by deleting, substituting and adding individual media elements. Unlike analogue media structures, which are fixed entities, digital media objects are not fixed because their structure is numerical coding + modular structure.

When theatre productions include digital technology an additional coding becomes present on the stage and is framed by the performance. Because digital media objects have a different ontology from non-digital media objects on the stage, so there is an empirical and qualitative difference between the digital and non-digital objects operative in the stage space. Thus, digitization plays a part in conceptualising the changing space of theatre performance. It creates junction points where the different media meet and it is there – at the point of their meeting – that we locate intermediality in theatre and performance, which in turn triggers a response in the observer.

A crucial element of digital media structures is *hypermedia*. In the computer, the multi-media elements connect through *hyperlinks* and, by following the hyperlinks, each individual user creates their own *navigation path* through a text and retrieves different versions of it. This leads Manovich to argue that the logic of the digital media corresponds to the logic of the post-industrial society, [...] "which values individuality [individual customization] over conformity [mass standardization]" (ibid., 41). We agree with him and Hadassa Shani explores this area in *Modularity as a guiding principle of theatrical intermediality Me-Dea-Ex: an actual-virtual digital theatre project*. Similarly, Birgit Wiens explores this and other related digital concepts in *Hamlet and the virtual stage: Herbert Fritsch's project hamlet_X*. Both Shani and Wiens explore inter-active technology as part of the theatrical process and the mental process that hyperlinks provoke in the minds of the audience. Others authors who utilise the concept of different pathways taken by the audience through a hypermedial text in theatre performances are Chapple (contemporary opera performance) and Boenisch (contemporary dance choreography).

Manovich provides also a useful conceptual model by identifying a *layering* within the *principles of digitisation*, which we relate to our theoretical model of intermediality in theatre and performance (see next section). The first layer in digital media is the material layer: *numerical coding + modular organization*. The second layer is *automation and variability*, which includes useful features such as hypermedia. However, the third layer is *transcoding*, which refers to the *layering of activities* between computer behaviour and human understanding. At the first layer of number + module, the computer works according to a "Cartesian co-ordinate system". At the level of *image representation*, the new media image has a 'dialogue' between the human user and the computer programming (cosmogony). At the level of *the new media*, there is an interface between the *cultural logic of media* and the *cultural logic of the computer* (ways of representing the world and thus of our understanding of reality). In addition, Manovich makes the point that:

> Because new media is created on computers, is distributed via computers, stored and archived on computers, so the logic of a computer can be expected to significantly influence the cultural logic of media. i.e. we may expect that the computer layer will affect the cultural layer (ibid., 46).

This pertains directly to intermediality in theatre and performance because, as Manovich points out, computers now have become *media machines*, (ironically, more like old media on the surface). However, the computer layer and the cultural layer are now being *composited* together, with the result that there is a new computer culture that is a *blend* of human and computer meanings – of traditional ways in which culture modelled the world and the computer's control over our ways of representing it (ibid., 46).

Clearly, Manovich posits an interactive model between human activity, and activity generated by computer programming. This seems to us to generate a space in-between several realities: in-between the computer-generated representation of the world, and the human user input to that computer-generated representation of the world. Theatre, as a hypermedium offers a staging space where such realities in-between performer, computer-generated realities and the audience perception of those realities is realised in performance.

Thus, the importance of the underlying structures of the digital to intermediality in theatre and performance becomes clear. The unseen elements of computer-generated texts await activation in the live performance. It is not too difficult to see why this type of structure appeals to contemporary avant-garde theatre. There is a real radical force waiting to be unleashed here, which is not dependent only on the mechanisms of the digital, but also on the underlying thought processes.

This brings us now to the importance of philosophical reflection to our concept of intermediality in theatre and performance. In particular to the concept of the rhizome as put forward by the French philosophers Gilles Deleuze and Felix Guattari in *A Thousand Plateaus: Capitalism and Schizophrenia* (1989). Although not such a new concept anymore, it still epitomizes the move from nineteenth century theatre based on dramatic representation, to the more conceptual post-dramatic theatre (Hans-Thies Lehmann 1999). The rhizome acts as an over-arching experience of intermediality in theatre and performance. The key point about the structure of the rhizome is that it is made of materials that seem, on the surface, not to have any logical reason to be together. The materials keep their own constituent elements and it is only by linking them to other elements that their purpose becomes a little clearer. However, it is never possible to stand back and view the whole structure because we are all in it, and operative within it – in the rhizome we operate in the sensual spaces in-between media. Thus, philosophy enters the intermedial stage and the concept of the rhizome seems to us to be a particularly useful way of thinking about contemporary intermediality in theatre and performance, where theatre is a hypermedium for all the different separate elements awaiting the activating and organising mind and body of the perceiver. The work of Deleuze is of particular importance to the theatre production of Guy Cassiers, as described by Sigrid Merx in *Swann's way: video and theatre as an intermedial stage for the representation of time*. However, in his essay *Sens(a)ble Intermediality and Interesse: Towards an Ontology of the In-Between* (2003), the Dutch philosopher Henk Oosterling relates the concept of intermediality to:

> the features of an artistic multimedial and interdisciplinary creativity [...] to the production of a (micro)political sensibility and to the application of an innovative philosophical conceptuality and interactivity. Intermediality [...] reconfigures arts, politics and science, especially philosophy, enhancing an experience of the in-between and a sensibility for tensional differences. [...] In the crossovers between arts, politics and science/philosophy new fields of research have constituted (Oosterling 2003: 30).

Although the group was not aware of Oosterling's work at the time of our research project, while editing this book we became aware that many of the chapters resonate with his thoughts as will become clear. Now, however, we turn from the work of other authors and their conceptual frameworks to present our own thesis on intermediality in theatre and performance.

Intermediality in theatre and performance

Working from the parameters of the intermedial discourse to date, we propose that intermediality includes within its constituent elements a blend of the art forms of theatre, film, television and digital media, which lead to an engagement with theoretical frameworks drawn from selected areas of performance, perception and media theories, and philosophical approaches to performance. We present now how we built to our concept of intermediality in theatre and performance: the conceptual framework and the limits of our investigation. In this section, we position ourselves in the intermedial debate and integrate key aspects of performance, perception and medial theoretical frameworks into a philosophical approach to intermediality in theatre and performance. There are two principles that underpin our conceptual framework, which in turn provide the form and structure of this book.

The first principle is that theatre is a hypermedium that incorporates all arts and media and is the stage of intermediality. This is explored first by Chiel Kattenbelt in his chapter, *Theatre as the art of the performer and the stage of intermediality* and then by the chapters that come in that section. The second principle is that intermediality is an effect performed in-between mediality, supplying multiple perspectives and foregrounding the making of meaning by the receivers of the performance. This is explored first by Peter Boenisch, in *Aesthetic art to aisthetic act: theatre, media, intermedial performance* and then by the chapters that come in that section. The third section of the book assesses first the contested history of theatre / film adaptation, the classical film debate, and then the turn to the new intermedial theoretical base of modularity, inter-activity and a self-reflexive process appropriate to postmodern theatre and visual performance culture.

Theatre

We use theatre as a collective term for all *live performing arts*, which implies that the performer and the spectator are simultaneously physically present in the same space. However, we recognise and specify that within this collective term for theatre there are different kinds of theatre that have their own ontologies, texts, narratives, genres and histories. One way to keep the ontology of the different art forms clear, but also to recognize that that they share the relationship of performer and spectator being present at the same time, and in the same space is to employ the semiotic code, and to define theatre on the sign systems of sound, image and word:

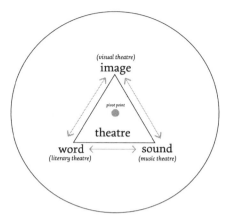

Figure 1
Theatre as word, image and sound

In Figure 1, we attempt to indicate the intermedial process through the pivot point and the arrows in the diagram. As the pivot rotates (and we ask that the reader use their imagnation here!) the particular intermedial aspect of the performers and the performance come into focus. At the first level of interpetation, intermediality is located (1) in-between visual theatre, literary theatre and music theatre, each of which is itself intermedial; (2) in-between the mediality of the performers and the mediality of the art forms; (3) in-between the performers and receivers of the performance. Thus, intermediality is not reliant on technology but on the inter-action between performance and perception.

Theatre and performance

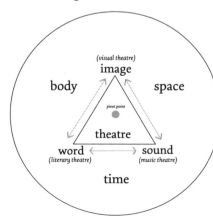

Figure 2
Theatre and performance

Figure 2 demonstrates the relationship between the semiotic coding of theatre to the concepts of body / space / time. The 'original' remains in place but may not be so visible in post-dramatic theatre, which moved away from the dominance of the text and reliance on *character driven action* operative in linear time and space.

In response to and as part of the changes to theatre during the twentieth century, performance-based concepts evolved, partly in order to refer to forms of theatre that go beyond the limitations of the dramatic representation of actions and characters. In 1997, Umberto Eco described a performance or a performative situation in terms of the *act of showing* (ostention) in the literal sense of the word regardless as to whether the performance takes place in a theatre building or elsewhere – objects/bodies, events and actions become *signs of signs*. Performance-related concepts form an important part of an intermedial approach because of their ability to move across traditionally ascribed disciplines and art forms. Recognition of the textual, the semiotic and the performative models in the same space, irrespective of whether or not one model or the other is dominant in a particular performance, is an important part of intermediality.

In post-dramatic theatre, manipulation of space and time is often, but not always, accomplished through other media operating 'as performers' in the performance space. Traces of text-based theatre and the more conceptually based post-dramatic theatre become a tangible intermedial force operative on the hypermedial stage. One consequence of this is that neither can assume authority over the other. The arrival of the post-structuralist debate opens for intermedial analysis the gaps and fissures *in-between* the texts, the signs, and the performance, and provides a location for intermedial discourse through the body and mind of the performer and receiver. Very much part of the post-structuralist debate, performance theory posits that the actor's body is a medium, and given that theatre needs the audience to complete its raison d'être, so too are the bodies of those observing. Between the bodies and minds of the audience, and the bodies and minds of the performer(s) is a medial exchange that is bigger than any technologically produced media may achieve.

We argue that the staging of intermediality activates a change of perception in the mind of the receiver to the constructions of class, race and gender, which we might refer to constructions of reality in the social and psychological reality of this world. However, it seems also to refer to *perceptions of reality* beyond the seen and into abstractions that impact on the body of the receiver. Forming an important part of our conceptual framework, this approach is explored in particular by Meike Wagner in *Of other bodies: the intermedial gaze in theatre* who adopts a phenomenological approach to intermediality. Here she concentrates on the materiality and immateriality of puppet theatre and its performers. Others who include this approach are Andy Lavender in *Mise en scène, hypermediacy and the sensorium* and Robin Nelson in *New small screen spaces: a performative phenomenon?*

Theatre, performance and technology: Live and mediatized, analogue and digital

We define live performance as the simultaneous physical presence of the performer and the spectator in the same space in the moment of here and now. However, we define *mediatized* representation as utilizing recording and playback technologies (or at least assume the intervention of a technological transmission device); no matter whether what is recorded is played back at (nearly) the same time or at a later moment. Mediatized is not the same as *mediated*, because all forms of communication are mediated by signs, but not mediatized by technology. In the strict sense, it is generally accepted that live and mediatized stand for a binary opposition: live means "absence of recording" and mediatized means "absence of live". However, often the concept "live" is used in a broader sense, namely for audiovisual media as far as the recording and playing back are taking place at the same time, that is to say without a perceivable time difference. In this broader sense, television and video can be live. In the case of live television, the performer and spectator are separated in space but not in time.

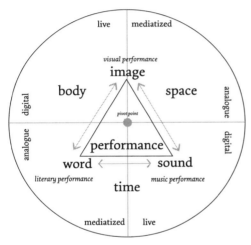

Figure 3
Theatre, performance and technology:
Live and mediatized / analogue and digital

Within the live/mediatized debate, we make a further distinction between *analogue* and *digital*. However, as Figure 3 indicates, as the live/mediatized categories do not always operate as distinct binary oppositions, so similar problems arise with the analogue/digital divide. For example, in her chapter on Cassiers' work, which makes extensive use of digital video and digital video cameras during the action of the performance, Merx demonstrates that there is a difference technologically between analogue and digital. However, the question remains as to whether the audience responds to an unseen technical different, or to the aesthetics of the images presented. Thus, we see that intermediality operates in the spaces where the strict formal boundaries become blurred. What is true is that the digital technology provides yet another coding system to share the space, and we see again the relationships between sign systems changing. In particular, we note that digitization changes theatre into a modular non-hierarchical inter-active non-linear process, where there is a layering of meanings present in the same space at the same time. This leads us into the world of many meanings, where we are uncertain as to the location of the referent and we are in a world of signs and media, which refer to signs, which refer to other signs – all of which are staged and framed by the performance.

Intermediality in theatre and performance

Here we see that theatre has become a *hypermedium* and home to all. It provides a space where the art forms of theatre, opera and dance meet, interact and integrate with the media of cinema, television, video and the new technologies; creating profusions of texts, inter-texts, inter-media and spaces in-between. It is in the intersections and the spaces in-between the intersections that we locate intermediality. Our model places theatre and performance at the heart of the new media debate, and locates intermediality at a meeting point in-between the performers, the observers, and the confluence of media involved in a performance at a particular moment in time, with theatre providing the staging space of intermediality.

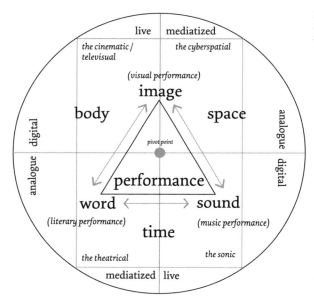

Figure 4
Intermediality in theatre and performance

In today's world, we all inhabit the intermedial – we are surrounded by newspapers, films, television. We live in-between the arts and media – intermediality is the modern way to experience life. Therefore, presented in chapters that follow are different understandings about *realities* and the place that creativity in theatre and performance plays in creating those realities. *Reality*, and inhabiting the spaces in-between realities is the proper subject for a philosophical approach to intermedial performance, which may help us also to perceive who we are in the 'real' world. It is an intermedial activity. Certainly, our concept of intermediality in theatre and performance is of a creative arena and mental space that operates in-between the arts, politics, science and philosophy. Intermediality is the whole recreated in performance: it is an everyday life experience of reality. This seems to us to be particularly appropriate to the twenty-first century, where we inhabit a world of the intermedial, within which we perform our lives and attempt to come to some understanding about our own reality.

Notes

[1] International Federation for Theatre Research: www.iftr-firt.org/firt/home.jsp

[2] www.theorie-der-medien.de (accessed 27/9/2005).

[3] We are aware that in some parts of the United States of America, there is a quite specific and different understanding of intermediality within media education. In this domain, the concept refers to media literacy and to the use of audiovisual media (technologies) in educative contexts. However, this approach is not central to our investigation.

[4] www.manovich.net (accessed 27/9/2005).

[5] Lev Manovich contributed to *The Digital Dialectic* (1999) Peter Lunenfeld, (ed.), which grew out of a conference on the convergence of technology, media and theory held in Pasadena 1995. Other notable contributors to *The Digital Dialectic* are George P.Landow and Brenda Laurel. The book is an extension of The South California New Media Working Group, *mediawork* founded by Peter Lunenfeld.

SECTION ONE
PERFORMING INTERMEDIALITY

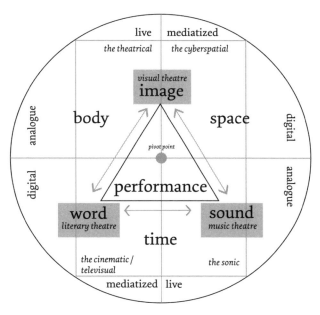

The chapters in this section share a focus on the performers in an intermedial performance situation, and the directors and theatre companies who produce multimedial and intermedial performances. They include an exploration of the experience of theatre actors moving to work in early cinema and performers talking about singing in music theatre. The way that the new technologies and multimedia performances remediate theatre space and time through manipulation of words, sounds and images is another theme that several of the chapters in this section explore. The effect of the manipulation of theatre space in intermedial productions on performers and audiences is the third theme that brings this section of the book together as a group. However, in common with the other sections, the chapters here resonate with themes and explorations in the other two sections.

THEATRE AS THE ART OF THE PERFORMER
AND THE STAGE OF INTERMEDIALITY

Chiel Kattenbelt

This chapter locates theatre as the stage of intermediality as a natural conclusion to the history of ideas about theatre. Set within the context of philosophical debate on theatre, the author questions first whether theatre is a secondary or composite art, or a primary and 'autonomous' art like literature, visual arts and music. Discussed with reference to the three most important representatives of German Idealism: Immanuel Kant, Georg Hegel and Arthur Schopenhauer, and explored further though Richard Wagner, Wassily Kandinsky and Jan Mukarovsky, the author argues that theatre is the paradigm of all arts, and a hypermedium that incorporates all arts and media. From this position, he moves to argue that theatre is the art of the performer and the art of presence. In order to clarify this assumption, the author compares theatre to film, which he regards as the medium of absence that hides its own mediality in accordance with the functioning of modern technology. Through an examination of theatre in the era of the device paradigm, the author assesses how film has taken over the function of theatre as dramatic art. However, rather than lamenting this fact, the author argues that the logical conclusion must be to re-define theatre: not as a composite art, nor as a dramatic art, but as the stage of intermediality.

Theatre as paradigm of the arts and hypermedium

There is a long tradition of thinking about theatre as a secondary, or 'composite' art as opposed to a primary, or 'autonomous' art like literature, visual arts and music. In the philosophical debate about the arts in the eighteenth and nineteenth century, the question about how the different primary arts related to one another played an important role in determining systematically the different expressions of the creative faculties of the human being.

  In 1798, Kant put forward his idea that words, images and sounds were the *ideal typical* or pure expressions of our experiences in thoughts (Gedanken) and intuitions (Anschauungen), which he subdivided into sensuous intuitions (Sinnesanschauungen) and sensations (Empfindungen). Kant considered *poetry* (Dichtkunst) as the highest art, because it was "the art of conducting the free play of imagination" (Einbildungskraft), which constituted the synthesis of thoughts and intuitions (Kant 1986: 257). Hegel, however, writing in 1842, suggested that *drama* (as in the dramatic text) was the highest art, because it constituted the synthesis of the subjectivity of *the lyric* and the objectivity of *the epic*. To be more precise, Hegel defined *theatre* as the highest art, because it is in the theatre performance only that the drama finds its completion through direct presence in action:

> The actual sense material of dramatic poetry is [...] not only the human voice
> and the spoken word, but the whole human being, who not only expresses
> sensations (Empfindungen), sensuous intuitions (Vorstellungen) and thoughts
> (Gedanken), but who also, being involved in a specific action, according to
> his total existence, affects the sensuous intuitions, intentions, actions and
> behaviour of others and who experiences similar reactions or defies these.
> (Hegel 1976: 535–536 – my translation).

From this, we see that Hegel's concept of theatre foregrounded the direct contact and mutual influence between the human bodies of the performers and spectators, and concerned primarily the art of the actor (Schauspielerkunst). However, in 1820, Arthur Schopenhauer argued that *music* was the highest art because he considered music as the most direct expression of the human 'will' to live (Urwille) (Schopenhauer 1988: 214–228).

Given this context, it is not surprising that in 1850, Richard Wagner defined poetry, dance and music as the three basic arts. He considered them as the natural expressive faculties of the human being and located them in the form of Greek *tragedy*, which represented in an almost ideal way the *harmony* of art within society. Wagner deplored the fragmentation of the Greek tragedy into individual components: rhetorics, sculpture and music, which occurred after the Greek polis declined, undermined largely through the position of slaves in the society, and at a time when art could no longer claim to be the expression of common consciousness (Gemeingeist).

Wagner wanted to revive the unity of the arts of Greek tragedy and conceived his idea of the *Gesamtkunstwerk*, "the artwork of the future" as he called it. He defined music as the heart (rhythm) that reconnects the head (poetry) and the body (dance) with each other. In the *Gesamtkunstwerk*, based on the logic that they derive from nature, rather than mankind, painting, sculpture and architecture only fulfil a supportive function. Wagner's ideas were, and still are for many artists from different disciplines, an important source of inspiration for crossing the borders between the individual arts: to re-integrate them in a new total artwork. Wagner's idea of the *Gesamtkunstwerk* as an autonomous *Totalkunstwerk* related very much to the striving for perfect illusion. In Wagner's Festspielhaus in Bayreuth, which opened in 1876, the orchestra pit is partially under the stage and hidden from the view of the audience by panels. Total immersion into the world that the performance represented was the aim – with nothing obscuring their view, the audience sat in the dark and watched an apparently real representation of the world. Ironically, this ideal and effect is realized in the Hollywood film where camera operation and editing are made invisible (completely motivated by an action-driven dramaturgy) to such an extent, that the represented world is accessible for the spectators without any interference. It is a pleasing flight of fancy to think that if Wagner had lived in the twentieth century he might have gone to Hollywood. Here he might have become an extremely successful film music composer, or an 'all-round' film director, pulling all the strings.

At the beginning of the twentieth century, a major revision of Wagner's ideas began. Wassily Kandinsky (1973b: 49-61, 79-83) observed in his essays *Über*

Bühnenkomposition [1912] and *Über die abstrakte Bühnensynthese* [1923] the decline of the theatre in its then 'old' forms. Kandinsky said that drama, opera and ballet were petrified into *museumforms*, which had lost their pulsating forces. He declared that the theatre needed a new form in which the individual arts, as developed over many decades according to their own rules of individual languages, be brought together. However, this time in their *pure forms* as *equivalent elements of colours, sounds and movements*:

> The theatre has a hidden magnet, which has the power to attract all these languages, all means of the arts, which together offers the highest possibility of monumental abstract art (Kandinsky 1973b: 80 – my translation).

We may notice a fundamental difference between Wagner's idea of the opera as *Gesamtkunstwerk* and Kandinsky's idea of the *Bühnenkomposition* as *monumental art*. In his operas, or music dramas as he called them, Wagner strove for a reunification and integration of the individual arts – in particular music, poetry and dance – under the primacy of music. The aim of his *artworks of the future* is referential illusion, that is to say the representation of a dramatic world in such a way that this world seems to exist on its own. However, Kandinsky considers the differentiation and autonomisation of the individual arts as a necessary condition for the arts to reach in the development of their own languages a pureness of expression.[1] According to Kandinsky, the specificity of theatre is its hidden magnetic power, which it derives from the fact that it provides a stage on which a dynamic play of pure expressive forms occurs as a representation of inner experiences – of the intensity of the "vibrations of the soul". Wagner's *Gesamtkunstwerk* is guided still by a dramatic mode of representation, despite the leading role of music as a synthesizing force that connects the head to the body; whereas Kandinsky's *monumental art* is pre-eminently guided by a lyrical mode of representation, by musical, pictorial and choreographed movements (Kandinsky 1973a: 125).

In a striking contrast to Kandinsky, and writing as part of the Prague linguistic circle, Jan Mukarovsky argued against the idea of theatre as a composition of autonomous primary arts. He thought that as components of a theatre performance, the individual arts lost their autonomy, and became a new art. Following Ortakar Zich, Mukarovsky considered the theatre performance as [...] "a dynamic combined play of all its components, [...] as a unity of forces as well as a whole of signs and meanings" (Mukarovsky 1975: 78 – my translation). Theatre performance was a hierarchical structure that consisted indeed of individual elements, but was more than just the elements. He defined the performance as a *Gestalt*: that is, more than the sum of its parts. Thus, all the elements of performance contain an aspect of the whole in them because they are determined primarily within the coherence of their mutual relationships. To put it differently, the theatre performance is a *contexture* (a weaving of strands together to create a texture) as opposed to a *composition* of individual elements. We understand their mutual relationships in terms of correlation and integration, as opposed to terms of equivalence of supplementation. According to Mukarovsky, the constituting components of a theatre performance are so closely related to one another, that it is difficult sometimes to distinguish them

31

from each other. However, if this is the case, then what is the distinctive feature that determines theatre as an autonomous art? Mukarovsky's answer to this question was quite radical: it is not possible to define theatre through its constituent components because none of them is decisive for defining theatre. Not even the art of acting or directing, although they relate to theatre very much. This is why theatre occurs in such an enormous variety and diversity of appearances.

For Mukarovsky, the *essence* of theatre was that it occurs [...] "in a changing tie of continuously rearranging immaterial relationships" (Mukarovsky 1975: 84 - my translation). Ultimately, the consequence of Mukarovsky's definition is that no specific theatre form or performance is a complete realisation of the theatre's essence. The consequence of this is that as soon as two or more specific arts connect to one another in the same artwork, they step over and overstep their constitutive moments. It is inevitable that, to a certain extent, they lose their specificity and autonomy and a process of *theatricalisation* emerges. This process derives its energy (tension) and dynamics from the continuously changing relationships between the spatial and temporal components, of which the theatre performance, as a transitory phenomenon, consists.

From here, we are only one-step away from claiming theatre to be the *paradigm of all arts* and thus a *hypermedium* that is able to incorporate all other arts and media. However, in order to do this we need first to return to Kant and his division of the arts (schöne Künste) into literature (redende Künste), visual arts (bildende Künste) and music (Tonkunst, which belongs to the category Kunst des schönen Spiels der Empfindungen). Kant based his division on the means of expression that we use in *verbal interaction* or, to be more precise, in face-to-face communication: the *articulation* of words, the *gesticulation* of the body (gestures) and the *modulation* of the voice (sounds). We know also that Kant regarded theatre as a secondary art, that is to say, as merely a connection of different arts in the same artwork, which meant that the theatre derived its '(right of) existence' from the primary arts of literature, visual arts and music. However, if we keep Kant's division of the arts but argue in the opposite direction, we can define theatre as the art of physical presence (face-to-face communication in a situation of here and now) and of expression in words, gestures/ movements and sounds. This is the basis of all other arts as they have distinguished and differentiated themselves into literature under the primacy of thoughts expressed in written words; visual arts under the primacy of sensuous intuitions expressed in frozen images; and music under the primacy of sensations expressed in sounds. Theatre is the only art capable of incorporating all other arts without being dependent on one of these in order to be theatre. We need to notice also that the autonomisation of literature, visual arts and music into separate and individual arts is a result of the *reification* (Verdinglichung) process. Literary, visual and musical works of art can exist or survive independently of the author, the visual artist and the composer or musician (although the latter in a mediatized form only). However, theatrical works of art remain connected to the artist without whom theatre cannot exist – namely the physically present performer. Derived from Hegel, and demonstrated in the diagram below, my position is that theatre is the art of the performer (Schauspielerkunst) and the art of presence (absolute Gegenwart).

32

Figure 5
Theatre as the art of the performer. Diagram by Chiel Kattenbelt

Unlike film and television, theatre always takes place in the absolute presence of here and now. The performer and the spectator are physically present at the same time in the same space. They are there for each other. The performer presents him/her self, while the spectator looks on. The roles they fulfil presuppose and support each other and they are exchangeable. The performer and spectator are necessary to each other because together they hold the responsibility for the realisation of the performance. This shared responsibility provides the performance with an aspect of collectivity and with an ethical meaning, enclosed in the social meeting between performer and spectator in the live presence of here and now.

Theatre in the age of the device paradigm

There is not only a long tradition of thinking about theatre as a secondary or composite art, but also as *dramatic art* per se. In this section, I argue that in the age of the device paradigm – of which film is pre-eminently the exponent – the theatre (re)discovered the special qualities of its liveness. For this purpose, I compare theatre to film.

In 1984, Borgmann (1984: 40-48) argued that our modern culture and society bear the stamp of technology, in which he recognized a *device paradigm*. A notable characteristic of the devices of modern technology is a strict distinction between ends and means. The end is the product and the means are exclusively in service of the product. Modern technology functions like a concealed machinery, which makes commodities, goods, services and experiences available without imposing burdens on us. For Borgmann, being technologically available, means that the technology has been rendered instantaneous, ubiquitous, safe and easy (ibid., 41). The strict distinction between ends and means has been internalised as a specific modern attitude towards reality as a far-reaching functionalisation. We really want the product and we are happy that we do not have to worry about the conditions that produce it. The device paradigm fits in seamlessly with the consumer society; but the ideal of effortless consumption carries within it the consequence that the increasing ease of consumption goes with less engagement:

> [...] The presence of things is replaced with the availability of commodities and [...] availability is procured through devices. Devices [...] dissolve the coherent and engaging character of the pretechnological world of things. In a device the relatedness of the world is replaced by a machinery, but the machinery is concealed, and the commodities, which are made available by a device, are enjoyed without the encumbrance of or the engagement with a context. [...] In sum, the machinery of devices, unlike the context of things, is either entirely occluded or only cerebrally and anonymously present. It is in this sense necessarily unfamiliar. The function of the device, on the other hand, and the commodity it provides are available and enjoyed in consumption (ibid., 47).

Film in its – still dominant – mode of classical narration is an outstanding example of the device paradigm. Classical film narration conceals all aspects of the cinematography in order to give optimal accessibility and *transparency* of the possible world that the film represents. Nothing may disturb the *illusion* or rather impression of reality. Even when the represented world is obviously unreal, everything that happens is plausible. Nothing may remind us of the fact that the film is just film.

Classical film narration defines the position of the spectator as that of an invisible and anonymous witness. In this position, only s/he is allowed to be present in the represented world, which seems to exist on its own. Situated in this position by the camera position and editing techniques, relatively little is demanded of the spectator in terms of activity, except that they identify with the hero. The need, the pressure or the seduction for identification is an effective strategy of neutralizing the heterogeneity of a mass audience. Indeed, the device of the camera determines that all spectators share exactly the same perspective, and so ignores the needs of those who might want a different perspective. Represented literally in an integrated range of projected images, the possible world of the film is easy and safe to believe in and experienced as being real: a world where one may be involved and feel immersed in it. *Transparency* and *immersion* are the two sides of the same coin: the more transparent the medium, the more we feel surrounded by the world that the medium represents.

Today, *virtual reality* is a new medium that comes closest to the ideals of transparency and immersion. Janet Murray suggests that the transparency of a medium is decisive for its success as a storytelling technology:

> Eventually all successful storytelling technologies become 'transparent': we lose consciousness of the medium and see neither print nor film but only the

power of the story itself. If digital art reaches the same level of expressiveness as these older media, we will no longer concern ourselves with how we are receiving the information. We will only think about what truth it has told us about our lives (Murray 1997: 26).

Jay David Bolter and Richard Grusin suggest that, at least in the case of digital technology, there is even "a need for transparency":

> The transparent interface is one more manifestation of the need to deny the mediated character of digital technology altogether. To believe that with digital technology we have passed beyond mediation is also to assert the uniqueness of our present technological moment (Bolter and Grusin 1999: 24).

Theatre, on the other hand, as live performance needs no camera to create a possible world and takes place in the closed continuum of the here and now. However, over its centuries long history, theatre developed all kinds of interruption techniques in order to escape from the restrictions of the actually given here and now. For example, there is the division of the performance into acts and scenes, which usually conform to the structure of the dramatic text; the use of a curtain; the changing of setting and lighting et cetera. Moreover, there is still the spoken word used to appeal to the spectator's faculty of imagination when the scenic possibilities of the stage are not sufficient for actually showing specific actions and events. The restrictions of time and space in theatre is an advantage because the stage provides the performer with an arena; that is to say an empty space in which he can use unrestrictedly all his expressive skills (Peter Brook 1986). As the only living and moving 'element' of the performance, the performer has complete control over the passing of time. By playing, speaking and acting, they can give every desired meaning and interpretation to the space. It is the predominance of spoken language, which liberates time from space. As long ago as 1947, Erwin Panofsky (1985: 218) regarded time as the medium of thoughts – ideas, memories, fantasies and emotions – evoked by the language of the actors. They are expressions of the internal world of experience, detached from the external world of actions and events.

    In search for more 'abstract' forms of theatre, which predominated in the early part of the twentieth century, but with a revival of interest in the form in the 1960s, *continuity* and *simultaneity* were (re)discovered as special qualities of the theatre performance. Directors like Robert Wilson and Jan Fabre used techniques of deceleration and repetition in order to intensify the experience of the passing of time, and to dispose the action of its functionality for the sake of its own dynamics. Directors like Gerardjan Rijnders and Alain Platel used techniques of montage (collage) in order to break through the unity and singularity of time, space and action, and to reinforce the consciousness – whether or not for the sake of fragmentation and deconstruction – of their simultaneity and relative independence.

    In retrospect, it is clear that Béla Balázs formulated concisely the basic principles of theatrical representation in 1938, in his essay 'Zur Kunstphilosophie des Films'[2] in which he falls back on his book *Der sichtbare Mensch oder die Kultur des Films* (1924). Here he posited that in the theatre the spectator sees the individual scenes of the performance in a spatial totality and from an unchanging distance and perspective (Balázs 1973: 157). From a fixed seat in the auditorium, every theatre spectator has a unique position with respect to the actions and events shown on the stage. No camera determines their perspective and, in principle, s/he has freedom of choice on what to focus his attention. True, the spectator's attention is guided to a certain extent, particularly by spoken words, movements and lighting, but in principle, they are able to ignore the guiding mechanisms. According to Balázs, the main consequence of the theatrical methods of representation is that the spectators remain outside the represented space. However, I would add that the space of the performance also contains the space of the spectators, which implies defining the spectators, to a certain extent, as characters in the represented world, and consequently that they are involved in the represented actions and events. This is born out by directors, notable Brecht, who tried to remove the separation between the stage and the auditorium, or at least to bridge the gap between them, in order to address the spectators as participants in the actions and events on stage. Notably, it was in order to characterize the emergence of film art, around 1915, that Balázs brought together the basic principles of theatrical representation, as Ralf Remshardt also notes.[3] For the film spectator, the represented space of the individual scenes is no longer given as a spatial totality, as in theatre, but as a concatenation of space fragments, which are welded together as a spatial totality (Balázs: "visual continuity") in the imagination of the spectator. Camera operation and editing made it possible to change distance to and perspective on the represented actions and events quite easily. Because the film spectator constructs a spatial totality in their own imagination, they get the impression of being 'surrounded' by the represented space and of being involved into the represented action. The spectator's ability to look through the eyes of a character had, according to Balázs, an identifying effect. He identified the close-up as being particularly effective in breaking through the distance between perceiver and object, and the closed totality of the work of art as a "microcosm" on its own.

The basic principles of *theatrical* representation – spatial totality and the unchangeable distance and perspective – identify the basic principles of *dramatic* representation, define theatre as a dramatic art per se and are valid in each case as theatrical norms. The dramatic principles of representation are *linearity* (succession), *concentration* and *selection*. In its dramatic mode, theatre is primarily action-oriented toward the *actuality* and *causality* (development) of the *action*, which is carried by the characters acting on their psychological motivations (linearity). The simultaneous presence of the spectator at the theatre performance limits, in terms of survey and endurance, the course of action – there is a limit to the amount of concentration and observation that an audience can provide. Because the theatre performance is taking place in the actual space and time of here and now, it is restricted in its capacities of actually showing actions and events. In this case, spoken language can be 'brought into action' in order to evoke in the spectator's imagination. However, it is necessary to select the decisive moments in the development of the action. Thus, we see that the unities of time, space and action are the 'natural laws' of the theatre. Conceived of as a dramatic art per se, the principles of the Aristotelean dramaturgy are usually regarded as absolute rules. In its dramatic mode, it is as if theatre is – by definition – all about the actuality and causality of action; and as if the intensity of experience and the reflexivity of thought – that is to say the lyrical and the epical dimensions – are of subordinate importance. However, if we look back over theatre history, we know that lyrical and epical tendencies are as old as the theatre itself. We know also that the absolute domination of the dramatic principles of representation described above, only started in the eighteenth century, reached its peak at the end of the nineteenth century and from there began to decline. To a considerable extent, film took over the function of theatre as dramatic art. From its earliest history, film demonstrated itself as more capable than theatre in presenting a possible world that seems to exist on its own, precisely because film is only projection. Moreover, film defines more clearly the position of the film spectator as that of an anonymous and invisible witness. Thus, we can say that film provides the illusion of reality (even in cases that we know that the represented world is everything but real), whereas theatre provides the reality of illusion.[4]

Theatre as the stage of intermediality

As I have discussed in the preceding section, in its simplest form theatre can exist without any technology. However, film, television and digital video are technology-based media that can record and play back everything that is visible and audible, within their specific ranges of sensitivity, but they cannot incorporate other media without transforming them under the conditions of the specificity of their own mediality. At the very most media can *remediate* (Bolter and Grusin 1999) other media, which implies in the end a *refashioning*. Clearly, theatre is not a medium in the way that film, television and digital video are media. However, although theatre cannot record in the same way as the other media, just as it can incorporate all the other arts, so it can incorporate all media into its performance space. It is in this capacity that I regard theatre as a *hypermedium*.[5] Theatre provides film, television and digital video a stage, that is to say a "performative situation" (Umberto Eco 1977), in which the other media are not just recordings on their own, but at the same time and above all theatrical signs. Operative as part of theatre, the other media become "signs of signs" as opposed to "signs of objects" (Pjotr Bogatyrev 1971 [1938]). To put it differently: as components of a live performance, film, television and video recordings are not only screened, but also and at the same time staged (which is not necessarily the same as refashioned).[6] Thus, because theatre is the art of staging *pur sang* it becomes pre-eminently a stage of intermediality.

Confirmation of this is in the stage language of theatre practitioners, where the concept "transparency" means the opposite of the same notion in media theory. Theatre is transparent because it foregrounds the *corporeality* of the performer and the *materiality* of the live performance as an actual event, taking place in the absolute presence of here and now. In the live performance, the use of media technologies is not to provide effects of immersion and illusion. On the contrary, very frequently the use of media technologies is to extend the lyrical and epical modes of representation, for the sake of the intensity of experience and the reflexivity of thought.[7] The dramatic ideal of the stage being a holodeck belongs more to the technology-based medium of virtual reality than to the live performance of theatre.

In our mediatized culture, technology-based media like film, television and digital media mainly function according to the mechanisms of the device paradigm, which as we have seen means that they hide their own mediality for the sake of their transparency and immediacy (illusion and immersion). At the same time, we may notice that the media in our mediatized culture – in particular since the emergence of the digital era – are characterized by *hypermediacy*, which is, according to Bolter and Grusin (1999), the opposite manifestation of transparency and immediacy:

> If the logic of immediacy leads one either to erase or to render automatic the act of representation, the logic of hypermediacy acknowledges multiple acts of representation and makes them visible. Where immediacy suggests a unified visual space, contemporary hypermediacy offers a heterogeneous space, in which representation is conceived of not as a window on the world, but rather as windowed itself – with windows that open on to other representations or other media. The logic of hypermediacy multiplies the signs of mediation and in this way tries to reproduce the rich sensorium of human experience (Bolter and Grusin 1999, 33-34).

Hypermediacy and immediacy are opposite manifestations indeed, but in the end [...] "of the same desire, the desire to get past the limits of representation and to achieve the real" (ibid., 53).

We need now to add to this and say that in our mediatized culture the media have become a substantial part of reality. Instead of providing us with representations **of** reality the hypermediacy of the media functions in the end **as** immediacy and transparency. In other words, our mediatized culture has become a *hyper-reality*, that is to say a world of signs that are more real than the objects, to which they seem to refer (Eco 1985). With Theodor Adorno, we could say "The more complete the world as representation, the more inscrutable the representation as ideology" (Adorno 1963: 71 - my translation). In 1985/86, Jean Baudrillard characterized our postmodern culture as a *hyperreality* of *simulacra* and *simulations*, which has taken the place of reality.

If the expression "all the world is a stage" is (or seems to be) no longer just a metaphor, but on the contrary a characteristic feature of our mediatized culture, then we really do need a stage on which the staging of life can be staged in such a way that it can be deconstructed and made visible again. My assumption is that theatre provides the stage on which this may happen and that is precisely because of the physical presence of the here and now in which the theatrical performance takes place. Thus, theatre becomes the stage of intermediality.

Notes

1 See Klemens Gruber's contribution to this book, in which he refers to the notion of "semiotic fundamentalism" as a characteristic feature of the historical avant-garde.

2 See also Thomas Kuchenbuch's contribution to this book.

3 See Ralf Remshardt's contribution to this book on the intermediality of the actor

4 The fundamental difference between theatre and film with respect to the relationship between reality and illusion (or fiction) is a central topic in *The Imaginary Signifier* by Christian Metz.

5 The concept of "hypermedium" is discussed also in the contributions of Peter Boenisch, Meike Wagner and Birgit Wiens in this book.

6 This assumption is also one of the underlying ideas of Andrew Lavender's contribution to this book, in which the 'awareness' of staging is related to the notions of *mise-en-scène* and *Verfremdung*.

7 See the chapters of Freda Chapple, Andrew Lavender and Sigrid Merx for examples of this.

THE ACTOR AS INTERMEDIALIST: REMEDIATION, APPROPRIATION, ADAPTATION

Ralf Remshardt

Taking as a point of departure the observation that remediation, as defined by Bolter and Grusin, involves a "redefinition of the real", the chapter traces the experience of stage actors in early films whose intermedial voyage integrated with an 'analogue crisis of representation' that redefined the real of performance. Film performance became what Walter Benjamin called a 'testing ground' for actors. The divergent responses to this challenge of the camera range from Sarah Bernhardt's *appropriation* of the medium for the assertion of overt theatricality, to Eleonora Duse's problematic adaptation to the demands of film. In a coda, the analogue crisis of representation is set into the context of the digital crisis occasioned by computer-generated performance.

If it is true that today "we cannot even recognize the representational power of a medium except with reference to other media", as Jay Bolter and Richard Grusin write in their book *Remediation* (1999: 65) then certainly the obverse holds true as well: any medium will to some degree define the *specific mediality* of the media that contextualize it. This figure-and-ground dialectic played itself out at the beginning of the twentieth century, when early film not only defined itself in contrast to theatrical representation; it defined also theatrical representation as itself. One test case of this shift was performance. What occurred when cinema began to absorb theatrical performers is that theatre itself became *medial* in a way it had not previously been. Prior to cinema, one might refer to the theatre's mediality as latent or *transparent*; film made the theatre's theatricality visible, or its putative *immediacy* visible as theatricality. Because theatre was no longer the sole location of performative or dramatic activity, film foregrounded theatre's *constructedness* and *contingency*. Nor was *filmic performance* as a category marked off as clearly as in the space of theatre, or tied to the body of the performer, since film itself, *as a medium*, performed – rather than to *mediate* simply a performance.

In rapid order, film achieved the status of a normative mode of representation. As the grammar of film integrated into visual discourses, and the homogenous viewer of the discontinuous film image replaced the dispersed viewer of the continuous stage image, film in turn acquired a certain transparency. At the same time, it threw the entire theatrical apparatus into relief and, in a move both hostile and curiously nostalgic, relegated the theatre to a position defined now by its antecedent function and its defective authenticity. We can assume a moment – transitory, almost ineffable – when early cinema audiences shifted from *stage seeing* to *camera seeing* and the point of reference no longer remained a previously seen *stage* performance (or an imagined stage performance which actors were obligingly duplicating) but a previous film performance which had lost trace, if subtly, of its stage antecedent. This is the moment at which the cinematic universe began to close:

to become self-replicating. Actors, too, viewed films with actors who were no longer acting as if on stage, and acted like those actors, only more so. With every subsequent film, the distance to the stage grew more pronounced. Cinema had, even in respect to performance "redefined the real" – and, as Bolter and Grusin observe, any new medium undertakes at first a "redefinition of the real" (ibid., 65).

In this chapter, I am interested particularly in the moment of transition when the apparatus of the early cinema redefined the "real" of the actor in the process of cinematic remediation of stage performances. The process of *remediation*, "the formal logic by which new media refashion prior media forms" (ibid., 273) is discussed more amply elsewhere in this volume and is here assumed to be common critical terminology. Leaving the bounded realm of bodies behind and entering into the space of images, actors were the original inter-medial voyagers who experienced the medial shift from theatre to film, not as observers but as participants. I will look at some early film performances by theatrical actors, in particular Sarah Bernhardt and Eleonora Duse, as documents of an analogue crisis of representation, where, what Roberta Pearson has called 'histrionic code(s)' (1992: 21) become visibly and visually problematic. Here a site opens up for negotiations between the shifting frames of theatrical performance and the no less dynamic frames of a cinema rapidly developing its own language.

Early films paid some superficial respect to theatrical tradition, but in fact, in their appetite for novelty, they aimed, as Walter Benjamin put it, at the "liquidation of the traditional value of the cultural heritage" (1968: 221). For actors moving from theatre to cinema the stakes were high, since films seemed to pose a manifest threat to the two categories indissolubly linked with theatrical performance: liveness and repetition. If cinema was able to duplicate the latter with mechanical precision, it seemed also to render the significance of the former literally immaterial, or rather, to redefine its own illusion of immediacy as an immersive non-liveness. Of course, to frame the problem simply as a conflict between liveness and mediatization would be insufficient. As Philip Auslander has observed, the opposition is spurious; there are "few grounds on which to make significant ontological distinctions" [...] "The historical relationship of liveness and mediatization must be seen as a relationship of dependence and imbrication rather than opposition" (Auslander 1999: 51, 53). It would take a more extensive account than is possible here to do justice to cinema's early phase, but with regard to performance, the literature has failed to acknowledge truly the complexity of intermedial influence, which, in its final effect, resulted in film's repudiation of the model of theatrical *mise-en-scène* and the creation of a more autonomous language of staging, montage, and acting.

A. Nicholas Vardac's *Stage to Screen*, which set the tone of the debate, positioned cinema as legitimate heir to the "pictorial realism" of a depleted theatre whose resources had run short of its aspirations, but paid little attention to acting. Nevertheless, he inaugurated a *narrative of displacement*, in which, by extension, stage acting figured as an outdated practice conceived for another aesthetic space, which stood as a kind of *body double* until a more commensurate mode of performance analysis emerged. Theatre scholar David Mayer has rightly taken issue with the notion of a singular master narrative of transition. "There are", writes Mayer, "in play at century's end a range of gestural systems or partial systems, some used in stage plays, some in various approaches to narrative or interpretive dance, some American in origin, some on the American stage arriving with British and European performers". The theatrical influences on early films are "multiple", and audiences would have viewed them "with a range of critical and aesthetic expectations" (Mayer 1999: 12).

Pursued in trade magazines like the *Moving Picture World* the earliest discourse on film and theatre performance, such as it was, took place almost entirely in a theoretical vacuum; an analytical understanding of their disparate representational frames and modes of signification developed only fitfully (Brewster and Jacobs: 99-110). The vaguely correlative qualities of film and stage performance, bound by a performative gestus (acting) and a collective system of reception (audiences), led to a kind of false analogy between the two that resulted in the many 'stagy' art films around 1908. Because traditionally acting is an "analogue technique" (Naremore 1992: 2) which relies on spatial and temporal continuity and presence, but cinema has the ability to transpose the actor's face "from space into another dimension" (Balázs 1970: 61), the implied notion that performance was media-neutral precipitated what might be called the 'analogue crisis' of acting. It emerged only slowly that performance was the tenuous thread that connected theatre and film as media, which otherwise pursued entirely different, even oppositional pragmatics (a fact that is recognized for instance in the critical work of Vachel Lindsay or Hugo Münsterberg).

The confrontation with the demands of silent film forced actors, who were accustomed to a dominant subject position on stage to accede to their objectification and commodification by an apparatus they understood only incompletely. In turn, they developed several characteristic and frequently anxious strategies towards the medium of film, some of which they marked by an implicit gesture of resistance. For instance, the American actor James O'Neill in *The Count of Monte Cristo* (dir. Edwin Porter, 1912) virtually performs his ambivalence about cinema in every frame. Bernhardt and Duse, as I will describe later, either attempted to force a theatrical logic onto the cinema in a gesture of *appropriation*, or forced themselves to *adapt* to film.

The earliest film document depicting a theatrical star, the American character comedian Joseph Jefferson III in his *Rip van Winkle* series (dir. W.L.K. Dickson, 1896), still seems free of all intermedial anxiety. Running at less than three minutes in total, the film is a series of tableaux from Jefferson's most famous role, the title character in the dramatization of Washington Irving's novella, which Jefferson had toured to great public acclaim since 1865:

43

Figure 6
Joseph Jefferson III in his *Rip van Winkle* series

On viewing, Jefferson's performance, with its loose and almost offhanded quality, surprises. Apart from a few larger gestures that punctuate the scenes as 'points', mostly for the sake of tableaux, his acting is deliberate and casual, even, as Stephen Johnson describes it, underplayed. He appears "very relaxed, perhaps lazy, with a stoop-shouldered frame, loping walk and gestures kept close to the body" (Johnson 1992: 115). Were it not for the outdoor setting, we could be watching a stage performance, much abbreviated but not substantially altered. Jefferson seems untroubled by any potential *ontological challenge* to his living self. Even if rigged for the camera, the event plays itself out on the cultural terrain of the theatre; the acting is an act of invocation of another performance to which it explicitly constructs a reference. It is neither exhausted with this moment, nor circumscribed by it, but because there is clearly no implied expectation that the apparatus is adequate to reproducing the full measure of the play, the camera is not all-consuming. The camera does not define and delineate the performance; it only registers a demonstration of sorts, calculated not to fulfil a desire but to summon it: the live performer's voice and body beckoning beyond the imperfections of the mute and flickering images.

As of 1896, the cinematic remediation of the stage had not occurred. Film could record actors, but one could not act in films. There was, at this point, no resistance to film by stage actors because, as far as they were concerned, as a site of dramatic expression there was no film. Within less than a decade, all this changed.

Perhaps it became obvious that film, in spite of its initial technical limitations, was what Walter Benjamin called a "transportable reflection" [*Spiegel*] (1968: 231) of the actor. In a profession keenly conscious of its transience, film could offer time regained. However, acting for the camera curtailed exactly the *dimensions of being*, over which stage actors exercised as their right absolute control — *space* and *time*. Naturally, or in fact unnaturally, the actors' command of space was compromised by the camera's fixed purview.

Josef von Sternberg provides some analysis of the dilemma faced by stage actors. Pointing to the difference between the actor's autonomy on stage and before the camera, he wrote in 1955:

44

> This mechanism [of cinema] not only distributes the actor like popular dolls turned out wholesale, but it actually makes those dolls look as if they could move and speak by themselves. A child, a shark, or a horse is made to act the same way as a great actor — easier, as a matter of fact, since they do not resist so much. (Sternberg 1974: 85)

The ease with which screen performers adjust to the medium's requirements for *objectification*, Sternberg suggests, is in inverse proportion to their investment in another medium and mode of performance. Stage actors were badly equipped to give what the camera most demanded: not performance, not the modelling of a character or the simulacrum of someone else, but rather a new kind of intimacy, the simulacrum (for it was scarcely real) of an authentic self.[1] Only in that way is it possible to play within, or against, what we might call the phenomenal self-givenness of the screen environment — the sense, as André Bazin puts it, that in film "man in the world enjoys no *a priori* privilege over animals and things" (1967: 106). Nevertheless, Sternberg's argument goes further; it constructs the apparatus of the cinema as one essentially of *alienation* for the actor, an argument that seems to echo Walter Benjamin's notion that:

> in the representation of man through the [cinematic] apparatus, his alienation from himself has been put to a highly successful use (Benjamin 1989: 369).

Both see the act of camera performance as a submission to control by outside forces, but to Sternberg the loss of autonomy film coerces from actors (while simultaneously trading on the phantasm of their autonomous image) seems more than vaguely sinister. However, in Benjamin's materialist analysis the actor trades the auratic presence of the stage for a manufactured, commodified "spell of personality". Here they are subjected to the critical gaze of the masses in the marketplace of images, masses who are no less than the camera's alter ego and the final arbiter and critic of the performance in which Benjamin sees a "testing ground" [*Testleistung*] (1989: 371).

Stage actors indeed often perceived films as a test, and one of the few to have given it extensive consideration is E. H. Sothern in an article for *The Craftsman* in 1916, where he tried to define "the New Art" of cinematic acting. Sothern found to his distress that:

> all the experience that I had acquired in years on the stage, the gesture, the voice, the expression, not only did not avail me, but rather stood in the way of the work (1998: 28).

We find similar insights in countless anecdotal statements by early migrants from stage to film, but Sothern casts it in an unusually frank language of *dispossession* that reflects a considerable state of anxiety. Without a responsive audience, without the stage's physical expanse and the effects of the voice, writes Sothern, "we do our acting before the camera absolutely denuded" (ibid., 28). Elsewhere in the same article, he observes:

> On the stage a man is within the bonds of nature, he is persuading his audience **45** as to the reality of his presentation. [...]. In the moving picture all these opportunities are wiped out (ibid., 29).

The terminology of *abjection* and *annihilation* is revealing. When he describes the act of performing for the camera, it is as if he himself must transform into the apparatus, or at least commune with it, and learn to speak dispassionately, as a machine to a machine:

> Your entire picture must come mechanically from your brain, you cannot acquire any inspiration, any stimulus [...]. A moving picture actor never tries to feel any emotion, only to help the audience to feel it [...] You may express the most abounding beauty, the profoundest emotion, the richest gesture, but if the camera is not making a note of it, you have not accomplished the task the director has set for you (Sothern 1998: 30-31).

The trope of the camera's coldness, its indifference to the expression of 'true' emotions, indeed, its cruelty, recurs in much of the writing on early films. There is an erotic subtext here, of course: the camera is fickle, it may spurn any advances, and accept only overtures from those it 'loves' — the very definition of movie stardom. Imperiously, it requires a total commitment to the moment of performance even as it makes no promises of deliverance. As George Arliss put it in 1923, "the camera has no mercy on the actor who is thinking of other things or is incapable of imagination" (Gledhill 2000: 22).

Silent film actors conversely were eager to distance themselves from the thundering physicality of the theatre; in their descriptions, film acting became the opposite of stage acting: a kind of spiritualism, a feat of consciousness, at home in an entirely different realm to which corporeality was incidental. An acting manual advised:

> It is not acting as we understand the word from what we see on the stage. It comes nearer to being a projection of the trained imagination [...] the portrayal begins in [the actors'] mind; they are conscious of it there, they concentrate on its mental portrayal, and the human body naturally conveys that mental conception to the audience (Klumph 1922: 104-5).

Or, as screen star Mary Fuller would have it:

> Old-style pantomime meant 'putting things over' by physical means; photoplay acting is putting things over in a mental way — the art of mental suggestion. *It is mental and emotional radiation* (Fuller 1914: 227 - her emphasis).

However, even if the actor was successful in courting the naked eye of the machine, in delivering Fuller's mental radiation or what Sothern calls "the essence of concentrated expression" (ibid., 29), that act of performance was only one part of a succession of steps. In the recording, fragmentation, reassembly, and distribution of the ultimate image their performance was merely the raw material out of which was refined, later and elsewhere, the final form.

Such alienation, as Benjamin recognized, is not incidental but integral to the process. In this sense Pirandello, whom Benjamin quotes approvingly, imagines the film actor as an actor in exile [...] "from himself" who finally surrenders not simply his sovereignty but his very physical being:

> [H]is body loses its corporeality, it evaporates, it is deprived of reality, life, voice, and the noises caused by his moving about, in order to be changed into a mute image (Benjamin 1968: 229).

Like Sternberg and Sothern, Pirandello sees in the fashioning of the cinematic image a peculiar metamorphic process at work that finally leaves the actor's material dimension behind as dross while it resurrects his likeness with unprecedented luminance and potency. This is a fraught transaction, a double transformation which is at once physical (indeed chemical, as silver nitrate reacts to light) and 'metaphysical'.

A Benjaminian 'testing ground' would certainly be the films of two iconic female stage actors of the early twentieth century, Sarah Bernhardt and Eleonora Duse. The stakes were altogether higher for these two than for most male actors. As women in an image industry, dependent entirely on public perception, they operated within a carefully calibrated environment of adulation. Film, by its very nature, jeopardized this system of charismatic stardom. It offered no possibility for the *narratives of redemption* that litter both careers, where a great second night might obliterate a miserable opening and avert an impending disaster; film's fixity rendered a bad performance irreversible. Cinema tendered no guarantee that it could convey that quality of stardom upon which their careers had been built – that of the *sacred monster*, almost institutional in their power, larger-than-life personages enshrined in the subconscious of their respective cultures, which pictures could only trivialize.

Sarah Bernhardt in *Les amours de la Reine Elisabeth* **(1912).**

Bernhardt's attitude towards film was one of unequivocal *appropriation*; her films were made in the service of perpetuating her cultural position and cementing the myth of the reigning stage actor. In her screen practice, she evinced no recognition that the medium required any adjustment from her. The vehicles she chose for herself were notably plays in which she had had prior theatrical success, with which she was firmly identified, and which were faithful simulacra of the stage performances, not adaptations — by her own admission, the actress often left her performances essentially unaltered, even insisting on speaking all the lines (Abel 1994: 314). The quintessence of Bernhardt's control of her cinematic image occurs in *Les amours de la Reine Elisabeth* (1912).

    Elisabeth was a kind of 'test case' by Bernhardt of how far she could extend the loyalty of her following into the new medium, and more importantly, how far she could make the medium extend itself to her. The film is a study of a woman as spectacle, the theatricality of power and the power of theatricality, but also of the blurred lines between the public and the private, the 'true' self and the performative self. Bernhardt succeeds quite brilliantly in creating an artefact that intentionally signifies ambiguously; everything and everyone in *La Reine Elisabeth* plays not only to Elizabeth, but also to her surrogate, Sarah Bernhardt. Her performance confirms Richard Dyer's observation that a star actor collapses the "distinction between the actor's authenticity and the authentication of the character s/he is playing" (1998: 21).

    The early part of the film is structured as a series of royal audiences, with Elizabeth/Bernhardt holding court, and the courtiers in the film function as a kind of built-in audience, modelling the reactions of the imaginary theatre/film audience. Through that device, Bernhardt not only negates the problem of a lack of immediate feedback, which contributed to the stage actor's Pirandellian sense of "exile" in front of the camera, but effectively creates a play-within-the-film, or at least a thoroughgoing sense of motivated theatricality within which not only her character but also her persona can thrive. Elizabeth/Sarah's act of observing and judging is itself the main theatrical action, the one worth watching to the film's audience. Here Sarah extends her control to both media by reappropriating the camera's strategy of surveillance.

47

Another assertion of theatrical prerogative, in the form of a double surveillance, occurs in a scene where Elizabeth watches through a window as the executioner and official attendants parade her lover to the Tower. Bernhardt, standing in the left middle ground in a rigid pose, arms at an oblique angle, hands with down-turned palms tensely hovering, stares upstage as the procession moves through an arch and off to the right. As Essex passes by, she makes a sudden convulsive movement then rapidly has the curtain drawn, as if in a theatre. Conventional cinematic resolution of such a dramatic situation would call for close-ups to monitor the Queen's reaction, but we are unable even to see the expression on Bernhardt's face in a scene that proceeds without edits for more than two minutes. Instead, in deliberate defiance of film's demands, Bernhardt plays out an instance of the *expressive immobility* for which she was acclaimed (Taranow 1972: 97). Perhaps she was aware that close-ups would challenge the supremacy of her physical idiom; to allow a close-up would have given the camera the power *to extract* the emotional moment, rather than authorizing the actress's body *to project it*.

It seems that even her pronounced limp, owing to an injury that would later result in the amputation of her leg, is revealed, as much as hidden, as if to challenge the audience to read the charismatic Sarah out of the wound. At several points in the film, she makes deliberate long crosses to enter or exit, usually supported by another actor. Judicious editing could easily have obviated these painful parades but they form part of the paradigmatic Bernhardt vocabulary of grand entrances and underline the ceremonial nature of the enterprise. Since they are cinematically superfluous, they force the audience to acknowledge the actor's presence as an essentially theatrical one. Bernhardt's flamboyant death scene, in which she falls face first into a conveniently placed heap of pillows after prolonged and agonizing leave-taking, was subject to ridicule even when it first appeared:

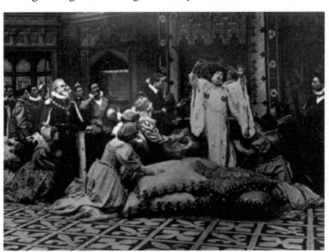

Figure 7
Sarah Bernhardt performing her death scene in *Les Amours de la Reine Elisabeth*

But this "regally attitudinized death" (Taranow 1972: 127) is entirely in keeping with a film that at every turn denies its film-ness; for an actress noted for her death scenes, that she seems very much alive at the end is exactly the point. Even at the last moment, Sarah Bernhardt reclaims the theatre from film in a gesture of disarming presumptuousness. Appearing for her curtain call on the set of the last scene, lest the audience believe her magnificent quietus signalled the end of Sarah, she accepts her imaginary ovations with a small shrug of feigned modesty. Bernhardt triumphs over death by restaging her death scenes as obviously living moments: grand, balletic, voluptuous. Her final appearance negates death and vindicates the theatre.

Thus, Bernhardt resists making the performance medially transparent by subordinating herself to film's naturalistic aesthetic and simply disappearing; in salvaging the theatrical she retains what Bolter and Grusin refer to as the medium's "hypermediacy" – essentially, the continuing visibility of film as a secondary medium through which theatre (as the originary medium) is mediated. It is only in the hypermediated mode that the performer's autonomy survives erasure.

Eleonora Duse in *Cenere* (1916)

In contrast to Sarah Bernhardt's usurpation of the medium, Eleonora Duse tried in her only film, *Cenere* (Ashes), made for the Ambrosio Company in 1916, to negotiate the divide between film and stage by creating a *hybridized cinematic derivative* of her stage style.

In fact, Duse was more sensitive to the needs of film than almost any other stage actor of the time. In 1915, she received an offer from D.W. Griffith's agents to propose a film project, which prompted her serious consideration of the cinema:

> The art of silence! The fever in my heart, ever since Griffith's offer, I have dreamed only of films (Weaver 1984: 309).

A devoted filmgoer, she was convinced also that films were not living up to their artistic potential, and she began to conceive of possible film projects for herself. Prescient in her understanding of film's aesthetic autonomy, Duse thought of cinema primarily as a pictorial and lyrical medium, not a dramatic one. Indeed, she fervently opposed the theatricalizing of the cinema and saw it as a chance to make a break with her prior acting career:

> I want to do nothing that resembles, even remotely, my work of the past. – The depths of the soul see the way, but it is almost impossible to clarify for others? (ibid., 304).

Her choice finally fell on Grazia Deledda's novel *Cenere*, written in 1904. The simple story tells of Rosalia, a poor Sardinian peasant woman who gives up her illegitimate son to his prosperous father. Years later, the son, now betrothed, seeks out his mother to bring her to live with him and his future wife. However, the fiancée rejects the

49

indigent and reclusive mother, and Rosalia commits suicide in despair – all turns to 'ashes'.

The scenario for *Cenere* was written in first draft by Duse herself, aided later by a professional screenwriter (ibid., 308). She invested so fully in its making that she directed most of the film herself, although officially the director's credits went to the actor Febo Mari, who plays her son. Several scenes were reshot at her request, severely trying the patience of the producer Ambrosio, and although she was unhappy with the film in its final state, she never attempted to have it obliterated, as has been suggested, and it still exists, although in apparently abbreviated form.[2]

The remaining film, approximately thirty minutes long, gives evidence of the struggles Duse endured in its making. Shot near Turin, the film is a cinematic hybrid, moving somewhat uneasily between a naturalistic idiom, the rough Sardinian terrain and its deprivations; and a melodramatic one, the son's futile quest to redeem his mother. There is evident theatricality in the middle section of the film, in the confrontation between Rosalia and her son and staged in a conventional fashion in the mother's paltry hut. In what she felt was her innovation Duse decided not to have the character speak at all, even though the intertitles render her dialogue. Thus, we never see her opening her mouth, and the lines assigned to her appear as if they were mental projections of her will. While on the one hand this gives the performance an almost monumentally lapidary and stoic quality, especially as seen against Mari's histrionically agitated son, the enforced muteness also threw Duse back on a vocabulary of gestures developed for the stage, which at times seems out of keeping with cinematic flow. Although she was widely regarded as a realistic actor, Duse had an idiosyncratic array of expressions, which, to the contemporary eye, often seem strained.

However, on some occasions, the film uses the landscape and the diminutive figure of Rosalia, who traverses it like a black crow, as an effective metonymy of the harshness and loneliness of her existence. Conveyed entirely in her forlorn posture and the play of her hands, her agony is clear as she bids farewell to her young son at the beginning of the film. Throughout the film, the camera returns to an oblique view of the actor, showing her in the background of the frame, or from behind, or at an angle that obscures the face, as if to underscore the character's essential abjection. In one scene, she is seen sprawled on the ground, drinking from a brook:

Figure 8
Eleonora Duse in
Cenere

At other moments, Duse turns or walks away from the camera, avoiding its direct gaze and refusing access to the viewer. Notably, this strategy of indirection was used also by Griffith in scenes of what Tom Gunning has dubbed "hidden emotion", where a strong response is played obliquely, with the actor's face obscured (Bowser 1990: 91). At those moments, the character's isolation and Duse's anxiety over the adequacy of her performance seem powerfully conflated. This figural conception of the character was Duse's idea; she insisted on a *chiaroscuro* treatment that left her adumbrated much of the time, fearful that the strong natural light used for film would dilute her performance. She wrote to Febo Mari after a rehearsal:

> Put me in the shadows! Put me in the shadows, I beg of you! [...] A film full of sun like yesterday's, even if done as a rehearsal, cannot be successful with me – of that I am certain. (Signorelli 1942: 138).

Contrasting with Bernhardt's baroque demise, Duse's most remarkable scene is the one she did not do – her death scene. In our last view of the character alive, she walks into the depth of the frame through a field. Later, a procession bearing her body delivers the coda; the character's intervening suicide is merely implied. Narratively, this reflects the character's complete self-abnegation, an atoning repetition of her original move of the abandonment of her son, now as self-annihilation. However, for the actor to manage her death as disappearance was not simply an aesthetic decision but also an acknowledgment of the devouring logic of film to which theatrical representation could not adequately respond. Duse literally felt she was failing the 'test' of the camera, and expresses this failure in the language of a kind of near-death experience in her urgent dispatches to Mari:

> I thought that I was so well prepared [...], perhaps it was only the fruit and error of solitude. Yet I saw myself in the shadows – in the distance – far, far away, as when children close their eyes in order to rediscover a world of make-believe (Pontiero 1986: 298).

Bert States writes of her ability to transform herself on stage: "[Duse's] disappearance was so complete that the artist reappeared on the other side of the illusion – that is to say, stunned the audience with the fidelity of the artifice" (States 1985: 167). However, in film, Duse found she could not pull off the feat of reappearance. She called film making a "spiritual problem" and complained that she felt "detached" when she saw herself on screen (Weaver 1984: 309, 311). In contrast to Bernhardt, she had succeeded in turning her stage self into an imaginary, as film demanded, but perhaps at the price of losing the connection with the acting she understood and surrendering to the *crisis of representation*.

Computer-generated performers

If for the actor films at the turn of the nineteenth century summoned the spectre of an *analogue crisis* of performance, the turn of the last century has given way to a potential *digital crisis* as computer-generated performances have come within reach. The notion of the *synthespian* or *vactor* [virtual actor] has gone from the realm of science fiction only a few years ago, when some quaintly fantasized about reanimating, say, Marilyn Monroe, to current reality. Digitally created performers are vying for recognition as serious actors. In recent releases such as *SimOne*(2002), about a manufactured cyberstar, Hollywood tries to manage its anxieties by making light of them. However, there is no denying that computer-generated performers, with their infinite pliability, trouble the ontological category of performance itself. "Celluloid cinema dramatically altered the relationship of the individual to reality", writes Barbara Creed (2000: 80), "the computer-generated image is about to change that relationship once again and in equally profound ways". If theatrical actors mustered a surfeit of resistance to cinema, the computer-generated performer conversely is submissive and affectless:

> Asked to identify with a cyberstar, the spectator would be haunted by a sense of the uncanny: the image on the screen appears human, and yet is not human. The glamorous other is a phantom, an image without a referent in the real, an exotic chimera, familiar yet strange. (Creed 2000: 86).

In the digital domain, even death is now no longer a guard against the forces of remediation. When the actor Brandon Lee died during the shooting of the movie *The Crow* in 1994, it became possible to create a posthumous performance by digitally painting Lee's face on a body double and so saving the film. Ten years later, a resurrected Laurence Olivier co-starred in a film ironically both futuristic and retrograde, *Sky Captain and the World of Tomorrow* (dir. Kerry Conran, 2004). Unsurprisingly, this state of affairs has given rise to some hand-wringing. Stuart Klawans in the *New York Times* worried about "the actor's soul":

> We are accustomed to think of the greatness of a performer as an expression of individuality. However, when Olivier is no longer captured on film but manufactured on the computer, perhaps in multiple versions, we lose the very thing that art was supposedly preserving: our point of contact with the irreplaceable, finite person. (Klawans 2004)

Klawans' objection is almost touchingly naïve and phrased in the terminology of a theatrical reality that seems inconsequential now. Even if, as in the case of the synthetic Olivier, there is a "referent in the real", which real is it? We might say, paraphrasing a Derridean idea, that in the computer-generated performance, *il n'y a pas au dehors du trame* — there is nothing outside of the frame. "In short," remarks Creed, "the synthespian does not have an Unconscious" (2000: 84). All live performance contains traces of the actor's biography and archive of experience, with memories and intentions, with acting choices *not* made as much as with those made, and so on. Even in filmed performance, these traces are present interstitially, between the frames, as ghosts in the machine. However, in computer-generated performance, there is exactly a sequence of 24 frames per second and nothing more. In the digital realm, the already vague distinction between liveness and mediatization has collapsed entirely;

there is no doubt that computer-generated performance is a post-actor, post-human "redefinition of the real" which has yet to be theorized.

Notes

1 The idea has been restated many times, for instance by Walter Benjamin: "For the film, what matters is primarily that the actor represents himself to the public before the camera, rather than representing someone else" (Benjamin 1968: 229).

2 There are vast differences, for instance, between the two versions I have seen of the film. One is an edit made for the Italian television station RAI and circulated on video tape in a very inferior copy. The other is the viewing copy at the British Film Institute. Although the BFI copy runs only 24 minutes as opposed to the 30 minutes of the RAI version, it appears narratively more complete.

MISE EN SCÈNE, HYPERMEDIACY
AND THE SENSORIUM

Andy Lavender

This chapter is about the production of pleasure in certain mixed-media performances, particularly with regard to phenomenological aspects of the combination of media. The use of two-dimensional projected images alongside live action immediately means that such images are 'staged' as well as merely screened. This gives them a different status than they have in film, television or in computer/monitor contexts. Certainly, they are not self-sufficient but contingent upon other frameworks – notably the live event, the moment of performance, the three-dimensional scenic space and the theatrical gaze. The effect is intensified where the screened (and staged) image is produced only through the immediate action of whatever is occurring onstage at that particular moment. Spectators often find themselves enjoying (marvelling at, drawn in by) the interface between the actual and the virtual, the corporeal and the mediatized, at the very point at which (re)presentation becomes artefact. The author turns to Jay Bolter and Richard Grusin's account of the relationship between hypermediacy and immediacy in order to explore these issues and relate them to a notion of contemporary *mise en scène*. He argues that effects of simultaneity in contemporary mixed-media theatre are part of a larger cultural turn that is predicated upon an interplay between synthesis and multivalence, the actual and the virtual, the here and the there. Mixed-media productions by The Builders Association and Diller & Scofidio, Klaus Obermaier and Chris Haring, and Complicite reference the exploration.

Hypermediacy and contemporary theatre

In their book *Remediation: Understanding New Media*, Jay David Bolter and Richard Grusin discuss the relationship between *immediacy* and *hypermediacy* in visual culture. They give a cogent definition of the two terms as they apply in a digital environment:

> In digital technology [...] hypermediacy expresses itself as multiplicity. If the logic of immediacy leads one either to erase or to render automatic the act of representation, the logic of hypermediality acknowledges multiple acts of representation and makes them visible. Where immediacy suggests a unified visual space, contemporary hypermediacy offers a heterogeneous space, in which representation is conceived of not as a window on to the world, but rather as "windowed" itself – with windows that open on to other representations of other media. The logic of hypermediacy multiplies the signs of mediation and in this way tries to reproduce the rich sensorium of human experience. [...] In every manifestation, hypermediacy makes us aware of the medium or media

and (in sometimes subtle and sometimes obvious ways) reminds us of our desire for immediacy (Bolter and Grusin 1999: 33-34).

As Bolter and Grusin make clear the two categories, *immediacy* and *hypermediacy*, are to an extent mutually linked. They argue that immediacy – a direct contact with the spectator – has been a project of artists since at least the Renaissance, in an attempt to give the viewing public an access to the work that is as apparently unmediated as possible. Meanwhile, effects of hypermediacy – producing an awareness of the constructed nature of the artwork and the presence of the media in play – are frequently encountered *simultaneously*, albeit sometimes as a secondary and more minor strain. The paradigm is rebalanced somewhat in digital culture as hypermediacy and its effects become more apparent – although the persistent tension between hypermediacy (plural, open-ended and involving links and interrelationships) and immediacy (embracing the spectator in a directly absorbing engagement) remains definitive. In many instances, hypermediacy and immediacy do their work simultaneously.

That this has become so apparent in contemporary culture should perhaps not be surprising. Hypermediacy is not simply a question of the multiplicity of sources, images or image systems. It is expressed through *simultaneity*: two or more sources, images, systems and effects in play at the same time in a shared ecosystem. Simultaneity has emerged as a significant characteristic of digital culture. In her book *Virtual Theatres: An introduction* Gabriella Giannachi supplies co-presences at almost every turn. Virtual theatre "allows the viewer to be present in both the real and the virtual environment." Orlan's "happenings" are "a montage of real and fictional, text and metatext". Stelarc's body in his piece *Extra Ear* is "both host and augmentation, passive and active" (Giannachi 2004: 11, 54, 56). Simultaneity is a defining mode of digital theatre and a structural characteristic of *hypermedial products*. What is noteworthy here is the simultaneous agency of *hypermediality* (structured around simultaneity) and immediacy. In passing, we might observe that both Orlan and Stelarc directly engage (absorb, provoke, repel) their viewers, albeit through less than conventional means.

56   Principally, my concern in this chapter is with the simultaneous co-existence, the mutual play of what might appear to be two distinct media – the screen and the stage – and the ways in which their very co-relation produces effects of immediacy that are deeply involving – more, deeply pleasurable – for spectators. Interestingly, Bolter and Grusin's book does not include theatre among the various media where the authors observe the effects of hypermediacy at work. However, their comments do describe well some of the effects that structure contemporary performance in which there is a combination of screened images and live action. In order to explore this more closely I shall describe briefly three productions that depend upon a relationship between stage and screen. These examples suggest a set of commonalities to hypermedial *mise en scène* – the arrangement of the stage and its spaces of performance – that I discuss later in the piece. Lastly, I consider how *mise en scène* works to guarantee effects of immediacy and pleasure, partly in phenomenal terms, through a sensual engagement with the spectator's experience of the event.

Case studies

JET LAG: "PART ONE: ROGER DEARBORN"
PRESENTED BY THE BUILDERS ASSOCIATION IN COLLABORATION WITH DILLER + SCOFIDIO[1]

Figure 9
Actual-fictional presence: *Jet Lag: 'Part One: Roger Dearborn'*

A performer sits on a stool at an angle of 45 degrees to the audience. A blank back-projection screen waits behind him. As the show begins, the back projection screen shows an image of the sea, with the horizon in the distance. Centre-stage is a single video camera on a fixed one-legged stand, pointing at the man, and therefore seeing him against the back projection screen. The camera's gaze takes in a couple of wires rigged in the space from floor to grid. The man's image comes up on a large screen across the back of the stage. Since the camera also observes the wires (which look like sail rigging) and the back-projected image, it looks as though the man is on a boat at sea. The impression is enhanced as the man starts to sway from side to side – as does the back-projection unit. (The back-projector is fixed on the same framework as the back-projection screen, so the entire image rocks from side to side, although independently from the man.) A sound design is introduced – ocean noises. The character talks to camera. We learn that this is Roger Dearborn and that he is making a video diary of his solo voyage around the world. If we simply watched the large screen, we would see a man at sea, talking directly to camera (an effect cheekily underscored when he puts his hand on the "rigging" to steady himself). Since we are theatre spectators, we see that this impression is fabricated by exploiting the camera's framing properties and the combined movements of the performer and set.

57

The piece concerns an actual event. In 1969 the British yachtsman Donald Crowhurst sent regular reports home plotting his apparent progress during a round-the-world race. He then disappeared, and when his boat was discovered it transpired that he had faked the reports. The real logbook showed that the boat never left the Atlantic during its 243 days at sea. Therefore the piece is about communicating untruths, contriving data and voyaging yet not progressing.

The production riffs upon this thematic of lack of authenticity later in the piece. Dearborn begins a Christmas Day message. The sea is calm. He stops, turns to the onstage vision-mixer operator and says, "This should be a stormy scene." He pulls on a bright orange oilskin and squirts water on his face with a spray-mister. The sound design changes from the environmental sound of the tranquil ocean to that of a raging storm. The back projection screen swivels exaggeratedly and Roger begins his address again, shouting to the camera. On the large screen, it looks for all the world as though he is in the middle of the storm-tossed ocean. As mediated by the camera the scene is convincingly real. As hypermediated by the theatre, the scene is palpably fabricated. The spectator delights in the fact that an actor and some technicians have cooked up the effect with a spray-mister and loud noise.

The piece draws upon a close relationship between its subject matter and its mode of expression. That is, the precision of the theatrical illusion – put together under our nose, so to speak – evokes the efforts to which Dearborn/Crowhurst went to manufacture his own false coordinates. The presence of the camera is diegetic. It is positioned centre-stage as the medium for Dearborn's diary. You could say that the screens are in some respects diegetic too. The back projection screen 'stands in' for the actual ocean and the large screen 'stands in' for the television monitor (presumably) on which Dearborn's family and colleagues will watch his strange personal video. On the other hand, the camera and screens are subsumed as part of the production's theatrical apparatus. The piece plays out in theatre-time and theatre-space to a theatre audience. A true story presented in the mode of fiction. A publicity flier for the production exclaims "Jet Lag examines how the media and new technologies compress our perception of time and space." This is fair comment, in terms of the show's content. However, in terms of *mise en scène*, the production exploits phenomenal differences between stage space and video space to stimulate the spectator's perceptual awareness of both. Time, space and presence simultaneously contract and expand.

D.A.V.E.
PRESENTED BY KLAUS OBERMAIER AND CHRIS HARING[2]

D.A.V.E. begins with a bare-chested, shaven-headed man in taupe combat trousers, turning slowly on the spot. Perhaps this is the eponymous Dave. As he revolves, the video image of a man turning slowly on the spot is projected onto his body. The dimensions of the image map precisely on to the performer. The man appears to speed up – and does so at an alarming rate. He turns so fast that he is a human spinning top. Actually, he has imperceptibly stopped in order to form a screen for his dervishly whirling digital video self. Rather, not quite self, for his digital video double has hair on his head. This hirsute cyborg slows and stops. The video projection fades, and we are left with Chris Haring, standing still, his back to the audience in pristine vertical blankness, a human screen coming into perspective as baldpate, bare back and beige combats.

So begins a game with the materiality of the body played with remorseless precision by Haring and co-creator, the video artist and composer Klaus Obermaier. D.A.V.E. stands for Digital Amplified Video Engine. Put like that he sounds rather more techno-geek than bloke-in-the-pub. Who is this D.a.v.e.? Is it Haring, palpable and present, a body which is also a screen? Or, is it the video body, placed parasitically on the flesh that it simultaneously obliterates? The question is left deliberately unresolved. D.a.v.e. is teasingly bi-textual.

There are no screens in the piece other than Haring's body. His corpus, then, is intimately interlocked with every single image, in a show that proliferates with other bodies. At first, it seems that Haring is really just doubling himself by means of his digitally manipulated doppelganger. It soon becomes clear that, by grace of editing software, Haring and Obermaier would prefer to stretch this second self and, with it, any notions we might hold of the coherence of the physiognomy that is its material root. Early in the show, for instance, Haring puts his hands over his eyes. New and extremely large eyes are projected on his hands, which are then vertically extended to create a bulbous alien-like effect. By the same principle, his ears and mouth are weirdly enlarged. Such distortions are merely by way of a warm-up. Later Haring's DV persona squeezes his head to half its width and pulls the sides of his stomach into an impossibly thin hourglass shape. He then lowers his shoulders level with his chest and then peels back his skin to reveal the red flesh underneath. He spins and ages, turning into a wrinkled body with grey hair. With his hands across his chest and groin he becomes a bare-chested woman. He takes his head, a red globe, and passes it around his body like a juggler, his own outlines etched in fluorescent white lines. This is the stuff of the fairground, the freak show of Victoriana rendered anew (and newly sanitised – no smell! no sweat!) by the gestures of digital video.

The programme notes suggest that "*D.A.V.E.* deals with potential future removal of limitations upon the body [...] a man will be able to find out what it's like to be a woman and vice versa". It is difficult to take this statement very seriously given that *D.A.V.E.* shows a series of digitally imaged body-alterations, rather than any more organic presentation of change and transformation. If anything, this is a body that is irreducibly urban. A more abstract series of images shows a travelling shot of the girders of a bridge. These are projected on Haring's flexed body as he kneels with his legs wide and his hands held in front of him. The effect of the editing and zoning the image around the torso suggests an irruption of the city's space from within. The hypermedial body digests and exudes the very fabric of metropolitan urbanity. Obermaier's sound design strengthens the technological embrace, providing an ambient, inside-of-the-head urban soundscape full of recurrent light-industrial motifs.

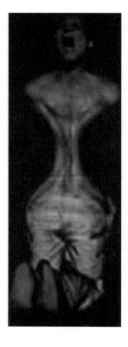

Figure 10
The virtually distorted body: *D.A.V.E.*

There is a curious video-game effect when the images play on Haring's body. Their heavy pixellation, the flattened colour contours of digital video and the slight mismatch of the edges of the image (for in spite of everything the framing is never quite perfect) mean that the video self is always clearly virtual. At first sight, this is also a virtuoso body, more elastic, distortable and wilfully grotesque, as it obliterates the flesh on which it disports. Yet Haring's originary body is valorised through his gymnastic performance of short controlled dance sequences, interspersed between the video segments where the performer is largely required to be still. Of course, *D.A.V.E.*'s actual body is with us throughout, an organic screen, an irreducible presence and a place of volatile mediation even whilst it is simultaneously erased by the digital cyborg that flexes on its surface.

THE ELEPHANT VANISHES
PRESENTED BY COMPLICITE AND SETAGAYA PUBLIC THEATRE OF TOKYO [3]

Directed by Simon McBurney, *The Elephant Vanishes* was developed by the London-based company Complicite in Tokyo with a group of Japanese performers. It draws on the urban short stories of the contemporary Japanese writer Haruki Murakami and depicts various characters and events by way of a mix of mundane detail and extravagant flights of fancy.

The stage-space conjures something of the Tokyo cityscape in which the show is set. Fluorescent lights and what look like telegraph wires run across the upper half of the space. There is a large projection screen across the entire back section of the stage. Two television screens hang at different heights in mid-air from scaffolding and at points in the show track sideways through the space. A fridge on stage provides a convenient white surface for projection, as do two pairs of Japanese screens that track in and out at intervals. This is a place of post-industrial communication and concealment, on and off, in and out, live and dormant.

An introductory collage of images, scenic movement and human action emblematises some of the motifs of the production. The back screen shows a tracking shot of Tokyo and, in particular, the facades of buildings with their colours slightly flat. It stills to a blurred focus shot of the neon lights of the city. Parts of the image are animated – a hoarding, for instance, and a light at a pedestrian crossing. The fridge shows people moving through the city. The TV monitors – themselves in motion

– contain a spooling montage of faces, TV interference, travelling shots. Members of the company move elements of the set and take up positions onstage. This is a flux of motion across different planes and media, multiple points of focus, simultaneous interactions in separable spaces.

Figure 11
Multimedia *mise en scène: The Elephant Vanishes*

At times, a very simple set-up becomes dynamic by virtue of its layered elements. A character sits on a chair as if driving. The Japanese screen behind him shows an image of an illuminated road tunnel, as if seen through the rear window of a speeding car. The image is doubled on the large rear screen, and trebled on a TV monitor high to the performer's right. The effect is of an intoxicating rush of movement, vivid, intense and pleasingly disproportionate.

 At one point, a man reads a newspaper. A top-shot from a camera in the grid shows the man's hand, along with his wafer and his mug on the back screen. The sound of him eating the wafer and slurping his coffee is magnified. The man jerks the newspaper across the table so that different parts come into focus – thus, in a way he performs his reading for the camera. He reads about the disappearance of an elephant. Stills showing a huge leg-shackle appear on the back screen. The first we see of the eponymous vanishing giant is by way of a close-up of an elephant's eye on one of the TV screens. The conceit is that this is the elephant itself, moving along slowly. As the TV screen tracks across the stage, the performers move four chairs as its feet, and a man dressed as a keeper, holding a long brush, keeps pace with the virtual beast. As implied by the opening collage, this particular stage is a zone of simultaneous perspective, fracture and synthesis. The virtual elephant – sketched by a theatrical combination of gesture and media imagery – is made out of a performed inter-relationship of transpositional and hypermedial parts.

61

Two screens, the sort that you find in Japanese apartments, are set onstage. They form a divider between kitchen and bedroom. A narrator flown by a harness stands on top of the screen. Then he lies along it as if in a boat, as the screen shows a green section of the sea, by way of a back projection. The man's arm appears in the image (pre-recorded, clearly) as he drapes it in the water, and then his face as he ducks beneath the surface. This a play on the transposition of live and recorded in a single image-field that recalls Robert Lepage's similar effect in *Needles and Opium*.

Later in the show, one of the characters talks to a camera on a tripod. A live relay showing her face plays on the TV monitor that is behind her shoulder. She takes the camera with her to the fridge and tells it that she has not been able to sleep for the past seventeen nights. One of the TV monitors shows a series of images on fast-forwards, and stills, detailing her life with her husband and son – a video diary. Appearing on both the TV monitor and the Japanese screen, the image of the woman doubles. She talks about her face, her insomnia, a dream. She puts her hand to the camera to black it out. When she releases her hand, the image returns from black and appears on the back screen as well – the woman is now tripled (or quadrupled, if you also count her corporal presence). She talks again and stands up, and it becomes clear that this part of the woman's speech to camera has been pre-recorded, for the actor in front of us is not talking. She describes a nightmare in which she sees herself. The staging enacts this, so that the woman-narrator onstage is joined by three actors playing the woman in her dream. Thus, she is serially present, as herself (played by a performer), her speaking self on the three screens and her three alter egos embodied by performers.

Earlier in the sequence, silhouettes of live performers appear behind the Japanese screen – a couple in the bedroom – whilst the flying performer stands in mid-air above them. This is a peopled stage, with up to ten performers and camera operators at times. The scenic objects shift around the space whilst the video imagery cuts across it by way of leaps in size and site. The digital domain participates in a play of perspectives, disembodiments, re-embodiments and simultaneous actions and presences in dissimilar planes, spaces and modes. The effect is a dynamic interaction of discrete elements held in relation by the *mise en scène*. Overlaps, interconnected movements, asynchronous patterns – we witness a form of fractal expansion in which images recur without being quite the same, are doubled without being quite identical. In a multi-dimensional space that denies fixity the flux, the transition and the travel become motifs. The hypermedial *mise en scène* evokes the hypermedial city, with its permanently oscillating interrelationships and constantly shifting permutations.

Mise en scène and hypermediacy

From the examples above, we can see that the hypermediacy of the staging gives both structure and texture to the event. We see the same space as both flatly pictorial and fully scenic, two-dimensional and three-dimensional. Likewise, we are presented with the meeting between the live actor and mediated actor-as-other, seeing the same person as two people and the human figure as both actual and expanded. The actuality of the actor's presence is heightened by the co-presence of his or her mediatized selves, which are themselves staged as part of the theatrical mix. We watch *Jet Lag*, for example, not as viewers of Dearborn's video, nor as viewers of the sea, but as spectators of a hypermedial mise en scène, alert to the layering of image, reference, context and meaning performed in the theatre space.

Mise en scène – literally, that which is "placed on the stage" – is more than merely a directorial arrangement of activities or an effect of the meeting of set and actor. It is the continuum that gives staged elements their effective relation one to another and, thereby, their affective relation to the spectator. The *mise en scène* that broadly derives from the productions above featured screened images in dynamic interaction with other elements and attributes of a theatricalised space (bodies, set, movement and lighting). The screen is folded into the live event and so into the phenomenal realm of theatre. The screens in each production cannot ever be 'full', cannot contain all their effect in the manner of a single mediation (theatre or cinema, for instance). They are contingent upon aspects of the staging and are themselves staged. The projected images have a different status than they would were they part of a uniquely screen-based environment such as cinema or TV.

Bert States suggests that "film removes the actual aspect of performance and leaves us with the record of an actuality into which we can safely sink" (States 1985: 19). However, the *evident* interface between media in the examples above means that rather than immersing in the world of the image we are made sharply aware of "the actual aspect of performance". The images are not self-sufficient. What might once have been separate media are not self-contained. They can only be fully decoded in relation to the *mise en scène* – a *mise en scène* that is flamboyantly hypermedial. According to Patrice Pavis:

> *Mise en scène* is the art of suggesting a series of enunciators, an atmosphere, a dramatic situation, all of which open up trajectories of meaning, only to quickly close them down [...] We employ aesthetic categories of *mise en scène*, its segmentation of the real, to orient ourselves according to our own cognitive and existential categories (Pavis 2000).

Mise en scène in this account is an engine for spectatorship, configured according to the press of the cultural moment. It organises space for spectating and thereby redistributes meaning and effect. In Pavis's terms, *mise en scène* is both historically specific and culturally grounded – it is the concretisation of affects that convey meaning in the epistemological sense – and no less, I would suggest, that convey the texture of modern experience in the phenomenal sense. It is always an activity of combination and synthesis. In hypermedial performance, *mise en scène* is a network of mediations that are also remediations, persistently playing back to its spectators both the modes of the piece and the culture's modes of aesthetic affinity. The effect is in many instances less to do with the direct production of meaning and more to do with the production of a (meaningful) texture to the event.

To return to Bolter and Grusin's contention at the beginning of this chapter: hypermedial theatre engages the spectator in an awareness of the interaction of different media, hence of media themselves. In so doing, the fabric of the event – its *mise en scène* – suggests a sensorium based upon flow, linkage, interaction and

63

simultaneity. By this means, the production evokes the experience of contemporary culture, and offers an immediate engagement with the form and felt texture of that culture. We have come full circle to the pleasurable conjunction of hypermediacy and its shadow twin, immediacy.

Immediacy, presence and pleasure

Immediacy depends upon a sense of contact with something that matters, something that affects you. What matters to you might be that you laugh, wince, flinch, cry, think, feel excited or simply get absorbed. When this is the case, you experience the event in a pleasurable frisson of commitment, an engagement that is deliciously rapt. I have argued elsewhere that one of the potencies of live performance is precisely its ability to involve the spectator in an awareness of the here and now, the uniquely present moment of current experience.

In this sense, hypermediacy in the theatre can usefully be seen through a phenomenological perspective.[4] Towards the beginning of *Great Reckonings in Little Rooms* Bert States mentions "the immediate absorption of the image by the senses" (States 1985). This characteristic formulation suggests that the things that we see – whether staged action or screened images – work on us not merely via our reasoning and as a result of vision, but through a broader sensual engagement. States finds such absorption "delightful". My interest here is not in modalities of perception or the relation between what is potentially and actually perceived, but in the visceral nature of spectatorship and effects of visible, acoustic, motional, rhythmic and textural aspects of the staging. The functionality of staged elements lies in the way they impact upon a spectator. This impact is likely to be in relation to meaning-effects – but it may also have a *felt* charge that structures our experience of the event.

It has become commonplace to ascribe something of this charge to the agency of presence – both the presence of the performer onstage and the presence of the spectator at the live event. Presence is a central concern of phenomenology. As Robert Sokolowski suggests, "When we appreciate the presence of a thing, we appreciate it precisely as not absent" (Sokolowski 2000: 7). Sokolowski is not writing about theatre – but the theatre's characteristic trade in liveness and embodiment situates it as a medium that is especially invested in presence. As we have seen, the categories here are not simply presence/absence but also actual/virtual, since performance can evoke presences through a variety of strategies that do not necessitate the concrete onstage appearance of the thing that is conjured. Certainly, the virtual can be spoken of in terms of presence. In *D.A.V.E.* the virtual body is made present through projection, attaining materiality through its imposition on an actual body. In *The Elephant Vanishes*, a virtual Tokyo is made present by way of actual staging devices (moving objects, moving performers, interjections of sound, specific images) that evoke a complex system of interdependencies (evocative of city life) whilst drawing attention to their hypermediacy. In *Jet Lag* a virtual storm is made compellingly present as a series of ingredients that together fashion a space and a setting.

In hypermedial theatre, a theatre of simultaneities, the actual and the virtual are simultaneously in play, simultaneously emphasising each other. In various ways, theatre practitioners have routinely plied their trade in the liminal zone between the actual and the virtual. It is the actual which underpins the virtual and which offers itself most readily to our senses. As Merleau-Ponty puts it: "Things [...] arouse in me a carnal formula of their presence" (Merleau-Ponty 1964a: 164).[5] Or, if you prefer, "actuality continually pressures representation / fiction / illusion with the phenomenal claims of an experiential moment" (Garner 1994: 41).

Spectators enjoy recognition of the edge between the actual and the virtual, the real and the fabricated. We are complicit in the moment at which artefact becomes presentation. I do not think that there is any diminution of whatever turn to "reality" might be attempted by the staging – simply that meaning-effects take their charge and become more immediately pleasurable in the friction between the artifice and its referents. This intensifies our *jouissance*, to use Barthes' term, in the face of performance. Of course, in Barthes' sense such pleasure is bound up also with poignancy and loss – there is something event-like and overwhelming about its onset. The hypermedial productions that I have examined generate a similar pleasure at the point of the interface between the live and the mediatized, at the moment of (re)presentation, where the thing that is conjured evokes unreachable contingencies that are outside the room (the stormy sea, Tokyo and elephants, fantasy bodies) and its own material manifestation before us. The interrelation of media emphasises the presence of what we watch in this particular sense: it enhances our experience of it as existing in the here-and-now.

The productions described above underwrite the "experiential moment", to use Garner's phrase, through the nature of their hypermediacy. Structured around simultaneously corporeal and mediatized elements they trade in a currency of the present and immediate because of their theatricality. They place the body and the object in spatial relationship with the screen, whilst screened images are contingent upon live embodiment. The logic of hypermediacy in performance draws upon the provocative simultaneities of live bodies, mediatized images, theatrical time and space and screen time and space – placed within the immediate time and space of the spectator to produce an effect, precisely, of immediacy. As Bolter and Grusin, suggest:

65

> digital hypermedia seek the real by multiplying mediation so as to create a feeling of fullness, a satiety of experience, which can be taken as reality (Bolter and Grusin 1999: 53).

I am not sure that reality is the key currency here, but rather experience and, more particularly in the theatre (for why else would we go?), the experience of a sort of pleasure at multi-texture. This is, after all, a theatre for an age of consumption.

Andy Lavender

Notes
1 I saw the production at the Barbican Theatre, London. The Builders Association is a New York-based performance company and Diller + Scofidio are architects.
2 I saw the production in 2002 at the Purcell Room, Queen Elizabeth Hall, London.
3 I saw the production on 5 July 2003 at the Barbican Theatre, London, as part of the BITE 03 festival.
4 For broad introductions to phenomenology, see Moran 2000 and Sokolowski 2000.
5 Merleau-Ponty writes in terms that are luminously theatrical in their application. His focus on corporality – the body as a site of experience – gives his work added resonance in view of criticism's current interest in bodies and embodiment. See also Merleau-Ponty 1962 and 1964b.

SWANN'S WAY: VIDEO AND THEATRE AS AN INTERMEDIAL STAGE FOR THE REPRESENTATION OF TIME

Sigrid Merx

This chapter concentrates on the performance *Proust 1: Swann's way*, which is the first part of a series of four performances based on the work of Marcel Proust, by the contemporary Flemish theatre director Guy Cassiers. It assesses the way time and memory are staged through the use of digital video technology, and demonstrates how the representation of memory and the process of remembering calls for an intermedial approach. Playing with size and scale, presence and absence, live and mediatized, creating simultaneity and intermediality are some of the aspects that are discussed in reference to the performance. The paper concludes by elaborating the dramaturgical functioning of technology in the work of Guy Cassiers. Working primarily from a lyric perspective, Cassiers creates a sensory inner world, which electrifies the imagination and memories of the audience. By opposing live video to the physical present actor, the negative space in-between the image and the process of creating that image – the intermedial – is located. The 'empty' space functions as a platform, a stage on which the individual experiences of all participants in the live performance can be staged and the invisible, or 'the forgotten', can be remembered and made visible.

Opening scene

An empty stage except for a string quartet downstage left and three small video cameras centre stage. Two large projection screens are flown in. One screen is downstage of the video cameras, the other upstage, which leaves just enough room for the actors to move between the screens so that they can act to the cameras without being visible to the audience. The downstage screen is flexible, consisting of loose, vertical strips of texture, but the upstage screen is solid. A string quartet is playing. A man enters the stage and listens to the music for a while. Then he moves centre stage and positions himself with his back to the audience. Slowly, he puts his head through the downstage split screen, towards one of the video cameras behind. As his physical head disappears from the audience's view though the split screen, his projected head appears on the upstage screen in a full screen close-up, which is coloured by a vague blue light.

The man starts talking. That is to say, we hear an amplified voice and at the same time see the mouth of the projected head moving. We hear the famous opening lines of the first novel from Marcel Proust's *A la recherche du temps perdu* (1913-1927). The narrator, Proust, tells us how, when he was a child, he used to read in bed before beginning to fall asleep without noticing it, only to wake up again thinking: 'I am falling asleep'. Looking at the man's back, with his head piercing through the projection screen

Figure 12
Proust 1: Swann's way: An example of the combination of the body of the actor and a video projection of his face in one stage image.

it is as if we catch him in the act of *remembering*. Proust, almost literally, takes a peek into his own memories, and we are allowed a glance of him in his inner world. As he recalls moments from his childhood, vague contours start appearing on the projection screen on both sides of Proust's face, and slowly sharpen into huge close-up faces of his mother and father. It is like watching a film being processed in a bath of photo chemicals – the photographic images steadily emerge and his parents come to life. What we can not see is how, upstage of the split projection screen, the actors representing the mother and the father, carefully move their faces closer and closer to the camera, thereby moving themselves into focus. When their images have sharpened, Proust slowly moves out of the image by drawing his head away from the camera. The memories live on autonomously without the person who evoked them.

Figure 13
Proust 1: Swann's way: The narrator Proust recalls his childhood. Memories of his parents appear as video images on the projection screen.

The moment the narrator Proust is no longer present in the video projections, attention is drawn to another actor who is physically present on stage, playing the young Marcel Proust. The video projections now no longer present only an inner world but function also as the representation of an outside world, experienced by a child.

The opening scenes of *Proust 1: Swann's way*, from the Flemish theatre maker Guy Cassiers[1] and his Dutch ensemble, ro theater, form an impressive example of how the almost intangible process of *remembering* can be presented through an *intermedial interplay*: the physical presence of the actors; the digital video images projected on a screen (live and pre-recorded); the live music performed by a string quartet on stage; all offering different perspectives of the complexity and layering of *memory*.

An intermedial approach

Swann's way is not just an eclectic collection of *fin de siècle* prose and high-tech stage sets presenting a dazzling multimedia structure – each medium retains their individual principles of representation while inter-acting within the performance. However, what interests me, in particular, is how the individual media work together to represent *time*, and, specifically, the experience of *remembering*. My emphasis therefore will be on the influence and effect of video in this performance, although text, music and light do play a significant role.

PROUST AND THE DIMENSIONS OF TIME

The historical period in which Marcel Proust (1871-1922) wrote was one where *time* and *movement* played a prominent role; and his works carry the marks of the time in which it was conceived. In his series of novels on lost time we see how coaches changed into automobiles, crinolines into gowns and magic lanterns into movies. However, apart from these manifestations the work of Proust, above all, represents the search for the representation of a new experience of time. During his lifetime, the dominant aesthetic in art was the conventions of realism, but Proust tried to develop his own poetic, which can be characterised as an expressive externalisation of the inner human conscience. Moving away from the representation of action, Proust explored the process of remembering, of memories being 'electrified' by sensory experiences. Time, as represented by Proust is revealed in all its different dimensions: the social-historical background against which aristocratic leisure takes place, the psychological development of a young boy into a grown man. However, there is also the time of love and jealousy, the mystical experience of being outside time, which can be felt in experiencing art. Representing these layers of time, the work of Proust becomes a philosophical writing on time itself.[2]

69

Because of the desire to show a variety of different dimensions of time the novels constantly change *narrative perspective*. The overall perspective is provided by the first person narrator, Proust, but within that perspective we see also the world that he is describing from different points of view; these are dependant on the position the narrator is taking in relation to the world of his construction. Sometimes he is acting in the world, sometimes reflecting on the world and sometimes he is experiencing it.

Sigrid Merx

CASSIERS AND MULTIPLE PERSPECTIVES

In *Swann's way*, Cassiers has emphasised the different dimensions of time represented in the novel. The world of thoughts, the world of childhood, the world of love, the world of art are all represented and held together by the narrator, Proust. Cassiers stays loyal to the literary first person perspective. However, the fact that the 'I' *in the novel*, refers to both *the author Proust* and *the narrator Proust* at one and the same time, is not only seen but also heard on stage, which provides an extra dimension. Cassiers explicitly shows the duality of the 'I', (author and narrator) by staging *the creator of the 'I'* and *the 'I' who is the result of the creation*. In doing this, Cassiers establishes a close connection between remembering and creating because remembering can be understood also as a *creative process*.[3]

The performance begins and ends with the narrator Proust talking. Proust's reflections on his experiences provide a frame, within which everything that is experienced will be understood ultimately as a part of, and even the result of this frame. All the worlds revealed in the performance appear as Proust's experiences of these worlds. Using different media and allowing them to inter-act is a key strategy in creating different worlds and dimensions. Cassiers is interested in purifying each medium, letting them neither illustrate each other nor work together to build a Wagnerian Gesamtkunstwerk, but to tell their own story, thereby generating different 'voices', different views. The space between the different media and the different perspectives they bring about, should be filled with the experiences of the audience.[4] Cassiers is looking for a point of view, or language, which will put the individual memories of the spectator into another perspective and will stimulate them to look at things as if they were mentally cross-eyed. The language he is looking for should, according to him, not be limited to the language of the spoken or written word, but can equally well be the language of music or light or sound or image.

By titillating the senses of the audience, Cassiers wants to intensify all those experiences and memories they already carry inside themselves. The special thing about making theatre, he believes, is the fact that through different languages and different disciplines it is possible to address the senses independently. The sensory stimuli that Cassiers offers to his audience do not necessarily have a logical relationship or hierarchy. He feels that the relative independence he is looking for in his performances, mirrors the way in which our perception, our senses function in everyday life. Each position implies a different sensory approach. Cassiers encourages his audience to choose and shift between the different positions being offered. He is not interested in a bombardment of the senses, he is trying to stimulate people to deal creatively with the signs he has given them. Address in the work of Cassiers is by nature sensory.[5] The audience become their own editors, through participation in an intermedial play of putting the different parts together in their mind.

Video and theatre: an interaction of principles of representation[6]

An intermedial perspective on *Swann's way* necessitates doing justice to the variety of perspectives that are represented and the relationships that are established between them. I will concentrate on the use of video in the live performance primarily because using video projections literally means creating *a new frame* within the theatrical frame; but also because video and theatre each have their own possibilities of representing time and creating time experiences as a result of their ontological differences. It is my belief that the intermedial relationship between video and theatre can open up new dimensions of time. Therefore, in order to do this I divert, for a moment, for a brief consideration of the different ways that theatre and video can represent time (space and action).

Theatre is a live performance in which actor and audience are simultaneously physically present and takes place in the absolute here and now. *Video* is an electronic device, which can record and play: image and sound are simultaneously recorded onto a magnetic tape, which are transformed into electronic impulses. Electronic materiality enables video to transform its recorded sounds and images to digital information. Video, like theatre, can be live because it has the possibility of instant playback. The difference between the *live* in theatre and in video is that image and sound are mediated through a technical device. Video can take place in the absolute now, but not in the absolute here of actor and audience.

As a result of its materiality, theatre as a direct communication process has some limitations. In general, but not always, the *performance space* is confined and the audience is given a fixed position, with, as a result, a fixed perspective. *Time* in theatre is a closed continuum. *Time and space* are the givens in theatre, which are filled in by the performance. This has led to a definition of theatre as a performance space in which *unity of time* is the principle structuring factor, and the actor is the dominant force, distinguishing himself from the static space in which he is moving.

Video in theatre, on the other hand is more flexible in terms of time and space, which can be constructed with the help of camera movement, camera framing, montage and digital manipulation. As a result different perspectives, distances and sizes can be realised in theatre. The audience, although physically in a fixed position, can relate to the shown images in different ways. The flexibility of time and space enables more complicated narrative structures. When video is employed within the theatrical frame, there is a potential for the static space of theatre to become more dynamic. Video can represent spaces, which enlarge, double, transform the theatrical space, as well as, in the case of live video, the performance space. Similarly, the closed continuum of time can be broken, as video can introduce a different dimension of time in the performance. On the level of narrative these possibilities concerning time and space enable theatre to employ more complicated narrative structures.

The dominant role of the actor in theatre can be affected by the use of video in theatre. Normally the actor is the main moving element in a performance, but he has to relate himself to the moving image of the video projection when it is active. The audience is also affected because they are confronted with different perspectives. They have their own perspective, which enables them to oversee the performance stage and a different perspective offered by the video projection. Video raises possibilities playing with the scale in theatre as well; especially in the use of extreme close-ups or grand establishing shots, where the physically present actor can be reduced to a tiny figure and the audience is confronted with different sizes of the images. Finally, one of the most significant consequences of the use of video is the aspect of simultaneity. Spatially separated, but parallel evolving actions and events can be performed simultaneously.[7] The aspect of simultaneity draws the attention to the relationship between the physically present and the mediatized.

Swann's way: a performance analysis

The Proust series of Cassiers is based upon a dramaturgy of time-images, and in *Swann's way* video and theatre work together to offer us a variety of *temporal images*. Therefore, I turn now to take a closer look at some of the scenes of the performance in order to reveal how, with the use of video, the *different dimensions of time* are represented in *different time-images* and which perspectives, or *positions to see*, are installed in the minds of the audience a result.

THE WORLD OF MEMORY

In the first two scenes, the audience is invited to take up the perspective offered by Proust as he searches his memory and is offered a *lyrical perspective*[8], which relates to the "intensity of the experience" (Kattenbelt 1994). The space behind the flexible projection screen becomes the domain of a Bergsonian "pure past"[9] . This is the *physical space* where the actor is looking into the camera and talking into the microphone and the *symbolical space* where Proust is looking for his memories. At first, the voice – as a stream of consciousness – seems to represent his thinking. However, the moment his thinking turns into remembering, we no longer have the voice to listen to or the talking head to look at, but we are confronted with images of his memories, which can be understood as coming out of the process of remembering. It seems that we have gone back in time.

THE WORLD OF A CHILD

From the moment we see the actor playing the young Marcel the character of the projected images changes. The actors playing Marcel parents are dressed in clothes we would expect in the *fin du siècle*, and positioned against the background of a furnished living room, with decorative curtains, a tea table with cups and cakes. Father is reading a newspaper, mother is knitting. The nature of the images presented by the actors and in the stage setting photographed image on the screen behind them tend toward naturalistic, playing with the codes of narrative Hollywood cinema. The projected images in this sense emphasise the actuality of time, space and action and help to create a dramatic world. Despite the scale of the photographic image, the dramatic features of the images are not dominant in this scene. Looking at the video projections it is possible to tell easily that the room in which the parents are present is not a three-dimensional room, but a photographic image in front of which the live actors are acting. There is no real tea to pour, no cake to eat. The stage lighting foregrounds the fact that you are looking at a construction and there is little possibility of loosing oneself in the illusion of the projected images, as would be possible in cinema. The *film-like images* are staged within *a theatrical frame* and they interact with other theatrical signs. The video projections are not independent but bound up with the physical present actor. In this scene, the projected images have become the perceptions of the world by a child.

Figure 14
Proust 1: Swann's way: The relationship of the young Marcel Proust with his parents expressed in the play through the scale of the human body and the scale of the video projection.

The huge projected images of his parents and the doctor refer to the outside world as Marcel seems to experience it: big, impressive, almost threatening. The audience has no choice but to look at this world from the point of view of Marcel and is offered again the opportunity to take up a lyrical position. The screen mediates and connects two different spatial dimensions. At the same time, it is the screen which separates the two worlds. Marcel and his parents do not share the same space. Marcel is alone and the actor is alone on stage.

THE WORLD OF LOVE

Young Marcel has three important women in his life: his mother, with whom he has an almost incestuous relationship, Gilberte, the love of his youth and her charming and enchanting mother, Odette. Most of the time his mother appears on the projection screen in huge close-ups. She is always near, so near that it tends to be suffocating. On one particular moment, she offers the young Marcel her cheek for a kiss, the actress bringing her cheek very close to the camera. For Marcel, his mother can be understood as the cheek to be kissed. Without this kiss he feels desperate, alone and insecure. The cheek is brought so close to the camera that, in its projection, it gradually looses its meaning of a cheek and turns it into a mere landscape of skin.

Although still operative in real time, the video creates an exciting tension between the live and the mediatized. The reality of a face is registered, captured and doubled so to speak, but at the same time transformed. The cheek of the mother turns into a new sensory image, which is able to conjure up an immediate sensation, and in so doing, it has the potential to trigger all kind of memories of the audience.

In his novels, Proust often meticulously describes how involuntary memories are intensified especially in those moments of intense sensory experience: a ray of light, a special scent, a certain tune or the taste of a Madeleine cookie. The impression that Gilberte has made on Marcel is shown in a blurred video projection of two bare legs in a field of flowers and in the image of a middle finger stuck into a mouth projected in slow-motion, which in its repetition takes on different meanings, ranging from innocence to sexuality and vulgarity. Both video projections are pre-recorded and have been manipulated to create a hazy look and denial of a total picture: the face is not presented and it is not even clear if this image really is Gilberte. When we consider the images to be perceptions and memories of Marcel, Gilberte seems literally to have been reduced to his 'vague' general notions of girlhood and blossoming sexuality.

On the other hand, Gilberte's mother, Odette is to Marcel the paragon of womanhood. She is the swish of her astonishing gown, the folding of her hands and her seducing smile, represented in a constellation of impressions visualised in a montage of fading images on the projection screen – parts of her body, a certain look, the fabric of her dress – which, exactly because of their fragmented nature, represent this one woman, The Woman.

Figure 15
Proust 1: Swann's way: An image of Odette, the mother of Gilberte, whose appearance mesmerises the young Marcel Proust.

With the use of video the body and appearance of Gilberte, as well as of Odette is fragmented and then put back together in a series of moving, dreamlike, highly subjective, images that reveal Marcel's inner experiences. They suggest that love brings about a completely different form of looking and remembering. An experience, which in reality only took seconds, is represented as an extensive moment, which starts to lead a life of its own.

The intermedial presentation opens to our interpretation the possibility that we do not necessarily love a person, but the image we build of that person in our mind. The fragmented images of the women and the actors impersonating them are simultaneously present and make us aware of this image-making ability in us. Apparently, the experience of lust and desire cannot be captured in the linearity of a narrative or adequately represented by the totality of the physical present actor. Because the images are detached from the total appearance of the actors, a space is opened up for the audience to experience these images as impressions of every woman they choose to see or remember.

THE WORLD OF THE SALON

After the interval, the upstage screen is left in place but the flexible screen has disappeared. The three cameras are now visible to the audience, breaking the illusion of the autonomous image. Thus, the construction is shown and it is not by accident that this visibility coincides with the situation on the level of the narrative. Presented on stage is the French salon of Madame Verdurin and her guests, where everything is about seeing and being seen. No longer is the focus on an inner world on stage and an outer world in video projections, but a social world of codes and conventions. All the characters are engaged in trying to make a specific impression.

75

Figure 16
Proust 1: *Swann's way*: The salon of Madame Verdurin. The actors present themselves directly towards the video camera and the microphone.

Similarly, the outside world in these scenes is not outside the characters: they are part of it and they are shaping it. This becomes clear in the way that they move their costumes in front of the camera, literally showing their outside to the public, creating abstract images with the colours and the shapes of the prints on their costumes and decorating their own salon. These images are frozen into stills, thus forming the background of their social life.

Whereas the characters are decorating their own salon with their bragging and small talk, the actors are seen creating a live image of a salon in front of the very visible cameras and the microphones. In a monologue, the character Madame Verdurin reflects on how the world of the salon and social interaction will never cease to exist. The face of the actor representing Madame Verdurin – who is delivering her monologue directly to a small camera – is recorded and projected into a seemingly infinite amount of transparent layers. We see a face on a face on a face and so on. As a result, a specific temporal awareness is installed and opens up a future.

Other actors also 'step out' of the situation of the salon. Representing their characters, they turn to the camera with reflexive monologues, which exceed the direct context of the salon and emphasises the epic tendencies in the performance.

TEXT-IMAGE

Epic tendencies continue in the shown projections of words, which appear between the scenes and echo early film captions and intertitles. They provide information concerning space, time, action or modes of expression and function as visible stage directions. The emphasis is on objectively describing (telling) instead of on showing. Short sentences appear, depicting, for example, historical time '1896', or a place, the 'Champs Elysée' thus creating an objective framework of facts and historical time, within which the theatrical action takes place. The separation of the media is a very important structural principle in the work of Cassiers. Word, image and sound are not used to create one illusion, but function independently and so are able to communicate different meanings, different stories. For example, Cassiers stages text projections, which show the kind of information you would normally find in the stage directions of a play: references to actions, occurrences, emotions.

Figure 17
Proust 1: Swann's way: An example of text projection. The text says 'knocking on a door'. The action of the actor is replaced by the words, which have become an image.

Like a reader of a play, the audience 'reads' these stage directions as they are shown as text in the video projection. However, the actions or persons to which those stage directions refer are not necessarily represented on stage. The space that exists between the physical action and presence on stage, and the projected text is filled with the imagination of the spectator. This allows for unexpected meanings to be created. For example, during the moment when the word 'piano music' is projected onto the video screen and the string quartet start playing.

Thus, although the media keep their own ontology, through theatrical performance and framing the boundaries between the media become blurred. Here is the space of intermediality where the media remediate each other. The intermediality works closely with the aspect of transformability: the word becomes image.

A very significant moment concerning the use of the text projection is during a scene towards the end of the performance. The front screen has been lowered once again and the perspective of the narrator Proust returned. Speedily the years pass by, together with a short description of the most important occurrences in these years: the invention of the telephone, the first Airplane. Literally, time is not only evolving but hurrying by, to finally slowing down and ending with the First World War.[10] With these projections, the subjective memories of Proust are enlarged to include a social and political perspective. The subjectivity of memory and the objectivity of history meet in a final monologue on the First World War. Gilberte appears on screen as the chronicler of a devastating period of time as well the first love of Marcel. Everything Proust remembered from his childhood played, as it turns out, an important role in history. The little road where he first met Gilberte became the front line of the war between the Germans and the French.

MULTIPLICATION AND REPETITION

The idea of repetition plays an important role: our experiences are shaped by the things we have already lived. However, every time we experience something, even though we have experienced it before, it is a new experience. The monologue of the character Swann – the husband of Odette, father of Gilberte and former friend (before he married Odette) of Marcel's parents – expresses this thought, and gives as an example the experience of listening to music. He says that every time you hear a much listened to piece of music you hear it anew: it will always be a première. What changes it every time is not so much increased understanding or knowledge, but the recollection of previous experiences of listening to the same piece.

77

This idea of *repetition* and *renewal* is not only referred to in this monologue but also expressed in the performance as a whole. Musical phrases of the live string quartet are repeated throughout the performance; the narrator repeats lines of his monologues, characters take up each others sentences; and video projections from the beginning of the performance are shown again later in a different context. A specific case of repetition can be found in the way the relationship between the adults Odette and Swann is mirrored in the adolescent relationship between Gilberte and Marcel. Both relationships are imbued with and determined by a doctrine of extreme jealousy on the side of the men.[11] Mirroring characters in other characters is one of the features of the work of Proust, and Cassiers makes the parallels visible. He intends to do so not only within the performance of *Swann's way* but also in all the parts of this theatre project. The mirror reflections work in two directions: they reflect the past and project the future at the same time.

The live and mediatized

Cassiers plays a deliberate game in creating an illusion and breaking it down again. Although in the first part of the performance the video cameras are hidden, which might encourage a suspension of disbelief, Cassiers skilful use of a variety of media ensures that the audience is constantly aware of the theatrical experience. The flexible strips of texture of the projection screen in the first part of the performance are not only like the cracks in someone's mind, but are also the shreds of the 'fourth wall' of the projection screen torn apart. They shatter the illusion by showing us glimpses of what is going on behind. The perspective of story telling is therefore not only taking place on the level of the fictitious narrator. The actor *presents* himself as an *instance of narration* as well on the level of the theatrical. Within a theatrical framework, the actor becomes visible as a constructor of images.

Factually, the demonstration of the construction of an illusion can be understood as the proposition of an epic perspective of the audience, and offer a possible critical stance. In the work of Cassiers however this distance between what is presented and represented, ultimately has to be considered as a space, which can be filled by the images, experiences and memories of the audience themselves. Thus, it becomes a totally intermedial experience, as the audience become constructors of images and create a lyrical perspective of their own in response to the inner world shown on stage. Intermediality is located in the creative process of Cassiers.

Not forgetting

The most important result of the interaction between live video and the physical present actor is the exciting connection that can be established between the past and the present. What else is remembering other than creating an image of the past in the present? When we are simultaneously confronted with the process of creating an image and looking at the image, which results from this process, we are able to experience the passing and preservation of the present itself.[12] It seems to me that the greatest potential of live video, not only in this performance but in every live performance, is to install in us an awareness of the liveness of theatre. Live video in the live performance can remind us of the fact that 'this is live', 'this is now'. Live video can make us remember that we are in the theatre.

It seems to be quite paradoxical that theatre does need the interference of a medium to bring to attention its ontological characteristics. However, it is not that strange perhaps when we take into consideration Auslander's account of *Liveness* (1999). He has tried to demonstrate that liveness should no longer be considered as an ontological feature of the live performance – a feature on which it has popularly been opposed to the mediatized. Liveness, as Auslander treats it, can be understood as an effect of mediatization, and television, in his opinion, is socially and economically more capable of creating an experience of liveness for an audience than the live performance. The tendency of the live performance to embrace the mediatization is an attempt to secure its threatened position. Cassiers once told me that theatre should be about "not forgetting". He was opposing it to all the mediatized forms in our contemporary society, which, according to him, seemed to have turned forgetting into an art – selling illusions without presenting them as such, delivering messages full of prefabricated meaning. When Cassiers employs live video in his performances he is not trying to save theatre from extinction, but deliberately using video to deconstruct this process of forgetting.

Video, or whatever medium, does not necessarily take over the live performance when it us used, as Auslander seems to suggest, because it is staged within the theatrical frame. Staging live video as a theatrical sign makes it possible to let it interact with the other theatrical signs, such as the physical present actor and thus become part of the conceptual framework of intermediality.

In *Swann's way*, through creating deliberate differences between what is to be seen live on stage and on the screen, through his choices in what not to illustrate, the focus turns to be *the invisible* - the mental space that lies between the two and connects them. Quite literally, the *intermedial* is the empty space in which the invisible can become manifest. Instead of using this space for an explicit media critique, which of course would have been possible, Cassiers tries his best to leave the space empty, or should we say full with possibilities. Possibilities that can be actualised by each and every one who takes up the invitation to enter this space and search for his or her time lost. Proust, who looks in the darkness behind the projection screen, the actor who is looking for his reflection in the lens of the camera, the audience looking at and simultaneously 'with' them; we are all looking for ourselves, taking a peek in our inner world.

Clearly, it is not only the spectator who is stimulated in to motion. The classical positions of the actor and the text involved are shaken as well. The text is torn apart and taken away from the actor who is supposed to represent it. Aspects of authority and authenticity, normally attached to the dramatic text are no longer there. The mimetic relationship between text and actor no longer exists. The illusion of one reality is broken to give way to the intensity of experience. As the spectator is tempted to create their own reality, the technique tempts the actor to construct his own identity in front of the camera. This search and experiment is similar to the search of the characters in the narrative experience, showing and presenting to the outer world.

It is in this way that Cassiers creates a world in which, brought together because of the situation, actor, character and spectator meet. They do meet. It is in the empty, intermedial space of the performance that all their worlds are staged. We might not share what we remember, but we do share that we do remember.

79

Notes

1 The theatre maker Guy Cassiers, artistic director of the 'ro theatre' since 2000 is known for his revolutionary use of (live) video in performance. Cassiers hardly ever stages dramatic texts but prefers to adapt novels. *Proust 1: Swann's Way* is the first part of a theatre series of four performances based on the seven novels of Marcel Proust *A la recherché du temps perdu*. The opening performance (Rotterdam, 5 March 2003), was followed by *Proust 2: Albertine's Way* (26 May 2003) *Proust 3: Charlus's Way*, (15 May 2004) and *Proust 4: Proust's Way*, (7 May 2005).

2 In his book *Proust et les signes* (1964) the French philosopher Gilles Deleuze distinguishes four categories of signs in the work of Proust. The worldly signs, which refer to the signs of the social world determined by the social codes; the signs of love, mostly referring to betrayal, adultery and homosexual feelings; the signs provided by our senses, referring to our lost time (the taste of a Madeleine cookie bringing Marcel back to his childhood); and finally the signs of the artwork, the highest order of signs in the Proustian hierarchy. In these signs, real truth can be found because they not only bring back to memory lost time, but materialise it as well in the work of art.

3 The concept of remembering is used in a specific way here. I link the ability of video to record events, to store them and to play them back (with or without manipulating the image) with the function of memory. An important difference is that in the case of a memory, 'the event' and 'the memory of that event' is separated in time. With live video the 'recording of the moment' and the 'occurrence of the moment' itself are simultaneously present. Remembering, in this case, means that live video used in a live performance *reminds* us of the fact that this is 'live'.

4 In his book *Postdramatisches Theater* (1999: 290) Hans-Thies Lehmann describes the "multiplication of frames" as characteristic for the post-dramatic stage. The result of this multiplication according to him is an emphasis on the "sensory qualities" and an increased "perceptibility" of the singular frame. This is certainly the case in the work of Cassiers.

5 In her book *The Locus of Looking: Dissecting Visuality in the theatre* (2002: 47) Bleeker advocates a new approach of the concept of perspective, away from the perspective in terms of framing, towards perspective in terms of an address, that presents a viewer with a point of view as to what is there to be seen. She understands address in terms of a setting up of positions, which invite the viewers to take these up themselves.

6 The comparison of the principles of representation of video and theatre is based on the comparison of film and theatre as described and elaborated by media theorist Kattenbelt in *Theater en Film* (1991). Kattenbelt bases his comparison on the writings of different film theorists, such as Lukács, Balázs and the Russian Formalists, who, in an attempt to legitimise film as an art form, explicitly opposed film to theatre. Groot Nibbelink, in her article 'Verhevigde werkelijkheid' (in: *E-view* 99 (2000) 1. http://comcom. kub.nl/e-view/99-1/groot.htm.) uses Kattenbelt's comparison of film and theatre to explore the influence of the montage of video and theatre on the principles of representation in theatre.

7 Kattenbelt (1991) argues that in this particular case time, characterised by the aspect of 'after each other', gets a spatial dimension and therefore is dominated by the aspect of 'next to each other'. He refers to this principle as the 'spatialisation' of time.

8 The use of lyric here refers to the different positions an auctorial instance can take in relation to a possible world constructed in theatre, or for that matter any medium. Kattenbelt relates the dramatic to the actuality of action, the epic to the reflexivity of thought and the lyric to the intensity of experience. Kattenbelt, C: 'The triad of action, emotion and reflection' in: *Kodikas/Kode: Ars Semeiotica*, Vol. 17, (1994), No. 1/2.

9 French philosopher Deleuze distinguishes between the movement-image, time-image and thought-image within a context of cinematographic modernity. His understanding of the movement-image and time-image is based on the work of Bergson, especially his *Matière et mémoire* (1896). See *Cinéma 1 – L'image-mouvement* (Paris 1983) and *Cinéma 2 – L'image temps* (Paris 1985).

10 Following Kattenbelt (1991) we could term this moment as an example of *temporalisation of space*.

11 According to Cassiers, as he told during a rehearsal, the relationship between Marcel and Gilberte is as mature as the relationship between Swann and Odette is immature. The language they speak is different, but their way of acting identical.

12 Following Kattenbelt (1991) we could term this as an example of *spatialisation of time*.

DIGITAL OPERA: INTERMEDIALITY, REMEDIATION AND EDUCATION

Freda Chapple

This chapter argues that the performer in opera is a medium of intermediality, and that intermediality, remediation and education are linked inextricably to each other. Referencing conversations with professional singers and the Kurt Weill and Bertolt Brecht opera *The Rise and Fall of the City of Mahagonny* (1930), the first part of the chapter explores how the singing actor performs *in-between* the medium of music and the medium of theatre. She argues that intermediality in opera is located in-between the medium of instrumental music (whether live or technologically produced), the sung lyric and spoken word performed by the singing actor, and the *mise-en-scène*, which may, or may not include multi-media representation. The second part of the chapter explores how the intermedial production of *The Forest Murmurs: adventures in the German Romantic Imagination* (Opera North, 2001) remediated Romanticism in opera in space and form, which allowed the audience to use their own imagination and thoughts to create their own readings and perceive the opera form differently. Here she argues that when intermediality is staged in a format that draws on the structures of the digital, it "cultivates humanity through *liberal* education", in the Stoic sense of "liberating the mind from the bondage of habit and custom" (Nussbaum 1997: 8). In the light of this, she suggests that there is a need for change in theatre and education research practices to take account of what contemporary opera performance identifies.

> Methods wear out, stimuli fail. New problems loom up and demand new techniques. Reality alters: to represent it the means of representation must alter too.
>
> Bertolt Brecht[1]

Contesting media

Opera and *theatre* have always had a symbiotic and often combative relationship rooted in conflicting claims of authority and hierarchy. There is a tradition of defining opera in a binary opposition to theatre, based on the difference of written text and spoken words versus music notation and sung words. However, live performances of opera and theatre both use the performer's voice, body and mind in the presence of an audience in the same space and at the same time. Therefore, I prefer to define opera as a part of *music theatre*, which includes within its form: opera, operetta, the musical, musical theatre, musical comedy, music hall and cabaret. Opera is an *intermedial art form* that has remediated the *medium of music* (instrumental and vocal) with the *medium of dramatic literature* (libretto) at various times in its history. In common with other art forms, opera has spawned a variety of generic variations related to historical periods and artistic movements, with the Romantic repertoire becoming the dominant operatic genre in the nineteenth century. Romantic opera is the genre most identified with Grand Opera, spectacular productions and the creation of the *Diva*. Drawing freely on literature, plays and philosophical and political ideas of the nineteenth century, Romantic opera expressed patriotic appeals to national identity and the desire for individual liberty in physical love and philosophical thoughts. Influenced by Gothic literature, aspects of Romantic opera revelled in its ability to indicate phenomena beyond the 'real world'. In this context, it is no surprise that Shakespeare's plays were remediated to the operatic genre via Verdi: *Macbeth* (1847), *Othello* (1887) and *Falstaff* (1893).

To some extend, contemporary opera companies still have to engage with the legacy of the Romantic repertoire because of its popular appeal to audiences and this was certainly the case at the start of the twentieth century. The two operas discussed in this chapter both remediate Romanticism in opera in different ways. The first is the Bertolt Brecht and Kurt Weill opera *The Rise and Fall of the City of Mahagonny* (1930). The second is *The Forest Murmurs: adventures in the German Romantic imagination*, (Tim Hopkins and Stephen Sloane, Opera North 2001). Both, I argue use multimedia and intermedial effects creatively to expand the language of the opera stage and explore intermediality, perception and education. Brecht and Weill raised the consciousness of the audience to their exploitation, and educated them to go and change the social system that produced their reality. *The Forest Murmurs* separates musical items from their traditional narrative context and expands *medial boundaries* within the operatic frame. These challenge audience expectations of opera and the operatic voice as a *live medium*. Separation of text from context and the expansion of medial boundaries trigger alternative perceptions about the representations of humanity presented within the theatrical frame. This is an important part of the *intermedial discourse* and integral to *education*:

> When we ask about the relationship of a liberal education to citizenship, we are asking a question with a long history in the Western philosophical tradition. We are drawing on Socrates' concept of "the examined life", on Aristotle's notion of reflective citizenship, and above all on Greek and Roman Stoic notions of an education that is "liberal" in that it liberates the mind from the bondage of habit and custom, producing people who can function with sensitivity and alertness as citizens of the whole world. This is what Seneca means by the cultivation of humanity (Nussbaum 1997: 8).

In this chapter, I argue that the singing actor in opera is a medium of intermediality and the interface between the intermedial form of opera itself and the audience, who are mediators of its intermediality in performance. Using *The Rise and Fall of the City of Mahagonny* and conversation with professional singers, I locate intermediality in opera. From there, I argue that *The Forest Murmurs* remediated the operatic space and audience expectations of Romantic opera by presenting the material to the audience in a performance mode that draws on the structures of digital technology. The effect of this is not only remediation of the operatic form, but "liberal" education. Given the ability of digital media to communicate instantly with "citizens of the whole world" this seems to me to be an appropriate model. In conclusion, I argue that if contemporary opera companies are leading the way in "the cultivation of humanity" through intermedial theatre practice, then the Academy must respond and change curriculum and research practices to put intermediality at the centre (not at the side) of theatre and education research.

Intermedial models / intermedial performers

In the early part of the twentieth century, theatre directors and composers moved easily across medial boundaries in order to create new art forms. Included within their ranks were Schoenberg (*Pierrot Lunaire*, 1912) and Stravinsky (*L'Histoire d'un Soldat*, 1924). Given the level of difficulty in their music, this was no 'dumbing-down' but rather an elevation and creative experiment in opera at the start of a new century. In retrospect, it is possible to identify that the phenomenon was particularly popular in European culture. In Russia, the poetry of Mayakovsky, the music of Shostakovich and the direction of Meyerhold created a physical and poetic form of intermedial theatre, which in its satiric form appealed directly to the masses. In Germany, the productions of Max Reinhardt and Erwin Piscator created the context for the music of Kurt Weill and words of Bertolt Brecht to create *Epic Opera*. *The Rise and Fall of the City of Mahagonny* has the city as protagonist expressed through the media of literature in poetic, utilitarian, capitalist, biblical and imperialist mode; music in classical, popular, religious, parodic and pastiche mode; and art in photographic, set design and caption mode. Separation of the medial elements in the structure created a model of twentieth century opera in performance that *remediated* the epic theatre of ancient Greece. The lyricism and the parodic elements of Kurt Weill's music set against Brecht's intertextual libretto and intermedial production techniques, remediated opera into a politically driven music theatre. The dialectic model employed setforce against force, which together with an intermedial and intertextual melange of cinematic, literary, poetic and profane texts, drove home the message of social revolution and indicated new ways forward theatrically.

The dominant opera model that Weill and Brecht remediated was Wagner's **83** *Gesamtkunstwerk*. Wagner conceived of music as the heart, which through its rhythms joined the poetry of the head to the body of the dance (thus uniting the three basic art forms) in his form of opera (music drama).[2] Wagner developed *Totalkunstwerk* – a perfect staged illusion, which nothing must intercept. Under the guiding primacy of music, which allows us to identify with the hero, the world represented on stage becomes an illusion. It is a place of fiction, set apart from the real world, where the audience suspend all disbelief and enter the space mentally for emotional fulfilment. Despite of, or perhaps even because of the constructed nature of the art form, nothing disturbs the illusion; the melody carries all through the singing voice and orchestral playing, which acts on our aural senses as an invisible dominant interface: which indeed it is.

On the other hand, Kandinsky's *Bühnenkomposition as monumental art* is where theatre provides a stage in which a dynamic play of pure expressive forms occurs as a representation of inner experiences. Kandinsky related this dynamic play of forms to the soul. Kattenbelt suggests that it is a lyric mode of representation, guided by musical, pictorial and choreographed movements.[3] I suggest that in Kandinsky's model, the singing voice becomes one medium amongst many. No longer the dominant medium, here the ear competes with the eye for the sense perceptions of the audience. The singer, no matter how lyrical the song s/he sings, may become dominated by the competing patterns of other media. Multiple perspectives become inevitable, as do multiple interpretations.

From this point, it becomes possible to relate opera to the Bolter and Grusin model of *remediation*. The tension between the twin logics of *immediacy* and *hypermediacy* are useful ways of thinking about how the performer acts as an intermedial agent in all opera performance. For example, there is a moment in *The Rise and Fall of the City of Mahagonny*, where Kurt Weill gives the small-time capitalist and extremely unpleasant Ladybird Begbick a musical moment of such beauty to sing, that it allows us to empathise with her universal situation. The aesthetics of the soprano voice and the lyricism of the orchestral accompaniment act on our senses so that we move into another reality beyond reason. Listening to the soprano voice, we ignore the medium at the same time as we are moved by the medium into what we feel is a transparent presentation of a real reality. This is a moment of immediacy, where:

> a transparent interface [...] erases itself so that the user is no longer aware of confronting a medium, but instead stands in an immediate relationship to the contents of that medium (Bolter and Grusin 2002: 24)

Figure 18
A moment of *immediacy* for Jennifer Westwood as Ladybird Begbick. *The Rise and Fall of the City of Mahagonny*

This is intermediality in opera. The singer mediates the music and, at the same time, mediates the audience experience of how the medium affects their perception of the world represented in the operatic frame. There may be a temptation to ascribe the intermedial moment purely to aesthetic appreciation, but singers tell us that, at the moment of mediation, they are very conscious of what their voice is doing and the impact it has on themselves, as well as on their audience:

Tom   Some of the big moments from *Rosenkavalier* or from *Bohème* will move you because that is the height of Romanticism, but I can get some of my biggest buzzes from singing what one could think of as simple, very clinical austere pieces of Palestrina. The feeling of singing a line of music that is interweaving with other lines of music, and so making again an overall sound picture is wonderful. It is not just because you are enjoying the sound of your own voice, but you are aware of being part of something bigger, and of how you fit into a whole, and it is incredibly emotional.[4]

What this tells us is that the singer knows instinctively and cognitively that the language of music has no necessary signified. The abstract nature of the form, based on mathematical structures (the length of the notes played are measurements of time) and harmonic conventions (combinations of notes according to different key signatures) relate to an awareness of another reality induced through combinations of sounds and rhythms. The singer is aware of what the medium of music is doing to them at the same time as they are performing the music. Singers are aware also of the power of music to move the performer and audience into another space, which allows the performer to be part of the represented world on the stage and, at the same time, to move into the 'unreal' sensed world beyond. They are literally *in-between* realities and mediating the music in the act of performance. Thus, the singer and the audience reference themselves on a deep acceptance of the unreality of the represented world.

However, opera represents 'the real', as in the social/political world as well and, it could be argued always has done. For example, *The Rise and Fall of the City of Mahagonny* presents us with a critique of the social world through the narrative of the plot in combination with theatrical devices drawn from many media and its formal musical elements (solo aria, duet, quartet, sextet etc), which explore in musical form the emotion of the moment. Ensemble singing is polyphonic and a vocal equivalent of the multi-windowed *hypermediacy*.

> If the logic of immediacy leads one either to erase or to render automatic the act of representation, the logic of hypermediacy acknowledges multiple acts of representation and makes them visible. (Bolter and Grusin 2002: 33-34)

Figure 19
Hypermediacy in music, song, dance and *mise-en-scène. The Rise and Fall of the City of Mahagonny*

85

The audience is acutely aware of the constructed nature of the polyphony, but it chooses to ignore the clearly ridiculous situation of many singers all singing separate thoughts at once, in a variety of musical lines. Furthermore, part of the pleasure of having so many 'windows' open at once is hearing the musical form moving underneath the individual lines, which many composers use to build a dramatic finale. All performers singing in any ensemble work become very aware of their vocal technique, which they employ to negotiate the intermediality of the medium of speech and the medium of music:

Rosie: There is a technique of being able to think ahead. You are thinking about the words that are coming up, maybe the next verse, even while you are still singing. There are lots of things going on in your head. I do not think that is the same in theatre - certainly with *speaking* the words that does not happen. The only time that happens with me, when acting, is when the other person is speaking, and I am thinking ahead then. But, I do not think ahead while I am speaking lines in a play – not the same way as I do when I am singing lines. I had not thought about it before but it is true. I can be singing a verse of a song, and while I am singing it, I could be thinking "what on earth are the words of the next verse?" – while I am automatically singing the first verse – and panic about it as well. But, nobody seems to notice it happening - it is very strange.

In doing all these activities, the singer is constantly mediating the intermedial form. They memorise the words and music, process the information for tone and pitch, rhythm and musical dynamics, and communicate the whole to the audience. (storing, processing, transmitting see Kittler 1992).[5] It is the mediation of their vocal technique to the composer's text, the words of the libretto, the conductor's rhythms and tempo and the concept of the director, which demands a high degree of technical skill. Situated *in-between* the influences of composer, conductor and director the singing actor is a truly intermedial performer, who has to retain a direct and emotional response to the music:

Tom: Because we are in the business, we are all, to some degree or the other, musical, and being musical means that you respond to music in an instinctive way. If you are using your musical talent to re-create a wonderful piece of Verdi, then you can not help but be moved by that, it is just wonderful to feel part of that, because it is making it alive. It is taking something off the written page and making it live again, so it is a live performance and that is incredibly moving.

Rosie: Opera live in the theatre is like Tom says, but you do not get the same feeling, for me, on television.

Tom: No. It does not translate to television at all.

Rosie: But the sound of live singers singing over a live orchestra, in the flesh, there is nothing like it. It is thrilling hearing people when they can make these incredible big sounds. [...]

Tom: It is totally primeval you know [...] Even listening to the trio in *Rosenkavalier* my response is to what is happening in the music. I cannot tell you why that is, it just is. There is something about the construction of the harmonies, the chords, the build up of tension - I suppose it is almost sexual, like reaching a climax and going somewhere.

Rosie: It is certainly physical.

Tom: It is emotional.

Thus, singing affects the whole body and not just the vocal chords. The singer operates *in-between* the cognitive and the affective domain. Their intermediality is located in *interplay* between the music and the words; the irrational (Dionysus) and the rational (Apollo), performed in the live space at the same time. The singers are the intermedial interface between theatre and music in performance. They mediate the mediality of music, and they are conscious of their position on the stage as being *in-between* the conductor and the director, as well as *in-between* the musical score, the libretto and the audience, to whom they communicate. *Remediation* comes at the level of remediating form. For example, in their epic opera Brecht and Weill remediated the hero of classical antiquity to become a voice for the working class:

Figure 20
Remediation: The proletarian hero, sung by Martin Hindmarsh *The Rise and Fall of the City of Mahagonny*

The dialectic structure of Kurt Weill's satirical and parodic music constantly re-mediates earlier classical and popular forms. The music alternates between high modernism, classical fugue and barbershop, from the Romantic proletarian hero's aria reminiscent of *Fidelio* to cabaret music.

Each musical movement is a separate element complete within the scene.[6] Musical separation echoes Brecht's episodic dramatic structure where every scene carries as social message presented as a social dialectic. The multimedial production effects of staging writing (captions) and integrating projections of the real world into the stage space expanded the medial boundaries and re-enforce the dialectic message sent to the audience of the need for revolution.

Brechtian epic opera became an ideological battlefield where the bodies of the actors and their singing voices gave shape to the battle between the classes in the boxing ring.

Figures 21 and 22
Competing ideologies *The Rise and Fall of the City of Mahagonny*

Opera North: intermediality and education

Whereas Brecht and Weill worked in the age of analogue technology and the rise of Communism, Tim Hopkins (opera director) and Steven Sloane (musical director of Opera North and musical director and conductor for *The Forest Murmurs*) are working in the digital age and in the world of postmodernism. Hopkins as opera director, and Opera North as a company are not attempting to provoke a revolution in the social sense but they are, I would argue, intent on remediating our understanding of the relationship of opera with other media. Through integrating other media into their work, they are opening out perceptions of contemporary opera. They have moved opera into the digital age and ask us to reperceive the opera stage as an integration of the live with the mediatized in a non-hierarchical intermedial model. *The Forest Murmurs* came towards the end of a season of German Romantic opera, which had included already major new productions of Schumann's *Genoveva* and Wagner's *Tristan und Isolde*. In the publicity brochure, *The Forest Murmurs* is described as "A staged event with orchestra, chorus, soloists, film and text, with music from Beethoven to Berg". It was set amongst performances of *Lieder: the Black, Black Earth, songs of love and death: Schubert, Schumann, Mahler and Wolf*; a performance of *A German Requiem* by Johannes Brahms in York Minster and Englebert Humperdink's *Hansel and Gretel*, which played in small scale theatres. The investigation encompassed also associated art exhibitions and a series of seminars, which makes clear the role of education within the creative work of the company:

> Opera North is England's national opera company in the North. The company has established itself as one of the leading arts organizations in the country and one of the most imaginative opera companies in Europe, with a reputation for bold, imaginative productions of both familiar and less familiar repertoire. Away from the main stage, our inspirational Education work takes us right into the heart of the community. Opera North's acclaimed chorus and orchestra lead an energetic life outside the opera house – on the concert platform and

other projects. As well as its large-scale productions, the company takes an innovative approach to making a broad range of music theatre and seeks out opportunities to collaborate with contemporary creative artists engaged in drama, film, the visual arts and literature wherever possible (General Director, Richard Mantle).[7]

This is education is its broadest sense, and resonates with Martha Nussbaum in *Cultivating Humanity: a classical defence of reform in liberal education*:

> The arts cultivate capacities of judgment and sensitivity that can and should be expressed in the choices a citizen makes. To some extent this is true of all the arts. Music, dance, painting and sculpture, architecture – all have a role in shaping our understanding of the people around us. But in a curriculum for world citizenship, literature, with its ability to represent the specific circumstances and problems of people of many different sorts, makes an especially rich contribution. As Aristotle said in chapter nine of the poetics, literature shows us "not something that has happened, but the kind of thing that might happen". This knowledge of possibilities is an especially valuable resource in political life (Nussbaum: 86).

Nussbaum's preference for literature over the performing arts is set in the context of *Interculturalism*. I develop her argument here by suggesting that in the age of the intermedial, the *digital technology* that is the *language of the new media* is the new medium appropriate to engage with interculturalism and globalization. Digital technology 'creates worlds' that cultivate capacities of judgement and sensitivity as well as facilitating almost instant inter-active communication with global communities. Opera in performance that utilizes the structures of the digital also creates worlds that cultivate capacities of judgement and sensitivity, as well as facilitating inter-active readings of the represented global communities on the intermedial opera stage. Through perceiving opera in digital format, we perceive, as Aristotle said "the kind of thing that might happen". The multi-layered hypermediated modular constructed mode of digital opera has the potential to change perceptions about the world and encourages, at the very least, the active citizen to participate in global events.

Perceiving the world differently is itself an act of education and this Opera North provides. In 2002, Opera North introduced a splendid *Winterreise*, where Schubert's song cycle, with words by Willhelm Müller was set to the accompaniment of a piano and original film made by Mariele Neudecker. In September 2004, the intermedial international experiment continued through a joint production with the internationally acclaimed dance company of Emio Greco and Pieter C. Scholten of Gluck's *Orfeo ed Euridice*:

> Like Opera North, EG/PC are well known both in their home country (Holland) and abroad (From New York to Singapore) for their dynamic programming and their appetite for artistic adventure. The collaboration between the two companies – one opera, the other dance – was brought about by a joint invitation for us to present Gluck's *Orfeo ed Euridice* at the Edinburgh International festival 2004 (Richard Mantle, General Director).

Here we see intermediality operating at the level of international programming and at the level of performance. The embedding of contemporary dance movements within the production, from principal singers to chorus and the integration of professional dancers with the company presented an excellent intermedial and educative experience. *Orfeo ed Euridice* won general approval for the high standards achieved and also tested the audience responses. The night I attended, there were some very enthusiastic members of the audience and there were those who remained uncertain. Notably, those who appeared to be most confused were the critics, who tend to be either 'dance' or 'opera' critics, and who may have their own agenda for resisting intermedial performances. It seems to me that the community of critics need to adapt to what is happening in contemporary theatre performances. In 2005, Opera North won the prestigious *South Bank Show Award for Outstanding Achievement in Opera*. This award recognises quality in performance and in intellectual excellence and this is what *Opera North's* integrative approach provides. Through their innovative repertoire and associated seminar series, where composers, directors and the creative team discuss productions with a wide range of people working in the arts and education, the company is engaging with education in a very specific way. Their company policy seems to me to embody the words of Michel Foucault:

> There are times in one's life when the question of knowing if one can think differently than one thinks, and perceive differently than one sees, is absolutely necessary, if one is to go on looking and reflecting at all (Foucault 1985 in Mills 2003: 6).

Becoming able to think in a different way from the traditions into which one is accustomed to think and perceive the world differently is a remediation of our own experience: it is an education.

Digital opera: towards a new model of perception

Notably, in *The Forest Murmurs* we did not have a teacher to tell us what to do. Nobody guided us – there was no dialectic to raise our consciousness and no Grand Narrative acting as an over-arching framework – however, as in the form of the digital media, we chose which connections to make and thus the mental journey we took. Although the audience viewed the fictional world of the stage through a traditional theatre proscenium arch, the choices of perspective offered through the arch were multiple through the manipulation of stage space and multi medial representation, which created a hypermediacy in performance. Devised by dramaturg Meredith Oakes, conceptualized and staged by opera director Tim Hopkins and conducted brilliantly by Stephen Sloane, *The Forest Murmurs* explored the music, poetry, literature and philosophy of the German Romantic imagination.

It presented an eclectic range of written texts drawn from the poetry of Goethe, dramatic extracts from Friedrich Schiller, non-canonical material such as letters written by Heinrich von Kleist and philosophical tracts of Friederich Nietzsche. In theatrical and musical texts, it spanned the historical period from: Ludwig Tieck's play (*Puss in Boots*, 1797); Beethoven's opera (*Fidelio*, 1805); Marschner's opera (*Hans Heiling*, 1831-32); the music drama of Wagner (*Prelude to Tristan und Isolde*, 1856-9). There were extracts from the tone poem of Mahler (*Also Sprach Zarathustra*, 1895-96); Berg's opera (*Wozzeck*, 1925): itself a re-working of Büchner's play, *Woyzeck* (1836/37) and a traditional marching song (*Edelweiss*). The intermediality of *The Forest Murmurs* is immediately apparent. The non-chronological presentation order of the material, plus the presence of original films, and an extract from Fritz Lang's film, *The Death of Siegfried* (1926), calls to the surface a model of hypermediacy. The performance had no single author, no sole composer, no focus on a central character, no driving narrative, but rather multiple fragments of plots from a variety of sources. This was appropriate to an enquiry into the multi-faceted concept of the German Romantic Imagination:

> the essence of Romanticism [is located] precisely in the interplay between the plenitude of its diverse elements – ranging from the picturesque, exotic, historic and archaic to the poetic, imaginative, mythological, symbolic, unique and expressive – and their underlying unity (Wellek in Daverio 1993: 2).

The Forest Murmurs delighted in the interplay and self-awareness of the different medial forms (instrumental music, sung lyric, cinema, theatre and radio) operating in lyric and epic mode, which expanded the boundaries of the stage and the represented world – all in the search of the underlying unity – *perception*.

Perhaps deliberately, the programme accompanying the performance was elusive about concept and content. It gave only the briefest outline of the German Romantic Imagination, and then presented the numbered items that constituted the content. Some items included their poetic text written in the programme and others did not, but no reason was given for the choice of presence or absence of text. There were a couple of brief theatrical synopses and a variety of paintings and other illustrative material. These ranged from the early work of Caspar David Friedrich to an abstract painting of *Mother and Child in the Woods at Night Fall* by Max Ernst (1953), several film stills and one optical-acoustic installation. Reading the programme was like reading hyperfiction: we had to try to put the pieces together and make the connections ourselves. Thus, reading the programme became part of the activity of the performance: it became an adventure, a journey through an intertextual forest for which we had no authorial guide.

The structure of the programme, of course, echoed the experience of the performance. It soon became evident that within the proscenium arch of the theatre there was a 'forest' of intermedial texts through which we were to wander. Here, music became one medium among many media, and the visual and recorded media dominated at the beginning of the performance. Immersed into darkness and silence, no overture played initially but three titles, like those used in silent cinema appeared on a screen. These gave us the title of the staged event, followed by the title of the archive *radio recording* of Lotte Lehmann, captured in sound as she sang at Covent Garden 'en route' to America from Germany in 1938. The recorded voice of a male interviewer asked Lehmann what she would sing and she, in reply, explained her interpretation of the story of the *Der Erlkönig* (The Erl-King). The 'fragment' – an echo of an artist talking about her beliefs in the importance of music – became shaped

91

in the intermediality of music, film and radio and resonated with history: factual and medial. Clearly, the foregrounding of the medial devices resonates with the self-consciousness of the device that is part of the German Romantic experience. Here, through the integration of other media it acted as a manifesto to the opera event – it foregrounded change in the opera form itself.

As a member of the audience, I was very conscious initially of the archive quality of the conversation on my ears, but only until the film started when the eyes took over. As Lehmann sang the words of Goethe's poem, *Der Erlkönig* to a piano accompaniment of Schubert's music, Sigune Hamann's silent film presented the image of a horse travelling through the trees. Intercut with brief sexual images was the device that made possible the illusion of a father and son riding on a horse through the forest – the pre-cinematic zoetrope. Thus, Hamann foregrounded the device at the same time as she filmed it, to create a double illusion and hint at 'other realities' behind the surface reality. As Lehmann's singing continued amongst the thudding rhythms of the piano, it melded with the text of Goethe's poem written on the screen and a glimpse of human eyes looking out at us. The eyes (and subsequently the face) moved towards us, and then moved away again, hinting at fleeting moments of presence and perception. The presence (and absence) of the eyes became part of the polyphony inherent in the Goethe poem (between the father, the son and the narrator) where only the son can see the absent, yet present, Erl-King. The history of this mythical character and his presence in German literature became an actuality in the staging of writing, a recorded vocalization of the music and a cinematic visualization of a Goethe poem.

Here is the *multi-layering* that is a key feature of digitization (Manovich 2001) and a key feature of the opera production. Working most strongly in the opening section was the eyes of people looking out at the audience as if inspecting us – as if inviting us to join them. Intellectually, we knew that the filmed eyes were not real and there was no presence attached to them – the eyes were only there because of the way in which light shines on an object to capture it on film. However, emotionally, we perceived human beings looking out at us – we were both inside and outside of the medium as we watched the images and listened to the music. It was possible, via the eyes, to catch glimpses of the universal theme of perception, which is inherent in the stage design and became explicit as the *Fidelio* overture of Beethoven took over from the Schubert.

Remediating operatic space

Immediately upstage of the frame of the proscenium arch of the theatre was a 'picture frame' false proscenium, which led the eye to the rostrum stage behind the frame, and thence upstage towards the plastic back-projection screen. This presented the audience with the perspective of frames, within frames, within frames. Made out of a low quality crushed wood pulp, chosen for its sculptural texture and colour of wood, the frames and a full stage flown panel upstage made of the same material, enclosed the singers in a forest of crushed trees. Downstage, a black transparent gauze / projection surface reflected light designed to alter our perception of the stage scene:

When used in combination, the plastic and the gauze created a moiré effect: this is where the focal point of the eye is deliberately confused as to which field of depth to focus upon – this was deliberately deployed self-consciously as a perception foregrounding device (Tim Hopkins in email conversation with me, 2001).

Hopkins divided the overture of *Fidelio* into four staged actions. The first section located his characters: 'devoted mother', 'loyal wife', 'excited maiden', 'primitive hero', 'hunter', and 'cerebral poet' within the fictional space of forest. Trapped in-between the fictional space by the front gauze, the stage characters began to see shadows play on the back-projection screen, giving intimations of an unseen 'something unseen' located within nature. In the second section of the overture, as the characters began to move around and inhabit the forest, so too did their shadow images – live and mediatized action was set within the frame of forest, which was itself set on a theatre stage.

93

Figure 23
Remediating operatic space. *The Forest Murmurs: adventures in the German Romantic Imagination*

In the third section of the overture, the downstage gauze flew out and the characters had the opportunity to leave the fictional (cinematic/theatrical) space of the forest and enter the live (but fictional) world of theatre. They moved off the rostrum stage into the space between the picture frame forest and the orchestra pit. Situated literally in-between the orchestra pit and the forest: in-between realities and in-between media, they appeared uneasy in the harsh white lighting associated with epic theatre. Here, laurel leaf crowns were thrown at them from the wings, tempting them to pick them up, which they did. As they crowned themselves, their future selves – the 'Gods of the Forest' looked on approvingly.

In the final section of the overture, the 'Gods of the Forest' returned in digital media format – the bright blue of the computer screen – and the role models of the nineteenth century came together, in play, with their doubles – who were dressed in the clothes of Germany in 1940. The irony is that this happened as the theme of freedom that foretells the end of the opera *Fidelio* played. Composed in 1805 as Napoleon's French troops occupied Vienna and Europe's monarchies reeled under the impact of the ideas and political ramifications of the French revolution, Beethoven's opera stands at the cusp of Classicism and Romanticism and established the first German Romantic operatic 'hero' who operated at individual, national and mythical levels. *The Forest Murmurs*, questions the impact of the Romantic hero, in love and in political and mythical mode on the German nation. During the overture, the movement from early pantheistic individual desires, through to its later fatal manifestation in German Nationalism is reflected by a similar move in medial transformation from early film stock to digital manipulation.

The acting area was divided into three separate spaces. (1) The space in-between the orchestra and the first picture frame was *in-between the realities* created by music and theatre: in-between the ontology of the two media that is opera. (2) The fictional space of the rostrum stage was an *intermedial stage area* that drew freely on theatre, cinema and music. Here the dramatic and narrative representation took place. (3) The back and front projection screens, which dominated the stage, created a *cinematic space*. Looking through the proscenium arch of the theatre was cinema. The scale of the screens and the use of the moving and static images dominated the operatic space. The screens defined the different areas of the stage and told the narrative of the relationship between the live singers and their mediatized selves on the screen. The orchestral music was one medium among film and theatre performance, with singers caught literally inter-media between the film projectors, the stage space and the orchestra space.

Digital opera - Remediating music

In part one, the staged numbers moved very swiftly, hardly giving the audience a moment to breathe and no opportunity to sink into a fixed perspective. This was partly because the presence of so many *Lied*:

> [ ] the Lied, or art song is surely the most paradoxical [...] at once the most private and yet universalizing of art forms the Lied, less than a century ago, stood at the forefront of late Romanticism. Together with orchestral and various types of instrumental music, and later the music dramas of Richard Wagner, it formed a part of a Teutonic musical juggernaut widely regarded as without peer (Parsons 2004: 3).

The intimate personal art song was expanded to give private expression of universal anxiety and was demonstrated by the direction of the men's chorus for *Flucht* and the women's chorus for *Mailied* (Schubert). The men first, and then the women entered stage right, presented themselves centre stage, assumed an expressionistic pose, sang and exited stage left. Thus, Hopkins enacted the 'wipe' action of silent cinema and indicated the psychological relationship of early film. The act of showing (ostention) on film and showing via the movement of the actors' bodies the emotional content of the music became a structure of the opera. At times, the immediacy of the music enticed us into the piece (as in the *Fidelio* quartet), at other times, the beauty of the image created an immediacy via lyric patterns. Immediacy and hypermediacy acted simultaneously, creating many windows to watch and listen to, and remediated our operatic experience. This culminated in the lyrical film accompanying 'The Chorus Mysticus' from Schumann's *Scenes from Faust*.

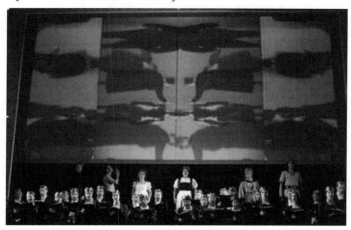

Figure 24
Lyric digital opera
The Forest Murmurs: adventures in the German Romantic Imagination

Framing the staging of the orchestra

In part one, the image dominated the stage space and remediated our experience of the music. In part two, the orchestra played within the frame of the stage, which remediating the theatrical stage space.

Figure 25
Framing the staging
of the orchestra.
*The Forest Murmurs: adventures in the
German Romantic Imagination*

During the interval, the orchestra moved to occupy the stage space and gave the audience an opportunity to concentrate on listening to the music, which redressed the emphasis of the image. Aural, as opposed to visual sense perceptions dominated. The orchestral players, now visibly interspersed between the audience and the back projection screen, usurped the singers from the narrative space. Staging the orchestra foregrounded the mediality of music, which is normally an 'unseen' element in the pit. It challenged us to ask why the orchestra in opera is usually the unseen element, like a film soundtrack. Framing the staging of the orchestra (hypermediacy) foregrounded the mediality of the orchestra players and their musical instruments as an 'extension of man' (McLuhan 1964). They became a medial device and their playing an act of ostention, which affected the audience's perception of the music. The normal experience in the Concert Hall became a foregrounded device on the opera stage and remediated the audience experience. The audience were located in-between the medial realities as the musicians remediated the opera space.

A feature of first wave German Romanticism is artistic involvement with nature, and their sense of a world beyond the scientifically known physical world. They felt they saw an indefinable 'something' beyond the known. In the first half of the production, the intermedial presentation gave us 'the something' visually – we saw 'it' too. By staging the orchestra and changing the balance from the visual to the aural, we heard but did not see 'the something' so clearly. This seems to me appropriate to the second wave of Romanticism, with its decreased interest in the individual and their 'visions'.

After the interval, the music of Mahler, Strauss and Berg expressed the collapse of belief and references to Nietzsche proliferated. Underlying the fragmented structure was sadness, loss and absence. A particularly painful moment came after the folk song, *Der Tamboursg'sell* (the Drummer Boy) from *Des Knaben Wunderhorn* (The Boy's Magic Horn), 1905 by the Jewish composer, Mahler. The group of soloists who had been facing upstage during the song turned, and in their blindfolded faces lined-up before us was the image of the firing squad.

96

Figure 26
Epic digital opera. *The Forest Murmurs: adventures in the German Romantic Imagination*

Note that for this song the orchestra and conductor were hidden behind the front gauze, which was now operative in its 'moiré' effect and foregrounding the act of perception. It allowed Hopkins to stage writing on the screen and place the role models of nineteenth century German society in epic lighting and the stage space of the intermedial. Thus, the values of the German Romantic imagination on German society were questioned as Romanticism in opera was remediated.

Remediating reading: intermediality, perception and education

Perception about the possession of knowledge was glimpsed in many of the individual 'fragments' (episodes) that formed the structure of the piece. This is a similarity with *Mahagonny*, but also a difference, for in *The Forest* the fragments operated more by way of free association made by the receivers. There was no obvious linking plot line or grand narrative present to drive home a message, which gives this piece more of a digital than social dialectical structure. The performers did make *links* between the fragments. For example, at the end of *Hans Heiling* the soloists held the gesture as they looked down into the pit where they had thrown the books away. In their ostended gesture, it was possible to see the bonfires of literature to come. A cinematic style edit linked their ostended gesture to the sound of the choir of the Leibstandarte-SS (Hitler's Bodyguard) singing the Volkish Fascist song, *Edelweiss*, which provoked images in the mind of endless and relentless soldier's feet marching in time to the driving military beat. Their target was the 1940's 'giants' who were 'lined-up' before us on the screen and literally written-on by superimposing the text of the song over their bodies. Watched from the stage by their 19th century counterparts, their images were minimized to the size of puppet dolls. Once reduced in scale, their 'live' stage doubles retrieved 'their' images from the film screen and tore the puppet dolls (themselves) apart, as we glimpsed the Nazi emblem passing behind on the screen: it was a chilling intermedial moment.

The music and multimedia elements were structured so that they became *hyperlinks*, which the audience had to activate in their minds by *making connections* to the unseen text behind the intermedial text. Hyperlinks are a feature of digital technology and an inter-active way of reading hyperfiction:

> A hyperlink creates a connection between two elements, for example, between two words in two different pages, or a sentence on one page and an image in another, or two different places within the same page. Elements connected through hyperlinks can exist on the same computer or on different computers connected on a network, as in the case of the World Wide Web (Manovich 2001: 41)

Activating the *hyperlinks* encourages a digital reading of the opera that is similar to a reading of *hyperfiction*, where the reader chooses which individual pathway to take through the presented fiction. It is true that the audience could only experience the opera performance in a linear fashion, in the same way as readers of this chapter

97

must experience the reading of this sentence in a linear fashion. However, the digital structure of the piece encouraged a *digital reading*, in the sense of alerting the audience perception to the unseen texts and the layering of interpretation available behind the surface presentation. The intermediality of music and other media drew on our sense perceptions and intellectual faculties and liberated (educated) us to look, read and interpret the world differently. This was particularly true of the final section of the opera where the recorded voice of Kathleen Ferrier sang Mahler's *Kindertotenlieder no.1*, 1901, during which the final film played:

> My colleague Pippa Nissen at the Nuremberg Toy Museum shot the film that accompanies the closing piece. I recalled a visit there before where I saw, in effect, a history of this same period in terms of toy production. I was struck by the artificiality and completeness of the nineteenth century dolls houses and the sinister effect of the toys from the Third Reich era, including toy dolls of Hitler and Goebbels on a saluting platform - these can be glimpsed in the film. As the war proceeded, the dolls reflect the absence of raw materials and the toys of 1945 are made of paper or grass. The idea of a creative fragment in a blasted lost world referred back to the Lehmann recording (Hopkins email).

Figure 27
Remediating the opera experience: digital opera. *The Forest Murmurs: adventures in the German Romantic Imagination*

The recorded mezzo voice of Kathleen Ferrier, the images of the toy museum and the singers huddled together at the edge of an empty orchestra pit tearing apart their toy puppet doubles, which they had earlier removed from the screen, provoked a powerful sense of pain and loss. The emotional response in the theatre was very strong, as a select audience left the theatre feeling that they had witnessed something quite extra-ordinary. Intermediality and perception are linked inextricably to each other in an act of education.

Reading the production from an intermedial perspective, I interpreted it on one level as a remediation of the Romantic Hero. However, reading it differently, revealed humanity lost in a world of intermedial connections, where citizens apparently have multiple choices but fail to realise that all are subject to 'programmability' – just like the programs of the computers that control our lives. My two interpretations are, of course, irrelevant. The strength of *The Forest Murmurs* is in its digital structure and intermediality, which allowed the audience to remediate their own readings of an operatic performance experienced within a communal setting. This was its power. It was an intermedial, intellectual and sensual experience, which remediated our perceptions about humanity represented on the intermedial operatic stage. It cultivated humanity through liberal education.

Conclusions

What we have seen is a change in the model. The Brechtian model placed the audience in the position of the receiver of the message, which instructed them to apply the message of the performance to the real world. Digital opera is multi-layered, non-linear and circular, which invites the audience to be intrigued, excited and alert to different perceptions offered in a variety of medial modes but does not instruct – it offers different possibilities. In contemporary life, we travel through intermedial and intertextual forests, and may be excited by the variety of possibilities, but we do not have a guide now that the grand narratives have been, at least to a certain extent, displaced.

Digital opera is not the inclusion of highly sophisticated media technologies in opera – *The Forest Murmurs* was definitely not a 'high-tech' production. Rather, digital opera functions as *hyperfiction*, as all computer interfaces do. Hyperfiction or in our case, *hypermediacy* is a 'windowed' presentation of individual units / fragments / modules / call them what you will, and the person who creates the meaning of the hyperfiction/hypermediacy is located in the reader – not in the sender of the message.

Crucially, digital opera displaces the traditional centre (authorial control   **99** of music and text) and all elements have an equal weighting. I recognise that *The Forest* was not strictly a digital model because it did not include an interface where the audience controls the order of the narrative and may change it – so that they experience the world presented in a non-linear mode. However, given that caveat, essentially, digital opera as I have used it, is a non-hierarchical multi-layered mode of performance, where all the elements of media, text and performance styles come together into an intermedial texture awaiting the organising mind and body of the audience. Intermediality, perception and education are inextricably linked to each other and they cultivate humanity through liberal education.

The structure of *The Forest Murmurs* brought to the surface the underlying force of the unseen – and it is a feature of the digital and the intermedial that we can never see the structure, or our individual place in it. When we perceive how lost we might become in the hypermedial forest of the digital age, and the potential for anarchy as communities break down into individual fragments, we too might like to stand back from the digital and reflect. Perhaps it is time to remediate our own thoughts about the digital and recognise that what we are playing with as 'artistic toys' in theatre practice, places us all in the *rhizome* – where we cannot see the beginning or the end.[8] Following Deleuze, I suggest that as a global society, we may not yet see the true awfulness of the digital age – although, through analogy the final scene of *The Forest Murmurs* gives an indication of some potential outcomes.

Through analogy again, we need now to make our final step, which is that given digital technology underpins global society, is it not time now to make explicit what is implicit through contemporary opera performance practice and in the philosophy of education? Following Nussbaum, Foucault, Deleuze and Opera North we need to recognize that there is a need for an integrated intermedial approach to theatre and educational research. I suggest that there is a need to remediate research connections between the arts and sciences, media and theatre, philosophy, history and the social world. Failure to make these intermedial research connections raises the possibility that we may remain forever in the rhizome.

Notes

1 Cited in Seldon, Widdowson and Brooker (eds.) 1997: 99.
2 See Chiel Kattenbelt's chapter in this book.
3 See Chiel Kattenbelt's chapter in this book.
4 All the extracts of conversations in this chapter are with Tom Marandola (professional singer and vocal coach) and Rosemary Ashe (opera and music theatre principal).
5 See Peter Boenisch's chapter where he talks about Kittler's definition of mediality. I see it as a very similar process to that undertaken by singers in rehearsal and performance.
6 Klemens Gruber talks about this also in his chapter.
7 This and the following two quotations are from *The Forest Murmurs* programme.
8 See Key *Issues* chapter for explanation of Deleuze's concept of the rhizome.

SECTION TWO
INTERMEDIAL PERCEPTIONS

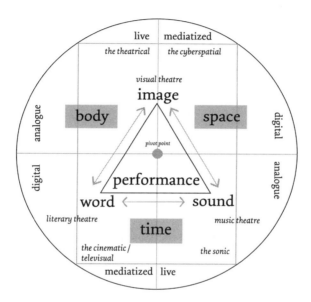

The perspective on intermediality in the chapters in this section is that of the audience receiving intermedial performances. One thematic link that draws their work together is an exploration of different perceptions of intermediality in audio theatre, puppet theatre, television and contemporary dance. A major feature of this section is the focus on the intermedial relationship between the body of the performer and the gaze of the receiver. Perceptions of intermedial performance take the audience into the space of the intermedial, which is located in-between their minds and the different realities created in the intermedial performance.

As with the other sections, chapters here resonate with themes
and explorations in the other two.

AESTHETIC ART TO AISTHETIC ACT: THEATRE, MEDIA, INTERMEDIAL PERFORMANCE

Peter M. Boenisch

This chapter puts forward the proposition of theatre as a medium and so reviews the vast field of contemporary media studies from W. Benjamin to J.D. Bolter and R. Grusin, via M. McLuhan, J. Crary and L. Manovich, to situate the key concepts of mediality and theatricality, before arriving at a new definition of intermediality. Foregrounding the crucial role of the observers in the process, intermediality as a concept is no longer reduced to being the mere use of various media technologies in live performance; nor as being confined to the computerized media-cultural economy in the early years of the twenty-first century. Rather, it is an effect performed in-between mediality, supplying multiple perspectives, and foregrounding the making of meaning rather than obediently transmitting meaning. Drawing on the Greek word *aisthestai*, to perceive, intermediality is an aisthetic act, which has close affinities to theatre – the place "to see and behold", as the Greek verb *theasthai* suggests.

Once upon a time, not too long ago, the division of medial labour appeared to be in perfect order. Film was one thing, clearly, theatre was another and a newspaper was something completely different. A direct consequence of this notion of *medial specificity* was an inexorable drive to set various media in opposition to each other, and to define them in contrast to each other, as if they all presided over their own distinctly defined aesthetic realms. Discussions about their distinguishing features led to claims of superiority and to the necessity for any so-called *new medium* to claim its own territory in the field of *the media*. Advocates of *the new medium* then attempted to dethrone any older media, while defenders of the latter braced themselves to protect their traditional claims. The advent of new pictorial techniques in the arts during the early decades of the twentieth century is a fine example of this process. Soon after cinema appeared on the screen theatre was asked to leave the stage by some critics and artists, while others promoted a re-theatricalization of the stage, concentrating on what they thought were theatre's very own and exclusive powers. It is possible to see the history of the theatre avant-garde in the first half of the century, from Craig to Artaud, in this light.

A similar scenario resurfaced when television, followed by video, entered everyone's living rooms. Theatre and the by then already *old medium* of cinema were placed on the list of endangered species, together with the contention that radio and its erstwhile stars had already allegedly been killed by video anyway. It is interesting to note that although endangered, at this time theatre was also praised as *the pure* and *immediate* anti-medium: the residue of *real* and *authentic* culture in a world of mass media and televisual daftness. Directors such as Grotowski, Brook, and Mnouchkine were celebrated as high priests of *pure theatricality*. Notably, over the period of the twentieth century, relatively few theatre directors sought actively to embrace and integrate new media, but Bertolt Brecht, Erwin Piscator, and more recently Robert Wilson and the Wooster Group, are excellent examples. However, given the historical legacy in academic analysis and theatre practice, it is not surprising that as soon as computers and the internet took over at the forefront in media technology, a fierce debate on *liveness* versus *mediatization* began to dominate theatre-theoretical discourses (Auslander 1999).

What is clear is that the invention and invasion of *electronic microchip-technology* has profoundly affected our ideas about what constitutes *a medium* because *digital information processing* undermines any clear-cut specification of sign-systems, genres, and media. Instead, microchip-technology subjects all texts, images, sounds, colours and movements to indifferent binary computation of zeroes and ones. At the same time, computer technology allows the merging of mechanical, electrical, and electro-magnetic systems into a single electronic system, while also short-circuiting industrial, technical, scientific, artistic and aesthetic networks. In this context, concepts such as *the cinematic* or *the theatrical* no longer make sense, because today all kinds of codes, data, and functions are all collected up into bits, bytes, and little silver disks. Clearly, we need now to look for a new conceptual framework that will facilitate analysis of theatre amongst the proliferation of the new media rather than proclaiming the demise of theatre. Ironically, we are aided in this project by the Canadian media philosopher Derrick De Kerckhove, who twenty years ago discarded theatre within the then emerging digital age, as no more than "an image of past cultures preserved in universities, which are the last strongholds of literacy" (De Kerckhove 1982: 152). However, despite this prophecy of gloom, theatrical performance has reappeared, as is evidenced in the debate over *Computers as theatre* (Laurel 1992); the electronic culture of digitized computerization as the age dictating performance, performativity, (McKenzie 2001); and, most recently, *Virtual theatres* (Giannachi 2004). This chapter will take the debate in a slightly different direction in that first I will discuss *theatre as a medium*, and investigate its relationship to what is commonly referred to as *the media*. From here, based on a review of contemporary media studies and their suggestions of what constitutes a medium and mediality, I identify *intermediality* as an effect on the perception of the observers. Drawing on the original meaning of the Greek word *aisthestai*, 'to perceive', which initially referred to more than just the beautiful and sublime, I identify intermediality as an *aisthetic act* located at the very intersection of theatricality and mediality. This approach goes far beyond merely quoting, borrowing or the incorporating strategies of another medium in performance, such as using the language of cinema on stage.[1] However, in order to conceptualize *intermediality* in theatrical performance we need first to clarify the definitions of *a medium* and *theatre* in turn.

Mediality as remediation

It may be somewhat surprising to realize that in twenty-first century society, where data highways, cyberspace and information management have become vital buzzwords, those who think about media at universities, academic institutions and research laboratories have not been able to come to a generally accepted agreement on what actually constitutes a medium. As may be the case with other academic disciplines, the various schools of media theory are at feud. Attempting to avoid fatiguing debates, I start from simple, common-sense intuition, and then I review and eventually take on board helpful insights, collected somewhat eclectically, from various branches of media studies.

The New Oxford Dictionary of English advises that a medium is "an agency or means of doing something" and, more precisely "a means by which something is communicated or expressed" (Pearsall 1998: 1151). While *communication* points at a minimum of a bilateral exchange of expression, where several parties cooperate to produce meaning, I like particularly the notion of media as an *agency*: a term that over recent years has acquired connotations of a less than innocent activity, and which draws on the ever-popular conspiracy theories. This underpins vividly one of the few notions held in common in contemporary media theory: that media are by no means a neutral means to communicate or express something, but, on the contrary, they essentially shape what can be thought, said and stated at all times. Far from being merely tools or machines, media play a central role in human communication and understanding. They are, in fact, a crucial foundation of our culture, of cultural change, diversity, and distinction. German media philosopher Walter Benjamin was seminal in taking into account the reciprocal effects of media, cultural discourses and *media users*, as we would say in today's terminology. The radical effects of photography, the cinema, and other new technical media on art and society as a whole inspired his writings in the 1930s. In his essays, whether discussing the age of mechanical reproduction, the works of French poet Charles Baudelaire or the origins of German tragic drama, Benjamin applied a critical perspective that was distinctly different from the dominant pan-European discourse. Instead of foregrounding intrinsic aesthetic values of *the beautiful* and *the sublime*, Benjamin prioritized the role of *technology* and *technological invention* over actual artistic form and content, and pointed to their fundamental effect on human perception:

> During long periods of history, the mode of human sense perception changes with humanity's entire mode of existence. The manner in which human sense perception is organized, the medium in which it is accomplished, is determined not only by nature but by historical circumstances as well (Benjamin 1968: 222).

105

We can see from this that Benjamin argues against the traditionally ascribed view of perception as a trans-historical given. His position, coming from within the context of a Marxist tradition was that our existence, in a very literal sense, informs our conscience, as media translate and infuse historical circumstances into our senses and thus into our bodies.

A few decades later, the powerful impact of media on human perception was elaborated in the work of the highly idiosyncratic, quite often mysterious and sometimes blatantly wrong Canadian academic and pioneer of contemporary media studies, Marshall McLuhan. He has become a 1960s legend, not the least for his flourishing metaphors such as "the global village" and his dictum that "the medium is the message". However, central for McLuhan's writings is his claim that "all media exist to invest our lives with artificial perception and arbitrary values" (McLuhan 1994: 199). He believed that "no medium is an empty container".[2] According to McLuhan, long before any communication takes place the very process of mediation:

> translates and transforms the sender, the receiver, and the message. The use of any kind of medium or extension of man alters the patterns of interdependence among people, as it alters the ratios among our senses (McLuhan 1994: 89).

Thus, McLuhan literally connects media to the body and the senses of their users. He conceived of media as direct "extensions of men", as ex-corporate functions that used to be affiliated with bodily organs or the central nervous system, as for example the foot in the wheel, and the eye in the camera. This is a contentious position to hold and some critics, notably Raymond Williams, arguing from a cultural materialist perspective and a continuation of the socio-cultural media research introduced by Benjamin, accused McLuhan of dissocializing media by reducing their effects to "simply physical events in an abstracted sensorium" (Williams 1975b: 127). Nevertheless, stripped from some of its oddities, McLuhan's approach seems to me acute and is compatible with much of the late twentieth century socio-cultural critique as fostered by French philosopher Michel Foucault and his method of discourse analysis. Interestingly, it was the German media academic Friedrich Kittler who brought together the approaches of McLuhan and Foucault in his studies on "discourse networks" (Kittler 1992).

Kittler, instead of condensing the effect of media on man in metaphorical "extensions", proposes a very handy functional understanding of media identifying the *processing, transmission*, and *storing of information* as the three ends to which media are the means. Clearly, this is a helpful intervention but it is important to recognise that the approaches discussed so far still root themselves in terms of medial specificity: investigating them as different extensions or looking at their discrete strategies of processing, transmitting, and storing. It was only with the advent of the computer as an integrative multi-medial device that media studies began to refocus on the common effects and impacts the media have on each other and, in particular, on the world they create and broadcast. Central to this line of enquiry have been US media academics Jay David Bolter and Richard Grusin. In their research, they have discovered that throughout media history, *the new media* have never radically ousted their predecessors; but instead they introduced themselves as improved versions of already existent technology: for example, presenting printing initially as refashioned manuscript, photography as revamped perspective painting. Similarly, radio, film, and television all posed as ultimate perfections of earlier media, which they absorb and *represent* within an altered framework. Bolter and Grusin term this strategy *remediation* and build their own definition of media on this concept, ultimately suggesting in a concise formula that:

> A medium is that which remediates. It is that which appropriates the techniques, forms, and social significance of other media and attempts to rival or refashion them in the name of the real (Bolter and Grusin 1999: 65).

If we accept their proposition, then it seems that what is new about the new media is not based on any inherent individuality guaranteeing their difference from old media. Instead, the new media build into the new format some of the existent features of the old; and in doing this they redefine the old media, who continue to survive very well in the updated versions. However, it is important to note that remediation à la Bolter and Grusin always works in both directions. As a convenient side effect, this mutual process of remediation helps media users to switch to new media almost instantly. Instead of having to learn entirely new languages for every new medium, apart from pioneering days when users had to have knowledge of MS-DOS or ASCII-codes to operate computers, their existing media competence can be swiftly transferred across the board of old and new media.

This idea of *mediality as remediation* is most obvious in present-day digital media. Not even the computer is a genuinely new medium; for several decades it served as an extended form of a calculator, typewriter and data processor. Only with their growing commercial availability were *digital media* marketed as ultimate perfection of and replacements for older media. Nowadays, we may listen to the radio, read e-books and on-line newspapers, and watch movies and TV channels all on our computer screens. Yet, some of the most prototypical features of digital technology, such as its *cut and paste editing*, revitalize much earlier medial strategies, for example, the montage and collage of cinema. Computer technology even remediates strategies of the not-exactly-old medium of television. Similarly, television is refashioned by the worldwide internet, and television screens more and more resemble computer desktops, as their various windows, textboxes, image-frames, open up simultaneously to provide plentiful textual, pictorial, and acoustic information. In another noteworthy contribution to the recent debate, Lev Manovich relates what he calls *The Language of New Media* to cinema, accounting for new digital media as well as for new cinematic forms as results of mutual remediation, even if Manovich himself never uses the term (Manovich 2001).

However, it is important to note that computers not only remediate other more recent media, but equally more traditional ones, such as books, the alphabet and 3-D perspective painting. It is quite fascinating to discover that at its very heart *digital data processing* is nothing more than a new gown for the very foundational principles of what McLuhan notoriously termed the "Gutenberg Galaxy": our Western tradition of the phonetic alphabet, literacy, manuscripts, and ultimately the printing press, which all rely on the same set of cognitive principles at the heart of Western cultural ideology. Digital data processing privileges linearity (of the sentence), clear-cut hierarchies (of clauses), and the clear succession of cause and effect; it relies on homogenic uniformity and self-identity that facilitates endless repeatability (of letters, for example, both in writing and in print); it is dominated by visual perception subsuming all other senses; and it favours passive consumption from a distance. These principles, epitomized in the world of the printed word, newspapers, and novels are very much present in the *interactive* cyberspaces of the new electronic world: the coding at the heart of the microchips and its scripts is still based on these language principles. "Computers are nothing if not hierarchies of encoded language", as Erik Davis rightly remarks (Davis 1998: 213).

As Bolter and Grusin demonstrate in their extensive research, similar points about the mutual effects between emerging and existing media could be made at any point in media history. Applying their idea of mediation as a continued process of perpetual mutual remediation redraws completely the map of media history. From their perspective, rather than a linear line of evolutionary progress, media history resembles an ever extending spiral; each seemingly radical progress in media technological development turns out as yet another remediation. Instead of an evolution of technological features and performance data in causal and linear ways, media history presents itself as an inter-linked field, disclosing genealogies where media, old and new, are mutually dependant and reciprocally related over various planes of the twisting spiral. A fine example of this process is given by US art-historian Jonathan Crary, who challenges the view of film and the cinema as a logical departure from the earlier moving images in the *camera obscura*-technology of the seventeenth and eighteenth centuries – as if the former had always been waiting in the wings to guide, direct and dictate the ever-advancing forces of invention and technological progress (Crary 1992). The similarity in technology – in this case, the focussing and projection of light – easily produces what looks like an evolution of ever more refined visual representation. Once we have arrived at our destination, all detours, wrong turns, and roundabout ways either seem like the most logical path, or they are simply forgotten and ignored.[3] With a similar thrust as Crary, Siegfried Zielinski suggests an equally not so straightforward and non-linear account of more recent media development, countering the popular myth of the 'natural' progression from radio to cinema, television and ultimately the all-absorbing computer. He describes all of these new media as mere medial *entr'actes*, and thereby introduces theatrical language at a very significant moment of a media-historical argument (Zielinski 1999).

Realities of the observer

We can see now that any medium will always remain *in-between* the various layers and never arrive. Even what seems like the most radical departure in media-technological development inevitably turns out to be another remediation rather than the ultimate, perfect *Über-medium*. Likewise, our own digital age, for all of the moment's enthusiasm, is just another transitional period on the move, an entr'acte. In Kittler's terms, we inhabit *Zwischenzeit: time in-between*. If this is the case then why should *intermediality* be a remote and artificial phenomenon rather than a default effect of any mediation? In his argument against traditional narratives of media history, Crary adds an important moment to our conceptualization of mediality. For him, the seemingly obvious similarities between the camera obscura and the cinematograph become largely insignificant as these two techniques literally project two thoroughly different mindsets. The impact of the photographic image and later of the moving image, according to Crary, were both pre-programmed by a change in the underlying cultural economy towards serialization and mass production, as well as substantially supporting *mechanical reproduction*. Thus, Crary subscribes to the inseparable correlation of symbolic representation and economic reproduction identified by Walter Benjamin, but Crary expands the reflection to include its *effect on media users*, and their *act of observing* paintings, pictures – and theatre. Pointing at the original meaning of the Latin root of the word *observer*, which remains in phrases like 'observing a law', Crary hints at the double meaning in that term:

> Though obviously one who sees, an observer is more importantly one who sees within a prescribed set of possibilities, one who is embedded in a system of conventions and limitations (Crary 1992: 6).

Crary is right in following the influential thinking of Michel Foucault and emphasizing seeing as a process "embedded in a system of conventions". However, his reference to limitations and to seeing as a less important part than observing, may lead us to misconceive the media-using observers as mere receivers: on a par with robots, obediently executing their pre-programmed scripts of conventions. I suggest that this would underestimate the active participation in any process of medial communication, which is to interpret data and information, because all media users remember, activate and apply their own experiences, knowledge, skills, prejudices, and backgrounds – all of which are certainly framed and impregnated by socio-cultural discourses. It is the essentially active role of the observer, that constitutes true *inter-activity* and this two-way process of observing is implicit in Bolter and Grusin's definition of *remediation* which, they argue, takes place "in the name of the real" (Bolter and Grusin 1999: 65). If this is the case, then technically reproducing, or artistically representing, pre-existing realities as *the real*, I suggest, is no more than an effect produced by observation. More generally, through connecting their observers to their cultural, discursive, and historic circumstances, the media *generate realities* – rather than *the reality*. The media, it seems to me, function in a similar fashion to the command MAKE WORLD in the Apple Macintosh computer programme script-language UNIX: the media (re-)integrate changes made to a variable environment into a single coherent and meaningful operating system. However, for the ones who perceive, whether they are reading books, attending theatre, or playing computer-games, the perceptions created by media, i.e. the effect on their *sensorium* of all the signs and symbolizations staged and performed – are always ultimately *real*. Whether virtual fictions, outright naturalism, or factual documentary style, these perceptions are always 'the case', as Wittgenstein might say, they are always "authentic" in the observers' experience (Bolter and Grusin 1999: 53).

With this in mind, we may now say that *representation* by the media is exposed as a powerful construct of cognitive-discursive conventions. If we foreground the undeniable ontological difference between *the factual* and *fictional* worlds, we can see that representation establishes a hierarchy between the two and assumes a mimetic relationship between the actual thing and its mediatized representation. Within this framework, the latter must appear as a "second order reality", whether as idealist representation of a crude reality in terms of the beautiful and the sublime, as a realist rendering of that actual thing, or as surreal invention of blatant Science Fiction.

However, what this hierarchic account of the factual and the fictional world does not take into account is the fact that the ontological difference does not necessarily translate into an equal hierarchy for the observers when they experience it, because the experience of both factual and fictional worlds is also a most authentic one.[4] The authenticity of any medial world-making includes a significant *spatial effect*, as 'making worlds' means creating spaces that are inhabited by the observers – some of which are quite literal, and others rather metaphorical. In addition, for the observers there is also the *sensorial layer*, which everyone experiences to a greater or lesser degree. If this is the case then we need to accept that *mediation is an act, a performance*, where both medium and spectator create meaningful spatial realities and invoke a sensorial, phenomenological experience, which adds to the semiotic reality, yet at the same time has the potential to irritate and disrupt. Mediation as an act and performance is induced in the non-semiotic, non-hermeneutical surplus of mediation, where the effects of mediatization become tangible in a most absorbing, albeit ever so subtle way. Roland Barthes, discussing films by Soviet director Sergei Eisenstein encapsulated this excess in his formula of the "third meaning" (Barthes 1977). Eisenstein himself speaks of "attraction", McLuhan, of course, mentions the "magic" of media, and we might well sense that it is right here where the loss of "aura", famously bemoaned by Walter Benjamin, will eventually be compensated. It is, above all, in this essentially *aisthetic process* where *intermediality is performed*. Given the importance of the aisthetic process to mediation, we need now to move to theatre, for theatre, as its very name suggests, is a prime space to observe, and thus provides a unique focal point for investigating any process of seeing and being seen.

The mediality of theatre

If, for the sake of argument, we do a checklist against the suggested defining factors of mediality given above, then we see quite quickly that theatre obviously qualifies as a medium. It processes, stores, and transmits. Theatre also combines aspects of representational media, which foreground the creation of realities such as film and computer-games, with strategies of media aimed primarily at real-time presentation and communication, like the telephone, fax, and live broadcasting. For the creation of a reality that is happening in real time theatre is a hard medium to beat; for it makes worlds that are in a very tangible way real for the observers and they experience that world in actual time.

From its very cradle, theatre has always relied heavily on re-mediating other media in order to achieve effects. In fact, it seems always to have been a medium to broadcast other media, such as, most obviously for our Western theatre tradition, the written dramatic text. De Kerckhove stressed the prime impact of the formal, media-technological setting of theatre, long before the content of the actual presentation and its discursive and ideological implications came into play, which have been the dominant focus of theatre research (Boenisch 2003). Specifically, De Kerckhove scanned the infant days of Western theatre in ancient Athens and demonstrated that the invention of theatre, as we know it, linked with the introduction of the phonetic alphabet at the same time. This brand new *media technology* of phonetics was more than just a convenient way of processing, transmitting and storing data. The phonetic alphabet informed the entire culture of classical Greece, its laws, philosophy, geometry, and any scientific and cultural innovation of that age – including theatre: they all heavily relied on the new cognitive strategies of presenting and perceiving information. Theatre, De Kerckhove argues, incorporated these new strategies into its spatial setting and implemented them into its largely illiterate observers, who were immobilized for hours, and kept visually focussed on a presentation, which was taking place in a single confined spot, the stage:

> The theatrical institutions of Athens extended to the non-literate community the effects, which the alphabet had to literate individuals: they established a gradual separation between the knowers and the known, and supported the practice of distanciation, which is the root of our typically Western dichotomy between subjective and objective experiences and references (De Kerckhove 1982: 146).

Theatre, along these lines, functions as a training ground for perception and as a place to observe: that literal meaning of the Greek *theatron*. Reading De Kerckhove, it almost sounds as if theatre was a place to brainwash thoroughly the spectators. However, this would be to underestimate the observers' essentially inter-active role in their acts of observing. Yet De Kerckhove is quite right to describe theatre as "a sort of prototype of imagination, a try-out space for new experiences, emotions, attitudes, and reflexions" (ibid., 149). It is for this very reason that throughout the history of our culture theatre has played a particularly important role at any watershed moment for media technology. This has been true for the introduction of the phonetic alphabet, the invention of perspective and the printing press, and finally the more recent computerization of society. I suggest that theatre turns into *a new medium* whenever new media technologies become dominant, and, in addition, that theatre adapts and disperses the new cognitive strategies, just as it did in ancient Greece.

This process is exemplified in fifteenth century Italy, when Filippo Brunelleschi formalized the *perspectiva artificialis*. This particular new media technology of perspective introduced cognitive capabilities, which proved vital for many aspects of modern culture, from the printing press to secularization, and capitalist production. Perspective objectified human perception, which then became bound to the exact mathematical laws of geometry: any space, any reality, from now on was an effect of *proper perspective* – and thus dependent on proper perception. Notably, theatre soon embraced these new virtual realities. The fundamental difference in the two contrasting spatial arrangements coexisting in the Teatro Olimpico at Vicenza vividly demonstrates a fundamental technological shift in theatre. It features a classical *scenae frons* as designed by Andrea Palladio in the 1560s, yet after his early death Vincenzo Scamozzi, who was appointed to complete the building, simply added the latest fashion of perspective technology right into the old setup. Eventually, the changeable picture-frame stage became the standard format of Western theatre architecture for several centuries. Here again we see how the basic spatial arrangement of theatre reflected conventions of how to see and how to imagine (the) world: as a framed picture, from a 'natural' point of view – as silent, scientific, distanced observer.

111

Should it then come as an utter surprise that at the most recent media-technological threshold, once again "the general response of live performance to the oppression and economic superiority of mediatized forms has been to become as much like them as possible", as Philip Auslander remarked. (Auslander 1999: 7) The advent of new pictorial techniques, and the eventual digitization and computerization of any kind of data over the past hundred years inevitably boosted a fundamentally new theatre as well: from the theatre avant-garde around 1900 to contemporary 'post-dramatic' theatre, all the way down to multi-media, live art and cross-genre performance. It was in the latter context where the term *intermediality* first emerged, or should we say re-emerged through Dick Higgins, one of the artists associated with John Cage's Fluxus-movement.

However, the effect of intermediality becomes particularly powerful in the socio-cultural environment of the twenty-first century, which has media at its ideological heart. I contend that intermediality plays out a curious and somewhat negative complementarity of theatrical performance and electronic media. Digital technology has exponentially advanced the effect of what Benjamin referred to as "mechanical reproduction": the possibility to produce identical copies of an "original". This causes the loss of the sacred aura of any work of art, being now no longer original and untouchable, but mass-produced and multiplied (Benjamin 1968). Digital media not only enable mechanical but also electronic reproduction: by a single mouseclick, they produce an infinite number of copies of any original, thereby ultimately eliminating the last remaining sense behind the notion of originality. This capacity of electronic media is supported by what Lev Manovich describes as *transcoding*: the translatability of virtually any kind of data, allowing blending various types of audio-visual information, and to store, access, display, exchange, and replicate them by means of a single machine (Manovich 2001: 45).

For that reason, many describe the computer as a *"meta"-medium*, which absorbs other media in its numerical logic of zeroes and ones.[5] Theatre offers what appears at first sight an ability to soak up and *trans-code* other media. It combines texts, sounds, bodies, language, imagery, various visual and other sign systems in ever-new mixtures to create ever-new performances. The effects on these media remediated in theatrical performance, however, could not be more different from their digital trans-coding: While computers indifferently digest any other medium in their giga-byte stomach of the microprocessor, theatre apparently very generously provides the stage to other media entirely according to their will. Theatre behaves as a fully transparent medium, a remarkable camera lucida, without any palpable fingerprints of its mediatization stamped on the primary media it relies on so heavily. Imagine, for example, the same actor appearing in a movie and on stage: on stage, he remains the physical actor and is never transformed into a projection of light on a screen. A photograph might be displayed as part of a stage set, and liking it, I might scan it and use it as a screen saver; yet that photo on stage still remains the photograph, but not so as my new screen saver. Alternatively, a video might be projected as part of a theatre performance, which is then recorded for TV; yet the video on stage is still a video, whereas on the television it will be the broadcast of the showing of a video. These other media seem to be theatre's "message"; without them it would cease to exist. Most essentially, in contrast to mechanical and, even more so, digital reproduction, where the originals disappear, theatre even seems to reinforce the very originality and materiality of that actor, picture, or videotape. So, let us tie together this noteworthy and, at first sight, rather untypical medial behaviour of theatre, with the theoretical package bundled up earlier.

Drawing on media studies, we have envisaged theatre as architectural arrangement (thus, a site) of cognitive strategies, a spatial extension of men and mental space. McLuhan's colourful metaphor of media as extensions now maps a way of conceptualizing that striking mediality of theatre. Precisely because it is the extension (or, "remediation") of the mind, it must differ vitally from any other such extension, as for example the extension of the foot in the wheel, or the eye in the camera. As opposed to these human organs, the mind is no biological given, but itself essentially an implemented quality fabricated by its socio-cultural environment: discourse fundamentally channels, shapes and manipulates cognition and perception. Thus, theatre extends a mental space that itself is consistently reinscribed and reconfigured by the users' *observation* of media, in Crary's double stress of the term. While all media remediate, theatre therefore (re)mediates (re)mediation. Before any world-making or content come into play, theatre always confronts its spectators with the ever-changing workings of perception: it is De Kerckhove's training ground for the latest cognitive updates.

Consequently, if there is any specific *theatricality*, it is not to be found in theatre's exclusive values and aesthetic qualities – but in its very impact on and over the perception of its observers. I feel strongly that this most vital aspect of understanding and defining theatre has been largely ignored by traditional attempts at conceptualizing theatre in representational and aesthetic terms alone. While stories, narratives, and their discursive impregnation are without doubt important features, the medium and therefore mediality as such, is in fact theatre's core message – beyond genre borders, any formal limit, and all cultural frontiers.

This has crucial ramifications. It becomes clear that it makes no sense at all to think of an originally *pure theatre* that has been invaded by technological media. Nor should we get too over excited about potentially exciting frictions of live theatre and media technology. We have to accept that there simply never has been a separate history of theatre and media in the first place. Theatre itself is a media technology that 113 utilizes, at its very heart, other media to transmit and store, while it highlights, at the same time, the process of processing information. Essentially, theatre is a semiotic practice, which incorporates, spatializes and disseminates in sensorial terms (thus: performs) the contents and cognitive strategies of other media by creating multiple channels, and a multi-media semiotic and sensoric environment. It is exactly through this door where intermediality enters theatrical performance.

Intermediality as an effect of performance

Theatre, as an aesthetic act, an artistic medium, and an aisthetic process, relies on its observers. Intermediality, I suggest, is an effect created in the perception of observers that is triggered by performance – and not simply by the media, machines, projections or computers used in a performance. I conceive of intermediality as much more than yet another aesthetic strategy to be simply devised, or than just the latest media-technological gimmick feature waiting to be switched on as explained by the instruction manual. We could use all of the latest computer techniques on stage without creating any intermedial effect, while intermediality might sneak into a most traditional text-only talking heads drama production.

To clarify this core aspect of my argument, let us rewind and reconsider that actor, picture, and videotape discussed a moment ago. Up to now, we had seen that their *theatrical reproduction* appears to transparently trans-code them on stage without any trace of mediatization. Yet, I believe that this trace has only been overlooked. Again, we must go beyond the domain of theatre's alleged aesthetic originalities to scent that microscopic, yet ever so obvious effect. It is no technical, no mechanical, nor a digital effect – but an aisthetic one, which does not transform nor physically affect the actor, photo, or video-tape, as their mediation by means of a camera, scanner, or TV screen did. This trace of theatrical mediation is produced in the observers' perception alone: the actor on stage is no longer the actor, but the actor exposed on stage. That photo becomes a photo placed on stage and strangely different from the very same photo hanging stored back-stage before the show, not to mention my screensaver version of it. That video projected on stage is no longer the same as the very same tape I watched at home. As opposed to the digital transcoding into bits and bytes, theatre leaves the thing itself intact, yet the actor, picture, and tape, at the same time, are *theatrically reproduced* into something beyond their mere (even less: *pure*) original presence. They become signs representing a character, or any fictional world and, at the same time, they are always also something presented on stage, something presented to someone, and that is – far more essential than any represented meaning – the quintessential function of a sign.

As a primarily semiotic practice, theatre turns all objects into signs to be perceived.[6] Compared with other media that transmit objects to another space and/ or another time, or store them to make worlds out of them there and then, theatre processes these objects into worlds here and now, while simultaneously leaving them as they are. Thus, theatre multiplies its objects in a remarkable way into objects on stage that are present and representations at the same time, and – above all – they are presented to someone who is perceiving and observing them. This means that theatre not only mimetically creates fictional worlds, but it does so by utilizing not only three semiotic layers (of presence, presentation, and representation) but also a whole variety of sign-systems. Any theatrical performance, thus, negotiates a multiple range of potential perspectives to be observed.

According to the standard, hegemonic logic of representation, all these simultaneous, alternative layers, levels and perspectives offered en-route would be homogenized again into a single, closed and coherent final product of representation: in the destination of the ideal viewpoint, the single sharp focused picture of the reading camera-eye, or the one defined meaning of the text. Yet, the plurality of the perspectives might also spill over, crack and produce an untidy mess of meaning – either as a calculated result or as a somewhat subversive side effect. It is at this busy multi-dimensional junction of perspectives that intermediality and theatrical performance meet on the same platform. Intermediality is triggered in performances as an effect in the perception of their observers. It is very literally located inter-media, inhibiting, blending and blurring traditional borders between genres, media, sign-systems, and messages.[7] The intermedial effect breaks the standard law of *observing* the media timetable, and interferes with their *normal* function of creating unified messages, linear narratives and homogenous worlds in the cognition of the observers. Instead of closing down the multiple semantic potential offered into one coherent meaning, intermedial performances derail the message by communicating gaps, splits and fissures, and broadcasting detours, inconsistencies and contradictions. Therefore, intermedial effects ultimately inflect the attention from the real worlds of the message created by the performance, towards the very reality of media, mediation and the performance itself. The usually transparent viewing conventions of observing media are made palpable, and the workings of mediation exposed. Thus, intermediality manages to stimulate exceptional, disturbing and potentially radical observations, rather than merely communicating or transporting them as messages, as media would traditionally do. It is exactly this *disruptive intangibility* in the continuous flow of mediatized information that is encapsulated in the formulae of the third meaning, attraction, and magic moment – and it is right here where intermediality becomes so eminently powerful within the omnipresent performance paradigm of twenty-first century culture.

In a more and more thoroughly mediatized socio-cultural environment, intermediality offers a perspective of *disruption and resistance*. Rather than dictating yet more propaganda, information, advertisement, news and messages to be decoded, understood, and observed, intermediality as an effect of performance, manages to perforate *the meaning*. It confronts the ongoing medial homogenization and globalized universalization of *the meaning* (that *one reality* forcefully inscribed in recent years, which so blatantly contradicts all the slogans of cyberspace democracy and manifold globes of virtual realities with equal rights) with heterogeneous splits and alternative fragmentations. It is precisely because of the diversity of perspectives it offers, that intermediality has become a fascinating, attractive, and much aimed-at aisthetic effect in many contemporary artistic performances, some of which are sampled in this volume. Intermedial performances, not only on stage and on screen, yet anywhere from digital design to literature and electronic music, create effects of *alienation* and *dys-referential* un-realities.[8]

In the case of theatre, intermediality seems to be particularly effective. Instead of treating the dramatic text, any other single medium, narrative or even any multimedia-installation used in a performance as a *transparent* means to a certain fixed end, the multiplication of semiotic levels (of presence, presentation, representation), along with the usual multi-mediality of theatrical performance offers a unique and productive potential for *intermedial intervention*, compared to other forms of mediation. Thus, intermedial theatrical performances aim to foster intermediality playfully, in order to re-define familiar forms – to take theatrical performance to *alternative spaces* and different worlds, far beyond well-rehearsed verbal interactions of acted characters and their represented actions. Intermedial theatrical performances activate the observers, who become invited (some will complain that they are left) to find their own paths through the pluri-focal networks of signs, worlds, messages, and meanings offered by the performances, often without being closed into the single, *unanimous meaning*.

In an ever more streamlined, rather bleak reality where you are either for us or against us, where alternatives are mutilated by the force of bombs and you are supposed to obediently "perform, or else...", and where media and many layers of mainstream culture have become key collaborators of this predominant pre-programmed ideology, the *intermedial effects* that any performance may prompt and spark off, offer a vision of theatre's potential future that had been built into its organism from the very first day.

Notes

1 Both Christopher Balme and Patrice Pavis suggest an understanding of intermediality as a somewhat extended variant of intertextuality, in terms of quoting aesthetic strategies and importing techniques of a technological medium, such as film or video, into theatrical live performance (Balme 1999: 154; Pavis 1996: 46).

2 It is curious to note that even digital technology, which supposedly brings every message indifferently down to a somewhat anonymous and faceless computable o/1-binary calculation, still gives various data their identity, at least as a class. Words, sounds, and images are all coded in their distinct formats, which can then only be read and processed by the relevant specialist programmes.

3 Two websites inspired by Sci-Fi novelist Bruce Sterling neatly compile information on 'dead media' throughout the centuries: http://griffin.multimedia.edu/~deadmedia, and http://www.deadmedia.org (last accessed 23.09.2004).

4 Consequently, postmodern deconstruction suggests an alternative understanding of 'mimesis'. For Jacques Derrida, exemplarily, mimesis "is not the representation of one thing by another, the relation of resemblance or identification between two beings, the reproduction of a product of nature by a product of art. It is not the relation of two products but of two productions. [...] 'True' mimesis is between two producing subjects and not between two produced things" (Derrida 1981: 9).

5 Manovich addresses the most common stereotypes about 'new media', such as their alleged 'inter-activity' and other buzzwords of digital-PR, and stresses the limits of viewing the computer as medium at all: "New media may look like media, but this is only the surface" (Manovich 2001: 49-61).

6 Theorizing cinema, Laura Mulvey suggested, with similar aisthetic thrust, the classic formula of the "to be looked-at-ness" especially of the female body in film (Mulvey 1989).

7 Oosterling 2003

8 The terms are Kodwo Eshun's, who suggested them in his inspiring survey of recent 'futuristic' intermedial sound-performances from Free Jazz to HipHop and Techno (Eshun 1998).

AUDIO THEATRE: THE
MEDIATIZATION OF THEATRICAL SPACE

Christopher B. Balme

Intermediality in the theatre is linked usually to the use of media technologies not normally associated with the stage. However, intermedial theatre can take place also outside theatre buildings. This chapter explores how experimental theatre groups are making increasing use of the walkman to expand the notion of theatre space. Experiments that happen in controlled spaces (museums) directed by acoustic instructions or send spectators out into the 'real' world, reconfigure fundamental definitions regarding spectators and spaces. The chapter concludes with an argument for reconsideration of traditional distinctions between theatre and mediatized space.[1]

The relationship between theatre and media discourses is characterized by tension and distrust. In the one camp, media experiences of film, television, and computer are regarded as inauthentic and vicarious; in the other camp, contempt usually reigns: the theatre, if it is regarded as a medium at all, is seen as an 'old' one that has had its day. Perhaps the key experiential factor separating the two camps is that of space. *Theatrical and performative space*, and I will be using these two terms interchangeably, is defined usually by a notion of contiguity between performers and spectators. The fact that both share the same space is regarded as a crucial, if not the defining element of the art form. *Mediatized spaces* on the other hand are created by visual and /or acoustic technology: they are always virtual, often overtly fictional while purporting to be real. This dichotomy – which I claim is generally accepted by theatre and media scholars alike – needs to be questioned because of performance practices that dissolve such a sharp distinction.

    My thesis is that theatre has seldom existed apart from and independent of what we could call the media – be they ocular or print, acoustic or digital. Theatre and performance have always fed off innovation and developments in technology. I shall explore this thesis by examining recent experiments with acoustic media, whereby spectators explore space through receiving verbal instructions and musical accompaniment. The technological medium required for this is the walkman or headset used by museums in audio-tours. To develop my argument I begin by reviewing briefly some of the literature that has emerged in the wake of Shuhei Hosokawa's seminal essay of 1984 on *The Walkman Effect*.

    In the main section of my chapter, I examine two recent performances staged at Munich's bi-annual Spielart festival that have made use of audio technology: *The Sound of Time* by Viviane de Muynck, a Belgian actress closely associated with Jan Lauwers' Needcompany. Together with the cellist Martin Vink, de Muynck guided spectators through the Glypothek, Munich's famous collection of Greek and Roman sculpture. The second example, *Kanal Kirchner*, sent spectators / participants on an extended audio-tour of a Munich inner-city suburb, guided by a fictional murder story. In the final section, I discuss both performances within the context of site-specific theatre.

The Urban Theatre

At a first glance, the spatial effects of the stage and the walkman would seem to have little in common. Theatre structures space along two main perceptual axes: the fictional space of the represented world on the one hand, and the collective space uniting spectators and performers in a variety of ways on the other; ranging from baroque theatre boxes to the fluidity of street theatre. The walkman, on the other hand, seems to embody an individualized listener rather than a collectivized spectator, and as a medium appears to be directly opposed to the fundamentals of theatre. Yet in his essay *The Walkman Effect* Shuhei Hosokawa described the walkman as a form of 'secret theatre' (Hosokawa 1984: 177). According to Hosokawa, this secrecy or what he terms its "triple cryptic expressivity" (ibid., 178) manifests itself on at least three levels. The first is one of form: walkman users and those who behold them are aware that the listeners have secrets, the content of which is irrelevant. While the content of the music listened to may be different, the form is the same. The second level concerns "the expressivity of the music tied up with corporal movement, the walk act" (ibid., 178). Walkman listeners are affected corporeally by an invisible acoustic source, which makes them interact differently from their surroundings. The third level is the music itself; its own secret "what even the holders do not know exactly" (ibid., 178).

Hosokawa argues that the act of listening to the walkman elicits an *aesthetic response* in the original meaning of *aisthesis* – objects are rendered perceptible to the senses and transformed in particular ways. This has nothing to do with aesthetics in the sense of beauty or value but refers to "provoking certain reactions [...] and transforming decisively each spatial signification into something else" (ibid., 178). This "something else" can have both semantic and theatrical dimensions. The walkman / listener "is able to construct and / or deconstruct the network of urban meaning" (ibid., 178).

Hosokawa is referring here to Michel de Certeau's notion of "walking the city", or creating an individual arrangement of paths and spaces out of abstracted and schematized 'place' (De Certeau 1984). De Certeau says that in its relation to place, space is like the word spoken, which is transformed into a term dependent upon many different conventions. Spaces are determined by historical subjects, by the users of places. Thus, the street defined geometrically by urban planning is transformed into space by walkers. The theatrical dimension comes into play because the walkman walker is ostended and draws attention to him / herself. The walkman renders the listener an actor and the uninvolved bystanders into (unwilling) spectators:

> Thus, with the appearance of this novel gadget, all passers-by are inevitably involved in the walkman-theatre, as either actors (holders) or spectators (beholders) (Hosokawa 1984: 179).

In a related publication Hosokawa examines *The Walkman as Urban Strategy* and concludes:

> The walkman makes the walk act more poetic and more dramatic [...]. We listen to what we don't see, and we see what we don't listen to [...]. If it is pertinent to the speech act it will make the ordinary strange [...]. It will transform the street into an open theatre (1983:134).

In his essay *The Aural Walk*, the cultural critic Iain Chambers extends Hosokawa's analysis to bring it within the framework of cultural and media theory "With the Walkman there is simultaneously a concentration of the auditory environment and an extension of our individual bodies" (Chambers 1994: 49). Here we are reminded of McLuhan's famous dictum of media as extensions of man, and according to Chambers, the meaning of the walkman does not lie in itself, in its technological specificities or special design, but rather "in the extension of perceptive potential" (ibid., 50). The walkman seems suspended in a curious paradox, signifying on the one hand manifest isolation, with the listeners apparently oblivious to the surroundings, but in fact creating a sociability of a different order:

> In the manifest refusal of sociability the Walkman nevertheless reaffirms participation in a shared environment. It directly partakes in the changes in the horizon of perception that characterise the late twentieth century, and which offers a world fragmenting under the mounting media accumulation of intersecting signs, sounds and images (Chambers 1994: 50).

This 'participation' takes the form of a creative activity in which each listener creates a personal soundscape of musical fragments. Thus, each listener/player selects and rearranges the surrounding soundscape, and, in constructing a dialogue with it, leaves a trace in the network. For Chambers, like Hosokawa, the walkman is the proto-typical postmodern technology. It is, like the mobile phone and credit card, a symptom of contemporary nomadism, of migrant populations finding their way in cities and simultaneously reconfiguring these spaces:

119

> As part of the equipment of modern nomadism it contributes to the prosthetic extension of mobile bodies caught up in a decentred diffusion of languages, experiences, identities, idiolects and histories that are distributed in a tangentially global syntax. The Walkman encourages us to think inside this new organisation of time and space (ibid., 52).

Both Hosokawa and Chambers regard the walkman primarily as a cultural practice in which individuals listen to music. Its aesthetic potential is recognized only in terms of a general aesthesis; a change in perceptual practices but not in the narrower sense of an artistic practice directed by artists. In keeping with their observation of the walkman as a cultural practice, Hosokawa and Chambers do not consider that individuals listen to anything other than pre-recorded music. Yet the aisthetic effects and features they describe: the ambulant / ambient practice, the altered perception of familiar spaces and places through the intensification of aural senses, the theatrical ostension created by an individual evidently experiencing phenomenon not accessible to other passers-by or bystanders – all these elements are in no way dependent exclusively on music.

Of course, the potential of a mobile listener has long been recognized by museums, which quickly adopted, for an extra charge, the walkman technology for their audio tours. Anyone who has viewed exhibits with a voice telling one 'what it means' or 'how the artist came to create it', is more than familiar with the informational function of the walkman. The two performances to be described below, one briefly and one in more detail, take as their point of departure precisely this openness or neutrality of the medium.

The Sound of Time

The first project did not strictly speaking use a walkman, although the effect was similar. During the 1999 Spielart festival in Munich, a number of actors were invited to create their own performances under the heading 'Actor's Choice'. In *The Sound of Time* by Viviane de Muynck, a Belgian actress closely associated with Jan Lauwers' Needcompany, spectators were guided through the Glypothek, Munich's famous collection of Greek and Roman sculpture. Through headphones we listened to de Muynck recite in wonderfully rhythmic and melodic English, together with live music performed by the cellist Martin Vink, a selection of texts revolving around the theme of time. Originally, she had planned to read from T.S. Eliot's *The Four Quartets* but unfortunately the executors refused permission to allow the texts to be read in this context. Nevertheless, for me at least, the combination of acoustic, visual and kinaesthetic impressions – listening, watching and moving – resulted in one of the most impressive experiences in the entire festival. Viewing the ancient statues and reliefs, themselves eroded by time, while listening to Bach and texts by poets ancient and modern intensified each of the basic sense perceptual practices in unusual and striking ways.

Because the texts and the acoustic music track were performed live, the medium was not technically a walkman; it relied more on the technology for simultaneous translation. However, in all other respects it achieved 'a walkman effect'. Spectators / auditors were free to wander among the exhibits. The musician Martin Vink, and the reciter, de Muynck, were stationed at different positions around the museum presenting spatial orientation points: movement to and from the voice or music allowed ambulators one means of structuring their individual paths through the exhibits. The experience was both collective and highly individual. It was collective because a group was moving and listening at the same time to the same text and music; and individual because of the confrontation with different statues and spaces at any given point in time. Although visually the listeners looked no different to any other visitor wearing headphones – indeed would not have appeared out of the ordinary – theirs was, of course, a 'secret theatre' too.

Kanal Kirchner – Real Space made Virtual

Following performances in Giessen and Frankfurt, the performance collective Hygiene Heute (Hygiene Today) created a third part to their project *Kanal Kirchner*.[2] Consisting principally of two former theatre students from the University of Giessen, Bernd Ernst and Stefan Kaegi, they term their concept an 'audio theatre play', where the viewer/listener, equipped with a tape player and headphones takes an urban journey. Following the instructions on the tape, the viewer/listener wanders through the real world of Munich and through the fragments of the story provided by the authors. The audio experience and real visual impressions combine to form a private experience on the streets of Munich. The story itself is of minor importance but can summarized as follows:

> The librarian Bruno Kirchner has been missing since 12 May 1998. One year later, his daughter Beate finds in her mailbox a package with a tape inside, and then she disappears without a trace. On 20 May 2000, the body of the cardiologist Markus Schlömer washes ashore on the banks of the Main River in Frankfurt. The police find the second tape under the Honsel Bridge. On 25 May 2001, Simone S. is handed an envelope in a massage parlor in Munich. Inside the envelope is a Walkman. She walks through Munich, following the voice's instructions on the tape, step-by-step. The prostitute Simone S. was last seen on the evening of 25 May in Kunstpark Ost in Munich.[3]

The performance itself began in a public toilet in the festival centre. Every 10 to 15 minutes a spectator/auditor, equipped with a walkman, set off on the one-hour tour following a route that took the auditor to various sites near the festival centre. These included the Gasteig, a large multi-purpose arts centre, an old church, along various streets, and into an underground car park. Peter Boenisch has described the effect of the performance as imposing a second, virtual reality on the well-known, or not so well-known, sites the audience walked through:

> Oddly designed radiators on the wall, a playground, fanciful architecture, decorated shop windows and graffiti all were connected with mysterious Big-Brother-like secret societies: the snail and the spider. The voice on the tape pointed out the evidence, and invited you to watch, to listen, to smell, to experience. At one point, it was implied that the listener was in imminent danger of getting trapped and caught by the snail. In the midst of the labyrinth of never used emergency exits in a huge underground car park, the voice said: "Run. Open the door. (Damn, another corridor). The snail is almost here, can you smell it? (Of course you did!) Run faster, open the door at the end of the corridor" - and the poor audience, who was alone and probably more and more lost at this point, found themselves in just another corridor! Numerous participants reported feelings of claustrophobia, extreme fear - and couldn't do but stop the tape (Boenisch 2002).

The relentless beat of the music combined with the urgent voice directing the spectator's attention to sights, fragments of reality, innocent bystanders who do not appear so innocent, function to redefine and reconstitute space. Hans-Thies Lehmann described it as a "narrative in a no-man's land between X-Files and Kafka" (2000: 28). The verbal script paid detailed attention to the spatial surroundings of the tour. It drew the spectator's attention to minutiae of the path to be followed. This continual interaction with the real world, as opposed to Kirchner's world, resulted in strange and unforeseen adaptations of the real world to the performance as the environment was subjected to a continual stream of walkman listeners moving through exactly the same spaces. In my own case, while walking through the arts centre I lost orientation briefly, but fortunately a group of window cleaners noticed my momentary disorientation and pointed me towards the right door. Thus, we can see how real life space is de-stablized and on occasions even totally replaced by the virtual, and where it is sometimes necessary to be returned to the virtual world by the inhabitants of the real.

Sound and Body-Space

The final question to be addressed concerns the theoretical assessment of such performances as *Kanal Kirchner* or *The Sound of Time* in terms of their special semantics. First, we must look at the similarities and differences and ask whether the medium of the walkman provides the decisive link between the two performances or if it is a mere technical device facilitating quite diverse spatial effects?

The obvious defining common element between the two performances is the use of specific, pre-existing spaces. Both conform to the broad definition of *site-specific* performances, i.e. performances that take place outside pre-existing and pre-defined theatrical spaces. Site-specific performances utilize natural features or historical spaces and buildings to provide a spatially determined semantic frame for the actual performance. Needless to say, the defining aspect of site-specificity is its rootedness in a particular place and hence the impossibility of transferring such performances to other locales. That such performances do in fact become transported has meant that the category itself has become too broad to accommodate the various experimental forms emerging under its conceptual umbrella. Indeed, a new subcategory has emerged, that of *site-generic* performance. These are performances that require a specific category of space but are not tied to one place. For example, the Brazilian group Teatro da Vertigem requires a prison, used or disused, for their piece *Apocalypse 1:11* which has been shown in Brazil, Portugal and Cologne.

Looking at these categories we can say that a performance such as *Sound of Time* is site-generic. It did not make any specific textual reference to the space of Munich's museum of classical art. It is clearly designed for a space in which time is made manifest, i.e. a museum, but of any kind. The encounter with aesthetic objects of the past was a crucial element of the performance, which resulted in an intensification of aesthetic perception. It was already highly aestheticized in the conventional sense but the performance imposed a different order of aestheticization on it.

Kanal Kirchner on the other hand was site-specific in the strictest sense of the term. The text led spectators through a precisely defined urban trail, in the course of which concrete references were made to buildings, streets, bus stops etc. The slightest deviation from this path led to complete disorientation and ultimately to a failure of the performance. Although the performance has been carried out in three different locales, it has been adapted in each case to the actual site. The story itself has been continued much like a television or radio serial.

An important effect of this walkman-induced or directed theatre was the almost complete effacement of the narrative in the traditional diegetic sense. The fictional story – the adventures of, or search for Mr Kirchner – moves out of focus as the listener/spectator struggle to follow the spatial instructions: "turn right, now left – watch the people carrying bags" etc. The overall effect of audio theatre is to intensify *spatial perception* in the sense of basic physical orientation. This is linked with what Hosokawa calls 'the walk act', the essential corporeal aspect of the medium's effects. Walkman theatre is body performance of a special kind, focusing as it does on a moving body that is itself perceiving rather than being perceived. On this level, *Sound of Time* and *Kanal Kirchner* do in fact meet – as they share this fundamental feature of foregrounding corporeal experience within a spatial environment.

The second common element resulting from audio theatre concerns the *ontological* status of the space represented and experienced. In traditional theatre theory, there is a clear phenomenological distinction made between *physical* and *fictional stage* space. Although in fact they may be identical as objects and constitute a kind of duality, the performance transforms the physical space into a fictional or metaphorical one.[4] Much contemporary theatre and performance practice challenges the dominance of metaphorical (fictional) space by making use of what Hans-Thies Lehmann has termed a trend towards 'metonymical' space, i.e. the fictionally or aesthetically organized space remains connected or contiguous with the real space of the spectator, instead of being clearly metaphorized and thus distanced.

The consequences of this trend towards *spatial metonymy* are manifold and fundamental for our participation. They lead, according to Lehmann, to a destabilization of the borders between work and frame, perception and participation. It highlights in particular the spectator's own presence as a central moment of artistic practice (Lehmann 2000: 27). In both of the performances considered here, the spatial organization is metonymical rather than metaphorical – we find no clear moment where a metaphorical space can be set apart. Yet, at the same time, the influence of verbal texts, music and sound effects do result in a transformation of the spaces, as we have seen. The red brick building of the Munich Arts Centre is transformed into the realm of the Spider and the Snail. The Greek and Roman statues can, under the influence of poetic, metaphoric language become metaphors within the individual's subjective consciousness.

If we return to Hosokawa's statement cited above – "The walkman makes the walk act more poetic and more dramatic [...] We listen to what we don't see, and we see what we don't listen to [...] It will transform the street into an open theatre" – we can see that the technical medium of the walkman, far from creating media experience distinct from the theatre, returns in fact to the theatre's most fundamental property: its ability to effect a *transformation of perception*.

Christopher B. Balme

Notes

1 A first draft of this paper was presented at the Korean Theatre Studies Association conference in October 2003.

2 The title is ambiguous in German. 'Kanal' can mean either a conduit for water or a broadcasting channel. Kirchner's Channel would be an approximate translation.

3 See www.hygieneheute.de (last accessed 28.09.2005).

4 See Gay McAuley (1999: 24-28) *Space in Performance: Making Meaning in the Theatre* Ann Arbor: University of Michigan Press

OF OTHER BODIES:
THE INTERMEDIAL GAZE IN THEATRE
Meike Wagner

Puppet theatre is an intermedial art form that brings a massive ontological problem to a clear-cut distinction of live performance versus media technology. Is the puppet a live performing body, present, perceptible and sensitive like the body of an actor? Or, is it an object body, a body image, or a medial representation of the human body? This chapter analyses the puppet staging of Müller's *Hamletmachine*, *Máquina Hamlet* by the Argentine theatre company El Periférico de Objetos, in which the photograph, staged figures, human actors and the puppet body present a visualization of intermediality in performance. The author argues that it is in the interplay between the perceiving and the perceived, the material and immaterial, the visible and the invisible, the self and other, that intermediality is located by the corporeally involved perceiver. In her discussion, she explores the intersection of phenomenology and media theory to locate the intermedial gaze in theatre, and introduces the notion of intermediality as a matrix, which shapes and produces theatrical bodies through a negotiation between the discourse on the body, the spectator as embodied perceiver and concepts of materiality.

The stage direction 'Family Album' given by Heiner Müller in his famous play *The Hamletmachine* materializes here through an intermedial *mise en scène*: a bright spotlight is focussed on a group of stage characters framed by the sharp edges of the light. They are posed as if they are in a nineteenth century family photograph. The men and woman, dressed in outmoded black suits and dark costumes have inexpressive faces.

It is hardly possible to distinguish a human from puppet figures. This 'family photograph' might be representing the living or the dead.

I was Hamlet. I stood at the waterfront and talked to the surf BLAH BLAH BLAH, behind me the ruins of Europe (*The Hamletmachine* 1995: 87).[1]

Figure 28
Family Album, video print from *Máquina Hamlet*

125

Hamlet's cynical and painful record of his father's funeral cuts violently through the rigid stillness of the 'photograph'. When the text turns to Hamlet's inner conflicts and his struggles against himself, the actors detach themselves from the photographic setting and start to re-enact bits and pieces of Shakespeare's *Hamlet*. They play a series of scenes with small nostalgic dolls as puppets, from which a section of the back of the heads are cut off to provide a grip for the puppeteers to manipulate them. The actors show the poisoning of the King and his funeral procession, the uncle's seizure of the throne and Hamlet's mother, and Hamlet killing his mother and uncle. It is only as the actors exit the photographic stillness to take up the puppets that the spectators realize that the 'family' is composed of human beings and human size mannequins. The complex intermediality of the opening of the play: the intermingling of photograph, stage figures, human actors and puppets is resolved here – briefly – for a moment.

The inter-relationship of the human actor and the puppet object has been a major concern in puppet shows since the entrance of the human actor onto the puppet stage in modern puppetry after World War II. This raised critical and theoretical issues about the ontology of the body in puppetry in the late eighties, which led to many puppeteers playing with the blurring of the boundaries between them. Thus, puppetry entered the postmodern discourse on the constructedness of the body. The puppet staging of Müller's *Hamletmachine* by the Argentine theatre company El Periférico de Objetos described above is indicative of the new trends in puppetry today. Their intermedial staging of *Máquina Hamlet* (1995) is part of this debate and is rooted in Heiner Müller's universe of suspended animation, apparent death and of haunting ghosts. The ontological status of the stage figures remains indistinguishable: all appearances are transformed into cyborgs – half mediatized technological objects, half-animated agents of human flesh and blood. *Máquina Hamlet* plays constantly with ontological blurring and so raises a number of issues relating to intermediality in theatre and performance. How does this intermedial set of objects, human bodies and photographs impact on the perception of the spectator? If mediality is considered as a transformed corporeal perception then how does this kind of theatrical performance shape a specific form of mediality? How does the object body of the puppet interfere as an alienating, othering body into the medial perception in theatre?

Live bodies versus mediatized bodies

As Peter Boenisch has argued at the beginning of this section of the book, there is a tradition of viewing theatre and media as two distinct domains defined by their opposition to each other. The live body of the actor, *corporeal presence*, has become the main criteria by which to define theatre. This argument links theatre to *incarnation*: if there are bodies present on stage then there is live performance; hence, there is theatre. The human body is set up as a shield to the mediatized body and there is a clear line between the two spheres: on one side of the line there is *live performance*, where the authentic human body is physically present. On the other side of the line, there are technical representations of the body as in video, film, television and the digital. The argument is based on the assumption that there exists *original corporeality* (natural human flesh), which can be distinguished from its *medial representations*. Looked at from this perspective, the argument is that theatre is not a medium because it deals with original bodies as opposed to their representations.

However, it is possible to conceive of a different notion of theatre, which is a fusion of *media* and *Gesamtkunstwerk* where theatre is considered to be a *hypermedium*, which integrates a variety of technical media into its performance. Viewed from this perspective, theatre is a large *medial framework*, which incorporates different media without negotiating the assumed live quality of the theatrical body. To me the model of theatre as a hypermedium is a compromise, which opens up possibilities of connecting to the ancient art form of theatre with contemporary notions of media, without renouncing the claim of corporeal presence in live performance. In this definition of theatre as hypermedium, the notion of media is conceived of only as a technical transmission – an apparatus that delivers images of bodies – but, crucially, does not include within its account the *corporeality of the media user*, the people who are observing – the *theatre spectator*.

I suggest that what is lacking in the current debate is a critical approach to the mediality of theatre as a performative and communicative space that can present a more elaborate conception. Therefore, I put forward here a phenomenological approach, which foregrounds the corporeality of the theatre spectator, and I use the art form of puppetry to explore and explain some of the issues involved, particularly as they pertain to intermediality in theatre and performance.

Puppet theatre is an intermedial art form that brings a massive ontological problem to a clear-cut distinction of live performance versus media technology. Is the puppet a live performing body, present, perceptible and sensitive like the body of an actor? Is it an object body, a body image, or a medial representation of the human body? Is it a combination of any or all of the above? One of the attempts to solve this dilemma is based on the assumption that puppet theatre differs essentially from live performance and theatre.[2] It would be very easy to support this belief if puppetry remained inscribed within its traditional framework: defined by the use of a castelet, the covered manipulation of the puppets, the use of a defined choice of materials like wood and textiles, and the pre-production of puppets before they enter the stage. However, contemporary puppetry cannot be pinned down within such criteria because it breaks out of the ancient framework and transgresses the old borderlines. Contemporary puppet performances mingle puppet bodies with human actors and mediatized bodies and so draw the human figure into an ambiguous position between an animated agent and an existential symbol of mediatization. We can see this in the human performer's interaction with the puppet bodies, which are constructed from a combination of material objects and human flesh. The performers enter into the puppet bodies and humanize the animated objects – they inter-change their human bodies with their object representations, until the sharp line of division contradicts itself. It is in the blurring of the border between the living and the dead, between live performance and the mediatized event that intermediality is located.

In postmodern puppetry, the notion of a coherent live performing body becomes problematic. The problem does not arise due to the narrative content of a puppet show but is generated by the *medial structure of puppetry*, which admits and, at the same time, also marks the productive rupture of the hermetic body image. Thus, puppetry presents on a stage, a *discursive notion of the body*, as theorized by Judith Butler (Butler 1990, 1993) who suggests that *the body* cannot be reduced to an original unintelligible *materiality*, but is crystallized through *discursive formation and inscription*.

I will argue that if we follow Butler's notion of the body as being more than a corporeal manifestation, which is constructed through discursive formations; then *the theatrical body* also is not *a given materiality* but emerges as a result of *performative acts*. In order to further my argument I will introduce here the notion of intermediality *as a matrix*, which shapes and produces theatrical bodies through a negotiation between *the discourse on the body*, the *spectator* and *concepts of materiality*. This notion of intermediality as a matrix does not subscribe to semiotic ideas of mediality as the signifying code of a technical apparatus. It does, however, accept that theatre is a medium and, in order to gain an insight into the intermedial production of theatrical bodies, I investigate the intersections of *phenomenology* and *media theory*, where theorists working in these fields consider *corporeal perception* as an *interplay* between *the perceiving* and *the perceived*, and thus introduce the spectator as a *corporeally involved perceiver* rather than only as a decoding and signifying mind whose position, traditionally, was to interpret a pre-existing message. In my discussion, I accept that the perceiving body and the body of an actor are mutually dependent. However, the potency of the puppet body is a potential troublemaker for the apparently coherent concepts of live performing bodies versus the mediatized body, and so functions here as a marker of theatrical bodies as a medium, through which we may visualize the intermediality of theatre.

The Blindness of Sight

The medial dimension of the theatrical body can be demonstrated with reference to Maurice Merleau-Ponty's conception of *seeing* as a *corporeal/embodied process* and as a *pure optical function*. In *La phénoménologie de la perception* (1945) Merleau-Ponty argues that the constant evasion of the body, the strangeness of the body itself crosscuts through the act of perception. This is rather similar to the fleeting, ambiguous intermedial moment at the beginning of El Periférico de Objetos' staging of *Hamletmachine* when, as a member of the audience, I saw that the 'family photograph' was composed of human beings and human size mannequins: in the alteration of my own gaze is the dwelling place of intermediality.

In his later works, *Le visible et l'invisible* (1964) Merleau-Ponty develops his thoughts on the *ontology of seeing* and *of flesh*, which contradicts hermetic concepts of subjectivity, Ego and presence. He articulates an understanding of *inter-subjectivity* as dramatically *inter-corporeal*. At this stage in his writings, seeing is not a subjective act, but an incidence of gaze, which enwraps the *viewer*, the *visible* and the *other spectator*. Merleau-Ponty put forward the proposition that the familiar and the other, the visible and the invisible form a chiasmic intertwining of the self and the other, endlessly reversing and redefining them.

If we accept Merleau-Ponty's later propositions, then one conclusion must be that a conclusion is always beyond one's reach, in this never-ending interplay of differences. Certainly, the possibility of ever attaining *a complete vision*, the idea of the entirely graspable visible is questioned by the paradoxical process of how human beings physically see things. We can never see ourselves in the act of seeing because what makes seeing possible at all is the blind spot in our retina where the optic nerve enters the eye. Thus, *the invisible* lies at the core of seeing. We only see ourselves and others through a reversibility of seeing and being seen, perceiving and being perceived. However, the invisible continues to trouble our perception, and in this sense, *the invisible other* becomes an irritation; an object that cannot be rendered visible through a simple gesture of, as it is often referred to, as 'lifting the veil'. The invisible remains a constituent disturbance, which troubles our seeing from within and acts as an alienation effect on our perception of familiar things.

It may be useful to make an analogy here. The puppet bodies in *Máquina Hamlet* function as an alienation effect on my familiar modes of perception because they connect with/are part of my relationship with my own body. *My body*, which I perceive as being an intimate, integral part of *my self* is disturbed through the encounter of the object body (puppet body) on stage – responding to my viewing with its dead eyes.

Unlike Jacques Lacan, Merleau-Ponty does not denounce *the invisible/ the other* in terms of loss or lacking, but rather he pleads for the idea of a *perceptive embodiment* of the invisible/the other. Correspondingly, he does not understand the invisible as *external to our world*; but pursues the invisible *within our world*:

> The idea is this level, this dimension, it is not something factually invisible like an object that is hidden behind another one, but it is also not an absolute invisible that is completely independent from the visible, but it is the invisible of this world, that which dwells in this world supporting it, making it visible, it is the inner, fundamental potentialities, the being of being (Merleau-Ponty 1986: 198, my translation).

Merleau-Ponty's idea of embodied vision marks the gap between *the look* and *the gaze* and thus points us to the *precondition of intermediality in perception*. Georg Christoph Tholen refers to Merleau-Ponty and to Lacan to demonstrate the impossibility of unmediated perception and to investigate the potencies of mediated vision:

> This medial splitting of the look and the gaze is not recognized by philosophy before phenomenology and psychoanalysis focus their attention on it. Both their reflection on the loss within the perception, which at first makes perception itself possible, is path breaking for media theory. Not to take into account the invisible loss or withdrawal in the perception leads to the dilemma of mistaking the loss of perception for which artificial vision machines are responsible, while distancing gradually from the human eye for a loss of supposed immediacy or naturalness of perception and of equalling this loss with the disappearance of the human being (Tholen 1995: 47, my translation).

Here, Tholen criticizes Paul Virilio's media theory, which postulates that vision machines could accelerate and substitute human perception. What is at stake here is Virilio's assumption about a 'natural' human perception invaded by technical media. Technical artefacts can substitute pure vision and the look – but not the gaze:

> The complaints about the technical substitution of the human eye overlook the fact that the gaze is not inscribed purely in the visual stream of the eye. Thus, it can not be replaced by the substitute of the eye. No tele-vision or mono-vision can take the place of the real. Because the real withdraws per definition from the images that we produce of it. The real remains different from its place, the images dwell at the margins of the impossible, which means they are movable clippings respectively medial therefore communicating frames (Tholen 1995: 68, footnote 5, my translation).

Phenomenology emphasizes that a *shifting borderline* cuts off the visible from the invisible but that it is the ephemeral permeable nature of the borderline that makes a difference. It is still a widely persistent illusion that a complete grasp of the visible, *a pure vision* is possible. However, as we shall see, whenever the visible is traced it is still inhabited by a newly defined invisibility. Tholen sees the function of art as its ability to approach the demarcation between the visible and the unseen, and to point at its shifting, its play of differences. Tholen makes the distinction between *seeing as a pure vision* and *the gaze embracing the other* and *the otherness of seeing* to help us to understand the chiasmic perception model, which relies on the reversibility of the visible and the invisible:

> Relying on the gaze, we are accessible only through an unforeseeable passiveness of being seen or being gazed at. It is the gaze that can be altered by art, when inscribing, shifting and distilling in the visible the unrepresentable chiasm of the invisible. To cut through pure sight, to unmask the illusionary perspectives and phantasms of holistic thinking is the strategy of art. It repeats like desire the order of symbolic and medial cross-cuttings, when questioning once and again the visible without ever abolishing it (Tholen 1995: 67).[3]

Clearly, this position differs from notions of media technology as a substitution for human perception. Such conceptions consider media as alien invaders of natural bodies who gain control over the human being. The phenomenological perspective does not subscribe to this idea. Phenomenological perspectives recognise that medial transmission is a space for the interplay of the visible and the invisible, which is the other space, the other side of human perception. The other, the invisible I am talking about could be linked also to the notion of 'transparency illusion' – a term coined by French film critics and apparatus theory.[4]

The distinction of seeing and the gaze can be compared with medial transmission but they differ in one important point. The gaze distinguishes the visible from the invisible, but is not a fixed perspective – it can be shifted by the demands of the other. Technical apparatus, on the other hand, set a constant limit and cut off a well-demarcated invisible. It is not easy to perceive the invisible dimension in such a well-defined technical setting. Only a radical break, the violent penetration of a technical disturbance or a medial operation, can rework the technical framing. This is the moment when the artist can appropriate and subvert the hermetic medial set-up. Artists can create disturbing structures to move, as Tholen (1999: 28) puts it, "the margins of the perceivable (the visible, the audible) and of communication" (my translation). I do indeed consider the use of the *object* (puppet) *body* in theatre as exactly such a medial operation. The use of the puppet body on stage can create disturbing structures that move the margins of the perceivable, and when we watch the puppet body on stage we become aware that we are moving into areas that we do not habitually perceive or inhabit.

Throughout his early work, *La phénoménologie de la perception* (1945), Merleau-Ponty already described the body as a non-static dynamic structure constantly fluctuating between object and subject, which crystallizes through perception. However, in his later works, especially in *Le visible et l'invisible* (1964), Merleau-Ponty develops the notion of 'the flesh' as inter-corporeality. Here he says that the body, inscribed in this inter-corporeality is always on the edge of turning over into the object hood of its environment without ever accomplishing this movement. This idea keeps reappearing throughout the whole book. What Merleau-Ponty is setting up is that *the flesh* and *the body* is self-identical and at the same time negates this identity. As a different body, it is a *sutured* body both concealing *and* revealing its seams, ruptures and cuttings. This idea is perhaps best understood through reference to Derrida and his concept of *difference/différance*, as Derrida and Merleau-Ponty inhabit some of the same conceptual space. *The flesh* operates in the ephemeral permeable borderline referred to earlier where, through interaction with the other, it constantly reconstitutes itself. The body as flesh is, at the same time, both the delimiting skin and the place where the inside fuses with/dissolves into the outside. Both appearances of the body – *the delimitation* and *the fusion* – crystallize for a little while, but only to vanish again; they are bound to an everlasting stabilizing and destabilizing *phenomenological interplay*.

Intermediality dwells in the margins between the look and the gaze and becomes perceivable *through the challenging of the other*. The tension between the look and the gaze sets the body as medial figure in motion and so negates any fixing of an essential corporeality. This idea of corporeality as Derridean *différance* can be linked here to contemporary puppetry, which in the interplay of materiality and performance, crystallizes for a moment fleeting and passing bodies.

What we have seen so far is that the body is part of the process when its gaze meets that of other bodies. The artificial object body, the puppet body on stage, decentres my own bodily perception in particular. I recognize obviously a human-like body, animated and moving like people are animated and move. However, the puppet body carries at its core *the artificiality of the other* that is its first principle of existence. When a phenomenological perspective is applied to the analysis of puppetry, it opens up the investigation to include not only that which one sees, but also the invisible. Crucially, the phenomenological perspective includes also *the spectator as a seeing and being seen body*. This is the point where intermediality and phenomenology meet and generate new understandings.

Contemporary puppetry is particularly preoccupied with investigating this *othering* aspect of the puppet, the object figure as a challenge for my own body image, by way of marking the underlying mediality of this process in the staging of puppet bodies. The notion of the puppet body as an othering body has to be linked here with my conception of mediality, which focuses on the medial conditions of my seeing this other body. Otherwise, my analysis would be constrained to the mere looking at those puppet bodies. Consequently, we need to move now to connect my notion of intermediality as a productive and generative matrix. Perception and materiality are discursive parameters entering jointly into this medial matrix – a mediality constructing and producing all bodies involved here: spectators, actors and puppets.

Alien bodies, machine bodies

Puppetry freezes the other of corporeal perception in the image of the other/the alien body. The puppet is very close to human beings; its features are familiar to ours. However, this familiarity is fragile and endangered – after all the puppet does bear the potential of radical alienation and othering: it still symbolizes death. In particular, the incorporation of this opposition – to be the carrier of the familiar other, of another human feature *and* the radical other, the dead object – inscribes the puppet into an undecidable (intermedial) status and creates an irritating image of the puppet as *the other body*. The splitting and ruptures in the puppet body image – they would be certainly deadly to human bodies – challenge my own corporeal scheme, my perception of my body and mess up my belief in an established corporeal structure. My own body itself becomes alienated and other when facing the other puppet body, like as Waldenfels (1998: 109) has said, "the experience of the other / the alien transforms the experience and all phenomenon into something other / alien" (my translation).

The constructed body of the puppet offers an insight into its intermedial structure. Its deconstructing potential demonstrated on stage causes an obstacle to the smooth perception of the body, a disturbance of its invisible inscription into the medial process. The gaze seizes the puppet body as an other/alien body because its intermedial materialization is obvious.

Máquina Hamlet produces a similar intermedial gazing through the crossing of the body with photography, as we have seen in the opening of the 'Family Album'. Equally involved in this intermedial folding is a human size puppet with portrait features of Heiner Müller himself. This puppet is constantly present on stage but generally remains uninvolved in the stage action. However, at one point, our attention is focused on the Heiner Müller-puppet and this is the scene 'Pest in Buda Battle of Greenland'. This scene is a depiction of the total 'mechanization' of Hamlet's inner freezing, which is the result of his inner conflicts between a revolutionary desire and reason of state. In this scene, the Müller-puppet is placed at centre stage, stripped of its clothes and then skinned to its wooden bones.

The dismemberment, the scattering of the author is a central theme in Müller's text, referring to aspects of alienation, of the existential situation between death and living. Müller describes the alienation, the splitting of the self into non-substantial positions, which culminates in the final tearing apart of the body in search of the absolute silence, of the deathly quiet in the otherness of his own entrails. At the beginning of this monologue, the actor denies his own stage figure: "I am not Hamlet. I have no more role to play" (90). The splitting of the role and the speaker, the fragmentation of the self reaches here another level. The self-alienation of the speaker is articulated, the dramatic situation of the splitting becomes virulent at the moment of revolt:

> My place, if my drama were still to take place, would be on both sides of the front, between front lines, above them (91).

Here the self considers itself both a revolutionary and a supporter of state interests; dramatically condensing the conflict the self transcends into the sphere of objects:

> I am the typewriter [...] The parts I play are spit and sputum cup knife and wound tooth and throat neck and noose (91-2).

The splitting of the roles leads to an unbearable paralysis, the historical events roll over the horrified author who is not able to move. The insanity of the alienating/othering splitting, results in the dismemberment of the flesh in self-destruction, in total objectification.

> I break open my sealed flesh. I want to live in my veins, in the marrow of my bones, in the labyrinth of my skull. I retreat into my entrails. My place is in my shit, in my blood. Somewhere bodies are being broken so that I can live in my shit. Somewhere bodies are being opened so that I can be alone with my blood. My thoughts are wounds in my head. My brain is a scar. I want to be a machine. Arms to grab legs to walk no pain no thinking (93).

The corporeal inside is a heterotopia, hidden from sight. Immersion in this other space promises an escape from the painful self. However, this desire to escape is filled with guilt and other bodies are scattered for this flight. However, this fleeing, escaping, hiding in the other space does not fully succeed; reflection is still full of pain. The longing for silence, for being other, being an object collapses into the wish to be dead and deadly: "I want to be a machine".

The stage action of dismembering the Müller-puppet counterbalances the text at this point. The intention 'I tear up my sealed flesh' is acted out by somebody else. Reacting to the stage direction 'Photograph of the writer', two actors turn the Müller puppet, which until now has been sitting on a chair, towards the audience. A bright spotlight focuses on the wooden skeleton. I watch this 'photographic portrait' until 'scattering of the writer's photograph' is heard. The actors are now beginning to dismember the puppet. They tear off arms and legs despite the struggling resistance of the puppet.

Meike Wagner

Figure 29
Dismemberment of the writer, *Máquina Hamlet*

Here again the photograph is equated with the photographed. The puppet is as dead as its photographic representation. However, still there is life, struggling against the dismemberment. Living and death, representation and object fuse in my imagination; the photograph becomes at the same time living and deadly. The fact that it is a verbal order to scatter the photograph, which leads to the horrible dismemberment of the puppet – up to that moment established as an inter-acting and sensitive being – refers to a scary medial transfer: at the core of the death of the puppet lies the imaginary textual scattering of the photograph.

The tension between the photographic medium and the puppet is created by the oscillating perception of difference and identity. When I equate the photograph with the puppet – the puppet is identical with the photograph – then its potential to become an animated body transgresses the frame of the photograph. When I distinguish the photograph from the puppet – the photograph seems to be completely independent from the puppet – then their interconnectedness is not logical, it seems to be an ungraspable, irritating, invisible umbilical cord. In *Máquina Hamlet*, the sophisticated complex relationship between the photograph and the puppet(s) creates a highly destabilizing tension that cannot be comprehended fully or explained. This brings us back again to the deferring, othering effect of the intermedial body in performance.

The irritating medial crossing between life and death bears a certain degree of violence. The theatrical representation of bodies that have to suffer from violent treatment has an even more horrifying effect on the spectator: in the performance of *Máquina Hamlet*, I felt, sitting in the audience, a collective release of the breath taking tension after these moments. The other body, the puppet, does not destroy itself – this crime is committed by other actors. This kind of violence, however, does not equate with the horror scenes of exploding bodies in so called 'splatter movies'.

The dismemberment of the puppet body does not show bloody entrails, there is no disgusting bloody mess, and after all nothing 'to live in'. The wooden skeleton is a hollow structure concealing/revealing nothing – its otherness is not inside but on the surface, persisting in the ungraspable status of the puppet between artificiality and liveliness. The puppet still possesses a living potential distinguishing it from sheer dead materiality. 'Breaking up the flesh' does not affect the puppet body unless the deadly aspect of materiality comes to the fore through theatrical performance.

The puppet seems to come very close to the ideal of being a machine. It is a metaphor of control, manipulation. However, what yet is lacking is total objectification. Scattering the Müller puppet visualizes the steps of reducing the puppet to an object. The puppet body is gradually dismembered without any effect on its actions. Stripping off the skin, tearing up the limbs wounds my imagination although the puppet stays unchanged. According to its logical matrix, the puppet struggles and fights against the treatment but as soon as the amputation is completed it does not seem to feel any pain, being at rest. Lacking a limb cannot yet destroy a puppet. Being alive springs here from its animation, follows a performative logic that is not dependant on corporeal coherence. The puppet is still living until the last cut – the head is still sitting on the trunk, arms and legs are hung up on the back wall – it is an intermedial entity being both animated and dead. It is only when one of the actors makes a purely 'technical' gesture that the puppet turns into a dead object: After tearing off the head, he lifts the puppet trunk with a purely technical attitude and pins it to the naked back wall next to the other limbs. Clearly, he is not acting on an animated being but storing away a thing, a material object. Thus, the self of the puppet is stripped of any living aspect; it is now a real machine.

This description demonstrates how the interaction of puppets and human actors produces temporarily varying degrees of object-hood and subject-hood. The same counts for Müller's Hamlet who is determined by the crumbling ruins of history: he becomes a machine according to the political conditions/events. The joining of the logic of the puppet and the logic of the machine in Müller's Hamlet creates a paradox. While the image of the machine offers fatalistic freezing (violence) or anaesthesia (flight inwards) as a solution to the splitting of the self, the puppet-machine represents a dynamic field, an interplay between the self/human and the other (animation and object hood); and this interplay crystallizes the image of the ambiguous puppet itself. The puppets visualize exactly what Müller intended: the mechanization of the body, the transcendence into the sphere of object, the scattering of the body, its fragmentation. But yet, in a way they also resist such a reading by demonstrating their mediality as a phenomenological interplay of *the own* and *the other*. The corporeal staging in *Máquina Hamlet* focuses exactly on this dynamic tension.

The crossing of the border is not only the transfer from life to death but it is also connected to the difference of *the own* and *the other*. The *mise en scène* of the other demonstrates the constant shifting of that differentiating limitation; it is indeed a dynamic borderline. Equally dynamic and shifting is the border between the own (my self, being alive) and the other (the alien artificial, dead) when I consider it as a phenomenological crystallization of interaction. The violent treating of the puppet should not be hurting me; neither I, nor my kind is endangered here. The suffering of

135

the puppet, however, is painful to me and even more dreadful when the difficult deed of its animation is made visible, when the performative production of life is shown in puppetry. My imagination interacts here with the animating performance, is itself in a way animated and cannot keep its distance to the object anymore. It transcends any borderline only to be limited again by the active border itself at work.

In puppetry, the border is always incorporated in the staging. This implies the fundamental paradox of human existence. The puppet mirrors the doubling of my own corporeal existence: the own and the other are interwoven in indispensable and necessary phenomenological interplay. The puppet is at once a material and animated being, and both modes of being depend on its performance. The splitting of the human self is concealed by identifying strategies and images which construct the evidence of coherence. However, it can be and is dismantled by the puppet's performative potential. When on stage, the puppet's mediality – the matrix of its existence relating spectator, materiality and discourse – is part of my perception. However, I am able to become conscious of this only when disturbance occurs, when the puppet is thrown back to its mere materiality and thus becomes clearly distinct from human actors. Accordingly, drawing the line between dead and living becomes questionable. Death is always part of myself: exactly as it is part of the puppet. Thus, the puppet-machine and the cyborg reflect the intermedial interplay of the border between the own and the other.

The puppet body does not therefore inscribe into the binary logic of live body vs. mediatized body. The seams of the puppet skin burst open and reveal its construction, giving an insight into the inter mediality of the theatrical body and marking visibly the intermediality of the gaze.

Notes

1 All citations of the play are taken from Müller (1995).

2 This debate is currently vivid in German puppetry where traditionalist views would like to preserve the 'specificity' of puppet theatre and do not want to open up the genre towards other theatre forms.

3 Bernhard Waldenfels (1991: 213) confirms this notion of art: "The picture, so to say, not only visualizes something *but rather makes visible visuality itself without ever leaving the sphere of the visible*" (my translation).

4 Baudry 1993 (1970), Comolli 1980.

NEW SMALL SCREEN SPACES:
A PERFORMATIVE PHENOMENON?

Robin Nelson

This chapter discusses first the impact of the proliferation of other small screens, notably the home PC and mobile phones, on the content and form of television texts. Informed by the Bolter and Grusin debate on Remediation in net art and digital culture, the author considers critically the application of their ideas to television. In applying some of their key concepts to contemporary Television Drama, he locates in particular an *intermediality* of television, theatre and PC culture. He notes that a feature of intermediality in televisual and digital culture is a change in the activity of those who construct the performance text and those who receive them and assesses how, through the introduction of the digital into an analogue medium, 'viewers' have increasingly become constructed as self-aware 'participants'. From there he moves to assess the different kinds of experience and perceptual shifts involved in a 'performative' culture. His concluding phenomenological discussion resonates with other discussions, which have located the in-between feature of intermediality.

New technologies of representation proceed by reforming or remediating earlier ones (Bolter and Grusin 2000: 4)

Introduction

The Bolter and Grusin conceptual framework of remediation involves "the twin preoccupations of contemporary media: the transparent presentation of the real and the enjoyment of the opacity of media themselves" (2000: 5, 21). They suggest that two elements: *immediacy* and *hypermediacy* together make up a model of *remediation*. The apparently un-mediated mode of immediacy appears to present the viewer with immediate access to *the real* but it oscillates with and is often presented simultaneously with hypermediacy – the highly *constructed* and *multi-mediatized* mode of presentation. It is with this model in mind that the chapter addresses first the impact of the proliferation of networked small screens, their viewing apparatus and television texts before moving to consider phenomenological and performative aspects of contemporary Television.

In one obvious sense, the small screen is not new at all, but so much part of daily life on a global scale that its omnipresence renders it unremarkable. In the economically developed world, most homes have more than one television monitor, and satellite antennae have been spied atop Bedouin tents in the desert (Dowmunt 1993: 1).[1] However, there is another sense in which the small screen is a recent phenomenon. Over two decades small screens, superficially similar to the television apparatus, namely computer monitors, have so rapidly become equally as ubiquitous as television screens that we tend to overlook both their relative novelty and their reciprocal influence on their older cousins.[2] More recently, even smaller screens have proliferated on mobile phones and elsewhere. The rapidly-attained ubiquity of PCs is having an impact both on the construction of texts to inhabit the television screen space and the disposition of viewers towards that space. Some commentators have proposed that computer culture will rapidly overtake and destroy television. It is too early to say whether or not this will prove to be the case, and this chapter concentrates on the present moment in which television is primarily responding to the advent of personal computers (PCs).

Bolter and Grusin observe that "both new and old media are invoking the twin logics of immediacy and hypermediacy in their efforts to re-make themselves and each other" (2000: 5). Signs that television is likely to endure and co-exist with PCs are evident in this reciprocal process. As van Vliet (2004: 1) puts it, "next generation television strives towards interactivity and connectivity [...] Both [television and the Internet] 'long for' what the other medium possesses". Whilst this chapter explores primarily the influence of the small screens of PCs on the older monitors of television, it is important to note also that the influence of remediation is a two-way, indeed multiple, process, through the channels of the network of small screens.

Traditionally, the television screen has been seen as a 'window on the world'. Though television theory has long since unpacked this 'naïve' view, a residual inflection stubbornly remains of the television set as *the medium* through which access is gained to the external world beyond the scope of any individual's direct experience. Early television discourse established this conception:

> People now look upon scenes never before within their range; they see politics as practiced (sic), sports as played, drama as enacted, history as it is made (Dunlap 1947, cited in Auslander 1999: 15).

Though seen by theorists today to be fabricated to the point where television constructs rather than reveals reality; *Broadcast News*, now available on television *as if live* twenty-four hours per day, retains nevertheless a core function of information. Indeed, outside the circles of theory:

> The discourse of the immediate has been and remains crucially compelling.... [C]omputer graphics experts, computer users, and the vast audiences for popular film and television continue to assume that unmediated presentation is the ultimate goal of visual representation and to believe that technological progress towards that goal is being made [in digital graphic imaging] (Bolter and Grusin 2000: 30).

However, I suggest that to trace the developing relationship between PCs and television is, in part, to trace the unsettling of one facet of the double logic of remediation. Therefore, in the second section of this chapter I discuss examples of contemporary TV drama to illustrate this tension at work, before moving to examine the phenomenological shifts in the experience of the small screen, that is, with a shift "in the manner in which it appears [...] as it manifests itself to the experiencer" (Moran 2000: 4). Given the importance of the effect of *intermediality* on the *theatre audience*, as contributors elsewhere in this volume have noticed, so the focus of discussion turns in section three to the performative elements of the PC and television, where the *viewers* are increasingly incorporated as *agents* in the medial process. Perhaps some small clarification is required here in that the relationship between television 'participants' and the small screen as *live* will be discussed in a related (but not totally similar fashion) to the Auslander discourse of *liveness* (1999: 54).[3]

I contend that an emergent habitus of *virtual spaces*, which afford experiences that are in part embodied, is shifting the *phenomenal relationship* with machines. Indeed, distinctions have become increasingly blurred between: the live and the mediatized; humans and machines; reality and representations/simulations; truth and fiction. The small screen, which under the constraints of its early technology was little more than a radio with indistinct images, is tending now towards a *multi-medial* and *inter-medial* space, promoting by turns an *inside-outside*, *immersive* and *interactive* information society.

This chapter then is ultimately concerned with *performance* and the *performative relations* between viewers and the apparatus, rather than performances within the televisual frame. The hypothesis explored is that, whereas viewers traditionally treated television as an object to be watched as if live, the habitus (in Bourdieu's 1979 sense) is changing to a disposition whereby viewers *engage* with the apparatus – to be in some sense *present within the medium* – while at the same time, being *consciously aware of the medium* with which they are engaging. It is proposed that the widespread use of PCs has played a significant part in this paradigm shift and that, in turn, television programmes have adapted to become more inclusive of their audience on several levels: to involve 'ordinary people' in broadcast programming; to afford digital interactivity with the television apparatus; to changing the conventions of *television drama*, from shutting viewers outside the 'fourth wall' to acknowledging their presence and participation.

In the 1970s, Raymond Williams remarked that "watching dramatic simulations is now an essential part of our modern cultural pattern" (1974: 53). A twenty-first century account of television culture must acknowledge both the continuities and discontinuities of this pattern. Audiences in millions still regularly watch performed on television visual narratives which parallel everyday life in offering 'real' (though fictional) representations. The popularity of soaps, of continuing serial narratives stand as testimony to the established culture of watching dramatic simulations, located particularly in domestic spaces, 'rooms in which life was centred' (ibid., 14). However, a number of factors in the force-field of contemporary culture are mobilising the shift in the relationship between spectator and apparatus. In one respect, the *realist paradigm* is giving way to a *virtual paradigm*; to simulations of worlds which are not real in any physical sense but which are taken for real, even more perhaps than television's previous constructions of illusions of real (though fictional) worlds. Along this trajectory, we might think in terms of a continuum of increasing depths of immersion, ranging from a temporary suspension of disbelief in a traditional television fiction, through a deeper immersion in a role-playing computer game, to full simulation of an unreal world experienced as if directly through sense-perception, but in fact through the wiring of a virtual reality head-set.

The implications of an implicit blurring of any clear distinction between virtual and physical worlds will be taken up in section three in a sketch of contemporary culture. My immediate focus however is the two facets of the double logic of remediation, which have been increasingly in tension for some time as generations have grown up with television and understand much more about its construction, many through study of the media in school and further education. The *as if live*, the very *here-and-now-ness* of the medium of television has undoubtedly been eroded amongst *media-aware audiences* since the 1970s. Cultural and technological changes have pushed both immediacy and hypermediacy into new dimensions. The focus here is on the space for play between the two facets.

Television texts

Given that the double logic of remediation resonates both with aspects of immediacy in the history of Western art and the hypermediacy of the newer media of today, it is not easy to predict the impact of any given text by describing its compositional principles alone. The dispositions of different viewers at various times need to be taken into account. In respect of television, some viewers today are likely to incline towards the first face of the double logic, immediacy, and take television in the 'window on the world' tradition as representing plausible worlds. Amongst a large audience, however, sub-divisions, or micro-cultures, will watch in various ways. Younger, media-literate viewers are more likely to bring to their viewing an irony, distinctive of a postmodern culture and aware of the text as text.[4] Though dispositions towards television inflect readings, features of the text that encourage certain ways of seeing rather than others may be delineated. Examples from the *windowed* television news or sports programme reveal a screen space structured similarly to the PC screen. To illustrate the tension noted above I propose briefly to discuss two examples of contemporary TV drama where the relation between TV and PC screens might be expected to be less overt: the comedy drama *Ally McBeal* and the 'real-time' drama *24*. The aim is to bring out *intermedial play* implicit in the textual construction. 'Play' here carries three resonances: *playfulness*, as in children's play, *play/slippage* as in the room for movement between socket and joint; and, particularly, the *inside-outside play* between medium and watching-listening participant.

ALLY MCBEAL (1997-2002)

Beyond the generic hybridity of comedy + drama, the narrative form of *Ally McBeal* is a hybrid (Nelson 2000) combining aspects of the series, the court-room drama, with the on-going serial, some would say soap, story, of Ally's quest to find the perfect partner. I have proposed that the high temperature, rapidly intercut form of what I dub *flexi-narrative* in TV drama resonates with a new affective order, based in an economy of intense but unsatisfying experiences turned over fast (Nelson 1997). These features in themselves approximate to the *windowed style* of hypermediacy. Although the screen space itself is not broken down into sub-sets of windows, rapid cutting between one dramatic mode and another has a similar effect of juxtaposing disparate information.

In addition to the rapidly intercut fragments of visual narrative, the texture of the text is enriched by an overlay of popular music as soundtrack. Serving as another example of *intermedial play*, the influence of MTV's commercially successful combination of moving images cut under popular music soundtracks (Kaplan 1987) has impacted upon a range of TV dramas. In an early example of a hypermedial tendency in television drama, the series *Miami Vice* (1980s) pioneered the use of pop music sequences, which "interrupt the continuity of the narrative" (Buxton 1990: 140).[5] By the beginning of the twenty-first century, the use of pop music to establish a dynamic or mood only loosely related to the dramatic situation or, indeed, simply for the pleasures it generates, has become commonplace as we recognise in the UK from *Heartbeat* to *Teachers*; and in the US from *Ally McBeal* to *The Sopranos*. Whereas music hitherto had been harmonised within the textual composition, where the systems of sounds semiotically supported the system of the visual and the narrative, music increasingly has a disjunctive relationship with the visual and narrative. In some instances, the relationship is almost arbitrary, whilst in others the different sign-systems might be taken to comment ironically upon the other. Elsewhere, (Nelson 1997) I have suggested that this postmodern bricolage aesthetic in television resonates culturally with the play of multiple windows on computer screens, which contain disparate information frequently expressed through different media: graphics, video and soundtrack.

Ally McBeal, though rooted in the plausible (though fictional) world of the Cage & Fish law practice, repeatedly breaks the televisual frame with its digitally-generated devices The *graphic imaging* techniques in *Ally McBeal*, illustrative of the intermedial influence of computer culture, are employed in the visual construction of the characters' fantasies, which playfully distort the integral world of the mise-en-scène. To take a famous example, Ally's tongue extends hugely to display her petulant dislike for somebody. In *Ally McBeal*, the digital effects offer a broader range of pleasures to those who are fascinated by hypermediacy and enjoy the sheer playfulness of devices. It affords, indeed, an opportunity to oscillate between an *inside* and *outside* position in relation to the text, paralleling a mobility that Bolter and Grusin observe in PC windows:

141

> [The user] oscillates between manipulating the windows and examining their contents, just as she oscillates between looking at a hypertext as a texture of links and looking through the links to the textual units as language (2000: 33).

I propose that the compositional principle of *Ally McBeal* affords the opportunity of a similar inside/outside experience.

The tension between immediacy and hypermediacy is evident also in the textual form of the series. Aspects of traditional narrative remain in *Ally McBeal* in the mode of the courtroom drama, which affords some series-style narrative closure in each episode as the specific lawsuit is concluded. In addition, narrative arcs on-going across several episodes of *Ally McBeal* echo those used in soaps. However, *Ally McBeal*, whilst retaining established aspects of established drama formats, adopts also the hypermedial features of computer graphics and MTV-style music video as part of the texture. These hypermedial features may be absorbed by the more established dramatic forms, or foregrounded, by way of textual play in any or all of the three senses noted above. Indeed, according to Bolter and Grusin, '[s]ometimes hypermediacy has adopted a playful or subversive attitude, both undercutting and acknowledging the desire for immediacy' (2000: 34). Thus, in the one televisual space *Ally McBeal* conflates constructions of *the real* (though fictional) world with constructions of *the virtual*, allowing viewers readily to slip between them.

24 (2002)

In contrast, 24 is a more conventional serial drama in many respects appearing to construct a real (though fictional) scenario. The story of the first series concerned an attempt to murder the black governor of California and prevent him from becoming the first black president of the USA. It is the destiny of Special Agent, Jack Bauer, to foil the plot. At the same time 24 is concerned with Jack Bauer, the family man, struggling to save his rocky marriage and to do the right thing by his daughter. Both wife and daughter get caught up in the action-adventure of Bauer's professional role. Both are in danger of their lives on several occasions. Indeed, the wife is ultimately murdered by Bauer's former colleague and lover who, quite improbably, turns out to be the mole in the CIA. In yet another hybrid drama exploring the tensions between domestic and professional life, 24 is distinctive and intermedial in aspects of its presentation. In particular, it is innovative in its use of television screen space; time; parallel worlds; intermediality and advertising – many of which have been adopted from the computer industry – and which together remediate the televisual experience.

Screen space and time

Computer technology has enculturated several generations in the use of multiple windows on the PC monitor:

> Each text window defines its own verbal, each graphic window its own visual, point of view. Windows may change scale quickly and radically, expanding to fill the screen or shrinking to the size of an icon (Bolter and Grusin 2000: 33).

24 was celebrated for its innovative use of split screens in the television screen space although it was not the not the first to deploy the technique.[6] It deploys a parallel multiple-screen windows technique, which offers inserts into the television screen space that reveal several dimensions of a complex and spatially dispersed action, which take place contemporaneously. Illustrating Kattenbelt's 'spatialisation of time' 24 shows time in a screen split four-ways: Bauer in the office desperately trying through new technologies to locate his loved ones (in-set frame 1), his kidnapped wife and daughter under imminent threat with no apparent means of escape (in-set frame 2), whilst the mid-European terrorist is authorising their deaths (in-set frame 3) and all along the real-time clock is ticking (in-set frame 4). 24 purports to be a real-time drama, the twenty-four hours of its title denoting twenty-four hours of both narrative and air time, one hour to be shown weekly over a six-month period.[7]

PARALLEL WORLDS

Interesting questions arise about a serial drama which takes to extreme the idea of the fictional spaces of television paralleling moment-by-moment the actual world inhabited by viewers. In Kattenbelt's terms, events are "next to each other" as well as "after each other". This *as if live* access to parallel worlds perhaps indicates a mutually reciprocal influence of early television culture on computer culture. Though the fragmented presentation of the split-screen may suggest hypermediacy, the emphasis placed upon the *as if live* resonates with the immediate access computers apparently afford to a range of parallel worlds. In *24*, the use of split-screen serves not to fragment and dislocate narrative coherence but to reinforce it through *spatial extension*.

> Hypermediacy offers a heterogeneous space, in which representation is conceived of not as window on the world, but rather "windowed" itself with windows that open on to other representations of other media (Bolter and Grusin 2000: 34).

24 in contrast used a structure of multiple windows within the screen space primarily to ensure that each window supports the others to confirm a *looking through* conviction in the diegesis. In evoking the *virtual territory* accessed through any single window of PCs, it serves to bind participants in to the experience of *virtual space behind* the television screen, in parallel with both the *virtual world of the Internet* and with *an actuality*. Having said that, the multi-window brings to some viewers an increased facility to *look through*, whereas to those disposed to hypermediacy a *looking at* provokes an *inside-outside* experience. The sense of occupying parallel worlds remains available.

INTERMEDIALITY: OTHER MEDIA

In its treatment of the traditional action-adventure thriller and domestic narrative, however, *24* illustrates another intermedial influence, that of cinema on television. Whereas the cinema screen space and the television space were once relatively **143** discrete, the advent of video and specialist film channels amongst the digital multi-channel profusion has softened the boundary between the small and big screen spaces. Technology has sought to bridge the gap in that the quality of digital imagery far surpasses that of its analogue precedents. Wide-screen television monitors, available to the wealthy in dimensions approximating to the big screen, have to an extent addressed the problem of the narrow scope and aspect ratio of traditional television monitors. The domestic monitor continues, however, to favour a range of shots between close-up and mid-shot in comparison with cinema's wide-angle vision. As a consequence of increased *intermedial exchange* between cinema and television in the distribution of films, a hybrid form of *film for television* has emerged combining aspects of both media as traditionally conceived. *24* affords a good example: to put it simply, the wide-angle, action-adventure sequences are inter-cut with the close-ups of soap's domesticity.

Robin Nelson

ADVERTISING

This is the final aspect of intermedial ebb and flow evident in 24. Unlike *Sex and the City*,[8] 24 does not foreground specific fashion items, but it does feature numerous technological gismos employed by its hero, Jack Bauer, and broadly encourages their consumption. Bauer escapes from extremely tight corners by the use of video phones, car-faxes and hi-tech GPS location technologies. At an historical moment when sales in the mobile phone industry are diminishing in a saturated market, the state-of-the-art feel of the split-screen device and Bauer's use of digital kit will have done no harm to the market for videophones.

Ally McBeal and 24 illustrate differing aspects of the complex process of remediation working through contemporary television and computer technologies. Though both TV series retain an option on viewing immediacy, perhaps required by the conservatism of the domestic medium, both incline in their textual composition towards hypermediacy, though to different degrees and perhaps with different impacts. In doing so, both afford a potential slippage between an inside-outside shift between viewing positions. Though it may evoke a caricature to suggest that the traditionally illusionist and authoritative representations of the television medium solicited a passive viewer, the sense in which today's viewers might be constructed as active goes way beyond the audience studies of the 1980s, which revealed that people adopted various viewing positions. In a culture of performance and performativity, today's *viewers* might better be constructed as *participants*. However, before discussing shifts in viewing experience, I turn briefly to *Reality TV*, further to illustrate intermedial practice in the twenty-first century.[9] This part of the discussion illustrates ways in which ordinary people are caught up in small screen cultural performances on a number of levels.

REALITY TV

Perhaps in reaction to the epistemic shifts which dislocate established bearings, *factual* television "became in the 1990s, one of the most dynamic, successful and rapidly evolving fields of production" (Dovey in Creeber 2000: 134). From *Big Brother* to *Fame Academy*, the formats make for cheap and popular television. So attractive are they to network executives and audiences alike that they are marketed and watched across the globe. In Reality TV, the fly-on-the-wall camera techniques lend a conviction to viewers that they are watching real life in real time, as it is being lived in the here-and-now, and gaining privileged insights into how people actually behave. CCTV surveillance technologies and confessional video diaries addressed directly to web-cams have become signs of authenticity in contemporary television culture, in which everyday life is mediatized as it is lived. In the perception of ordinary viewers, the very sense that it might have been themselves 'in the house' (the domestic location is significant), had they only been selected, at once confirms both the ordinariness and extra-ordinariness of what viewers know to be a highly artificial construct but which, in the moment of viewing, they may take for real.

The opportunity to participate in voting by telephone or text message to evict participants, by watching on the Internet or by selecting a camera as a digital viewer of E4, opens up spaces for active virtual involvement. As Lavender remarks, "[t]here is apparently a greater degree of control on the part of the audience of *Big Brother* both in determining the outcome and in the construction by individuals of their personal viewing partner" (2003: 6). Viewers can thus simultaneously be both inside and outside the small screen performing a state of *in-between-ness*.

In *Big Brother*, there is an evident tension between the democratic impulse to give ordinary people access to - and some influence on - the medium of television and the commercial impetus to control programming. Far from a random group of individuals being allowed to play out their social interactions observed by fly-on-the-wall cameras as in earlier documentary traditions, *Big Brother* is constructed as a TV drama. The selection of participants is based on a core principle of traditional drama that characters must be in conflict.[10] Selection of a small number of participants from thousands of applicants is informed not only by strong, individual personality traits but on the basis of potential for conflicts between members of the group.

With hindsight, one young woman selected for the first UK series of *Big Brother* realised she had been chosen for her perceived sexuality and that, in the editing of the programme, the selection of shots of her encounters had emphasised her sexuality (Channel 4, 2000). Thus, character and a narrative involving amorous conflicts had been pre-figured for her, and she inadvertently played a role in a strand of steamy romance. The tasks set to the participants in *Big Brother* are designed to inject conflict when everyday social encounters in the house fail to provide them. It should not be forgotten that the driving narrative principle of the programme, affording its meta-narrative arc is a competition for survival leading to a significant cash prize. As in a drama serial, smaller narrative arcs overlap under the shaping force of the meta-narrative leading to ultimate closure.

In the discussion of texts above an increased tension between immediacy and hypermediacy is evident. It is suggested that, in the process of remediation, television has been forced to adjust to the challenges posed by computers for leisure time in the domestic environment. Television viewing figures have been diminishing in America and in the UK, whilst computer usage in the home, particularly by young people, has grown exponentially. However, the intermedial influence at a technological-textual **145** level is not all one way. Usage of home computers did not accelerate until the word-based command line was transformed into a (tele)visual iconography. Aspects of early television's window on the world have been echoed in computer usage as PCs strive for the holy grail of immediacy to which, according to Bolter and Grusin, the dominant tradition of western art since the Renaissance has aspired (ibid., 2000: 30). At the same time, but pulling in the opposite direction towards hypermediacy, there is a tendency amongst an increasingly media-literate population towards awareness of textuality and viewing pleasures in its play.

The final section of this chapter proceeds to locate technologies and texts in this broader frame of culture. Whilst influential, new digital technologies do not determine cultural phenomena but rather function as one factor in a force-field of influences; so an attempt at an account of small screen usage necessarily involves a discussion of viewing dispositions in the context of broader conceptual shifts. The texts and the technologies under discussion, like those that have gone before them, might serve, in Huhtamo's summary of Benjamin:

> [...] as inscriptions which could lead us to understand the ways in which a
> culture perceived itself and conceptualized the "deeper" ideological layers of
> its construction (2004: 02).

I am concerned now to touch upon how the intermedial relations between technologies
and texts in recent years may have brought about phenomenal and discursive shifts,
which might ultimately emerge as a new configuration of our experience of the
world. This is, of course, a vast topic and I can do no more here than explore aspects
pertaining to the small screen, with an emphasis upon viewing experience. The brief
exploration that follows might be taken together with the several other contributions
to this debate on intermediality in theatre and performance, which have recognised
the impact of intermediality on the audience experience.

Viewing experience - a new phenomenon?

As indicated above, in the early twenty-first century many viewers are more media-
aware and perhaps more aware of themselves in viewing. Encouraged in part by the
processes of *interactive* computer usage, they want more than ever to do something
with television. In using computers, they speak to them, give them commands, and,
in turn, are addressed by them. The relationship approximates to a dialogue. With
the extension of digital technology to television, in symbiotic relation with the home
computer[11] the medium's mode of address and engagements need no longer to be
predominantly one-way.

Audience reception studies of television in the 1980s (Morley 1993)
established that sub-sets of viewers negotiated the meanings and pleasures of
television from different ideological positions, relative to such factors as class, age,
gender and ethnicity. Though not questioning the continuities of this kind of active
engagement, my interest here is in other kinds of *inter-activity* in which people
participate, on different levels, in an active manner in the realisation of the final
text.[12] Where direct address to the audience was relatively rare in early television,
and delivered from a position of constructed authority - mainly in news and public
service broadcasts - informal chat shows of all kinds now abound, including ordinary
viewers literally on-screen as participants, but overtly embracing others off-screen
through a virtual discourse of social inclusion. Notably, the new engagements are
technological as well as discursive. Digital facilities open up an inter-active, virtual
space in which a formerly passive audience of consumers may become literally active
in contributing to the construction of what is shown on their small screen.[13] In this
context, the established discourse of small screen 'audiences' (who hear) and 'viewers'
(who watch) becomes increasingly inappropriate. In analysing a new phenomenon
we should indeed speak of participants as proposed above. Behaviour has been altered
by the physical aspects of the processes of engagement with new technologies,
most prominent amongst which is the pressing of small buttons. From the remote
control of the television monitor, through the computer mouse to the mobile phone,
much of contemporary life is activated by dextrous fingers and thumbs.[14] Corporeal
movement - or the lack of it - is a feature of engagement with digital technologies. We

need now to locate these into the broader cultural context of the past twenty years.

Three key factors inform a culture of active *engagement* as opposed to *passive reception*. First, post-Watergate, there is scepticism about received wisdom and about the integrity and commitment to the greater good of public figures. Establishment institutions are no longer to be taken at face value. Doubts in this domain are disseminated through popular television in TV dramas such as *The X-Files* and resistance to a top-down authority has increasingly opened up possibilities of dialogic negotiation on all levels. In principle, this questioning opens up the possibility of greater agency on the part of the broader populace. Secondly, on a theoretical level, poststructuralist accounts of language have emphasised the slipperiness of communications systems. Derrida's construction of *différance/difference* (1978) neatly catches the sense of deferral of closure in an endless chain of signification. Thirdly, feedback in the production-transmission-reception loops of media systems suggests that even the most sincere attempts objectively to *record reality* are confounded.[15] There is increasing awareness that the news is made as much as reported, and that digital technologies, in converting images to a series of os and 1s, are even more liable to distortion than analogues. This technologically-based factor, challenging immediacy, is compounded by the theory of Baudrillard who has argued that, in a media-saturated culture, it is impossible to distinguish fact from fiction at all since *the real* has imploded through an excess of media constructions of it. Thus, it is no longer possible to negotiate the difference between a true and false state of affairs. In *Simulations and Simulacra*, Baudrillard (in)famously summarises four 'phases of the image', in the last of which the image "bears no relation to any reality whatever: it is its own pure simulacrum" (in Poster, ed. 1989: 170).

Baudrillard's theories seem to be very pertinent for Reality TV shows and they, in turn, are emblematic of a cultural moment in which boundaries and hierarchies are undergoing a shift in formation. Blurring any sharp delineation of fact from fiction, *Big Brother* is a hybrid of the documentary, the game show and TV drama. From within, from an in-house participant's point of view, there is an ambiguity of experience. On the one hand, in *Big Brother* and shows like *Fame Academy*, participants find themselves inhabiting a confined space and negotiating their everyday lives for real, but, at the same time, they are permanently under the watchful eye of the surveillance camera and are thus continually in performance mode. In addition to its broadcast television airings, *Big Brother* was available on-line 24/7 on the Internet both extending the sense of an *as if live* parallel world and affording another level of inter-activity. As Lavender has argued:

> The programme – and others like it – would be nothing without an economy of liveness and (this isn't quite the same thing) an insistence upon a certain sort of presence. It depends upon people 'being there' – in terms of the live presence of the house-mate-participant, studio, audience, Internet user and TV viewer (2003: 3).

This account of the Reality TV experience brings out how a viewing position discursively constructed in the past as passive, may now be constructed as active participation. The sense in which the participants are being kept constantly under

Robin Nelson

scrutiny depends on the 'being there' of participants in their own homes. This relationship gravitates towards self-awareness amongst people at home that they too are active participants, *performers* in the event. This inside-outside mode of being in the actual-virtual world is an aspect of what some commentators (notably Lyotard 1984) have termed *the performativity condition*. In intermedial digital culture any sharp distinction between the actual and the virtual in the experience of large numbers of people is dissolving. In Morse's summary:

> [w]e are increasingly immersed inside a world of images – acoustic iconic, and kinaesthetic – capable of interacting with us and even directing our lives in the here-and-now, or rather, since the advent of instant decompression and processing via computer, in virtual space and "real time". *Images have been transformed from static representations of the world into spaces in which events happen that involve and engage people to various degrees in physical space* (1998: 21, Morse's emphasis).

Morse's account brings out part of the new and complex experience of a world conceived in terms of *spaces* (virtual-actual) and *times* ('real'-imagined) in which people participate in events. They are, so to speak, *actors* in those events; performers, not passive recipients. This last observation is by no means new. In his influential book, *Perform or Else*, Jon McKenzie, building as he acknowledges upon Marcuse and Lyotard amongst others, proposes that:

> performance will be to the twentieth and twenty-first centuries what discipline [in Foucault's account] was to the eighteenth and nineteenth, that is an onto-historical formation of power and knowledge (2001: 18, McKenzie's emphasis).

It is neither possible nor necessary to rehearse again here McKenzie's ambitious attempt at a general theory of performance. The aspect of relevance in the context of my account of *intermediality* is that all the specific *inter-relations* between the small screens of television and those other small screens are taking place in the framework of a broader epistemic shift in which *performativity* replaces the traditional goals of knowledge, truth and/or liberation. As Schechner has observed:

148

> [t]he words "performative" and "performativity" have a wide range of meanings. Sometimes these words are used precisely. But more often they are used loosely to indicate something that is "like a performance" without actually being a performance in the orthodox or formal sense (2002: 110).

In concluding this chapter, I am seeking just to locate the increased sense of active participation characterised above as an inside-outside play - an informal performing encouraged by engagements with contemporary media - in the broader context of performativity. Under this term, Schechner writes of:

> a whole panoply of possibilities opened up by a world in which differences between media and live events, originals and digital clones, performing onstage and in ordinary life are collapsing (2002: 110).

It is the latter kind of performance, which I have tried to bring out in the discussion of the examples above. At this particular cultural moment, in which, according to poststructuralists there can be no innocent truth-language, such as philosophy, science and documentary, history may have been conceived in the past; and where the grand narratives of science, religion or the progress of history are revealed to be no more than fictions, everything becomes less fixed, more playful. At such a moment in time, where established conceptions of identity and agency are called in question and, where identity might be deconstructed and reconstructed, performance takes on a new significance. *Performance*, in its widest conceptual framework does seem to me to be *a feature of intermediality* in the televisual and digital media.

However, I should not wish to overstate the case for an inexorably liberal future that my account above may be taken to imply. Besides resistance to the forces of oppression which performance opportunities may afford, McKenzie recognizes a downside of *the performative condition*. The sense in which we are called upon to 'perform or else!' under late capitalism's drive for ever greater efficiencies, is derived from instrumental rationalism. The inter-related small screens that afford *play* are linked up also with the automats, which record our whereabouts at the cash machine and in the supermarket, and they, in turn, are networked with the surveillance cameras in the car park. From the *panoptic perspective* of the digital control tower, the notion of *agency* as used above in a liberal manner needs a gloss. The sense in which it implies that individuals are freed up through play in *intermedial spaces* to determine their own fates and futures must be qualified. I have in mind a softer sense of well-being in the world, achieved through a dialogic entering into the playful spaces, which are opening up. The continued opening up of productively playful spaces *in-between* small screens will depend upon a range of influences in a force-field, over which the control of liberating – as opposed to techno-rational – impulses cannot be entirely assured. However, the performative condition in which contemporary television viewing is located at least invites couch potatoes to slip out of the role of 'sad-act' and to try on new facets of a more complex identity.

Notes

1 A current 'digital divide' is acknowledged from the outset of this paper. Though there is considerable disparity between individual ownership of televisions and computers in the economically developed world and the developing world, network access is increasing worldwide at least on a communal basis. In that the drive of global capitalism informs the technological revolution, it is assumed that individualized digitalization will, for good or ill, become in time a global phenomenon. This paper addresses the current situation in the economically developed world.

2 Digital image production became dominant in graphic imaging only at the very end of the 1980s. (see Morse 1998: 21).

3 Auslander argued forcibly against an ontological distinction between 'the live' and 'the mediatized'. I hold, and Auslander might not disagree, that the physical proximity of performers and audiences in a space may offer a phenomenologically different experience from, say, that in the cinema. However, in arguing that television, patently a recorded medium is increasingly experienced as if it were 'live', I am pursuing an argument about television that builds on Auslander's collapse of an ontological binary but looking at the viewers' experience in the social imaginary.

4 For a discussion of 'Gene X TV' in this context see (Owen 1997).

5 '*Miami Vice* was the first series to make use of neurophysiological research on the viewing process: research carried out in the Communication Technology laboratory of the University of Michigan has shown that (American) viewers tend to become impatient with overly elaborate stories or characterisations' (Buxton 1990: 140).

6 Lynda LaPlante pioneered this technique in the first of a series of dramas entitled *Trial and Retribution* (ITV)

7 Ironically, the advertisements (not included in its UK airing on the non-commercial BBC2 channel) reduced narrative air time to approximately forty-five minutes per episode).

8 Expensive fashion shopping is a favoured activity of the protagonists in *Sex and the City*. Carrie Fisher is addicted particularly to Manolo shoes.

9 For a discussion and definition of 'Reality TV' see Dovey in Creeber, ed., 2000: 134-136.

10 On *The Making of Big Brother, World of Wonder* (Channel 4, 2000), as Lavender reports, "the programme's Executive Producer states that her aim is to compile a house full of characters from the pile of CVs and demos which flood in each year" (2003: 8).

11 Though not yet available on a wide scale, the computer and television have been combined in one small screen space through digital technology and this 'combie' may well become the domestic norm over the next decade.

12 Van Vliet cites Michael Joyce (in De Mul 1997) who "argues that true interaction is only the case when the medium responds as often on the user as vice versa" (2004:18). This is a stricter definition than mine in that I ultimately take 'text' not to denote the material object of production but the significances of negotiations in the engagement with readers.

13 At present, admittedly, 'interactivity' in television is limited to choosing between one camera angle and another, or to register a vote at the press of the red button on the remote handset. The principle having been established and enculturated, however, the possibilities to extend interactivity through digital technology are considerable. Though widespread interactivity in the construction of broadcast television by millions of viewers may lead to a very postmodern text indeed.

14 It should be noted that texting is a cultural phenomenon not common in the United States in the way in which it is in Europe.

15 For a fuller discussion of how "news become the immediate or apparent cause rather than the report of events" see (Morse 1998: 15).

MEDIATION UNFINISHED: CHOREOGRAPHING INTERMEDIALITY IN CONTEMPORARY DANCE PERFORMANCE

Peter M. Boenisch

This chapter argues that intermediality in contemporary dance performances is located at the point when the bodies of the dancers intersect with their role as a medium, as opposed to the dancing bodies inter-acting with technical media machinery. The latter is acknowledged only as one part of the intermedial process and not a necessary condition for intermediality. The author's discussion moves from the traditions of classical ballet, where the focus was on the 'natural' marriage of sensual movement, music and semiotic mediation, to the contemporary work of Xavier Le Roy, Merce Cunningham, William Forsythe and Lynda Gaudreau. Here, he explores how these choreographers and their dancers fracture the habitually closed circuits of medial representation by re-membering presented physicalities and by transcoding movement, sound, space, and speech. The resulting intermedial effects involve dancers, choreographers and observers alike in an inter-active process of offering, negotiating, and editing yet undecided pluralities of meaning.

DV8's *Happiest Day of My Life* culminates in a most memorable moment when a performer, as if dancing with her own memory, interacts with the film image of another person as it is projected onto an actual waterfall on stage. In *Anaphase*, by Batsheva Dance Company, projected onto the skin of a dancer are faces and bodies. Wim Vandekeybus, in almost any of his choreographies, includes entire acts as screened films that are usually shot in surreal dreamlike other worlds. If we add to the above numerous other experiments with film, video, electronic music, digital editing, interactive set ups, and even internet performance in contemporary dance performances, then we can see that dance artists have played a pivotal role in using *new media* and their displays, software, and interfaces on stage. Dance, it seems, has become the ultimate multi-media avant-garde theatrical form, ever since Merce Cunningham launched his performance events in the 1950s. In fact, probably ever since the early days of the twentieth century, when Loïe Fuller staged her synaesthetic dances at the Folies Bergère in Paris; not forgetting the most sensual Gesamtkunstwerk-spectacles of the Ballets Russes. But then, one might as well think even further back to the legendary *Ballet Comique de la Reine*, which in 1581 combined poetry, music, theatre décor and dance in a seminal innovative way, eventually giving birth to the Western theatre dance tradition later called ballet. By becoming adept at using the latest technological innovations on stage, dance has always been most successful in marrying the mediation of semiotic meaning with the performance of physical and sensual motion. It is for this reason that I doubt the validity of the fashionable argument that living, organic dancing bodies act as a *natural counterpart* to all technological media machinery. Nor do I accept physical movement and dance

151

as privileged means to 'de-scribe' the standard socio-cultural codings and all the other discursive inscriptions from our skin, or to subvert the global commodification of bodies as marketable products. However, I do suggest a very particular affinity of dance to the processes of intermediality, which in my perspective is an effect that does not result from a performance simply because bodies and media are involved. While both may indeed interact in these processes, I argue that the performing body itself functions *as a medium*, which in addressing an observing audience facilitates the expression of a plurality of meanings – and thereby generates intermediality in dance.

That the dancing body is indeed a medium is most obvious in the traditional balletic body: it was disciplined rigidly into speaking an exactly *codified language*, with the figures and technique of the academic dance style supplying its *vocabulary* and *grammar*. The strict rulebook of balletic beauty not only granted the body its identity, but also guaranteed its *homogenous uniformity* with other bodies. The audiences, most certainly at the times when ballet was institutionalised at the French court of Louis XIV, and when it later reached its full bloom at the court of the Russian tsars at St. Petersburg in the 1890s, were able to read ballet performances like a book. In contemporary dance, the less disciplined and far from conditioned bodies still function as a medium: all the 'normal', untrained, un-perfect, deformed, aged, in many other ways 'non-traditional dancing bodies', even the (metaphorically or quite literally) bare, nude, and non-moving bodies are still choreographed, and they are presented on a stage to their observers. However, rather than the singular clarity of technique and discipline, they present the plurals and ambiguities of *sheer physicality* and *corporeal existence*; as André Lepecki rightly remarks, deviance, otherness, and nakedness "thickens, rather than dissolves, the body with semantic mass" (Lepecki 1999: 137).

It is in this semantic plurality of physicality where we may locate intermediality in contemporary dance and look to identify its effects. These will be found when the choreography interferes with mediation and undermines the medium's function of signifying and transmitting a single *authorial* and authorized meaning; when choreographic strategies and dramaturgic decisions reconfigure standardized body-images; when the choreography *translates*, and *transforms* corporal representation; when they present to the audience *a laboratory space* rather than a narrative line of aesthetic beauty; when dancing bodies irritate, unsettle, even frustrate acts of spectating and observing.

This essay discusses such *aisthetic effects* and their challenge to the conventional roles of choreographers, dancers, and observers alike. It explores also the processes of *de-mediation* and *transcoding*, identifying *three prime domains of intermediality* in contemporary dance performance, which are described as *corporeal*, *spatial*, and *sonic intermediality*. To illustrate these effects, I focus on productions and moments in a variety of dance pieces that do not display or foreground their use of new media technology, in order to avoid the utterly misleading binary notion of media versus bodies. At the same time, although my discussion has a focus on recent choreographies, it should be stressed again that intermediality in dance is not an exclusive privilege of the present cultural formation of digital networks and globalized electronic economies.

Sculpting Bodies: Corporeal Intermediality

The traditional matrix of representational media, in which our modern theatre is situated, prioritizes the logic of the logos and is dominated by principles of coherence, causality, and identity. Dancing and all performing bodies are part of this wider picture. Even in non-dramatic spectacular shows, the performers' bodies become texts to be read, and objects to be perceived. All of the bodies presented in performance primarily function as representations of bodies and related attributes of corporeality, and physical behaviour. Thus, with their bodies, dancers, actors and performers remediate individual traits, literal, psychological and symbolic physiognomies, movements, actions, speeches and thoughts – and all of these aspects are mapped onto a single point where they meet, intersect and come together into the coherent, causal and self-identical modern *character*, or to no lesser degree, the more recent post-modern *persona*.[1] The one present body of the performer (dancer or actor) is presented as a precise *representation* of that one other body.

Corporeal intermediality intervenes in this straightforward linear projection and identification process. It explores and exploits alternative configurations and in doing this it produces a shimmering reflection shining back on the usually transparent workings of mediation itself; above all, it literally re-members the body and "thickens its semantic mass" beyond the norms and standards of straightforward representational mediation (Brandstetter 2000). The fascination of most of the innovative European dance performances produced since the late 1980s by artists such as Jérôme Bel, Rui Horta, Emio Greco, and Vera Mantero, results from what can be identified along these lines as genuine corporeal intermediality.[2] Their choreographies have shifted the focus from *the products of representation* to the *processes of presentation*, and consequently to *the presence* and *materiality* of the dancing medium – the body – itself.

One of the most captivating performances of *re-membering* a body right in front of the observers' eyes comes from French molecular-biologist-turned-dancer Xavier Le Roy. His 1998 début solo-piece *Self Unfinished* emerged from a lecture performance of his PhD-thesis on microbiological concepts of the body. Consequently, in *Self Unfinished*, Le Roy confronts the audience with a dazzling white stage, lit by uncountable neon tubes, evoking the clinical setting of a sterile research lab, an operating theatre at a hospital, yet likewise the bare atmosphere of an industrial workspace. In this laboratory environment, Le Roy gradually rids his performing body of any of its usual significatory potential. In the course of less than an hour, he fractures and alienates his body. Casting off his pedestrian blue shirt and his sneakers, the performer eventually strips off any everyday, standard corporeal habitus. At one point, Le Roy wears trousers around his legs and pulls a skirt over his head and torso. What the audience witnesses is a body cut apart and reconfigured into two bodies apparently welded together in the middle. As the performance progresses, the head and the hands of the actual performer seem to disappear and four legs and feet stoop in front of the white backdrop.

Figure 30
Demediating the performer's body: Xavier Le Roy performs his *Self Unfinished* (1998)

After he removes these clothes as well, this naked body-scape goes on to form ever more utterly un-real (yet profoundly corpo-real) sculptures. The performer models his skin and bones almost like plasticine, shaping and embodying alternative physicalities that transcend standardized representations of the one body and its clear-cut physical identity. Thus, Le Roy prompts recognition of *corporeal intermediality*. Undoubtedly, his body – being presented on stage and in performance – still functions as a medium: it is evidently communicating and expressing something, transmitting, and signifying to its audience. Yet none of the alternative corporealities sculptured in flesh by Le Roy is streamlined into a projection of an actual or metaphorical unified self. His body more and more interferes with its role as a medium that would perform ornamental aesthetics, choreographed narratives, and danced representations of a finished self. In being presented on a stage (and thus mediated), the so tantalizingly present one body is split and multiplied: the one performs many, even any. Even though the body is nude, it is anything but emptied. Homogenizing concepts such as *character*, *identity*, *self*, even *persona* are no longer applicable in the face of a multiplied, thick semantic mass, to use Lepecki's terms. In performance, Le Roy *de-mediates* his body, leaving the process of mediation unfinished because it refuses to produce *a meaning*. If we take this to its logical conclusion then what it means is that *interpretation* no longer springs from decoding and observing some message that is already there, instilled as *the author's intention*. The observers have to give (rather than receive) meaning to the sculpted, ambivalent body-signs.

Le Roy's performance marks a most significant moment in recent dance history. Exemplarily for a number of choreographers in the 1990s, some of whom have been mentioned above, he set out to destabilize an ultimate and largely untouched norm of the traditional logic of mimetic representation. As prominently flagged in the title, *Self Unfinished* cuts what used to be presented as the natural link between the body and the self. Throughout the twentieth century, dance has tended to replace the Cartesian doctrine "cogito ergo sum" - René Descartes' proposition from his seminal 1637 *Discourse on the Method*, which launched modern philosophy and encapsulated the image of enlightened man: "I think, therefore I exist". The new credo of moving bodies could then be paraphrased as *habeam corpus ergo sum*: 'I have a body, therefore I exist'. The mind as the prime site of logic and rationality, which was at the heart of humanist and bourgeois ideology ever since the wake of the Renaissance, had become increasingly challenged in the face of industrial mass-production and mass media, while the organic body seemed to promise the natural remedy for all that. This shift, however, left the notion of an ultimately true and unmediated self intact; it had merely shifted from the brain and the mind, to the flesh and under the skin.

Initially, the body and its movements, whether seen in physical exercise or in a new uncodified dance, were taken to stand for ultimate self-expression and as warranty of individual identity. Continental Ausdruckstanz exemplarily juxtaposed the 'free body' with the shackles of both industrial physical labour and the regime of the traditional ballet codes. US-American Modern Dance, itself heavily influenced by Freudian and Jungian ideas of a psychology beyond the rational mind, sought to visualize the subconscious super-ego in the moving body that, according to Martha Graham's famous dictum, 'never lies'. Post-Modern Dance, then, propagated as its trademark more authentic and democratic everyday bodies and movements, as opposed to trained bodies, and artificial and spectacular choreography. At the same point in the late 1960s, Pina Bausch and Johann Kresnik invented their radical Tanztheater in Germany, similarly putting the *real selves* first and relying on their dancers' individual backgrounds, personalities, and experiences, thus on their *self*, for their choreographic works.

Throughout the twentieth century, dancing bodies have been envisaged as privileged sites for *authenticity*, *true reality*, *genuine identity* and *presence* that confront and oppose medial representations and simulations – an idea that largely ignores or at least circumnavigates what I stressed at the outset, namely that any body presented on a stage ultimately becomes absorbed in the working of theatrical remediation.

On the way into the twenty-first century, dance performers eventually ceased accepting notions of *privileged physical veracity*. They no longer saw the workings of a globalized economy of *subjection*, *commodification* and *signification* as affecting only the *cogito* of the mind, but equally having severe implications on the body as well. From that position, they began to challenge, expose, and exploit the *habeam corpus* ideology of earlier twentieth century choreography. The problematic trap that glued the revolutionary, yet very appropriately termed Post-Modern Dance to a modern dance ideology dating back to the Renaissance, was the insistence on the *first person singular*, on that *ergo sum* that was only too dear to most dancers and choreographers, no matter to which philosophy they subscribed. Utilizing the effects of corporeal intermediality, "new choreography in the society of the spectacle", as Helmut Ploebst tentatively describes it (Ploebst 2001), cut the dominating direct line from the body to an *attached self*, and ultimately re-membered the body beyond its projecting of

155

coherent identity, meaning, and *representability.* As Xavier Le Roy demonstrated, the danced self remains unfinished, not because it does not signify and mean a thing, but because the ambivalent plural of potential signification is left in tact. Thus, *De-Mediating* the body means over-coding and over-loading the body, and admitting that the skin is never bare, empty and simply present once it is presented and someone observes this presentation.

Broadcasting Bodies: Spatial Intermediality

On different continental as well as conceptual ground, US-American Post-Modern dance engineered its attempt at de-mediating dancing bodies; it vociferously voiced a programmatic "NO" to spectacle, mediation and representation, as Yvonne Rainer did in her famous *No Manifesto* in 1965 (Rainer 1999). Working in the US since the early 1950s and coming somewhere in-between George Balanchine's Neo-classical ballet, Martha Graham's Modern dance, and postmodern visions of the dance of the future, Merce Cunningham pioneered intermediality in US-American dance. Far beyond the obvious effects of his choreographic explorations of film, TV and computer technology, Cunningham shifts and breaks up fundamental standards of mediating bodies, space, and time. Famously accepting any movement as suitable raw material for the dance stage, and experimenting with the use of the *LifeForms* software, as well as *Motion Capture* technology in the choreographic process, Cunningham sculptures quite radically the moving bodies of his highly trained dancers far beyond any existing convention and technique. In doing this, he sometimes hits the very limit of human physiology and the bodies' motor capability. Through deliberately trespassing on the ground between artistic and everyday corporeal behaviour, Cunningham demonstrated that the conventional version of human physiognomy and behaviour is only one option amongst many. This has become a stock feature of various choreographic strategies ever since. Moreover, he put his finger on the fact that the categories of every-day movement, and artistic movements exist primarily as effects in the eyes of the observers: performing bodies display, in the first instance, mirror images of our own expectations. They are art-effects of medial representation.

However, as well as and beyond building basic strategies of corporeal intermediality into his choreography, Cunningham also opens up, quite literally, *intermedial* spaces. What I describe as *spatial intermediality* in his works only results partly from the actual architecture of the stage designs. Up to the present day, Cunningham has regularly commissioned from equally innovative visual artists such as Robert Rauschenberg, Jasper Johns, Andy Warhol, and, most recently, Turner Prize-nominee Catherine Yass. More significantly for our discussion, Cunningham translates and reinforces these artists' novel concepts of *(de)picturing space* by means of choreography – not unlike when he factually embodied the radical principles of musical composition conceived by his close friend John Cage.

In terms of space, Cunningham abandons the clear-cut hierarchy that used to be imperative for dance. First and foremost, this attributed a special 'royal' privilege to the spot centre-stage, reserved for the main ballerina, with an entire, sub-structured and hierarchic commuter belt of supporting moving bodies encircling that one central spot of power. Notably, Cunningham does not focus the action on stage on a single central event; there seem to be a million things and movements going on simultaneously. It is the spectators' choice where they direct their gaze; no single point in the space is in any way privileged and thus would guide the observers' vision and perception – not even the framed stage as such. In Cunningham's larger-scale works, dancers seem to cross the stage accidentally, no longer determined by clearly marked points of 'entry' and 'exit', or of, for example, beginning and ending their Pas-de-deux. They are no longer the protagonists but resemble accidental passers-by. The choreography not only fills the space but also spreads over the proscenium frame.

Cunningham abolishes the basic spatial principles of medial represent-ation: the unifying coherence of the fixed-point perspective that used to connect a privileged point of view with a central point of projection. Spatial intermediality no longer projects one clearly focussed space – which might either realistically depict, render a metaphorical space, or carve symbolic landscapes. Cunningham defies such traditional, unifying options, just as he replaces the choreographer's prerogative of choice by 'rolling the dice' and other 'chance' principles. Nonetheless, he still presents the observers with very well chosen and highly structured spaces but they are no longer reducible to *a single coherent, unified topology*: rather than creating a universe, Cunningham puts *multi-verses* on stage.

The observers face a multitude of simultaneous actions that do not even seem to stop at the edge of the stage. Many different perspectives are possible at any single moment, which, it should be noted, probably makes the assumption of a no less unified subversive perspective a rather unlikely option. The observers are encouraged to make their own choices, and to focus away from centre-stage to the distant background, or even beyond the limits of the actual stage-space.

157

Figure 31
Erasing the fixed perspective: The Merce Cunningham Dance Company, performing *Split Sides* (2004).

Peter M. Boenisch

Although the audience still sits in a traditional arrangement opposite the stage, it is the stage space that has changed: Cunningham no longer uses the stage as a picture-frame, but instead it is offered as a film or TV screen. From the fixed perspective of the armchair, or theatre seat, the observers are not presented with the singular framed entity of a picture, but face a continuous flow of multiple images taken from mobile, ever changing perspectives. In Cunningham's works the traditional depth of the picture-frame perspective is replaced by the flat screen of immersive home entertainment setups. He montages spaces and fades them into each other on the single space of the actual stage, with the audience zooming in and out. Cunningham's dance installs the equivalent of *Dolby-THX* surround-sound effects in choreography, aesthetically shifting from sculpting dancing bodies to *shooting* corporealities and *broadcasting* movement.

In the examples discussed so far, aisthetic effects of intermediality result from aesthetic strategies fracturing the normally closed circuits of mediation and representation. While multiple perspectives have opened up for the observers, the dancers have not quite had their share yet. Although no longer representing finished selves, and displaying mere accidental morsels of fixed choreography in an infinite number of new combinations, they still have to function as a somewhat transparent medium. Even if the intermedial effects foreground that very process, their bodies are still bound up in the medial triangle of sender (the choreographer) – transmitter (them) – receiver (the audience).

Editing Bodies: Corpo-spatial Intermediality

Whereas Merce Cunningham combines layers of corporeal and spatial intermediality, William Forsythe closely intertwines both strategies by no longer placing bodies in space, but treating them as space. In his choreographies, the dancers get their equal share of intermediality: now it is no longer 'rolling dices', but the dancers' own bodies that decide the choreography. Forsythe revisits key principles of the influential movement-research conducted by Rudolf von Laban in the early decades of the twentieth century. Laban, the leading theorist of German Ausdruckstanz, distinguished the architectural space of the stage from the individual kinesphere of the body, which refers to the individual space each and every body 'owns' and continuously carries around, which is determined by the points we can reach with our extremities without changing place (Laban 1992). Whereas Laban investigated the order and logic of the body's kinesphere and how it is organized from a clear geometrical perspective around the body's centre of gravity, Forsythe radically reorganizes it. He experiments with, for example, shifting the centre of the body to any limb, ankle, or muscle, and even with assuming several centres in a single body. Using the interactive CD-Rom documentation of Forsythe's approach to aid my analysis, it became clear how he exploits the common unifying logic behind *perspective space* and *corporeal individuality*, and projects the de-hierarchical spatial multi-verses identified in Cunningham's stage arrangements, into the dancing body itself (Forsythe 1999). Strategies of spatial intermediality are applied on to the kinesphere of the body-space, thus achieving a very specific corpo-spatial de-mediation of the body.

The highly individual practice that Forsythe created during his prolific residency at *Ballett Frankfurt* from 1984 to 2004 is no longer to be mastered by dancers, as they would traditionally master classical, modern and even post-modern techniques. Forsythe trains and triggers an active physical response in the dancers' bodies by creating unusual pulls in their muscles, playing around with gravity, making them use the back of their heads as focal point for their movement, exposing them to a continuous flow of outside impulses from which to choose. No longer moving as if on auto-pilot they *present* instead of *representing*. Thus, his technique *demediates* the body, allowing it to act as an agent – but one that is still working within clearly defined limits, as Forsythe's own somewhat oxymoronic description of his technique as *Improvisation Technology* indicates.

Ideologically, this choreographic approach shows striking similarities to late twentieth century directions in Performance Management that sought to replace earlier Fordist workspace monotony with, according to some buzzwords, "interconnected system thinking" and "low-level decision-making processes". Nowadays, each foundation textbook on Business Administration recommends to the potential manager that s/he should empower, motivate, and tap the creativity of the workforce, rather than bureaucratically dictating their performance from the top (McKenzie 2001: 55-94). Forsythe would deserve a first, with distinction, for his supreme choreographic management of his company.

Aesthetically, his technique displays an affinity to post-modern 'task-based' acting practices as explored by the Wooster Group; they also activate physical response, thereby avoiding traditional identification and character building (Auslander 1997: 39-45). Through analogy we can see that in Forsythe's experimental approach choreography turns from artistic authorial creation and the sculpting of someone else's body, into the *construction of complex systems*. These choreographic systems free the performers from their traditional ballet tasks of executing, as perfectly functioning machines, exactly pre-determined physical forms, shapes, poses, and fixed patterns, which transparently mediated set movement scripts. With Forsythe, the dancing bodies *run*, like a computer programme, or that allegedly empowered creative work force that present-day manager-training talks about: ever attentive to minute details and reacting to constantly changing inputs.

Former Ballett Frankfurt-dancer Nik Haffner illustrates these principles describing the complex choreographic interface-structure of *ALIE/NA(C)TION*: The title suggests the piece's association with the Science Fiction movie series *Alien*. There are, however, no evident allusions or references to its plot and characters. Instead, in a unique way, the choreography directly *transcodes* the moving images into corporeality. On monitor screens that are visible only to the performers, a constantly changing somewhat accidental selection of clips from the *Alien*-movies is shown each night. The dancers' task is to transcode this input into individual *movement patterns*, as Haffner explains describing how fellow dancer Ana Catalina Roman used colour as her input trigger:

> The chosen colour, let's say red, helped her to decide her movements in space. When a red tablecloth appeared in the upper left-hand corner of a movie frame,

Figure 32
Transcoding movements: Christine Bürkle, Dana Caspersen, Helen Pickett, and Jacopo Godani
(left to right) in front of the TV screen showing movie clips, in William Forsythe's *ALIE/NA(C)TION*
(1993).

she would transform this unto the stage by lying down flatly stage-front-left.
She thus transmitted the space from the screen, mapping it on the stage. She
caught her movements, her pauses, the various positions on the stage all as
information from this colour system (Haffner 2000: 31, my translation).

For any new piece, Forsythe developed new and ever more complex sets of similar
interface strategies. Ballett Frankfurt performances thus put on show individual
choices, decisions, and translations, rather than a prefabricated choreographic or
semantic product. The dancers cannot but relive and re-embody the choreography
with each night's performance. Forsythe's pieces therefore change with every new
performance, too, as Nik Haffner states tellingly:

William Forsythe rarely comes to us after a performance and says: "Great
dancing". But he comes very often to tell us: "Good decisions." [...] Forsythe's
task has now very much shifted to be an "editor" of various layers of movement,
of text, of visual elements of the stage (Haffner 2000: 34, my translation).

Thus, the *corpo-spatial intermediality* embedded in Forsythe's choreography not
only challenges the role of the dancer, but also redefines the choreographer's own
responsibility. Neither the dancer nor the choreographer is submitted to the
supremacy of representational mediation.

While all of these strategies must certainly impress avid spectators, they
are no less tested in their own right. Forsythe does not allow the audience a moment
to lean back and merely savour the sheer complexity and masterly effort of his
performers' 'good decisions'. Just as the dancers are no longer transmitters, just as

the choreographer is no longer the sole creative sender, the audience is no longer at the receiving end only. Forsythe embeds his choreographies in an all-encompassing dramaturgy of the intermedial: stage design, lighting, music, costumes, and texts are all interwoven without ever being allowed to become part of a single, plainly coherent narrative, as Forsythe explains referring to his *Eidos:Telos* (1995):

> The 'elements' are just there, and I can't explain why, although in the logic of the piece they are absolutely necessary. Of course, you can come up with explanations afterwards, but that's after the fact. There tends to be a universal desire to project narration into dancing, and one of the things I always want to say is that you don't have to understand this, you just have to watch it, and then maybe something will happen to you without thinking (quoted from Sulcas 1998).

The aisthetic moment of performing intermediality is nicely pinned down in this quotation. In prescribing neither exact movements nor exact meanings, Forsythe invites his dancers and spectators alike to make their choices within his edited edifices, and to select the stimuli they prefer to follow. The observers' job description has changed from decoding, interpreting, and understanding to *experiencing* a densely woven, sheer infinite network of most minute signs which, rather than coming together in the one centre-point of a represented meaning, *present mediation*, present *the making of a medium*, and present *the very working of theatrical presentation*. While still conventionally bound to their seats, the audience must make their own 'good decisions'. The message has not already been made and is waiting in the wings to be decoded; signs do not represent, but only ever more forcefully *present* their yet undecided meaning: intermediality is indeed mediation unfinished. It becomes clear that the 'inter' of intermediality is not performed in-between dance and technology, in-between live theatre and mediatized screening, but touches directly on the very process of mediation.[3]

Transcoding Bodies: Sonic Intermediality

William Forsythe's final full-scale production with his Ballett Frankfurt, *Decreation* (2003) sums up the effect of intermediality in its very title. Rather than creating works as an author, the choreographer edits texts, according to the infamous distinction by Roland Barthes:

> The text is not a co-existence of meanings but a passage, an over crossing; thus it answers not to an interpretation, even a liberal one, but to an explosion, a dissemination. [...] The Text (if only by its frequent 'unreadability') decants the work (the work permitting) from its consumption and gathers it up as play, activity, production, practice (Barthes 1977: 159, 162).

Writing in the 1970s, Barthes referred to aesthetic strategies he identified in his readings of literature, going on to hint at their aisthetic effect of what he termed jouissance, the pleasure of the reader-as-collaborator in the activity of meaning making. Contemporary dance involves the observers in a similar 'textual' practice: right in-between sensual texture and semiotic text, experimenting with – as Forsythe has described for *Decreation* – "unintentional movement" and "undirected action", in the double sense of the word 'directing'.[4]

Apart from the moving bodies, which traditionally have been conceived of as the opposite of the one fixed meaning of the logos, music seems also to privilege textual jouissance and play in a space beyond interpretation. Therefore, it is no surprise that once the two textual realms of the corporeal and the sonic are brought together, the potential for an even more powerful double 'explosion' is created. Dance and music, thus short-circuited, reinforce each other to twist mediations of clear-cut meaning and one-dimensional interpretations – they split the uniform self-identity of the performing body, and playfully fold traditional medial conventions against each other. I suggest the term sonic intermediality is used to describe such effects, which are triggered by sound, music, and other acoustic means. In this context, I will focus on the potential of sonic intermediality in dance performances.

Traditionally, music provides the default soundtrack to the silent theatre form called dance. Just as any *dance music*, from the Royal Courts of the Renaissance to twenty-first century clubs, ballet scores, or music on any basic level, beat the time and supply the rhythm of the movement, so any dance movement, in the tradition of dancing to music, is determined from the very outset: the movement is pre-scribed and pre-written by the music, before any more tangible process of making meaning or choreographing of the bodies has come into play. One of the achievements of the *Grand Ballet* era of the late nineteenth century was to attach a *dramatic finish* to the functional aspect of dance music. Composers such as Piotr Tchaikovsky and Alexander Glazunov introduced *narrative* and *emotional structures* into their compositions for the Franco-Russian ballet tsar Marius Petipa. Neo-classical dance eventually turned movement into *large-scale symphonies*, with choreographic and musical form and structure intimately knit together, turning the dancers into *visualizations* of the music score, and in the works of the mastermind of neoclassical choreography George Balanchine, even into *embodied ornaments* of a single musical instrument (Jordan 2000).

Following some *pure* dance experiments danced in silence on both sides of the Atlantic in the early years of the twentieth century, it was once again Merce Cunningham who most forcefully cancelled this medial contract between music and dance. He insisted on the sovereignty of each sign system, and stressed their accidental coincidence in space and time, by regularly teaming up music and choreography only at the night of the performance itself, again employing chance procedures. Ever since the legendary cooperation of Cunningham and John Cage, the relationship of music to movement has changed fundamentally.[5] Perhaps this is best demonstrated in the radical choreographies of French choreographer Jérôme Bel. He uses, for example, Stravinski's legendary *Sacre* as the score for his self-titled piece *Jérôme Bel* (1995); yet rather than being played, or replayed, a performer has to do his best to hum and buzz that huge orchestral composition in its entirety. Half a decade later, in *The Show Must Go On*, Bel treats the music with utmost reverence and choreographs it very literally

– but he does so with well-known popular music from a Strauss Waltz, to a Beatles evergreen, and then to the Marcarena-party-dance (Ploebst 2001: 190-208).

However, even if dance has started to exploit and undermine the traditional "feel-good harmony between what we hear and see" (Jordan 2000: 61) somewhere underneath, there is, from Cunningham to Bel, still that close affinity of dance and music, albeit with a minus sign. For example, Xavier Le Roy plays with this deeply rooted convention in his *Self Unfinished*: The performance begins with Le Roy walking up to a portable CD-player placed on the stage facing the audience, and pressing the 'start' button. Yet no music starts to play; rather, the acoustic perspective is inverted, and the audience hears what would usually be covered up by the music: tweaks and noises surface from Le Roy's moving body as he performs simple movements, sitting down on a chair behind a desk like a dancing office clerk. Then, this dancing machine gets up and travels in slow motion through the stage space, still whirring, screeching, clattering, and uttering a robot-like rattle. In this episode, Le Roy acoustically mimes the sounds of a perfectly programmed dance robot that are normally whitewashed by the music. At the end, we hear 'proper' music: Diana Ross's *Upside Down*, whose chorus of course goes on "inside out".

While Le Roy uses an illustrative, fictional body-sound produced by his mouth and his vocal chords, other choreographers have applied more radical strategies to make movement audible by transcoding dance into sonic movement.

For her piece *Document 3* (2002), Canadian choreographer Lynda Gaudreau uses a sound installation designed by Alexandre St Onge and Christof Migone. Each of the four dancers in the piece wears a highly sensitive microphone attached to their shirts. Consequently, each rustle of the cloth, every single breath, and each resonance of their dancing bodies is immediately transcoded into sound and projected in oversized dimensions, with the sounds loudly amplified on the public address system, while being additionally transformed through using reverberations, echoes, feedback noise, and other sound effects. Even without highlighting the use of the lavish sound technology as such, *Document 3* creates a striking *acoustic dance*, allowing the observers to be an actual audience of a dance piece by listening to the performers as they utter body language via the microphones. Their clear-cut movement isolations, along with the minimal, yet ultra-sharp and fast splinters of dance gestures, which are typical of Gaudreau's choreography, here seem to articulate rigidly montaged syllables.

The stage design by Annie Lebel heightens the references of the piece to various processes of mediation. An amazingly huge sheet of white, lucid parchment paper is set up across the stage, functioning as backdrop and carpet alike, and eventually unfolding like an empty book. The dancers move as black shadows across and before the parchment as it is lit from behind, their bodies thus visually writing on paper, while sonically speaking their movement phrases. When some of the dancers escape the vision of the audience behind the huge sheet, the observers all of a sudden realize that they have already become fluent in the body language. As the same patterns of movement keep reappearing throughout the piece, the spectators are now even able to see the sentence the performers dance when they are hidden behind the parchment, as the audience identifies vocabulary it had heard and learned before.

Figure 33
Listening to the bodies as they write the dance: Sophie Lavigne, Guy Trifiro, Tanya White, and Mark Eden-Towie in Lynda Gaudreau's *Encyclopædia: Document 3* (2002). Photo by Georg Anderhub.

Far beyond reading and deciphering it, the observers thus register Gaudreau's document in their sensorium. Transcoding movement into language, *Document 3* re-directs mediality. Accordingly, language, traditionally the privileged medium of human communication, is stripped of its licence as words become transcoded into a subtly choreographed dance. Earlier on in the piece, the male protagonist confronted the audience stammering burlesque fragments of a monologue about, amongst many other things, his "super-fast" cat. Later, he will attempt but fail to deliver an absurd lecture on black holes in the universe. Gaudreau continues to demediate language, gradually emptying it of even the last bit of useful and reasonable representational value. Towards the end of the piece the performers hold in their hands some dictaphones whose tapes replay in 'super-fast' speed; the recording is consequentially rendered into a non-understandable, shrill cartoon-character language, which the performers additionally mouth and overdub. In this moment, this dance says more than the proverbial thousand words, and every minute that is.

Document 3 was the third instalment of the Canadian choreographer's *Encyclopædia* project, which has a focus on processes of transcoding the bodies of her dancers. Gaudreau's initial point of departure was images and plates taken from the actual Didérot/D'Alembert-*Encyclopédie*, as well as choreographic snippets she sampled from existing pieces. Later, she commissioned short movement bits from fellow choreographers, such as Jonathan Burrows, Meg Stuart, and Akram Khan. However, instead of quoting their collected source material, or physically miming the images, she prefers to *transcode* them into movement. *Translation* for Gaudreau is more than a movement from one page to the next or from one text into another text in a different language. For her the encyclopaedia is not only a useful metaphor to describe her distinctive aesthetic strategy of collecting and commenting upon existing material, rather than authoring original artworks. It also encapsulates the fundamental aisthetic effect on the observer:

> The potential for hallucination is so great when reading an encyclopaedia. We don't always understand what we read. It's always a creative process for the reader. There's lots of approximation going on, so we hallucinate to a large extent. You see something that you don't understand completely, so you fill in the blanks with your imagination (cited in Szporer 2002: 9).

Again, we are pointed towards a process of observing that has become far more than passive reception.

Conclusions

The various strategies for triggering corporeal, spatial, and sonic intermediality in dance performance discussed in this chapter do not primarily bring innovations to the theatrical form of dance by providing the dancers and choreographers with new movement aesthetics and techniques, although that, of course, is some side effect of the process. They rather, in a first and somewhat radical instance, redefine fundamentally the relationship between the stage, the performance, the choreographer's task of editing fluid textural spaces, the dancer's act of spelling choreographies, and the spectator's feat of seeing and observing.

Thus, intermedial dance performances engage the traditionally clearly separated and mutually distanced senders, transmitters and receivers in an inter-active dialogue, where meaning is neither choreographed nor performed as a finished work of art according to causal, coherent, and linear structures, but negotiated by fairly equal partners in a process of meaning making. One result of this is that the performances are imbued with the energetic power of a secret, which constantly keeps revealing itself: in Forsythe's paradigmatic case even for the performers themselves.

We have seen also that bodies, sounds, and spaces refuse their usual **165** directedness and completeness of reassuring referential identity, of commodified coherence and unified perspective. They rather thicken the semantic mass of these pieces into a dense, yet incredibly fluid mash that no longer feeds the observers' appetite for clear, unambiguous meaning, which Peggy Phelan in her inspiring reading linked with the psychological quest for unspoilt self-identity (Phelan 1993).

From us who go to see these intermedial performances, they demand of us an active involvement and the willingness to make interpretative "good decisions", rather than decoding pre-determined meanings and silently gazing at beauty. This osmotic process of communication between stage and audience is where intermediality demediates, transcodes and de-creates uni-directional artistic transmission, and instead performs potentialities and ever-shifting perspectives. Indeed, it resembles a dance of meaningful alternatives, negotiated by moving bodies.

Notes

1 Philip Auslander introduces the concept of the "performance persona" discussing Willem Dafoe's acting in the Wooster Group's *L.S.D.* (Auslander 1997: 39-45).

2 Helmut Ploebst provides a detailed account of what he describes as the 'new choreography in the society of the Spectacle' by these and other dance artists (Ploebst 2001).

3 This is particularly valid for Forsythe's *Kammer/Kammer* (2000) where six monitors are suspended in the traditionally seated auditorium, as well as on stage, and where scenery more and more obstructs and eventually totally blocks the audience's sightlines. First and foremost this throws the observers back on their own, becoming more and more irritated, confused, and eventually frustrating attempts at seeing, watching, observing, and making sense, rather than foregrounding any conflict (or concord) of live and broadcast bodies.

4 The terms were used by Forsythe in a rehearsal for *Decreation* I was allowed to witness in March 2003.

5 The changing relationship between music and theatre is documented in 'Theatre and Music' (*Theaterschrift* 9/1995), which includes a discussion with choreographer Anne Teresa De Keersmaeker and her regular musical collaborator Thierry De Mey.

SECTION THREE
FROM ADAPTATION TO INTERMEDIALITY

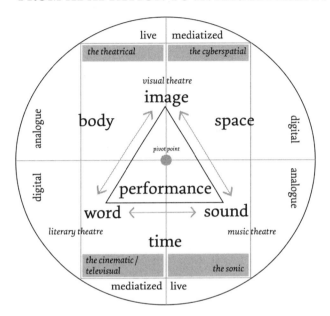

There is a chronological spine to this section, which begins in the 1920s and ends in the twenty first century. Running through the historical perspective is investigation into the changing relationship between the art forms of theatre and cinema, which concludes with investigations into the interaction of theatre with cinema, the digital media and the internet in theatrical performance. Several of the chapters engage with a retrospective view on the historical period of the intermedial avant-garde as evidenced in contemporary cinema and television. A major feature of this section is the move from a linear hierarchical theoretical approach to theatre/film adaptation to a new theoretical model based on modularisation, hypermediality and inter-activity. The chapters here resonate and inter-connect with ideas and themes explored in the other two sections.

THEORETICAL APPROACHES TO THEATRE
AND FILM ADAPTATION: A HISTORY

Thomas Kuchenbuch

The chapter presents an overview of key theoretical approaches to theatre and film from the beginning of early cinema to the arrival of the digital media. The author argues that from the beginnings of cinema there was a controversial relationship between the practice of filmic adaptations of theatre plays, and the debate about the aesthetic value of the new medium. After presenting the empirical and the aesthetic positions in the debate, he explores the avant-garde theory of the twenties and thirties. From there he moves to the discussions provoked by the wave of filmic adaptations of Shakespeare's plays after World War II and hence to investigate translation, reception theory and performance theory before engaging with the deconstruction discourse. He concludes with an analysis of the remediation discourse of Bolter and Grusin in which he argues that the fundamental questions of the period of early cinema remain pertinent to the practice of remediation.

A new art form does not simply appear (Vardac 1949: p. VIII)

Controversial beginnings: the empirical versus the aesthetical

The emphasis in this chapter is the relationship between theatre and film set in the context of contrasting theoretical and critical approaches to the new medium of film. The blurring of boundaries between art forms is a key feature of intermediality and this chapter gives the theoretical background to the phenomenon in an historical perspective, from the days of early cinema through to the arrival of the digital. Many critics have argued that from the very beginnings of cinema, the artists working in the new medium were inspired and influenced by stage events. Film artists copied the theatre actors and their performances: Sarah Bernhardt acting as Hamlet in front of the camera, Méliès showing magic performances in his films, Max Linder imitating boulevard theatre scenes in his screen comedies (Sadoul 1982: 61,113). Elsewhere in this book, Ralf Remshardt and Johan Callens discuss the theatre actor's relationship to film acting, and Klemens Gruber raises the issue of the staging of writing in theatre productions, thus emulating film's use of inter-titles in 'silent' cinema. It could be argued that the emergent practice of film production soon dissolved the boundaries between theatre and film, giving way to co-existence and collaboration until technical development enabled film production to adapt complete dramatic play texts, and even stage performances (Hickethier 1986; Lenk 1989). Despite many heated discussions about the aesthetic validity of the new medium of film, its quality as a medium to conserve and to transport events, including theatrical performances was obvious. As early as 1930, the adaptation of entire screenplays into film seemed to be so common and even profuse, that Pudowkin noted, with contempt "This may be useful for business but it is artistically unsatisfying" (Pudowkin 1973: 126). However, Pudowkin stressed also the empirical nature of the co-existence of theatre and film, and this approach has continued; as is demonstrated in a wide number of empirical studies, ranging from early sociological mass communication research from Emilie Altenloh (1914) up to more recent statistics of stage performances by television programs.[1]

The classical aesthetic distinction

In 1913, Georg Lukács raised the point of the different artistic dimensions and expressive possibilities of the new medium of film. His essay 'Gedanken zu einer Ästhetik des Kino' (in Witte 1973) is an impassioned plea for acceptance of film as a new art form. This approach differed from the discussions in France and Germany, where hesitating acceptance or even complete refusal of film was based on cultural and anthropological resentment (Kaes: 1978). According to Lukács "everything is possible" and, for Lukács, the possibility is the philosophy of film. Because film technique seems constantly to prove the empirical reality of each moment that is shown, the categories of *possibility* and *reality*, the real and the possible appear to be univocal: "Everything is true and real, everything is at the same time equally true and real" (Lukács 1973: 145).

That is what the pictorial sequences of film seem to tell us and it builds up a new homogenous and harmonious world, which has a status similar to fairy tales and dreams in our empirical life and in poetry. Film is mere surface and movement; therefore, it is in film that motorcars and pursuit races ascend to poetic qualities. However, according to Lukács, theatre reveals and emphasizes the reality behind the surface "The theatre is the realm of uncovered souls and of fate" (ibid., 145). What we can see from this brief intervention is that discussion of essential aesthetic differences between theatre and film, here initiated in dialectic Hegelian terms, began a tradition of theoretical discussion about theatre and film that would set the two media in stark opposition to each other. However, three years later in 1916 in Harvard, and from a very different point of view, Münsterberg pointed out in *The Silent Photoplay* that there is a fundamental difference between the flat *screen picture* and the stage *picture* offered to the theatre spectator:

> The theatre stage is broadest near the footlights and becomes narrower toward the background; the moving picture stage is narrowest in front and becomes wider towards the background [...] whatever comes to the foreground therefore gains strongly in relative importance over its surroundings. Moving away from the camera means a reduction much greater then a mere stepping to the background on the theatre stage. Furthermore lifeless things have much more chance for movements in the moving pictures than on the stage and their motions, too, can contribute toward the right setting of the attention. (Münsterberg 1970: 34-35).

The possibility of focusing through selective camera shots increases expression and narrative ability. Clearly, the increased sophistication of the camera as an apparatus and the skill of the camera operator led to more expressive possibilities. Furthermore, the sudden change of focus, made technically possible by camera work and in editing, enabled in filmic narration an epic ubiquity of the moving pictures, including all situations of modern life and communication by telegraph, telephone, gramophone, and even travel by trains, motorcars, ships. However, it is important to recognise that, for Münsterberg, the film picture was ambiguous. It was both naturalistic as a mirror, and spiritual in the whole construction as a two dimensional, artistically crafted technically produced illusion of a three-dimensional reality:

> The essential point is rather that we are conscious of the flatness of the picture and [...] the photoplay sacrifices not only the space values of the real theatre; it disregards no less its order of time (Münsterberg: 77).

Thus, as far as the artistic possibilities of film were concerned Münsterberg's conclusions tended towards a naturalistic or an impressionistic opening of possible *sujets*, including everyday items. However, at the same time he recognised their potential spiritualization as aesthetic objects. This may reflect "the encyclopaedic ambitions of the impulse of the early cinema" (Gunning 1977: 126). For Münsterberg, the most important function of film was the shaping of time and space in film for artistic purposes:

> The pictorial reflection of the world is not bound by the rigid mechanisms of time. Our mind is here and there, our mind turns to the present and then to the past: the photoplay can equal it in its freedom from the bondage of material world - but the theatre is bound not only by space and time. Whatever it shows is controlled by the same laws, which govern nature. This involves a complete continuity of the physical: no cause without a following effect, no effect without a preceding cause [...] This fountain like spray of pictures (sc. in film) has completely overcome the causal world. [...] The theatre would not have even the technical means to give such an impression, but if it had, it would have no right to make use of them (Münsterberg: 79-80).

Lukács and Münsterberg coincide in postulating a strict difference of the artistic principles that should, in consequence, govern theatre and film production. This strict distinction of the artistic principles continued in the discussion held in the era of Russian revolutionary film. Taking the debate on further and summarizing the discussions, in 'Zur Kunstphilosophie des Films' (in Witte 1973), Béla Balázs emphasizes the new visual dimension of filmic perception offered to the audience, in comparison to that of stage events offered in the theatre. In his writings, Balázs includes a variety of film *aspects* and their possible effects on how the observer might interpret the film narration: The expressive and narrative (diegetic) possibilities of sudden changes of perspective, the all-aboutness of film in the visual world, hence the epic qualities and the modern revolutionary spirit of film are adequate to a new industrial era (Balázs 1973).

171

From the number of times that Balázs quotes Sergei Eisenstein's *Dialectic Theory of Film* in his own writings it is clear that Eisenstein as director and theorist was an important reference point for Balázs in his search for new means of expression (Eisenstein 1971).

The Russian Formalist "Laokoon project"[2]

Following a similar approach to Münsterberg and Lukács, those working within the context of the avant-garde and linguistic circles, looked to ascertain the inherently specific qualities of film and theatre, and their work resulted in enthusiastic statements about overcoming the expressive and diegetic restrictions of the stage by film. Amongst the techniques available and identified as offering new possibilities were new methods of film editing (montage), new dramatic effects (contrast and acceleration), and diegetic versatility (cross cutting, time lapses, changing the order of events, etc.). Later on and working from the Prague linguistic circle, Jan Mukarovsky, talked in 'Die Zeit im Film' about the possibilities of film to modulate time and space, and this led Mukarovsky to situate film between *epic* and *dramatic art* (Mukarovsky 1974: 131-138). However, in general Mukarovsky worked within the formalist discourse and, following Lessing's tradition, makes a plea for a new Laokoon project. It is important to notice that he demands the absence of *normative implications*: thus, Mukarovsky endeavoured to create a basic aesthetics of film, which he derived from thinking about the possible means of expression available in different media (Mukarovsky 1974: 119-130).

The 1930s: Film and theatre as political and psychological media.

As the century progressed and cinema became a popular form of mass entertainment in the 1930s, the film theoretical debate moved to the conflict between capitalism in its democratic version on the one side and its Soviet Union version on the other. Meanwhile theatre, being less dependant to quite such an extent as film on financial support, spawned theatre directors and theatre theorists who generated a field of aesthetic and political experiments that incorporated film as well as theatre. Notable in the field were Vsevolod Meyerhold, Erwin Piscator and Bertolt Brecht who happily spanned theatre and film in their artistic and theoretical adventures. The importance of the political dimension of film in general, with its aptitude for mass communication became known as the *distribution aspect* and this, together with film's ability to provide mass information alongside mass seduction, the *psychological aspects*.[3] Both aspects are vitally important (Kracauer 1947) and in the highly charged political atmosphere it is not surprising that a renewal of interest in Eisenstein's and Vertov's theories takes place. Neither is it surprising that this was the period in which emerged a new type of constructive thinking, as evidenced in the theories of Tretjakof and Brecht, who emphasize the investigatory and analytical qualities of theatre and film. They developed concepts that were realised by the film pioneers in their works (Vertov 1973).[4]

This was also the period when the essays of Walter Benjamin on the role of the avant-garde in cinema played a trail-blazing role for later media theorists. In his writings, Benjamin stressed the *mind-forming qualities of film construction* and the respective *film reception inducing a mental state in the observer*, as opposed to the authoritarian cult of aura and adaptation. Furthermore, Benjamin defined film as *a medium for mass reproduction and mass consumption* (reproduction aspect) and therefore a particularly pertinent medium for those charged with inspiring revolutionary zeal amongst the masses (Benjamin 1972). Furthermore, according to the criteria developed by Benjamin, to convert a theatre event into a filmic version has a positive value.

Other notable discussions already begun before the Second World War and continued after its conclusion were those between Rudolf Arnheim and his fellow emigrant Kracauer. These seem to reflect again the ambiguous tendencies of film as both naturalistic and spiritual due to the dialectic relationship between photography (the cinematic image as raw material) and its embedment in the highly artificial procedure of the artistic aspect of filmmaking (Arnheim 1974: 4; Kracauer 1973: 37, 99). These discussions are a notable contribution and perhaps as an enrichment of the classical theory of general aesthetic distinction of media specificity, which influenced the discussion of the fifties and strengthened the idea of film being as valuable as theatre.

Post World War II: theatre in the film industry
A re-thinking of the aesthetic differences and intrinsic possibilities of theatre and film built up again after World War II through theatre's intervention into international film culture. A new era of cinema in all European countries, but especially in France and known as *The New Wave* resulted in the publication of André Bazin's essays on the relationship between film and theatre. Bazin, one of the most brilliant critics of international film of the time, remarked there remains a basic difference between both media: the immediacy of the actor's presence on stage and its aesthetical consequences. But, on the other hand he admitted:

> The drama is the soul of the theatre but this soul can live in other forms too **173**
> (Bazin 1975: 72).

Key cinematic productions were the film adaptation of successful plays from Broadway, in particular those of Tennessee Williams. These coincided with notable film adaptations of Shakespeare's plays in England (Laurence Olivier, Peter Hall, Peter Brook, Roman Polanski) and America (Joseph Mankiewiez and John Houseman, Renato Castellani, Orson Wells), and Italy (Franco Zeffirelli) as well as later in Japan (Akira Kurosawa) and in Russia (Sergei Yutkevich, Yan Fried, Grigori Kozintsev), all of which provided another stimulus for aesthetic discussions. Filming Shakespeare was proof of artistic maturity for the film industry in those days (Kosintzev 1967).

Translation theory

The arrival of Shakespeare's plays in the cinema raised many issues for film and theatre theorists, not least that of authenticity. How could a stage-based drama be *translated* into the medium of film? Comparing the original literary texts with their filmic adaptations, scholars searched for cinematic *analogies* with literature, and struggled to define them because film at that time was not regarded as another language per se, but rather as a system of audiovisual aesthetic means (Schneider 1981: 119). The analogy, they thought, could be found in the very individual stylistic solution of a filmmaker. Therefore, it could exist in the system of camera perspectives, in the way of editing, in the iconic character of the pictures and so on. Thus, looking for a filmic *analogy* of a literary narrative was an academic expression of the problem, without defining what and how the translation of theatre into film should be defined.

Several scholars tried to adapt Chomsky's *generative grammar system*, postulating a *genotype* of a story (plot) and a *phenotype*: the latter being the actual literary text (Eco 1971; Kristeva 1977). For these critics, adapting a literary text into the medium of film was only to transform it into another phenotype, no violation could be charged as long as the inadequately defined genotype remained intact. Again, the problem seemed solved. However, this proved not to be the case because reducing the genotype of a story to a mere abstract narrative structure, similar to the reduction formulas of fairy tales, (Bremond 1973) did not enable the critic or imitator to specify the intrinsic rules of the aesthetic display in relation to the totality of a work of art or literature. If that was one shortcoming, then another was that it was unable to reveal what forces could shape the surface and the rules for its work into a very strictly defined generative grammar (Chomsky 1965). Other critics attempted to stratify the stylistic levels: for example, the structure of the plot, the number and order of events, character design, historical situation and incorporated philosophy. However, the interacting levels meant the return to the totality and to hermeneutic holism (Schneider 1981: 126; Frank 1977). In the opinion of some scholars, the generative construction caused more problems than it could resolve.[5]

It appears that the filmic *translation* of a literary text still seems to go beyond all well-known generic formulas and that translation resides in the casuistic solid work of an individual person with large philological knowledge, wide aesthetical experience, and a great intimacy with filmic means and/or of intuition: the result of a complicated cybernetic process. It is possible that some translators are able to discover the nucleus of the aesthetic organisation of the original dramatic literature and to find a *filmic analogy* as a result, but not as a *petitio principii*, or a mere formula to appease the aesthetic discussions.

The analysis of adequate means to incorporate the filmic analogy can have a highly dialectic result. It can state, for example, that some theatrical values in a filmic adaptation are supported or even revealed by specific filmic means. This includes selective views and artificial, contradictory, rhythmical editing. Bazin noted that in some adaptations the spectator, in spite of all specifically cinematic means, still knows that he is invited not to a film but to a filmed theatrical stage performance; even if there is no fourth wall and the camera moves around the actors like a spirit or a co-actor (Bazin 1975: 79, 90). Good examples of such moments are found in

Peter Stein's television version of *Orestia* (1982), and Marivaux: *La Double Inconstance*, television version by ORTF and ZDF 1980. From these we can see that there must be other signals that indicate a theatrical intention, and that they can come from several semiotic systems: decor, make-up, language, rhetorical attitudes, or body language. Clearly, for whatever reason, the *inner kothurn* is considered to be distinctive. However, I suggest that much casework remains to be done. This may be on a new level of semiotic research, or by means of contemporaneous approaches, but it is necessary to resist the seduction of all-encompassing formulas. Certainly, research must focus on the excellent examples as well as the failed ones, since aesthetic judgment is unavoidable.

Reception theory and types of adaptation strategies

Discussion over the filmic analogy of a novel or a play (Iser 1976) led to the development of reception theories and adaptation strategies, where a gradation of adequacy was taken for granted. Grimm distinguished five degrees of adequacy: (1) The reconstruction of the text in terms of the intention of the author. (2) The reconstruction of the potentiality of the text in a supposed contemporaneous communication. (3) The adaptation of the text according to Mukarovsky's model of changing dominants, including allowance for actualisation within the given faculties/possibilities of the text. (4) Subjective-individual interpretation. (5) Integrated critical and historical view, which incorporates at least 1 to 3, as well as important historical interpretations (Grimm 1977: 57).

Starting from these basic assumptions, it is possible to stratify several implemented acts of reception and adoption in radio, film, video, television and into the digital recording system in order to construct a pragmatic system of adaptation types: (1) A distinction based on the *distribution system*: cinema/film, radio, television, world wide web, others. (2) A distinction according to *production formulas*: instant recording of theatre performances, composed recording, gathering several recordings of various performances. (3) Filming, electronic or not, in *the mode of film production* and postproduction, with the result of a theatre look or a film look. (4) Beyond the play itself, one can distinguish between several contexts recorded in addition to the play, for example, auditory reactions or interviews with theatre and filmmakers, actors or spectators. Recording public reactions is usual in some types of television adaptation of drama, but also in situation comedies and includes hearing the laughter of the supposed spectators. Interviews with artists or spectators are sometimes part of hybrid versions or documentations.

The end of distinctive aesthetics?

Seen from today's perspective, the emphatically formulated positions developed in the times of the developing film industry seem to belong to another age. Should they be remembered as a binding legacy in the current discussion or have they, and have distinctive aesthetic reflection in general, become ultimately obsolete? This question is appropriate to the dissolution of generic boundaries and styles prevalent in the postmodern attitudes of *quotation*, *irony* and even *carnival transformations* of art systems, as discussed by Ihab Hassan, Leslie Fiedler and Umberto Eco (Welsch 1988). In the audio-visual field, the spirit of aesthetic distinction seems to have weakened, and, at a first glance for some good reasons. On one hand, there is the development of stage technology, with its increasing number of optical and visual technical devices including laser-represented props and sets. These technical possibilities have helped stimulate the import of famous film subjects, and even well known plots, to the stage, for example, stage versions of *Citizen Kane* (*Rosebud* Müller, 1980; *Citizen Kane* Fabian, 1998). Furthermore, there are corresponding changes in stage design brought about by new aesthetic formulas in "non-dramatic theatre" (Lehmann 1999:126). The dominance of visual expression as opposed to language-centred drama performance and the collage of different heterogeneous texts within the theatrical frame all demand our attention.

On the other hand, there is the tremendous development of film technology, which creates three-dimensional experience and ranges from Stanley Kubrick's illusion of weightlessness in *2001 - A Space Odyssey* (1968) to the three-dimensional perfection of dinosaurs and Godzilla's, or the all-surrounding impression of jungles in *Rambo* (1982) and *Terminator* (1984) films. Contemporary cinema tends to dissolve established notions, for example, film imitating or re-imitating pictorial and theatrical expression systems (as in the films of Peter Greenaway, like *The Draughtsman's Contract* (1982), *The Cook, the Thief, His Wife and her Lover* (1989), *Prosperos's Books* (1991). The elimination of narrative realism and verisimilitude in favour of self-referential techniques also play their part in breaking down the traditionally ascribed notions of specificity and political intent (Jim Yarmush, *Mystery Train* 1989, David Lynch *Lost Highway* 1997) and others. Finally, the reciprocal adaptation of film subjects on stage, the multiple cross-over productions that incorporate film, video and holograms and other hybrid formulas in theatre practice, are signs of vanishing boundaries between the media – at least in a practical and empirical sense.

Over and above this plethora of generic blurring in theatrical and filmic performances is the omnipotent and omnipresent *television feeling*. Television – the main and dominant formula of world representation – may unify the aesthetic experience of the performing arts and thus overshadow the classical distinction of theatre vs. cinema. If we put the growth of television together with the rapidly emerging and increasingly dominant medium of the Internet, we can recognise the similarities as well as discontinuities of the periods of Modernism and Postmodernism. The presence of many visual and aural effects, including theatrical and filmic effects in *the new digital media* is beginning to change the feeling of reality in favour of the new dimension of *virtuality*. There is much speculation over future techniques and possible experiences transgressing and transforming human perception (Bolter and Grusin 2000; Levinson 1997, Baudrillard et al. 1989), and there are a variety of theoretical answers to the changing landscape of a technically mediated world representation - electronic or not, digital or not. However, in order to understand fully the new mediated world and its profoundly changed aesthetical discussion, we need now to think about some of the following discourses and consider some of the most outstanding ones in this select survey.

The deconstruction discourse

Derrida posited a theory of language analysis and philosophical reflection based on interpretations of *text*, which, he suggested, always refer to a never-ending and permanently delayed line of signifiers. Recognition of the interwoven and sub-textual nature of the combined discourses in a given philosophical or literary text helps the analyst to unveil their historical mythological, metaphysical and hence ideological implications (Derrida and Kristeva 1990: 140-164). *Deconstruction* means to look behind the elaborate opaque or reflecting surface of a work of art and make it transparent in order to see the polyphonic chorus in the background that enabled its genesis, and defined/traced at the same time its metaphysical implications. In criticism and in performance this implies a transcending attitude to look over the boundaries of one defined meaning and form. Deconstruction promotes the transcending of boundaries and abolishes the fixation on a separate notion of medium inherent aesthetic qualities, giving more weight to the potentiality of a text (of a work of art in general) and even a medium, than to its defined form. Performance theory, contemporary theatrical performances and even whole concepts of theatrical art have been affected by the *deconstruction discourse*, which has been influential in interpreting contemporary and past theatrical performances.

A deconstructive perspective enables us to see that Wilson's *Golden Windows* is at the same time the deconstruction of the melodrama as a whole genre, combined with and under-woven with the deconstruction of Beckett's existentialistic mythology. Deconstruction theory may give also a new understanding of patchwork - techniques and combination of costume and décor in *Orestia* (Peter Stein 1982) or *Troilus and Cressida* (Hansgünther Heyme 1983). Deconstruction theory highlights the combination of historical references in both of these productions. The spirit of deconstruction can explain also the intention of a work as *Shakespeare's Memory* (Peter Stein 1980) showing in an extended film a panoramic view of the world, which Shakespeare could have had in his mind when writing his dramas. This idea of displaying the background of a work of art is present also in *Prospero's Books* (Peter Greenaway 1991) and in *Russian Ark* (Sukorov 2002) where decades of history pass by in one filmic instant. Another outstanding aspect in Greenaway's postmodern modernity is the implementation of ancient art constructions and inventions into the filmic context, alongside the display of iconographic and theatrical tradition in his moving tableaux. These effects are due to new electronic media *composition* and *paint box programmes*, which allow a multitude of simultaneous layers and hence new and sophisticated configurations. Therefore, it is essential to come now to the influence of electronic media.

177

The Remediation discourse

The discourse of media history and diverse constellations of the permanent embedding of older media in new ones, thus *Remediation*, seems to parallel some aspects of the postmodern idea of repeated revolutionary or evolutionary circles in art history. Bolter and Grusin have given the widespread word *remediation* a definitive and specialized definition:

> We have adopted the word to express the way in which one medium is seen by our culture as reforming or improving upon other. This belief in reform is particularly strong for those who are today repurposing earlier media into digital forms. They all tell us, for example, that when broadcast television becomes interactive digital television will motivate and liberate viewers as never before; that electronic mail is more convenient and reliable than physical mail; that hypertext brings interactivity to the novel; and that virtual reality is a more "natural" environment for computing than a conventional video screen. The assumption of reform is so strong that a new medium now is expected to justify itself by improving on a predecessor (Bolter and Grusin: 59).

The term *remediation* promises a grasp on electronic media and its amazingly fast technical development and so it is appropriate to set it in the context of a historical survey. *Remediation* is the common business of media-history, the intrinsic logic of media-development. As this chapter announced in its preface, a new medium is always assimilation and perhaps an improvement but it never develops in isolation. As Bolter and Grusin point out, from painting plus the letter, to the illustrated book, from theatre to film, from film to television, from television to computer games, each new embedding tries to achieve an improvement and a surplus of interactivity. A notable feature of digital developments is the augmentation of distribution, and ease of access, thus the widening of participation from the few to the many, from the elite to the masses, and finally and globally to all. (Benjamin).

Another feature of digital art is the improvement of realistic illusion from the renaissance perspective, to photography, to film, to computer design and computer animation, and last but not least to devices for virtual reality experiences. In each case, mutatis mutandis, the medium tries to provide *transparency*, like Alberti's window, and *immediacy* insofar as it is *erasing* itself and attempts to make itself unseen. Thus, immediacy is a highly artificial product. A further significant impulse of digital technology is the augmentation and concentration of information, for example in a web site where multiple layers and 'windows' contain letters or pictorial elements. This *hypermediacy* leads to another form of pure mental immediacy, telling us that the apparatus (computer and software) is existent and real and the source of a surplus of information (we are aware of the reality of the apparatus). This raises important issues with the somewhat questionable parallelisation with the progress in modern Art:

> Modern Art played a key role in convincing our culture of the reality of mediation. In many cases, modern painting was no longer but about itself. Paradoxically, by eliminating the "real" or the "world" as a referent, modernism emphasizes the reality of both the act of painting and its products (ibid., 58).

However, I suggest that the assumption of permanent progress is only sustainable as far it concerns the aspect of mass distribution, and hence the velocity of spreading information even visual ones. The aspect of new media improving their predecessors is only sustainable in so far as a full illusion of realism is achieved or at least intended – mostly for technical reasons, for example, in architectural models presented via computer graphics, or virtual reality. This line of progression has been shared, more or less with the history of art until the nineteenth century, but certainly not since the invention of photography and phonograph recording. All the aesthetical discussion and art forms of a scrutinized realism and broken and reflected immediacy, and their critical interaction with pure technical media improvement, seem to be marginalized by Bolter and Grusin. Of course the authors criticise the mere technological aspect of progress (Levinson 1997) and admit: "Remediation can work in both directions: older media can also refashion newer ones, the process of reform and refashioning is mutual" (Bolter and Grusin, 59). Indeed, this case would be interesting in the history of theatre and film adaptations: a mutually inspiring process. One wished to read more about those mutual processes.

An initial impression of the *remediation discourse* is that it appears to be a technologically inspired survey of media development of improved world representation, in the sense of an illusionary realism. Thus, it seems to be a discourse that tells us that we are sitting, more or less, in the same boat since the Pompeian or the Renaissance culture, and which reassures us of permanent progress. However, the authors are ambiguous about this and seek to connect to various prominent theories and their respective discourses as they situate their re-discussion and re-evaluation. The *distribution and reproduction aspect* of Benjamin is accepted with precaution (ibid., 73). The *medium is the massage aspect* of McLuhan, inspiring in details is rejected insofar as it establishes technological determinism, and Raymond Williams is quoted in this sense. The critic of media technology, uttered by the so-called Frankfurt School, is quoted and rejected – both in a simplified form:

> We believe that the cultural significance of the new digital media cannot be condemned or praised in isolation [...] to condemn new media is to condemn contemporary culture itself (ibid., 78).

The feministic aspect of the male gaze, certainly present in the history of painting and other representational arts, is considered as longing for complementarity (ibid., 79). All in all, the separation and isolation of special aspects: the economic, the sociological, the technical, the iconic representational and the semiotic in general, seems to be the main concern of the authors and there is certainly an open mindedness towards further developments. Thus, the remediation formula inspires re-thinking media actuality in the terms of *media history* and, at the same time, it demonstrates the necessity of distinctive criteria. So, what can we conclude? It seems that, after all, film remains the medium that enables a shifting point of view: "only film can offer a mobile shifting point of view" (Bolter and Grusin: 80) and thus film enables/provides very intensive experiences. However, Bazin still is right in saying the immediacy of the actor's presence on stage is not to be achieved by film (television and so on) and separates the stage event from all reproductional products, which populate our communication system (Bazin 1975: 85).

Therefore, we are obliged to rate the advantages of the translation and transmission to several indirect media, and media combinations, in every defined historical moment – using a combined set of technical, aesthetical and political questions – without falling back into an enthusiastic optimism concerning media development.

179

Thomas Kuchenbuch

Notes

1 Kaes (ed.) 1978; Waldmann 1977; Dübgen 1977; Kreuzer and Prümm (eds.). 1979; Hickethier 1980; Knilli, Hickethier and Lützen (eds.). 1976; Albersmeier and Roloff (eds.). 1989.

2 Georg Lukács 1963: 509 "Die höchste Affintität zur Literatur besitzt der Film zweifellos gegenüber der Novelle", *Ästhetik. Teil I. Zweiter Halbband*. Neuwied/Berlin. Gotthold Ephraim Lessing: 1974, *Laokoon oder über die Grenzen der Malerei und Poesie*. In: Gotthold Ephraim Lessing: *Werke*. Vol. 6, Darmstadt: 7-188.

3 Lasswell 1950; Festinger 1957; Klapper 1960; Maynard (ed.) 1975.

4 Tretjakoff 1972, 57-73; Brecht 1967.

5 Irmela Schneider (1981: 276) recognizes the problems of this approach: "Insgesamt ist natürlich die Übertragung von Denkmodellen einer Grammatiktheorie auf fiktive Texte nicht unproblematisch" ("All in all, the transfer from a linguistic concept of grammar to a ficitional text is somewhat problematic"). This statement is placed in the current rejection of linguistic parallels between film and language (Bordwell 1992). "Das Schlüsselproblem der Filmsemiotik der 6oer und der frühen 7oer Jahre, die sich an Modellvorstellungen der Linguistik orientiert hat, war, das im Film keine Strukturen aufgefunden werden können, die dem sprachlichen Formenbau analog sind" (Wulff 1999: 290-291).

180

THE STAGING OF WRITING:
INTERMEDIALITY AND THE AVANT-GARDE
Klemens Gruber

This chapter takes further the discussion of the Russian avant-garde and German theatre artists established in Kuchenbuch's theoretical review of the intermedial relationship of literature, theatre and cinema. Set in the context of the first decades of the twentieth century, where art and technology drove forward many changes in perspectives, the discussion centres on fundamental approaches to letters and writing as a sign and a medium of communication. The author discusses how the historical avant-garde explored the relationship of words to pictures everywhere, not only in painting, but also in theatre, in cinema and in everyday life: Writing had invaded the modern city, word and picture jostled in a complex texture. Gruber shows that avant-garde artists discovered the liberation of writing from narration, the free existence of the alphabet, and the intensification of lettristic impact. He argues that this aesthetic strategy, focusing on intermediality, not only provides us with signs as expressive means, but also makes them perceivable as signs. Gruber then, in a second step, traces the intermedial inventions of the avant-garde to the present time, in the work of Alexander Kluge, where, once again, the medium of writing subverts the power of a predominantly image-based medium: this time – of television.[1]

> L'écriture est faite de lettres, soit.
> Mais de quoi sont faites les lettres?
> Roland Barthes, *L'esprit de la lettre*

The field of letters and writing gives us acute access to the dynamics of intermediality. Throughout the twentieth century, with its blurred genres, mixed materials and fragmented codes, the congress of art and technology has bred figures of expression that are entirely new offspring that can no longer be described by familiar categories of creative effort. The elements of change were there from the beginning, in the wilful efforts to subvert any aesthetic tradition that so characterized the early decades of the twentieth century. The universal demands of the *Gesamtkunstwerk* and the *fin-de-siècle* Symbolists' attempts at combining media were followed by a counter movement of the international *avant-garde*. What mostly seemed to be an arbitrary break with artistic convention – and, as in the case with Malevich's *Black Square*, a break too with conventions of reception – was rather an encounter with the new conditions under which signs were being made; in other words, with the industrialization of the production and distribution of signs. The analytical methods of the historical Avant-garde were the result of a crisis in the role of art, originally set in motion by the proliferation of photographs with their power of verisimilitude. "Non-mimetic painting and non-referential poetry," said Roman Jakobson about the trip he planned with Kasimir Malevich in 1914, "these were the slogans with which we wanted to set out for Paris" (Jakobson 1976: 293).

Around 1910, the predominance of the narrative, illustrative, and figurative began to be replaced by a kind of "semiotic fundamentalism" (Hansen-Löve 1992: 40), a going-back-to-basics in each art form. In painting, this meant colour, texture, and composition. In theatre, it meant a rediscovery of the body, of movement and of the staged voice, an abandonment of the script, and the liberation from the dominance of literature. In literature itself, attention turned to the physical qualities of language: "Stubbornly we tried to avoid meaningful words". The goal was a systematic presentation of aesthetic raw material; in language, this meant a paring away of connotation and a focus on *The Word as Such*,[2] in painting – abstraction; in theatre – an emphasis on space and construction, instead of decoration and storytelling.

Technological innovation amplified these basic explorations. Technology now could isolate the perception of each sense, to convey it in pure form: the telegraph transmitted only writing, the telephone only voice, the gramophone only sound (Moebius 2000: 251). However, turning the attention towards the inherent characteristics of their specific media did not lead to the isolation of their fields of work. Avant-garde artists investigated the intersection of art and daily life, of practical and poetic language, of word and image. Contrary to the amalgamations of Symbolism or Art Nouveau, they developed a clear-eyed awareness of borders; they consciously marked the moments of fracture, of transfer, of exchange. This allowed them to work out a set of procedures and practices for a project that involved an entire generation of artists and intellectuals in what Annette Michelson has called a "generalised epistemological euphoria" (Michelson 2004: 116), which was closely connected with nothing less than the transformation of the human condition – the project of Socialism.

The most general of these procedures was *Verfremdung*, a stance of critical detachment, the most generous, the disclosure of procedure itself, the "laying bare of the device". This latter became a major critical preoccupation of the avant-garde. In fact, the procedures themselves, as Roman Jakobson put it, became the "heroes" of modern art. No longer a human being or a fabulous creature, but the artistic, aesthetic device itself was admired and emulated, detached from its material, its media, and its epoch: "Method" wrote Viktor Shklovsky in the early twenties, "left home and started to live its own life" (Shklovsky 2001: 34).

So it was that everywhere, not only in painting, but also on the stage, in cinema, and in advertising, the avant-garde turned its attention to the written word and began to explore the relation of words to pictures. They sought the liberation of writing from narration, the free existence of the alphabet, and the intensification of the lettristic impact. The simultaneous emergence of writing in several fields – fields that had been either quite oblivious to writing, like painting, or even hostile, like theatre, which itself stages a text and thus cancels out the letters, or conversely, somewhat dependent on letters - as silent film, with its reliance on written titles – leads us to a series of questions as to the nature of this astonishing phenomenon.

A lettristic flow

To begin with, why did writing appear in painting? Even if writing had, in a sense, always been there, at least by title and signature or as annotations on the canvas back (Butor 1969), why exactly, at a certain moment in the winter of 1911, did writing suddenly appear in a Cubist painting, in an absolutely new way, one never seen before? Why was there suddenly an invasion of letters on a painter's canvas, in the form of newspaper clippings, tram tickets, left-over menus, but also single bits of lettering, beautifully shaped and without any meaning, a kind of lettrist flood that took over, once the naturalist landscape was left behind.

These paintings force us to deal with the fundamental dualism of writing, as both image and as a signifying element of language: "All writing has the capacity to be both looked at and read, to be present as material and to function as a sign of an absent meaning" (Drucker 1997: 87). However, as Petrucci points out in *Public Lettering, Script, Power and Culture* (1993) the letters contain also other tensions and paradoxes: First of all, the difference between material and object disappears the moment that letters are glued onto pictures and painting becomes non-mimetic. "Why should something be simulated, if it can be shown?" Juan Gris asked (Kahnweiler 1958: 91-92). In addition, writing entered the field of Cubist painting as a means of calling attention to "the questionableness of handed down techniques" (Einstein 1981: 236) and the conventions of pictorial codes. Further, it was obvious that the de-personalization of drawing, through the use of industrial materials, heralded a change in the status of the artist and of art altogether.

Shaken loose from a verbal context, the words and letters in Cubist paintings burst forth into multiple meanings, and, in the variety of their typography, they took on a visual character in their own right. In an assiduous attempt, some have tried to detect the literal meaning of these letters. Besides the overt propaganda present in Futurist collage, some have discovered, for example, that many of the newspaper clippings Picasso[3] used in his collages in late 1912 concerned the Balkan War (Leighton quoted in Poggi 1992: 25). Rosalind Krauss has dubbed those efforts "semantic positivism" (Krauss 1981: 32). Certainly, these paintings carried verbal messages. More relevant, however, is that the jarring placements and abrupt juxtapositions of images and words, torn from their familiar syntax, in both Cubist collage and the Futurist *Parole in libertà*, produced unexpected new meanings.

With the use of non-artistic materials in collage – headlines, theatre tickets and city maps – written characters became icons and messengers of everyday-life. It is there, in everyday life, that we can glimpse some conditions of the early twentieth century's aesthetic innovations. The diffusion of writing reached a new level with the explosion of advertising that began to transform the modern city. Letters left the white pages of the book to invade the city, to grapple with the metropolitan scenery. "Locust swarms of print, which already eclipse the sun of what city dwellers take for intellect, will grow thicker with each succeeding year", wrote Walter Benjamin in his *One-Way Street* at some time between 1923 and 1926 and published in 1928 (Benjamin 1996: 456).

Writing found a new, industrialized, form in neon signs. Although still made by hand, their radiant power caused an enormous proliferation of letters and demonstrated the dominance of the word over all other forms of life. We have in our mind's eye pictures of two historical cities covered with writing: The Athens of antiquity, where everything was written in stone; and the modern city, whose public spaces have been taken over by neon signs and billboards many times larger-than-life.

Figure 34
Man Ray, *La Ville*, 1931.

As advertising spread throughout the public sphere, so the invention of the typewriter domesticated the printing press, mechanized handwriting, making it anonymous, as it liberated single letters from their context. Words dissected into letters were freed from meaning; one thought with one's fingers. While, in their other famous manifesto of 1913, *The Letter as Such*, Khlebnikov and Kruchonykh could still claim "Our mood alters our handwriting as we write" (Khlebnikov 1987: 257), the typewriter had meanwhile altered writing speed and error rate.

A related and third invention was psychoanalysis, in which narration in the form of talking was methodically freed from sense – at least, the sense fixed by writing. Psychoanalysis made a complete break with the privileged status of the written word, a break from the linear arrangement of the great nineteenth century novel, so fundamental to bourgeois identity. So at the same time that signs floated their way into Cubist painting, the psychoanalysis' talking cure was encouraging nonsense in its use of enigmas for healing: as with dreams, desire was and is outside daily logic. It appears on the couch as a rebus, a picture puzzle[4] to solve:

Figure 35
Bragaglia, *Dattilografia*, 1911.

Critical spaces

Soon enough, letters reached the theatre. Paradoxically, the appearance of written characters on stage was related to the diminishing importance of language in theatre. The text had already lost its dominant role to the human body, to the staged voice, and to the space itself, by the time writing short-circuited its way onto the stage. For centuries, theatre has been a book-wanting-to-be-a-scene and a scene-wanting-to-become-a-book; now letters took a direct route.

By 1914, letters have taken over the entire set in Giacomo Balla's sketch for the ballet *Machina Typografica*. While traditional printed matter hangs askew and unreadable from the soffits, the letters are mobilised in a futuristic manner. "12 automatons" must, with hard, mechanical gestures execute the movements of an "enormous machine". With a sure instinct, Balla gave the key role in the typographical revolution of the *Parole di libertà* to the linotype-setting machine, presented as a "weeping onomatopoeia" on stage.[5]

Figure 36
Balla, Sketch for *Macchina tipografica*, 1914.

By contrast, the Ballet Suédois in Paris performed *Within the Quota* in 1923 to the music of Cole Porter. The décor for this "ballet-ciné-sketch", in which a cameraman filmed the action on stage, was designed by Gerald Murphy, who attacked American immigration policy and tabloid journalism by showing a gigantic newspaper front page full of over-sized lettering.

Figure 37
Gerald Murphy, *Within the Quota*, Choreography by Jean Börlin, Paris 1923.

In a form allegedly derived from Cubism (Levin 1995: 120) – analytically inspired by Dadaism however – the visual irony of the headlines turned the sensational into the satirical, and the seriousness of the facts into the ridiculous. The photo-illustration on stage compared the ocean liner, 'the Queen of the Ocean', turned up on end, with the Woolworth Building in New York. Christened the 'Cathedral of Commerce' by the Reverend S. Parkes Cadman, at its opening in 1913, it remained the tallest building in the world until 1930.[6]

186

Such decorative presence of letters on the set was probably one of the less irritating aspects of their use. However, something else seems to be going on in the famous constructivist staging of *Le Cocu Magnifique* by Meyerhold in 1922.[7] Here Popova's legendary abstract machinery replaces traditional decoration. This machine, with its platforms, slides, stairs, window flaps and scaffolds, held no mystery, required no explanation – it was a perfect "workbench for acting". Indeed, the letters painted in Latin script on the big wheel explained nothing, and hid no secret – at best they were a kind of trademark or signature, the consonants of Crommelynck, the play's author's name. However, we might understand the desegregation of his name as a telltale sign of the eroded status of the text in early *Regie-Theater*. Perhaps the missing vowels, with some futuristic panache, increase the speed of the revolving wheel. It is certainly not the case that the detested decorative had simply retreated into the form CR ML YNK.

Figure 38
Liubov Popova, *The Magnanimous Cuckold*, Moscow 1922

Subsequent constructivist theatrical productions showed a shift in the use of writing on stage from a non-narrative composition with architectonic potential, that is, from formal experiment, to pure political propaganda. The printed banners with painted solutions and projected slogans however always led an independent aesthetic life, penetrating the widespread illiteracy of the new audiences. When people could not read, graphic forms of writing could still awaken their interest where letters acquired their own physiognomy. To top it all, the slogans – like many advertising blurbs today – were known to everyone – as Aksyonov remarked in 1925 (Sarabianov, Adaskina 1990: 257).

Figure 39
Ljubov Popova, Slogan for Meyerhold's *The Earth in Turmoil*, Moscow 1923.

187

In Germany, Erwin Piscator also used the written word extensively on stage, primarily to intensify the expressive potential of his multi-media aesthetics and to install pedagogical and propagandistic links to reality. Elements or fragments of reality – newspaper headlines on stage or banners in the auditorium – enter his theatre, and then rebound on the outside world as political agitation. Bertolt Brecht was the first to develop an authentic dramaturgical concept for the use of writing on stage: his intention was neither to hypnotize the audience with media projections of suggestive spectacle, nor to persuade it with slogans. On the contrary, he tried fundamentally to alter all the relationships between the constituent elements of the theatre – including the passive role of the audience.

Like other procedures for establishing distance, writing interrupts the plot by commenting on it, or explaining connections, situating it in an unfamiliar context. In the economy of perception, the written word interrupts ongoing reception, and demands increased alertness and great presence of mind from the spectator. He or she must do much more than read. "Complex seeing must be practised", as Brecht put it in a comment on *Die Dreigroschenoper* (Brecht 1991: 59). The spectator's inner voice superimposes itself onto the action on stage, and activates the viewer to action.

To oscillate back and forth from one medium to another is, in a sense, an initiation into intermediality. Sometimes words on the wall act to disturb the image. Initially, written words on stage were surprising, automatically producing a distancing, *Verfremdung*. The confrontation of two representational modes destroyed the illusion of the immediacy of what was seen. Through reference to its made form; the scene could be identified as an artificial construction. The best-known formulation of media consciousness of this type may be the sign held up to the audience in *Trommeln in der Nacht* (*Drums in the Night*) Brecht's very first theatre piece, performed in 1921 for the Münchner Kammerspiele: "Don't gawk so romantically" (ibid., 14).

The aesthetic quality of Brecht's use of writing on stage also derived from the materiality of writing. Brecht preferred handwritten characters and antiquated typefaces – he had a weakness for the Luther Bible – and wanted to display traditional cultural skill. Brecht's writings on stage perform a dramatic, a perceptual and an aesthetic function. The inscriptions, notices and placards of his set transform the theatre's visual-and-fictional space into a semantic, abstract one. They corrode the space of illusion, opening up a space of critique.

An international language

Strangely enough, while in theatre letters appeared on stage, in cinema the goal was to get rid of them. Text frames entered the syntax of cinematographic narration early on – as early as 1900 – as an important element of being able to tell a longer story. However, even before the advent of sound, they began to be seen as structurally un-cinematic. "Perfect film doesn't need intertitles", noted Stephen Bush in 1913 (Savio 1956: col. 660).

Silent film effects a connection between the seen image and the read intertitle. To tie them together as closely as possible, Dziga Vertov, in collaboration with Aleksandr Rodchenko, conducted a series of experiments in 1922 into the status and potential of the written image in film. Son of a theatre prop man, the constructivist painter who called himself an engineer, shifted the audience's attention from the semantic to the graphic aspects of writing. Rodchenko created new forms for titles, treating them as graphic images and drawings. No longer interrupting the cinematographic motion with stationary lettering, as had been the practice, his titles were transformed into elements of montage, "equal in importance to camera shots" (Wertow 1967: 275). Treating titles as integral parts of the cinematic whole,

Rodchenko devised three types of titles, which were reported in the first edition of the avant-garde magazine *LEF*: those in large type, slung boldly across the screen; titles in which the letters receded in size creating an illusion of depth; and moving titles, which unfolded as the film progressed. In this way, their role was transformed: "from being a dead point in the film, the titles became an organic part of it."[8]

The Russian word "skwos", as we can see, means "through":

Figure 40
Aleksandr Rodchenko, Intertitle for Dziga Vertovs *Kinopravda*.

All three of these levels of experimentation in film intertitles – redesigning the titles, giving three-dimensionality to the letters, and creating movement – aimed for visual intensification. Some of the procedures complicated the act of reading, but the goal was always to win the heightened attention of the viewer, not only for the text but also for the entire, visual rhythm of the film's composition. In order to give some dynamism to the title optics, Rodchenko cut the letters into a dramatic form. He designed new letter types, compositions of letters and words (like the diagonal above), and geometrical signs (points, lines, arrows) to transform elements of writing into visual statements, so that, as Gilles Deleuze put it "the word formed a block with the image, a kind of ideogram."[9] Contemporary commentators called this procedure "speaking graphics" (Lavrentiev 1981: 77-78).

Paradoxically, these experiments ultimately culminated in the abandonment of intertitles. By 1923, Vertov himself had tried to reduce the importance of the titles, in an effort to dissolve all foreign elements out of the moving image, to shift from written into film language. His public was not, in any case, an audience of readers. In a country with an illiteracy rate of up to 90%[10], removing the titles was a critical ambition for the development for film. "We have significantly weakened the importance of intertitles", he wrote, "in so doing we have brought the movie screen closer to the uneducated viewer, which is particularly important at present" (Vertov 1984: 38). After having explored the possibilities of titles with Rodchenko for years and having given them a value of their own, Vertov dispensed with them altogether in his masterpiece, *Man with the Movie Camera*. Here, all titles – explanations, exclamations,

189

narrative or dialogue – vanish in favour of the rhythm film can create with its own means, with a film language that has been "totally freed from the language of theatre and literature".

Even without words, even without sound, Vertov succeeds without a single title to explain his moving pictures, without words to go along with the story. Instead, we see an awakening of perception, "to a language comprehensible to all, replacing the culture of the age of print". As we read in the film's opening titles, it is a work "in the language of film, which is an international language".

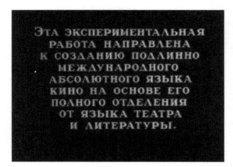

Figure 41
Dziga Vertov, *Man with the Movie Camera*, 1929.

"This experimental work is directed towards the creation of an authentic international absolute language of cinema on the basis of its complete separation from the language of theatre and literature."

Against linearity

Modernity meant the full extension of literacy, widespread typographic technology, alphabetisation of the relation between man and machine. With the predominance of the written word, the text itself is the declared battleground of semiotic strategies. "So we tear the letter out of its line, its one-dimensionality", wrote Kazimir Malevich to Alexei Kruchonych in June 1916 (Marcadé 1979: 185). If writing becomes the dominant form of cultural expression, linearity is its universal law – and the place for manoeuvre in artistic experimentation. Again, semiotic fundamentalism not only provides us with signs as expressive means, but also makes them perceivable as signs. The availability of these means creates a new performativity, a decisive change in the whole notion of the performance of aesthetic signs. Thus, the staging of writing offers a double pleasure: performative delight and analytic exuberance, which the avant-garde artist captured in one simple question. "How is it made?" With the same curiosity, determination, and ludic pleasure, with which children take apart their toys, or any other machines, even books, the Russian Formalists commenced to lay bare the structures of the artwork, its functional laws and aesthetic procedures.

We can trace the intermedial inventions of the early avant-garde down through the twentieth century. Practising Brechtians among the Beat Generation of America's 1960s transmitted Brecht's media-consciousness (provoked by contrasting means of expression) to the young Bob Dylan. Allen Ginsberg brought Brecht's books to Dylan's bedside after an obligatory motorcycle accident. In the first video-clip film of pop history, we see the "separation of elements": the music made off-screen; the lyrics on signboards (drawn by Joan Baez) and the performance, entirely Brechtian, falling artistically out of the role. Dylan simultaneously demonstrated: that his music must not be illustrated - neither by sun, wind, nor dancing girls; that this was an ad for his new album; and that lyrics are made of words, which disappear "in the mud of the asphalt" (Charles Baudelaire).

Figure 42 and 43
Subterranean Homesick Blues, 1965

Freeing letters from linearity allowed them to become pictures again. Today, as images have become the prevalent content in social communication, the experiments of the avant-garde may seem antiquated, almost obsolete. However with the progressive decentralisation of literacy, and writing's comeback on the web (after a period of secondary illiteracy caused by the hyper-consumerism of mass media), new relations between written language and visual culture are emerging.

The German writer, filmmaker and TV-partisan Alexander Kluge represents one of the avant-garde's "tiger leaps" (Walter Benjamin) into the present.[11] Long before CNN and other news channels, he used running titles extensively in his tri-weekly TV cultural journals. Intertitles, as in silent movies, punctuate his programs. These writings allow him to focus on transitions or about-turns. With the help of these titles, Kluge is able to advance an idea, to mark a turn, to pause. He distils the intertitles from what is happening on screen. The writing heightens viewer attention. A talk with Ulrike Sprenger, author of the *Marcel Proust-ABC*, about the Clinton-Lewinsky affair is ushered in with the title "Was Special Investigator Kenneth Starr badly prepared by his studies in Harvard?" This intervention interrupts the fatality of a television evening, paralleling the interruptions of Epic Theatre which break up the story against its own automatism: Brecht wanted to convey the immediate feeling, that everything could be different – and should be so; that, when we see something happening, or shown in a story, it should surprise us. Suddenly we think, why is that so? What planet do we live on? This is Brecht. Astonishment multiplies the possibilities of the course of history.

Figure 44
"Desire which rules the world /
Clinton, Starr, Ovid and Marcel Proust"

Figure 45
"It's all about a cultural organ"

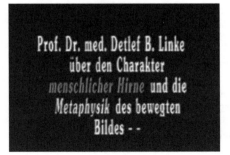

Figure 46
"Prof. Detlef B. Linke, M.D., on the character of human brains and the metaphysics of the moving image"

Kluge presents a kind of 'epic television'. Every now and then he transmits an entire program of *News & Stories* (the title of one of his shows) comprising only of writing. Imagine watching half an hour of TV with nothing but written words on the screen, hand-cut and set letters never seen before, which unroll a hymn by Friedrich Hölderlin, or Elfriede Jelinek's rhythmical prose. Kluge stages a certain kind of language, which we can observe being composed, can watch being thought. "We work with words", said Mayakovsky. Sometimes we begin to read someone's mind. Writing subverts the screen.

Notes

1 An earlier version "Die Inszenierung der Schrift. Eine Skizze" appeared in: *Theater Kunst Wissenschaft. Festschrift für Wolfgang Greisenegger zum 66. Geburtstag*, Wien, Köln, Weimar: Böhlau 2004; and a longer version will be part of my *2 oder 3 Dinge, die Sie von der historischen Avantgarde wissen sollten*, Wien: Böhlau 2006.

2 The title of the famous 1913 manifesto by Velimir Khlebnikov and Alexei Kruchonykh; in Velimir Khlebnikov, *Collected Works*, Vol. 1: *Letters and Theoretical Writings*, ed. by Charlotte Douglas, Cambridge, Mass.: Harvard Univ. Pr. 1987: 255-56.

3 Immense is the literature on how to read Picasso; recently Anne Baldassari, *Picasso working on paper*, London: Merrell 2000.

4 Freud called the dream a "picture-puzzle". Sigmund Freud, *The Interpretation of Dreams in The Standard Edition of the Complete Psychological Works of Sigmund Freud*, ed. by James Strachey, vol. IV, London: The Hogart Press 1953: 277.

5 Balla presented this ballet only once, totally improvised, in 1916 in Diaghilev's salon. See Giovanni Lista, *La scène futuriste*, Paris: CNRS 1989, p. 317; see also Maurizio Fagiolo dell'Arco, *Futur-Balla. La vita e le opere*, Milano: Electa 1990: 52.

6 Unusual amongst skyscraper, it was financed in cash, and in 1998 changed hands for the first time in its 85 years history. See also Stephen Jay Gould, "Restoration and the Woolworth Building", in *Natural History* 110, 10A, Winter 2001/02: 96-97.

7 Ivan Aksyonov, Popova's husband, who translated the play and prepared it for this production, ironically characterised the staging as "passing itself off as the staging of *Le Cocu Magnifique*" Iwan Axjonow, *Sergej Eisenstein. Ein Portrait* (1933), Berlin: Henschel/arte 1997: 32.

8 "Konstruktivistiy" (Constructivists), in: *LEF*, No. 1, 1923: 251, quoted in Hubertus Gaßner, *Rodchenko Fotografien*, München: Schirmer/Mosel 1982: 22; see also Christina Lodder, *Russian Constructivism*, New Haven/London: Yale Univ. Press,. 1983: 201.

9 "Vertov faisait de l'intertitre un usage original où le mot formait un bloc avec l'image, une sorte d'idéogramme." Gilles Deleuze, *Cinéma 1. L'Image mouvement*, Paris: Minuit 1983 : 119.

10 In 1929, The International Statistical Bureau in The Hague reported the following numbers on illiteracy in European capitals: Berlin 0,43%, Prague 0,69%, Vienna 2,04%, Paris 3,36%, Budapest 4,76%, Rome 10,95%, Leningrad 13,81%, Moskow 22,42%, Kiew 44,62%. (*Der Große Herder* vol. 2., Freiburg 1932: col. 738). If one takes into account, that in 1931 23, 6% of the population of the Soviet-Union lived in cities (ibid, vol. 11, Freiburg 1935: col. 143), the illiteracy rate of 90% becomes more concrete. See also Varlam Chalamov, *Les années 20*, Paris: Verdier 1997.

11 Yet in 1970, Pasolini called Kluge's work "un revival dell'avanguardia classica". Pier Paolo Pasolini, "La mancanza di ogni perplessità", now in: Sergio Tuffetti, Giovanni Spagnoletti, *Alexander Kluge*, Torino: Museo Nazionale del Cinema / Lindau 1994: 34.

Translated by Dardis McNamee

For criticism and inspiration, I wish to thank András Böröcz, Freda Chapple, Dieter Federspiel, Susanna Heilmayr, Chiel Kattenbelt, Antonia Lant, Roberta Mazzola, Monika Meister, Helmut Peschina, Werner Rappl, and Robbin A. Silverberg.

SHADOW OF THE VAMPIRE:
DOUBLE TAKES ON NOSFERATU
Johan Callens

This chapter contextualizes *Shadow of the Vampire*, Elias Merhige's movie on the making of Murnau's *Nosferatu*, in order to interpret the framing of the staged film production as a self-reflexive means of exploring the medium-specificity of theatre and film. The chapter relates *Shadow of the Vampire* to a variety of remediated representations, but in particular to Murnau's *Nosferatu*, Coppola's spectacular *Bram Stoker's Dracula*, and Ping Chong's theatrical stage adaptation, *Nosferatu: A Symphony of Darkness*. As conveyed by the horror movie's central metaphor of the vampire, intermediality is located initially in the technical and psychological realms before acquiring intercultural significance. The intermedial perspectives offered, alert us to viewing the vampire as 'other', whether the post-colonial subject or object. Thus, we are presented with a persuasive argument for the non-polarized interpretations which are a key feature of intermediality and contemporary culture.

Ostensibly, Elias Merhige's *Shadow of the Vampire* (2000) presents itself as a movie on the making of F.W. Murnau's *Nosferatu* (1922), which was itself an unauthorized adaptation of Bram Stoker's vampire tale, *Dracula* (1897). Steven Katz's script for *Shadow of the Vampire* develops the conceit that Max Schreck, the character actor who played the vampire in Murnau's *Nosferatu*, really was one. In the Merhige film, Murnau has contracted Schreck secretly to play the role of the vampire and promised him the lifeblood of his movie counterpart, Greta Schroeder, but he passes the creature off to the film crew as a student of Stanislavsky who is totally immersed in his role, onstage as well as offstage. Murnau, already credited with innovations like location shooting, now appears obsessed with achieving the highest degree of realism. However, by staging the shooting of key scenes in all their multi-coloured theatricality, Merhige, with the latest cinema technology recaptures the texture and visual aesthetics of Murnau's silent classic, seamlessly shifting media and time frames, and even including original b/w film sequences for comparison's sake, as well as for the viewers' delighted perplexity.

In *Shadow of the Vampire* the complexity of intermediality is immediately apparent and this chapter explores how, through the central metaphor of the vampire, the illusionism of Murnau's classic film (*transparent immediacy*) is welded to Merhige's fascination with the theatrical and cinematographic means of producing it (*hypermediacy*), without, however, subsuming one to the other.

Building on Murnau's and Stanislavsky's contributions to representational realism in theatre and film, *Shadow of the Vampire* involves references to, borrowings from and echoes of several media: the cinematic (*The Hunger, Bram Stoker's Dracula, King Kong*); the theatrical (*Route 1 & 9, Nosferatu: A Symphony of Darkness*); the literary (Stoker), operatic (Wagner), and even painterly (Knights Templar iconography during the opening credits). Merhige's intermedial practice resembles that of Murnau: a man who started out as actor and assistant to the German theatre director, Max Reinhardt; but who in his subsequent films staked out the independence of the new artistic medium; yet who had an architectural conception of space, and freely borrowed from painters like David Caspar Friedrich. However, far from being a simple way of besting the master in an innocent *Spielerei* or superfluous remake, *Shadow of the Vampire* allows Merhige to explore the specificity of the media involved, especially film and theatre, their historically shifting rhetoric (manipulative identification vs. critical distancing), metaphorical discourse (lifegiving vs. lifedraining; artificial vs. lifelike; presence vs. absence), cultural productivity (consumerism; colonialism) and counter-productivity (the demonization of science and new media in particular).

Intermedial Progeny

Steven Katz conceived of his story as a screenplay right from the start of the project: film appeared to him quite simply as the only appropriate medium for his central conceit and the intermedial exploration to work successfully (Cohen: 31). While the stage can incorporate screenings, it can only approximate film's illusory effects temporarily. Katz wrote the part of the vampire with Willem Dafoe in mind. In his early days as an experimental playwright, Katz had known Dafoe as a founding member of the Wooster Group (a renowned intermedial performance company) but in the meantime he had become a popular screen actor. Interestingly, when Dafoe auditioned for the lead in *Bram Stoker's Dracula* (1992, dir. Francis Ford Coppola) (Duynslaegher: 13) he had been bypassed in favour of Gary Oldman, but the associated connection was there. Other connections were in the making when, after several unsuccessful attempts at selling the script, Katz's agent, Crispin Glover, made an auspicious move by sending it to Coppola's nephew, Nicolas Cage who, with Jeff Levine, had just established an independent production company, 'Saturn Films', and who had an acknowledged interest in Murnau. Accompanying the script was a video tape of *Begotten* (1989), a pseudo-documentary horror movie directed by the then unknown Elias Merhige, performed by his own stage company 'Theatreofmaterial' and filmed on experimentally processed stock. It was on the joint merits of Merhige's first feature film and Katz's script that Levine and Cage sealed the deal (Atkinson: 29; Mottram).

Playing opposite Dafoe would be John Malkovich, a man with an equally extensive stage and film experience, some of it providing excellent practice for their joint venture and, with hindsight, seeming to forecast their parts as alter egos caught up in the psychological and intermedial tangle. Malkovich hails from Chicago's 'Steppenwolf Ensemble Theatre' and doubled the male leads in *Mary Reilly* (1996, dir. Stephen Frears), based on *Dr. Jekyll and Mr. Hide* (1886). Dafoe later played the scientist Norman Osborn and his evil alter ego, the Green Goblin, in Sam Raimi's *Spider-Man* (2002), based on Stan Lee's Marvel Comics. It was two years prior to *Nosferatu* that Murnau himself finished *Der Januskopf* (1920), a movie a.k.a. *Schrecken* and *Janus-Faced*. Based also on Robert Louis Stevenson's tale of a split self, it featured Conrad Veidt and Bela Lugosi, and later on, Lugosi would star as the vampire in Hamilton Deane and John L.Balderston's 1927 Broadway version of Stoker's novel, before repeating the part to much acclaim in Tod Browning's *Dracula* (1931). Thus, we can see a pattern of 'doubling' in a group of actors and directors working at the beginning and end of the twentieth century, and combining their interest in tales of the fantastic, with an exploration of the film medium.

A notable example of such metacinematographic concern is seen in *Shadow of the Vampire* during Malkovich's monologue, which is heard over exterior shots of the train during the ride from Germany to Czechoslovakia. Quite apart from Malkovich harping on about the immortality cinema grants, this sequence involves a self-referential allusion to the theory that train travel presents an analogue, and thus prepared the ground for cinema by parcelling the panoramic continuity of reality into discrete windows or viewing frames (Schivelbusch: 52-69, 188-197; Kirby: 6-11, 42-48; Vardac passim). The images of Malkovich's face, which Merhige super-imposes over the train, document the early cinema technique of "spirit photography" which Murnau relied on in *Nosferatu* (Thomas: 301). These now turn him into an equally spectral figure as Schreck the vampire, with a corresponding dubious ontological status. Elsewhere, Dafoe's facial image is indeed frequently reduced to a ghastly mask. Quite paradoxically, then, the train sequence documents early film's uncanny powers, by which Murnau already appears to have been consumed in his search for artistic immortality. Merhige construes the medium of film as both para-psychological and technological, building on early cinema's reputation as black magic (Moore and Sconce), as well as on the mesmerist scenes in Stoker's novel. Notably, mesmerism is reprised by Merhige in his opening scene where Murnau almost hypnotizes Greta Schroeder through his acting advice. Murnau was passionate about the occult, just as his producer Albin Grau dabbled in para-psychology and wrote a treatise on the use of colours in decor and lighting in b/w films – all of which anticipate Merhige's preoccupations with media (in the double sense).

Media Consumption

Merhige's depiction of the relationship between cinema and theatre is informed by two earlier projects of Dafoe's featuring some famous *revenants*. First, there was Dafoe's brief stint in *The Hunger* (1983), which was Tony Scott's directorial debut, starring youth-icon David Bowie as an ageing Undead, as well as Catherine Deneuve (Miriam) and Susan Sarandon (Sarah) in a lesbian tryst. *The Hunger* tapped into the American health-fad and allowed for repeated AIDS similes. From the opening sequence onwards, set to the song "Bela Lugosi's Dead" by the Goth rock band Bauhaus, the movie also betrays Tony Scott's previous experience directing music videos. Merhige, too, has made some controversial videos for Goth rock icons Marilyn Manson (*Crypt Orchid, Antichrist Superstar*) and Glenn Danzig (*Serpentia*).

As far as their stories are concerned, Scott's and Merhige's movies share a central male character (John Blaylock and Schreck), who grows old following a broken promise from his female lover. Scott's social critique of the youth-culture's consumerism and materialism dominating Reagan's 1980s and its aftermath includes the class basis of the potentially homoeroticism—a privilege of Miriam's yuppie

Johan Callens

leisure, which the new bourgeoisie represented by Sarah can only aspire to, until the latter revolts and assumes her former mistress's place. Similarly, in *Shadow of the Vampire* the aristocratic manners of 'Herr Doktor' Murnau, presented as a bisexual vampiric double of Schreck, are at odds with his artistic progressivism, and detract from the cyborgian potential which Rob Latham (111-119) considers to be the reverse side of the vampiric exploitation of the mass media supporting youth culture.

A similar metaphorical use of vampirism marked the Wooster Group's last act of *Route 1 & 9* (1981), featuring Dafoe and based on Thornton Wilder's *Our Town* (1938). This is a highly self-reflexive play in which the dead Emily Gibbs is allowed to return to earth. *Route 1 & 9* relied on vampiric masks to express an outburst of sexuality and to criticize the repressed emotionality of the small town setting. The use of vampiric masks expressed also how the stage performers are preyed on by roles, whether the roles prescribed by Wilder's drama or the stage persona of Pigmeat Markham, whose scatological blackface routine the Wooster Group incorporated in order to subvert the small town's racial discrimination. Regardless of the medium in which such parasitic role-playing occurs, it foreshadows Schreck's Stanislavskean based identification with his part in Merhige's movie. This approach to acting is resisted by an intermedial performance company like the Wooster Group who prefer to go for the actuality of task-based acting. The stage vampires emblematize the inhabitants of the cemetery, the undead state of Wilder as a canonical dramatist, of Pigmeat Markham as a performance model, as well as a more general dissolution of traditionally polarized categories (man/woman, black/white) signalled by the production's blackface and drag (Savran: 36-39). It is the dissolution of traditional boundaries that *Shadow of the Vampire* formally and thematically extends to the intermedial, whose realm is peopled by the abject and marginalized.

Media Imperialism

Since Nicolas Cage produced *Shadow of the Vampire*, his uncle Francis Ford Coppola's 1992 film adaptation *Bram Stoker's Dracula* may have functioned as a benchmark and we need to consider this. In the conservative 1980s, which were notable for the AIDS ravage, the marginalized clearly included homosexuals. Given the speculation about Bram Stoker's suppressed love for the Lyceum Theatre's star-actor, Henry Irving, in whose employ he was, and the reflection of their forbidden love in Jonathan Harker's relationship with the vampire in the novel *Dracula*, it hardly surprises that in his movie adaptation Coppola has been said to refer to AIDS, notably in the microscopically magnified shots of blood cells. By making visible repressed fears like those of AIDS and female sexuality (as embodied in Lucy), the Coppola movie arguably fosters a liberating acceptance of them (Dika: 395-6). There are several twists, though, to Stoker's novel. For example, in the prologue Coppola identifies Dracula with the historical Vlad Tepes and turns Mina into his reincarnated wife, Elizabeta (both parts doubled by Winona Ryder). The latter gives herself freely to liberate him, much like Ellen in Murnau's movie (albeit less passionately).

Katz's original script has Schreck believe in a similar reincarnation of his wife, but in Merhige's final cut Greta will have none of her handsome lead, so she must be drugged into submission to play the ultimate sacrifce for love. Also, insofar as the vampire and director have become doubles, Greta is an unwilling victim of Murnau, preferring what she calls the stage's life-giving powers to the cinema's life-draining ones. She only gives in after a b/w flashback, life already drained of blood and colour, in which the director argues: "It is the role that will make you great as an actress [...] consider it a sacrifice for your art". In an ironic reversal, her stage performance signals her literal death *and* her immortalizing through Murnau's movie.

It has been said that Coppola turned the horror story into a romance, and that he appropriated Victorian patriarchal morality in the service of contemporary conservatism and an all-too-commercial spectacularization, only thinly disguised by the movie's postmodern self-reflexivity in celebration of the first hundred years of cinema (Sharrett: 265-6; Dunbar: 64). For these critics, the reference to AIDS, in combination with Dracula's monogamous, marital love, symbolizes a moral and religious lapse from romantic love and Christian abstinence (Sharrett: 267-8). Others construe Coppola's full title, *Bram Stoker's Dracula*, together with his reliance on the historical Vlad Tepes, less evidence of the movie's self-referentiality (Thomas: 299) than a fraudulent legitimization, given the script's derivativeness from Dan Curtis's 1973 TV movie (Auerbach: 135, 213). If we accept that perspective, then Coppola's version is a re-authoring and re-appropriation of a two-centuries-old tradition, bridging high and low culture as well as different media and genres. However, both critiques omit that the message of redemption through love pervades Stoker's novel as is evidenced by allusions to Arthurian legend (Leatherdale: 216-23; Hughes: 54-96) and Wagner's *Flying Dutchman* (1843). True, Harker's visit to the Munich opera on the eve of Walpurgis Night did not survive Stoker's working notes (348-9; Leatherdale: 121). The published novel makes do with a reference to the ghostly ship from *The Rime of the Ancient Mariner* (1798) by S.T.Coleridge, whose mesmerist tale offers a variation upon the vampiric powers of Christabel in his earlier eponymous poem. Adding to the intermedial mix, Coppola and Merhige dutifully recycle Wagner's music, as Tod Browning had done in 1931. Dan Jones's soundtrack for *Shadow of the Vampire* uses excerpts from the overtures to *The Flying Dutchman* as well as *Tristan and Isolde*, works which also inspired respectively Murnau's *Nosferatu* and *Taboo* (Collier: 111-131; Elsaesser 2000: 230, 255n32).

In defence of the second criticism levelled at *Bram Stoker's Dracula*, that of the alleged spectacularization, it needs to be said that Coppola added a new sequence to the novel's material, in which the Count's arrival in London is made to coincide with that of the Lumière brothers' Cinematograph. The careful montage, together with the Count's mechanical walking and the sequence's sepia colour, actually identify him with the new medium (Thomas: 303-4). In Browning's version of *Dracula*, which like Balderston and Deane's Broadway adaptation updates the events of Stoker's novel from the 1890s to the 1920s, it is the advent of the *sound* film rather than the cinema proper, which is highlighted. Ironically, this is done by letting Dracula visit the opera house for a *live performance* of *The Flying Dutchman* by the London Symphony Orchestra.

Taken together Browning's, Coppola's, and Merhige's meta-cinemato-graphic concerns all remediate Stoker's preoccupation with the technological means of transmitting Dracula's tale – typewriter, phonograph, telegraph, and newspaper.

Thus, vampirism becomes the perfect emblem of the mechanical, quasi-authorless reproduction embodied in the novel's technologies and the cinema medium. This emblematizing was aided by early psychoanalysis, which displaced authorial control to subconscious drives. True, Coppola's double re-authoring of the vampire tale, i.e. his appropriating Stoker's name in the movie's title and his authorial directing, does run counter to a triple drift: that of the novel doing without an omniscient narrator, of cinema as a technology of reproduction, and of the vampire film as a genre inviting ever more remakes, distributed on ever more supports (celluloid, DVD) (Wicke: 467-493, Kittler: 143-173, Elsaesser 2001: 15).

The implied consequences of letting Dracula's arrival in London coincide with that of the cinema are attuned to interpretations of Stoker's novel as expressing the western fear of a reverse colonization (431-444). This is confirmed in Dracula's near-assault of Mina in the movie theatre during footage of a train assaulting the public at large. In interviews Merhige admitted that the megalomania of his Murnau consisted in using movies as a means of post-colonial domination and global conquest, not only as an innocent means of cultural exchange. Just as the train had been both an instrument in the development of tourism and an imperialist tool, eradicating othernesss:

> In *Nosferatu*, the death ship that arrives in Bremen is sort of like the cinema, in the sense that we export ideas, philosophies and culture to every corner of the globe, and some of the more delicate cultures are sometimes shattered by that (Merhige quoted in Magid: 75).

Coppola's ideological and metaphorical association of vampirism with the railroad and cinema confirms Merhige's cinematographic allusion in the superimposition of Murnau's spectral face on the train, rather than on the coach or cars used for the final leg of the journey. The cinema, says Merhige, is "an artefact of the Industrial Revolution that changed the world as surely as the steam engine changed the American West" (quoted in Stephens: 104).

It is no coincidence, then, that his Murnau uses a colonialist vocabulary, when complaining to Albin that "a native has walked into [his] frame." Similarly, Schreck's fascination with the film projector and his insistence on flying rather than sailing to Heligoland are partly motivated by his imperialist interest in technology. Having lost many of his powers through old age, Schreck needs substitutes. He may no longer be able to cross walls and locked doors, as in *Nosferatu*, but the camera can – as several follow-focus trackings demonstrate, offering in the process a spatial embodiment of the intermediality suffusing *Shadow of the Vampire*.

Media Persuasion

The relevance of the colonialist interpretation of the media is reinforced through one of Katz's acknowledged sources: Merian C. Cooper and Ernest B.Schoedsack's *King Kong* (1933) (Cohen: 31). After all, both movies feature documentary filmmakers (Carl Denham and Murnau) embarking on trips to similar exotic locations where they encounter a monstrous creature (Kong, Schreck) which they abuse for a globalized mediatic conquest. Denham believes that Kong, whether live or mechanically reproduced will make him and his partners millionaires. In keeping with Stoker's anticipation of the power shift from British bourgeois capitalism to U.S. monopoly capitalism (431-44), Kong quite appropriately terrorizes the Western world from the top of New York's Empire State Building. Denham seemingly undoes his capitalist dream by doubting the truthfulness of documentary cinema and by substituting the risky stage spectacle of the live Kong for the safer spectacularity of the cinema. At the most, sore eyes are what the old society lady expects to get from seeing at close range the 'darling monkeys and tigers' of a Denham moving picture. Yet, thanks to the special animation effects of Willis O'Brien (stop motion, dimensional photography, and rear projection), which caused patrons at the première to faint, Cooper and Schoedsack's picture reaffirmed cinema's illusory power – the very power that Merhige's Murnau equally doubts by engaging a real vampire. For the West End version of Stoker's *Dracula* in 1927, the lobby nurses and patrons were paid to faint, thus only creating an artificial hype (378-9).

In *Shadow of the Vampire* and *Nosferatu* a painted image of Mina in Jonathan's locket, with the force of a speech act pragmatically concludes the real estate deal, and exposes that she is in fact the object of exchange, as much as its medium; whether in Stoker's psychic sense of allowing the vampire hunters to track down Dracula, or in Kittler's technological interpretation as the operator of the late nineteenth century innovations featured by the novelist. The mercantilist spirit, which the exchange bespeaks, somehow qualifies the romanticism spelled by the redemption-through-love theme, though it remains in line with the monetary concerns and patriarchalism of Stoker's *Dracula*. The novel's positivistic portrayal of technology, by contrast, is inverted in the movies' presentation of the cinematographic image. In their respective films, the two monsters are destroyed by the technology underlying Western imperialism, whether this is achieved by gas bombs, chrome steel, biplanes or the cinema itself. According to the witchdoctor, Denham's filming of the bridal ceremony spoils it, just as Schreck is trapped by the mesmerizing camera that allows dawn with him—the very camera, Merhige playfully insists, which the real Murnau used and is now in the private possession of the director of Munich's motion picture museum (Stephens: 101). The metaphorical monsters escape seemingly unscathed, as if indeed "it was beauty killed the beast" (the "old Arabian proverb" prefacing *King Kong*). However, in the long term both Kong and Schreck survive Denham and Murnau, if only as consumerist commodities in the era of the spectacle fostered by the cinema.

Media Bricolage

If Coppola's *Dracula* adaptation is a more than likely source of inspiration for *Shadow of the Vampire*, and *King Kong* an acknowledged one, then the intermedial stage version by Ping Chong (no pun intended) surely is a possible one. Since the first draft of *Shadow of the Vampire* dates from 1987-88, Katz, who was then an experimental playwright/ director operating from San Francisco and New York, must have been familiar with Chong's *Nosferatu: A Symphony of Darkness* (Banes: 276-7), which premièred in 1985 (LaMama, New York) and was revised in 1991 (Easton, PA).

In this show, the Asian-American director pursued his intermedial stage practice of drawing inspiration from classic movies. Thus, his earlier production *Fear and Loathing in Gotham* (1975) is a tale of child-murder based on Fritz Lang's *M.* (1931), whereas Chong's *Nosferatu* incorporates slide-projected stills and title cards like those from Murnau's silent classic. These visual quotes are utterly ignored by four New York yuppies, named after Stoker's characters (Nina, Lucia, Arthur, Jonathan), who converse in the clichés and non-sequiturs taken from contemporary popular magazines like *Interview* and *Rolling Stone* (Neely: 123). This media "bricolage" as Chong has called it (Auslander: 83), was his rather inventive, depersonalizing take on Stoker's narrative mix of diaries, medical reports, newspaper clippings, telegrams, etc., all meant to enhance the alleged objectivity of his fantastic tale.

Chong's intermedial *Nosferatu* involves an investigation of "what it means to be an outsider" (Gussow: 127). This applies to the Asian-American playwright/ director, whose widely shown slide lecture, "Vampires, Doppelgängers and Aliens (Residents and Otherwise)", puns on US Immigration Codes (Allardice). However, it applies also to Stoker, an Anglicized Irish novelist, and Murnau, a homosexual film director launching his film career in the homophobic Weimar republic. According to Joseph Valente, Ireland is the novel's Other, underlying the Balkan or Eastern question, casting no reflection in Jonathan Harker's British mirror because this Other is erased by paranoid racist prejudices, often couched in sexual terms. However, the false hierarchies established fail to hide the similarities between so-called vampire and victim, and hence the solution to the Anglo-Irish conflict. This does not lie in military bloodshed nor in a vampiric economic exploitation but in the reconciliation embodied by Mina Harker. Her mediating figure ultimately represents a modernized and technologically enhanced version of the myth of Mother Ireland, as analyzed by Ernest Jones and possibly alluded to by Merhige and Katz by shifting their movie's finale to Heligoland, an analogue for Ireland and the Pacific Isles where Murnau found peace.

On the other hand, Nosferatu is the Other within, "an allegorical figure for the unacknowledged darknesses beneath the smooth surface of Reaganite America" (Auslander: 83), a realm already explored by Scott's *The Hunger*. The 1991 revision of Chong's play exemplified these forces with added references to plagues—Exxon, AIDS, right-wing death squads, and nuclear waste. All of them stress the audience's complicity in the creation of "political and ecological 'monsters'" (Westfall: 372, n5), a complicity conveyed by the fog (Dracula's disembodied shape), which engulfs the house and stage before the play's opening, and by the strange balls of black matted fur which at the end of the play bridge their divide.

In a formal prelude to the play, the very first black matted ball features as a metaphorical tumour or heart of darkness disembowelled in a choreographed battle between two puppet-like, Angels—"a cross between Pre-Raphaelite gravestone and Kabuki warriors" (Banes: 277). This battle takes place on a blue inner stage (heaven?) in front of a black curtain, which subsequently opens to reveal the projection screen. Later on in the play, during a brief absence of the characters, slides from Murnau announce the outbreak of the plague and performers dressed in skeleton-costumes similar to those used on the Mexican 'Day of the Dead' take over the stage to the accompaniment of Gregorian chants, which later change into a mambo. Chong's allegorical figures at the play's opening and end establish a frame, which is rather like Stoker's two editorial notes (5, 326-7). In both cases, the frame becomes a paradoxical precondition for exposing what lies beyond its immediate purview. Through its explicit staging of the filming of *Nosferatu*, *Shadow of the Vampire* retains such a frame and its intermedial function. During the opening scene, localized in time and place by an intertitle, Merhige even wanted the director and his film crew in their lab coats and goggles to appear like gods looking down on humanity from the studio rostrum (Stephens: 103).

Several of Chong's intertitles (which double the frame) harp on Jonathan's financial motive and equate it with the plague threatening the happiness of Nina. The inset proper begins and ends with his checking, much to Nina's displeasure, stock exchange figures from around the world recited over the answering machine. In his final phone call, he takes advantage of a business contract in order not to be held accountable. Both scenes convey the communication media's collusion in the economic reification, as does the media collage of the speeches, and the distortion of the mailman's voice over the intercom, a 'convenience' which allows Arthur to avoid the man from the safety of his flat.

For the rest, Chong's intermedial self-reflection pertains to the combined verbal and visual means of construing meaning and to their evolving twentieth century context. Thus, the provenance of Chong's "bricolage" (a term coined by Claude Lévi-Strauss in his research on South American myths) is highlighted by the belittling reference to "a structural anthropologist" (ts. 10) and by the Mexican 'Day of the Dead' interlude. The structuralist method is further exemplified in the game-playing with the indiscriminate paradigmatic list of culinary terms. These foreign-sounding names of drinks and dishes representing Western consumerism as the rationale for economic imperialism, mediatic or otherwise, lead up to Freudian play on "Schreck" and "Dreck", before breaking down in meaningless minimal units ("Yeck", "Eck", "Heck") arbitrarily cut short ("Check") (ts. 21-23). In psychoanalysis, anal retention commonly stands for acquisitiveness, yet within the post-colonial context of Chong's play, the yuppies' verbal defecation Others or racializes the vampire, in an attempt to keep their own darkness at bay and reaffirm their (Western) superiority and/or difference.

For Chong, the babble leads to an investigation into the very structure of language, as if a preliminary cause of contemporary ills might be found there. Voice-over questions accompanying the slides shift the attention from the anecdotal contents of Stoker's tale and Murnau's movie to the very processes of linguistic and intermedial signification: "What is misunderstood"? "What is contagion"? (ts. 23). When intertitles and stills from *Nosferatu* alternate with slides of "fish, a baby buggy, an axe, a seltzer bottle" and "coffins", the manner, in which "equations are made of the different images" (ts. 28) and the words, is of equal importance as the meanings thus established, much as in Merhige's clustering of vampirism, cinema, and trains.

Chong's widening of intermediality's scope seems to indicate his intention of bringing to the surface the intercultural and racial issues in his home country, the relations of North America ("US") with its immigrants ("THEM") (ts. 29), whether Asian-American, Filipino /a, or Latino/a. As a result, he refocuses Stoker's opposition between western civilization, on the one hand, and the vampire and his gypsy allies, on the other. Thus, the staging of the Mexican 'Day of the Dead' is peopled with an American Express Man, a Klansman, cheerleaders, a Chevrolet Silverado Sign man, even an Uncle Sam, bunny, cowboy and Indian, which gives the whole performance a bitter cartoonish and agit-prop atmosphere with chases and shootings. True, the cities and regions featured in the stock exchange data still spell out the global reach of capitalism and its detrimental effects, since a similar list relegates the metaphorical darkness to the furthest corners of the world, to Cathay, Delphi and Ravenna as well as Nairobi and Africa (Freud's 'dark' continent with its 'dark' populations) (ts. 33).

The omnipresent yet ignored, silent figure of the "Red Bride" (ts. 15 and ff.) represents an allusion to Poe's "The Mask [a.k.a. Masque] of the Red Death" (1842), which enhances the topicality of Chong's allegory, while re-infusing the endless parties of his socialites with the theatrical ambience of Poe's short story (buffoonery, improvisations, ballet, music; Prince Prospero's name, derived from Shakespeare's colonialist play, *The Tempest*). Simultaneously, the reference again fleshes out the vampiric and intermedial concerns, because "The Mask of the Red Death" derives from the tuberculosis of Poe's wife, which also engendered the aptly entitled "Life in Death" (1842), in which a painting's lifelikeness is extracted at the expense of the model's life (Silverman: 179-181, 246), much as in *Shadow of the Vampire* Greta Schroeder is victimized by Murnau's obsession with realism.

Conclusion

All in all *Shadow of the Vampire* proves far more than a simple docudrama on the making of Murnau's *Nosferatu*, providing a critique of the director's ruthless ambitions, whether self-interested or artistically motivated. We can now see how the movie's theatrical framing of Murnau's classic in fact doubles the remediation, and defines intermediality as an ongoing media struggle vehicled by the vampire metaphor in all its consumerist, racist, and colonialist ramifications.

Furthermore, these ramifications extend into the intermedial progeny, which Katz and Merhige had at their disposal, and so marks the erasure of postmodern performance's integrity and discrete boundaries as a fundamental feature of intermediality. Erasure may also characterize intertextuality, but the latter concept and term are quickly losing their legitimacy in our televisual age. For if Merhige first staged the filming of *Nosferatu*, thereby anchoring the events in the theatrical sphere, his filming of that staging marks cinema's re-appropriation. Intermedial theatre like Ping Chong's *Nosferatu* may be capable of incorporating visual media, yet *Shadow of the Vampire* ultimately suggests the migratory character of visual images, certainly iconic ones like those from *Nosferatu*, which refuse to be stilled or colonized once and for all.

Insofar as the process of mutual re-appropriation can never be prevented or stopped, Merhige's remediation signals the postmodern loss of an originary site (Stoker's novel) and the levelling of artistic media, which in Murnau's days were still fixed within a cultural and ontological hierarchy. This was demonstrated when Stoker's widow, Florence Balcombe, vetoed Murnau's unauthorized film adaptation in favour of a Broadway adaptation, for she not only exposed her desire financially to control and exploit her husband's heritage, but also the theatre's lingering artistic prestige. Her attempt to protect her husband's work also downplayed the extent to which it was already inscribed in a long-standing vampire tradition, with oral roots in folklore and beckoning further adaptations across media, as a way of guaranteeing the vampire motif's continuing dissemination.

However, none of these media can claim or establish ontological priority, not even Coppola's movie, through the use of a title which deceptively insists on the truthfulness of his adaptation or by adding a sequence that returns to the invention of cinema. Similarly, Merhige's 'documentary' movie, like Cooper and Schoedsack's *King Kong*, remains a fiction no matter how historically informed it may be. Even Stanislavskean acting or performance art, to take the two extremes, are always framed: temporally, architecturally, institutionally or by the audience. Finally, whereas Denham harked back to the immediacy of the live performance to step up Kong's spectacular effect, in Coppola's age the spectacular may have devolved more radically onto the cinema, even if his movie's costumes definitely display a theatrical opulence. It is as if the media keep infecting and preying on each other remediating our understanding through a complex intermediality. All of which goes to show how appropriate a movie on the making of *Nosferatu* proves to be to explore the interdependence of theatre and film in our media age.

MODULARITY AS A GUIDING PRINCIPLE OF THEATRICAL INTERMEDIALITY.
ME-DEA-EX: AN ACTUAL-VIRTUAL DIGITAL THEATRE PROJECT

Hadassa Shani

In this chapter, theoretical investigation into digital media and theatrical performance are investigated together. In her discussion of the *Me-Dea-Ex* project, the author puts forward modularity as a model for theatrical intermediality and presents a reflective commentary on the process. She argues that the model is a network of discrete modules, activated by the audience to create one pathway through the event, which takes the performance beyond the theatrical space. The complex network of hyperlinked modules required the audience to make free and associated mental links and, by looking at the subject matter in a non-linear way, to re-assess it. The author concludes with an assessment of the success and some of the problems associated with the attempt to integrate the actual with the virtual in theatrical performance, and in staging the technology and conceptual framework of the digital.

The neologism characterizing the world of digital visualization is not the product of new objects or items; on the contrary, it is the fruit of new connections created between existing objects and entities (Aronson 1999: 192).[1]

Me-Dea-Ex was an experimental theatrical project, which premièred at Israel's well-known and popular Fringe Festival held in the Old City of Acco (Acre) from 10-14 October, 2003 (www.MedeaEX.org). *Me-Dea-Ex* was an *actual-virtual* performance combined with *video-projection episodes*. It was *immersive/interactive* theatre, which employed the latest technologies in an actual performance in an attempt to integrate *the actual* with *the virtual* in new and meaningful ways. From its inception, the project sought to integrate the conceptual framework of the new media and use the potential of the digital for guiding thought processes, rather than simply relying on the use of new technology. Thus, of central concern to the creative process of the project was the question of *theatrical boundaries*. Specifically, it examined new theatrical connections constructed amongst the participants actually present in the theatrical space; between the various worlds that inhabited and comprised the extended and actual theatrical space; and the different adaptations based on the original play texts. Thus, it dealt with the means with which we can assimilate new media techniques and concepts in the medium of theatre in order to produce a *theatrical intermedial* work of art. In the modular structure of the *Me-Dea-Ex* theatrical *intermediality* is located as a conceptual framework for the performance.

When introducing perspectives originating in the new media to the world of theatre, it is not surprising that the connections captured by artist-spectator, spectator-artistic work, artistic work-artist dyads are expressed differently. Applying the spirit of neologism to a performance project allowed the team to create new types of connections between existing stage adaptations and other art forms based on the same original theatrical work and, as this chapter will demonstrate, the new connections flowed from *free and associative links* rather than from *linearity and hierarchy*. This approach encouraged perception of all the art works related to the same original as a complex whole, and thus allowed for a 're-reading' of the opus.[2]

The project was based on a free adaptation of the classical tragedy *Medea* by Euripides (431 BC) and included parts of Euripides' original text, as well as parts of the original story that were transformed into a new version, in Hebrew, Arabic and English. Additional texts were taken from Seneca's *Medea* (First half of the first century AD) and Heiner Muller's *Medeaspiel* (1974). Extant adaptations of the original tragedy in various art forms were presented or re-presented in a variety of ways. Working as the dramaturge, I brought to the project my own professional practice in theatre and film, specialist knowledge of the *Medea* texts and the theoretical knowledge of an academic working in the field. Neora (.com), a web specialist, artist, writer and cyber-culture lecturer was the initiator, adapter, and 'soul' of the project. As a computer professional, Neora was designer and activator of the virtual worlds. The main – and only 'flesh and blood' – actress was Khaula Elhaj-Dibsi, an Israeli Arab.

Central to the construction and reception of the project was the concept of *hyperlink*, which is integrally connected to *hypermedia*:

> Hypermedia is another popular new media structure, which is conceptually close to branching-type [...] In hypermedia, the multimedia elements making a document are connected through hyperlinks. Thus, the elements and the structure are independent of each other – rather than hard-wired together, as in traditional media (Manovich 2001: 38).[3]

Surfing and navigating among websites is a phenomenon belonging to the information age, the digital media and the virtual age. Navigation along a pathway is derived through *association*, and the pathway is built according to the *neologism* of the *virtual-digital age*, i.e., along a *network of hyperlinks*. These different types of links simulate the human mind in many ways and they resemble trails activated mainly by association.[4] It was this type of navigation that became the theoretical base of the *Me-Dea-Ex* project and available within the framework at a variety of levels. *Hyperlinks* were available between: *Classical tragedy* and its adaptations in a variety of art forms; theatre as an *art form* based on the parallel existence of two worlds – the actual and the fictional, and between different *communication systems*, for example, the digital medium and video art; and the *cultural context* in which the original work was written - Greece of the fifth century BC, and *contemporary political-cultural contexts* – particularly the continuing conflict in the Middle East. The network of hyperlinks expanded the boundaries of the project along three different dimensions: the *textual*, the *medial* and the *socio-cultural*. I suggest that the manner in which the project attempted to implement the thinking behind digital visualization was expressed primarily in the application of *modularity*:

The modular model connects separate units by means of hyperlinks rather than on the conventional logic of cause and effect. These new connections are the result of the structural/technical process of the new media, the effect of which is to simulate the dynamics of the human mind, and give expression to the fact that ideas tend to connect themselves in a nonlinear path (Manovich 200: 30,41-42).

I shall argue also that the modular structure of hyperlinks, applied as an overall concept applicable at various levels in the project, created *Me-Dea-Ex* as a paradigm of *virtual theatre* because of the way it implemented a *process of remediation*. The project remediated other works of art; it remediated similar cultural instances; and it remediated several media through the medium of theatre itself. *Remediation* is a fundamental characteristic of virtual theatre:

> [...] virtual theatre is therefore subject to a process not only of mediation but of remediation. This implies the use of a certain degree of intertextuality and metatextuality, but also of intermediality and metamediality. [...]Hence, virtual theatre is a form of theatre which remediates – which means that it is always also about media (Giannachi 2004: 5).

The *Me-Dea-Ex* project

THE PLOT: CONTINUITY

Medea, a Palestinian, is from an established family in her village. She was a teenager when she met Jason, the son of a German Jewish religious couple who had immigrated to the US. At the age of 18 Jason decided to come to Israel and serve in the Israeli army. After Jason arrives at Medea's village during the war, they fall in love. Medea's hot-blooded brother finds out about their relationship. He determines to kill Jason. Medea, terrified of losing her beloved, frames her brother and, in effect, hands him over to the Israeli authorities, who imprison him. They destroy her family's house, forcing them to move to a refugee camp. The situation becomes unbearable and dangerous for both Medea and Jason, each in their "homeland exile". The couple leave for the United States of America to get married and both study there. Medea becomes a computer specialist, Jason a successful financial expert and broker on the New York Stock Exchange. They have two sons. When Jason gets involved in a financial scandal, they escape the American authorities by returning to Israel.

Jason succeeds in arranging their papers for the trip with the help of the Israeli General Creon. Medea, torn between her life with Jason in Israel and her family, visits the refugee camp and struggles with the paperwork that will allow her to become a fully-fledged Israeli citizen. In the meantime, Jason has an affair with a young Israeli girl, Glauce, Creon's daughter. When the second Intifada starts, Medea is found back at the refugee camp with their children; Jason as if helpless to respond to her plight, stays in central Israel. Jason eventually divorces Medea and marries Glauce. Medea's anger over Israeli oppression and her frustration at being a betrayed woman, convince her to send her boys on a suicide mission as shahids (martyrs). As a result of their attack, 13 people are killed, including Creon and his daughter.

EXPOSURE OF THE PLOT

The actual performance indicated the main themes of the story through texts from Euripides, Seneca and Muller, chosen, adapted and organized as *nine units*: Introduction, Shahids, Love, Sacrifice, Exile, Betrayal, Eviction, Collision and Chaos. The plot was never explicitly stated in the text itself; it was revealed only through information shown on screens; related by the chorus, or exposed as a *meta-story* between the units. The units could be organized in a different order at each performance depending on how the audience voted. At the end of each scene, the spectators were asked to choose the next scene to be presented to them from the remaining scenes. Thus, as a rule, all the spectators, those actually in the hall and those who entered as avatars within the virtual world, together chose, on the basis of the majority, the order of the events and, as a result, their meanings. The following selection tree illustrates one of the several optional possibilities:

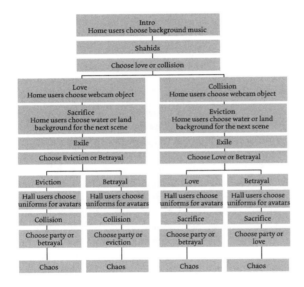

Moving from one unit to another changed the scene's *skin*. Slight changes in design, lighting, sound, music, graphs and charts were introduced on the screens. Medea attempted to convince the spectators, virtual and actually physically present, to help her jump to *previous screens* in an attempt to *debug* her past. The idea expressed here was that in this *hypertextual* 3D environment, Medea could re-design / re-engineer her identity and her position in the myth, although she needed the cooperation of other participants to do it. Occasionally, the spectators chose texts delivered by the chorus among the options offered to them, and these were displayed on the screen; some texts were repetitive, others contradictory. The spectators could choose until the programmed timeout. Home users could also add their own texts. These texts were added gradually to the *databank* of chorus parts. Several *Information Screens*, sign objects, displayed in the 3D environment delivered the following information: continuous subtitles of all the languages being used (current language was highlighted); graphs and charts showing the options chosen by the virtual audience; texts of alternative adaptations and productions of *Medea* as well as chat texts between users.

THE PROJECT'S UNIVERSE

Me-Dea-Ex was a 3D universe projected onto the 360 degree environment surrounding the audience. The spectators sat on swivel chairs that allowed them to interact with their 360 degree environment, and this fostered the illusion of being part of the virtual space, and vice versa. There was no actual lighting or decorated set – the set was controlled through the virtual world of screens with the projector lights dominating. The design concept of the projected 3D universe was that of a classic play, but also of computer art and games; one of the units was designed like the New York Stock Exchange. The multi-changing aspects of the project were offered to the spectators via each of its *units*, or *modules*. The choice of the modules and their integral medial aspects led the spectators to new spheres of action and place. The medial aspects of individual modules included video films and pictures of different productions of *Medea*, flashes of citations that frequently appear in the virtual world, data about terrorist acts and murdered children, among others. Sometimes, the modules included images of the audience, or of the *avatars*, sitting in the *virtual space*, and who became an inseparable part of the production for the spectators in the actual theatrical space. All spectators could choose between the options they selected or, alternatively, they could adhere to the *actual-virtual events* dominating the scene. Each module expanded the meaning of the events and projected the spectator to new spheres and associations, opening the door to new types of experience.

Medea was the only live character. She sat in a wheelchair throughout the **211** performance. The wheelchair had a control panel from which she acted, as if she was activating the projectors and the 3D universe, and this resembled her mind, her history, her myth. The choice of the wheelchair is explained by Neora:

> On the most concrete level, that is the office chair on which I sit day and night opposite the computer. Medea is pushed into corner and can do nothing: She is in exile from her village, from her family, from her country, from her home – it is as if she functions from a chair for the disabled (Shochat 2003: http://medeaex.org/haaretz_eng.html, last accessed 28-09-2005)."

Figure 47
Khaula Elhaj-Dibsi (Medea) on her wheelchair,
with its control panel.

Figure 48
Medea and spectators during a performance, the set is controlled through the screens with the projector
lights dominating.

Jason was represented as a 3D avatar. He was a pre-programmed 'bot' who spoke via
pre-recorded sound files, as opposed to Medea, whose speech was live, and unlike the

chorus, who spoke with synthesized voices (text to speech). The chorus was a virtual audience, grey male and female avatars who declaimed texts belonging to Euripides' original texts for Creon, Igeus and the Nurse. Movement around the 3D environment was reserved for home users. The inter-action tools were cellular/SMS, used by the live audiences in order to interact with the performance (vote, etc.).

Modularity as a guiding principle

Manovich refers to modularity as the "fractal structure of new media" (Manovich 2001:30). The concept of modularity, in its broadest sense, indicates the organization of elements according to loose or unstable connections, in which all of the elements continue to maintain their separate identities. This type of organization enables reconstruction through shifts in direction, often by jumping or skipping over different sections of a complex structure. The main characteristics of modularity are: multiplicity of options, independent units, free associations, personal choice, continual change, the opening of unanticipated horizons, and accessibility.

A theatrical approach based on modularity does not translate into multiple focal points or into parallel, simultaneously occurring events. Instead, it becomes one single pathway, which is the result of a continuous process of choosing between options. In *Me-Dea-Ex* movement along the pathway was accompanied by various hyperlinks that could be used to expand the action's context and meaning. Each choice, as a defined event within the greater modular network, led to new territories unfolding untold possibilities. At almost every point of the path, a series of connotative or associational leaps, fortuitous or semi-controlled were planted as an environment net and became accessible to users. These leaps, appearing in a variety of ways, helped users to arrive at an altogether different (from each other) experience.

Thus, a key feature of modularity in performance was the inability to anticipate more than a few steps in advance, or to exercise pre-planned control over this elaborate structure. Moreover, it was impossible to characterize a homogenous experience, despite the fact that all participants move along the same pathway chosen by the majority.

The modular model was expressed along different dimensions: in the way in which several extracts from different versions of *Medea* were combined together to establish the *Me-Dea-Ex* text; in the changeable order of events in each and every performance as a result of the audience majority vote; and in the selection made by any spectator to concentrate on different items in the dynamic *environment net*. The complex structure allowed development along the *three dimensions*: the textual, the medial and the socio-cultural. Shochat in her criticism summarized the experience in these words:

> The Acre festival show is a meeting between ancient Greece and the modern world, between the virtual world and live theatre, and between Jews and Arabs (Shochat 2003).

Thus, a project constructed on a network of hyperlinks between different productions is a project that operates within a domain of theatre where every production retains its unique identity, its originality, at the same time as functioning as a part of a whole. The result of this structure was that instead of progressive action and reaction we received feedback and inter-active inter-action between the different elements within the module.

It is important to note also that *the originals* and *the adaptations* were all individual factors in a global network *in the same normative position*; but together they formed the entity *Me-Dea-Ex*. A notable feature of the modular structure was that instead of a linear causal relationship of one explicit socio-political-cultural event, all the socio-political-cultural events were placed within a structure of *modular-associative relationships*. The modular structure revealed a network of instances displaying similar treachery, terror and repression, while avoiding the vitiating power of one explicit, extreme case.

I believe that meaningful and effective political theatrical work is a work that does not place its referent solely in the generalized context of human nature as such, but stages the complexity of the problem dealt with by the work, and emphasizes its individual character in an inclusive socio-cultural plan. Only a work such as this can make a significant outcry; and a work such as this can be achieved by adopting the modular-model.

Expansion of textual boundaries

Treating a variety of adaptations and stage interpretations of the same original theatrical work as a modular network of hyperlinks offers an alternative to the model of linear, normative, hierarchical control of the relationships woven between the original and its adaptations. Although this capability already exists conceptually, in practice the original on which the adaptations are based often has a preferential status. We refer to it, compare it, and we do consider it as the model. In contrast, a network that includes the original and its various adaptations is rooted in collaboration, a value that other technological cultures repress (Landow and Delany 1991, 2001: 215-216). Thus, the modular approach alters our attitude toward the authority that originality exercises over us.

In *Me-Dea-Ex* a variety of *Medea* versions were included, directly or vicariously, by incorporating parts of their texts in the work in the form of *quotations* and *links* either relevant to them, or to any direct or vicarious mention of them. The works from which verbal text were taken included *Medea* by Euripides, *Medea* by Seneca, and *Medeaspiel* (Medea-play) an adaptation by Heiner Muller. Other works were taken from theatre, film, television, dance, opera, and prose: Two cinematic adaptations of the tragedy *Medea: A Dream of Passion* (1978) by Jules Dassin, and *Medea* (1970) by P.P. Pasolini: A television production of *Medea* (1987) by Lars Von Trier: An Israeli opera *Medea* (1997) by Zipi Fleischer with a libretto by Rivkah Kashtan: A ballet *The Cave of the Heart (Serpent Heart)* (1946) by Martha Graham based upon the *Medea* tragedy: The painting: *Medea about to kill her children* (1838) (*Medea Furieuse*) by Eugene Delacroix: Prose works: *Medea: a modern retelling* (1998) by Christa Wolf, and *Modern Medea* by Steven Weisenburger (1998). These works appeared as part of the world of *Me-Dea-Ex* through either being used to construct the virtual world, or through introducing various themes that connected directly, or indirectly into the *Me-Dea-Ex* world. Together they constructed a network of themes, which operated as a framework of available associations surrounding the individual case of Medea's story.

The modular network allowed every spectator to experience the story woven in the project in a unique way and from a different perspective. For example, in his film *Medea* Pasolini shows the sacrificial murder of a youth as an offering to the fertility god of the earth. The association offered on the visual level by the scene, together with its intermedial connotations was that of the land – the territory – as the core of the Middle East conflict. The associations offered by the intermedial module projected the spectator into the connotations implied by the Israeli and Palestinian mothers, who give birth and send their children to the army to be bombed, to become cannon fodder and sacrificed for the sake of the concept of 'nationalism'. The *anthropological aspect* of Pasolini's work foregrounded Medea's alien status in Corinth and the contradiction between Colchis and Corinth: the old and the new, the sacred and the profane, the male and the female, the same and the other, and these served as hyperlinks for the elements in the project's specific story of an Israeli, a Palestinian and an American. This combination is depicted also in the character of the space, which shifts from the ancient (Greece) to the local (Middle East) to the foreign (the New York Stock Exchange).

Duality as a concept in Delacroix's *Medea about to kill her children* (1838) — the mother as protector and the mother as executioner — was expressed via connections with the combined image of Palestinian and Israeli mothers who bear children in a world where they become sacrifices to a cause (shahid'im) or sacrificial victims of terrorist attacks. The source of the light in Delacroix's painting, which is also the possible source of salvation as well as the entrance to the cave from which Medea's pursuers will erupt, enriched the duality that permeated the entire project as an exchange of identities — betrayer and betrayed, one who threatened and one who is threatened.

The epilogue to the opera *Medea*, composed by Zipi Fleischer with a libretto by Rivkah Kashtan, appealed to Euripides, who supposedly sat amongst the audience in order to revise his tale – to include a rumour that it was the Corinthians who actually committed the act of killing Medea's children. This element was referred to within the larger context of the electronic media and its role in the conflict, as well as by the constantly repeated attempts of Medea/Khaula Elhaj to re-design Euripides' plot of the myth.

Re-design was seen also in the module based on Martha Graham's *Cave of the Heart*, where Medea and Jason's love was portrayed as a pure love story, free of any political or other innuendos. The 'wireless' construction in the *Me-Dea-Ex* love unit, which was designed quite differently from any other unit, brought the precision of movement and the power inherent in the story's purification through Graham's choreography. Photographs of a performance of Graham's work found a place in the virtual environment and transformed that space into an actual environment. Similarly, the different forms of infanticide enacted in Dassin's *A Dream of Passion* dealt with a variety of Medea characters, each with its own individual story, each with its own particular form of child-killing, whether literally as abortion, or symbolically as choosing to remain barren.

This *duplication*, like other themes and connections found within Dassin's film, dominated the *Me-Dea-Ex* production. Newscasts that reported the explosion that had caused the deaths of dozens of children were heard repeatedly in several of the project's modules. In effect, the broadcasts opened up the performance: children of various nationalities; children who happened to be at the site of the attack; and those who bear the cross of death on their shoulders penetrated the *Me-Dea-Ex*. A mother who kills her children in order to keep them from entering a world with no hope – a dominant aspect of Steven Weisenburger's *Modern Medea* (1998) – was chosen to enrich the meaning of the conflict at the heart of the project. Strangeness, rejection of the 'other', the mother who gives as well as takes life were elements stressed in the various adaptations, and they appeared as connotative and associative connections at various levels of this multi-levelled production.

Thus, textual boundaries were expanded through the combination of verbal and visual versions of the *Medea* story, with the effect that the expansion created an entire world that could be used as an informative, associative and connective network. The new and old media modular *Medea* network was presented as part of an individual, local event and navigation. The network allowed enrichment of the individual narrative's context on the one hand, and freedom from the linear adjustment of this to other texts on the other. Some of the textual expansion was not necessarily immanent in the course of the events themselves, but rather in the numerous and changing possibilities flowing within the *virtual world*. The spectator was not required to observe or to choose them, only to select or ignore them as desired.

Despite the multiplicity of texts and hyperlinks, the story was presented as a single, coherent unit through the continuity of the *meta-story*, which was explored *in-between* the modules and evolved through the identities of the characters, which were consistently characterized throughout the project. Expansion of the textual boundaries enhanced the project's coherence, and it allowed the framing story of *Medea*, the computer professional, and Jason, the Jewish American Israeli, to unify all the components into a whole.

Expansion of medial boundaries

This was a key feature. The integration of actual space and virtual environment; between the human and recorded voice and 'text to speech'; the integration between a traditional theatrical performance with a live actor revealing a character before an actual audience found in the same physical space, and a situation transmitted between a live actor and an avatar; the integration of a spectator actually present and the representation of a spectator by means of a virtual image-avatar; the integration of a digital/virtual world and video projections. These represent only a smattering of the aspects that expanded the medial boundaries of the *Me-Dea-Ex* project.

The various inter-active levels that existed in the project symbolized, in particular, the transgression of medial boundaries. Nevertheless, the range of inter-actions available foregrounds the argument related to the expansion of medial boundaries: for we are not discussing a *multimedial* work but rather a *theatrical intermedial work* remediating other media. I use the term *remediation* according to Bolter and Grusin, who expanded McLuhan's statement that the content of any medium is always another medium, and who argue that:

> McLuhan was not thinking of simple repurposing, but perhaps of a more complex kind of borrowing in which one medium is itself incorporated or represented in another medium (Bolter and Grusin 2001: 45).

In this sense, they define remediation as: "the representation of one medium in another" (ibid.).[5]

It is not the function of this chapter to establish the credentials of theatre as medium. That function is undertaken by Peter Boenisch elsewhere in this book, so I shall not repeat his arguments. Rather, I concentrate here on the digital / theatrical relationship, with the tacit assumption that both are accepted as media. The position that I shall now argue is that in terms of categorization, the *Me-Dea-Ex* project clearly belongs to the theatrical medium rather than the domain of multimedia.

Every medium channels the spectator's reception of the phenomenon (event) transmitted in a different and distinctive way autonomous of the accepted, deductive logic applied when we interpret ordinary phenomena in everyday life. However, in the *Me-Dea-Ex*, once the separate modes of communication are examined we can see that the project is not controlled by the digital-virtual as a distinct medium. Comparison of the virtual world with the fictional theatrical world regarding their relationship to the actual world reflects this argument (Shani and Belkin 2002: 67). Relations between the virtual domain and reality, and between the fictional theatrical world and the actual world, are substantially different. The illusion of a virtual reality is not the same as the illusion created in the theatre, and therein is the differentiation between the *two aesthetic bases*.

On the operative level, as far as the characterization of *space* is concerned, virtual thinking constitutes an attempt to bring users into the virtual world: 'To be there' (as in the theatre), but there alone (different from the theatre). In theatrical terms, the illusion of reality in a virtual world is a delusion – complete oblivion versus reality. In contrast, the world of theatre rests on logical links, many of which do not meet the logical criteria for deciphering the phenomena of reality. (e.g., the actor talking in an aside to the audience while the other actors on stage 'do not hear'; saying 'moon' only to observe stage time turning into night). However, the fundamental requirement for *theatrical aesthetics* is the co-existence – parallel and simultaneous – of both worlds: the fictional and the actual, the here and now, and the there and then, while the relations between them remain flexible and constantly varying. The viewer is required to enter a state of illusion, not delusion.

The literal, primary translation of the shared presence of both worlds is their separate existence in one single space, no matter how divided. To admit the viewer into the fictional space, not just as a matter of perception but in actual fact, while both worlds continue to co-exist in parallel and simultaneously is the primary and necessary pre-condition for a theatre resembling the virtual world. This is accomplished in the project through the way that it immerses the actual with the digital. Thus, *Me-Dea-Ex* is a *theatrical intermedial work* in which decoding principles from digital media and video art are assimilated into the theatrical domain and function under the dominance of theatre as a medium.

It is appropriate here to note that this approach to the term *intermediality* meets Balme's third definition of intermediality as cited in Boenisch (2003: 35) and by Chapple and Kattenbelt in the introductory chapter of this book. In the *Me-Dea-Ex* project, the actual spectators were invited to connect to the virtual environment only through participation in the events occurring in the space where they are found. The fictional world created throughout the project is a continuous world, crossing the boundaries between the actual and the virtual. Khaula (the actress) does not represent Khaula (the actress) in an actual world and Medea in a virtual world. She is both Khaula and Medea and in both worlds at the same time. The fictional world that operates concurrently with the actual world in the theatrical situation, whose simultaneous presence is responsible for the special type of communication distinguishing theatre as a medium, is encountered in the project as well. Here it is observed as a fluid world, existing parallel to the actual world and in response to that world.

Expansion of the medial boundaries, that is, use of the digital medium and video art served the actual theatrical inter-action. They expanded the existing situational possibilities of the here and now, but they did not alter the dominance of theatrical communication. Nonetheless, the theatrical spectators not only observed a space replete with advanced technology spread out before them on the *Me-Dea-Ex* stage, but they themselves became involved as part of the virtual-digital environment.

This phenomenon was inherent in the attempt to create a theatrical experience different from traditional theatre, an experience nourished by aspects of the new media, aspects whose essence rests on navigation through a network composed of dynamic, changing features. At any given moment, the fictional and actual domains co-existed; at any given moment, inter-actions were initiated between those who initiated actions and those who observed and consequently interpreted those actions. In the *Me-Dea-Ex* context, it was the dynamism of the events that replaced the dominance of each separate component in turn.

218

Expansion of cultural boundaries

Broadening cultural boundaries was one of the main purposes of the *Me-Dea-Ex* project. Hence, the project related to the Arab-Israeli conflict in the Middle East by introducing a Jewish-Israeli identity facet to an Arab-Israeli identity. However, the project also placed the Middle East conflict into a broader inter-cultural context of aggression, global terrorism and the dominant materialism of the new world order. It is important to note, however, that the broader context did not function as an integral part of the story; rather, it was there as an inter-active component waiting to become part of the environment.

The tragedy *Medea* encapsulates important universal issues, amongst which are: the faceless identity of the foreign, the presentation of the self when confronting the other, 'child sacrifice', the materialistic inclination inherent in human nature, and the effect of unrestrained aggression as well as arrogance. All these and other issues served the project's socio-political orientation. Some of these separate aspects of the original work have already been alluded to in various productions of *Medea*. By now it is clear that referring directly to the Middle East via the ancient precedent placed the location into the broader context of the history of human nature. However, placing local events into the context of global terrorism acted as a boomerang for the creators of the project: for it presented the local conflict as just another case among many in the history of human nature and which are currently found in other countries – as reflected in various works of art alluding to similar events. So, the general context served to explain the particular phenomenon by its characterization as integral to the human condition, or as rationalized by the argument that there have always been wars, hostility and tyrannical rulers and always will be. This represented problematical reasoning that weakened the protest aroused by the insufferable socio-political situation, which inspired the project. While mitigating the protest voice itself, it undermined its effectiveness.

The dichotomy was resolved by establishing a *global network of associations and connotations*. Hyperlink connections introduced dialectic rather than linear-logical synthesis of the relationships holding between its parts. It invited recognition of a broader context for the local political issue, while permitting the formation of a network about the particular case. The *global network of associations and connotation* enabled every spectator to select the most pertinent self-connections and to permeate the Middle East case with numerous associations. Although the meanings associated with the specific Middle East case were deepened by connotations found in similar cases, those same meanings avoided the loss of significance that generally follows logical and linear comparison. The placement of an individual event in isolation, yet in in-direct relation to additional, similar events, guaranteed that the event was perceived in all its force, while, at the same time, the additional network of associations broadened its implications.

Applying a modular perspective, originating in digital-computer culture and its assimilation into a theatrical work, enabled not only the combination of several art forms and texts, but, more specifically, many cultures in one work. On the one hand the project is made up of *fragments* and thus has an important characteristic of virtual theatre:

> Virtual theatre, like the reality it allows us to view, is made of fragments, segments of information. In Deleuze and Guattari's view, life is 'spatially and socially segmented'. Virtual theatre too reflects and exposes this signification (Giannachi 2004: 11).

On the other hand this process operated within one well-defined domain of meaning, *the theatrical*. This duality honed the project's unique theme. Moreover, *Me-Dea-Ex*, by incorporating texts from numerous adaptations of the original tragedy, with the help of various media, and by connecting an apparently never-ending stream of socio-political and cultural cases, intensified as well as expanded the explicit case's boundaries. This enabled an incisive analysis of the intolerable situation in the Middle East: the individual case depicted in the project. This holds true, in particular, when referring to the remediation characteristic of the project: its remediation of other media, texts, works of art. As noted by Bolter and Grusin, the word remediation derives ultimately from the Latin remedi –"to heal, to restore to health" (Bolter and Grusin 2001: 59). "Remediation, [they claim] is *reform* in the sense that media reform reality itself" (ibid., 61).

I claim that replication of the case on various levels by means of different textual connections, art forms and cultural meanings invites authenticity. The multiplicity of media – *hypermediacy* – returns us to reality, to the authentic, the actual. Hence, the replication of the individual case – that is, extension of the event's boundaries by means of a diversified modular structure – made it possible to rage against the individual case on the one hand and still arrive at its universal truth on the other.

Post-performance reflections

Despite the power and potential inherent in this innovative project, many of its aspects were unrealized in its first performances. A gap still existed between its potential and its actual. The technical problems that accompany projects of this sort, and probably will continue to be a factor in future productions of virtual theatre, caused frequent disturbances during the performance, to the point of preventing execution of several of the features at the project's foundations. Moreover, today's theatre audience is not accustomed to taking the initiative or responsibility for its theatrical experiences. The activism created by audience participation motivated by the actors within a stage scene, something I would term *dynamic inter-action*, is quite different from the inter-activity at the core of the inter-actions where spectators are not only activated by the work's artists, but they are also required to take responsibility for their experience and to take the initiative.[6]

The *Me-Dea-Ex* project invited the most preliminary level of inter-activity but failed to meet the creator's expectations. Perhaps the main barrier to the project's fulfilment was the non-linear connections by means of which the story unfolded. The evolution of the events in an unanticipated manner, entailing unfamiliar connections that were themselves not constructed according to the building blocks of cause and effect, made it difficult for the spectators to grasp the performance's complexity, and eventually relate the components to form a uniform whole. One response repeatedly heard was that the domain of *Me-Dea-Ex* offered more than the spectator could comprehend. This frustrated, rather than inspired participation in a complex, rewarding experience. However, I will conclude by saying that the performance began with a death, murder and terrorist attacks and ended in chaos. There is no logical order within this maze but only the distant connections between 'sampling' in the digital spirit, with high resolution between the samples and without the possibility of simple 'quantification' of the data can serve us the way that digitization can.[7] This implies a degree of complexity that can be uncomfortable:

True [claims Neo] we live in a confusing era and only those who are willing to accept this confusion can feel comfortable in it (Shohat 2003).

Finally, in its entirety, with all its dynamism and complexity, its hyperlinks and the way it assimilated the new media into the domain of the theatre and established a theatrical intermedial work, the *Me-Dea-Ex* modular structure contained more power than all the familiar connections we know and with which are familiar, such as: love-disloyalty-revenge; hostility-war-conquest; originality-adaptation; theatre and the new media-multimedia.

Notes

1 Arnold Aronson applies the concept neologism in connection with the perception of cyberspace.

2 It is interesting to compare this process to Jonathan Miller's thoughts on the afterlife of an artwork (Miller 1986: 23).

3 For those who wish to read further, an elaborate description and implementation of a particular case of Hyperlinks and Hypertext, is given by Charles Deemer at: http://www.uv.es/~fores/programa/deemer_essay.html.

4 On the trails of the human mind and their connections to the notion of these different types of links, see Vannevar Bush: [...] "with one item in its grasp, it snaps instantly to the next that is suggested by the association of thoughts, in accordance with some intricate web of trails carried by the cells of the brain" (1945, 2001: 149).

5 On this subject, see also Giannachi 2004: 4.

6 On the different types of interactions found in theatrical events, and the role of initiative as the main factor of the division, see (Shani 2004: 114).

7 "Digitization consists of two steps: sampling and quantization. First, data is sampled, most often at regular intervals [...] The frequency of sampling is referred to as resolution. Sampling turns continuous data into discrete data" (Manovich 2001: 28).

HAMLET AND THE VIRTUAL STAGE:
HERBERT FRITSCH'S PROJECT *HAMLET_X*

Birgit Wiens

Intermediality in theatre and internet art is discussed in this chapter through a critical analysis of *hamlet_X* – a long-term research project by Berlin-based actor and multimedia artist Herbert Fritsch. The central question driving the project is whether it is possible to locate Shakespeare's *Hamlet* in an intermedial dramaturgy, using the tools, language and narrative structure of digital culture. Fritsch's *hamlet_X* employs theatre, video and animated film, to transform the themes of *Hamlet* into a non-linear narration of multiple identities, electronic masks and fakes. The artist's attitude toward the media is a playful but critical one: Hamlet, with the hesitations and doubts for which he is famous, turns into a sort of computer virus. Contextualising the project within the avant-garde aesthetics of the Volksbuehne theatre, the author suggests that it can best be interpreted from the position of theatre as a hypermedium, and argues that *hamlet_X* is centrally concerned with the strategies of intermediality: exploring the energy *in-between* the different media.

Rescuing Hamlet

For me, electronics have always been connected to storytelling. Maybe because storytelling began when people used to sit around fires [...] Electronics are modern fires.
(Laurie Anderson in McKenzie 1997)[1]

It will not be easy to rescue the theatre into the third millennium. Particularly considering all other problems on the planet (Carl Hegemann 2003)[2]

hamlet_X is an ongoing artistic research project conceived by the German actor and multimedia artist, Herbert Fritsch and based in the Volksbuehne theatre complex at the Rosa Luxemburg Platz in Berlin. The Volksbuehne is one of Germany's most renowned playhouses, which became famous for its radical aesthetics during the nineties and, more recently, through its special interest in intermedial experiments.

When starting the project in 1998, Fritsch "felt he was in a crisis with theatre and theatrical modes of acting and representing stories".[3] This feeling was strong enough for him to leave the proscenium stage and to begin a systematic exploration of the artistic potential of the internet. To accompany him on his trip he chose Shakespeare's Prince Hamlet. To Fritsch, Hamlet is not only the iconic figure of European theatre but, according to Fritsch's reading of the Shakespearean tragedy, the prince lived in a fundamental dilemma that perfectly reflects the digital condition: 'To be, or not to be', (*Hamlet* III. 1, 56) which Fritsch related to the basic *digital code*: 0 and 1. Although at first sight this appears to be a strange analogy, a closer look reveals that it is more than just a joke. The attempt to bring Hamlet onto a *virtual stage* meant dealing with the complex theatrical structure of the play, and with the fact that Hamlet never really decides between 'to be or not to be'. Despite the appeal of the analogy, the way in which Shakespeare's Hamlet moves, particularly in performance but also in the play's written text *between* the two options, the way his doubts, hesitations and avoidances are acted out, do not appear initially to fit easily within a medium that only offers the binary o/1 coding. Therefore, the research question became whether Hamlet could be communicated in the digital. From the very beginning, it was clear that in attempting to answer this question, Fritsch was engaging with the larger question that had caused him to quit the proscenium theatre, which was whether it was possible to rescue *Hamlet* from a cultural context dominated by the *written word* and move him into *modern media culture*.

A central question that the project raised for the Volksbuehne was how to translate *theatre language* into the *language of hypertext* so that Hamlet could be performed in the mode of *Internet performance*. The research project that has developed over the last five years and gained wide attention in Germany is an *intermedial project* involving theatre and media research, and inevitably, intermedial projects cross over financial as well as aesthetic boundaries. This necessitates never-ending complicated footwork and hampers the work on it immensely. Acquiring financial support for intermedial projects appears to be quite a problem in Germany. Most theatre companies have a web site for advertisement and public relation purposes, but do not really care about the digital medium as a platform for artistic experiments. Similarly, museums and media art festivals tend to have their main focus on internet and/or digital art, but suffer collective amnesia when it comes to inviting artists from the field of theatre, dance or performance art as part of their shows. The rhetoric of internet art is of an interdisciplinary field, but this is not necessarily implemented in practice. In Germany, this may be because of the separate traditions of theoretical investigation. Some media theoreticians, for example, Berlin-based journalist and author Tilman Baumgaertel define internet art as an art form without historical preconditions and thus something entirely new:

> It has been repeatedly emphasised that the first and most important subject of Net Art is the Internet itself. Net Art has to do with its own medium; it deals with the specific conditions the Internet offers. [...] It is only sensible within its medium, the Internet (Baumgaertel 2001: 24-33).

By this definition, net art is a purely formalistic art, which uses the levels, codes, protocols and programs of the internet as its material. Baumgaertel identifies further characteristics of net art as "globality, connectivity, immateriality, inter-activity, egalitarianism and multimedia". Other theoreticians, namely those who come from the world of fine art, recognise the aesthetic prerequisites in art history, namely in the *object art* of the avant-garde since Marcel Duchamp, and in *video art* created by artists such as Nam June Paik.[4] Comparisons to theatre in this context are rare as net art is defined as a non-physical, "immaterial" art form.[5] However, it needs to be noticed here that in order to describe the ever-changing, dynamic interweaving of heterogeneous systems of symbols on the internet, and also the possibility of masquerading and simulating other identities in chat rooms, some writers tend to refer to the 'theatricality of the Internet' often in a more or less metaphoric manner (Goettlich 1998: 209-227). Only a very few theoreticians refer explicitly to theatre and the internet. Up until very recently the most cited theoretician was the programmer and software designer Brenda Laurel. In her book *Computers as Theatre* (1993) she charts a future of *interactive digital technologies* in which theatre plays as important a role as computer science.[6] For Laurel, theatre could serve as a model for designing virtual space because in both media one has to deal with the concepts of character and dramatic sequences of action, space and time. Although Laurel was criticized strongly for a too narrow concept of theatre based on 'old-fashioned' Aristotelian aesthetics (McKenzie 1994: 83-106) her insight may still prove her right in the end: the human-computer interface should not be dominated by the performative values of efficiency, quick decision-making and profitability. In *Virtual Theatres* (2004), Gabriella Giannachi provided an excellent explanation of theatre operating in digital and internet performance. Certainly, establishing an intermedial research project designed to assess *theatre performance* and *net art* and the *spaces in between* was very necessary at the time, and remains important today.

Enter *hamlet_X* - conceptual frameworks, intermediality and financial constraints

Fritsch was very clear about the intermedial status of the project through his definitions of what the project would not include. The project was not designed to *inter-connect* one or more different performance venues; nor did it aim to provide a *multimedia* version of *Hamlet*. Neither would it compose a digitally presented *lexical-didactical archive* that offered facts and information on *Hamlet*. Instead the *hamlet_X project* would reflected the variety of ways in which cultural heritage is *channelled* and *changed through different media*. The project description reads:

> Shakespeare's *Hamlet* is a wild fantasy that has been connected in various northern cultural societies. It was passed on by word-of-mouth, and always found new pictures and turns. It is a legend, a myth that demands to be continued onwards. It is a myth that cannot be satisfied with a few interpretations. Hamlet was presented by Shakespeare as a civilised myth, and after centuries of stiffening and fossilization, due to misunderstood loyalty to the text and intolerant exegesis. He wants to be ripped apart, chopped up into separate parts and spoken by many voices. The modern network offers this possibility. 225

hamlet_X attempts to develop an *electronic dramaturgy* to tell Hamlet's story by the means of the internet. Fritsch describes the piece as "a large electronic mosaic, a labyrinth of scenes, conversation reflexes, interviews, portrait of people" (Fritsch, ZKM 2003). He wants Hamlet to be transported into contemporary culture through the use of a variety of media: little films, short cuts, animations, comics, on-line games and chats. *hamlet_X* was created and launched as an intermedial project based on the non-linear narrative structure of the internet, with mediatized and live presentations. The intermediality of the project defined the cosmos of the artistic resources and the rhizome-like structure:

> My dream would be a huge exhibition with 111 rooms, and in every single one, a *Hamlet* film would be showing, or actors would be performing, or there would be an installation present. And the visitors could move between these 111 rooms infinitely, totally non-linear and full of unplanned linkages (Interview with Fritsch, *tip Berlin* 13/2003).

One of the first things that were completed as part of the project was some of short films, and quite a lot of the *hamlet_X* film material has already been shown. Some of them were presented in a walk-in interactive installation (Prater 2001); some in a lecture-demonstration (ZKM - Centre for Art and Media Karlsruhe 2003); and a series of the films has been released on three volumes of DVD (Volksbuehne films). There has been also a co-operation with television. The theatre channel of ZDF, Second German Television, showed interest in an artistic co-operation on the topic of interactive television, and invited Fritsch to design the concept and to create a television interface of the project together with them. On the 19th January 2003, at the conference *Future Theatre at ZKM Karlsruhe*, Wolfgang Bergmann, chief editor of the ZDF theatre channel, gave a lecture, *Operation Theatre Channel: Electronic Stage – Media Compound for the Theatre – Cultural Memory* in which he presented the following reasons for his interest in the project:

> *hamlet_X* is 100% that what we understand an electronic stage as being, it is a theatre project that can only take place in such a manner on the electronic stage, that exploits a new effect level for theatre material that can't be created on stage, that deals with its audience in a different, in a new way and that at the same time does not lose the age-old joy of playing in front of the world's mirror out of one's sight. The linking of the television interface with the Internet, though, is a well-tried means of bringing this new electronic stage to the audience and to give it a quite far-reaching window.

This augured well, and on an evening in June 2003 the Berlin Volksbuehne, the ZDF television and the internet were connected with one another, and the project seemed to achieving some of its aims through creating the *television interface* between the three media. However, the same evening showed also some of the problems and limits of the project. Having designed and implemented the *television interface*, ZDF, as partner and financer, reserved the right of choosing what was television-compatible from the material at hand and, perhaps inevitably, they chose the already completed films and invited many of the acting stars for interviews.

Figure 49
hamlet_X, scene from
the short film *The
Crown*, featuring
Martin Wuttke and
Margarita Broich.

The internet based interactive elements, such as the *karaoke game* and *chat* in which
the audience at home in front of the television or computer could participate, were
only given a fraction of the time during the three-hour broadcast. The audience in
the Prater room of the Volksbuehne could not participate at all, except for being the
audience, and in this case acting as extras. Everything that could not be calculated
within a financial budget, in particular all elements that go together to make up
inter-activity, were excluded from this variant of the *hamlet_X* project – because of
the dominant position of the public broadcasting television station.

We have to recognise that the Volksbuehne theatre itself cannot shoulder the project
on its own. Certainly, the project has struggled to gain financial support elsewhere.
Attempts to get support from film funds, for example, have been unsuccessful and
this appears to be partly because of the intermedial status of *hamlet_X*, because it is
not defined as a separate film project.

     The other element that may be an inhibiting factor in attracting sponsors
is the *trash aesthetic* of the project, which is part of the ethos of the Volksbuehne
theatre complex but which scares away a lot of people, especially those that are not
in sympathy with the policies of the Volksbuehne. The version on the Internet [www.
hamlet-x.de] is incomplete and will require more time, plus financial support before
it can be (re)launched in its conceptual version as an "electronic mosaic". However,
the idea of presenting Hamlet in the internet is still the guiding concept and main
aim of the project.

227

Hamlet and the Machine: Electronic Dramaturgy

> "Thine evermore, most dear lady, whilst this machine is to him, Hamlet…"
>
> *Hamlet* II. 2,122-123

Herbert Fritsch aimed to produce his intermedial *Hamlet* in the non-linear
narrative structure of the internet. He decided to use some of the central themes
of *Hamlet*; multiple identities; the search for identity; the experience that the

world is a delusion; as well as the aesthetic strategies inherent in the drama, for example, a play within a play; appearances of ghosts. From this, he produced discrete medial units that were tangentially associated with the themes and aesthetic strategies to expand and explode *Hamlet* into myriad pieces. Clearly, this is a similar structure as used in the *Me-dea-Ex* project described by Hadassa Shani in the previous chapter of this book. Fritsch's working process was as follows: The Shakespearean text of *Hamlet*, translated by Schlegel/Tieck, was split into 111 fragments, to which was added a few passages from the original English version. The short scenes work as quotes, paraphrases and commentaries on Shakespeare's *Hamlet*. Fritsch then started to interpret these text fragments in 111 short video films (each film has only a few minutes running time), and he invented 111 new characters from Hamlet's surroundings, such as a cook, a housekeeper, Ophelia's gynaecologist, a nurse and other characters who offer 'social commentaries' in filmed little interviews. No actor was to appear twice, and every video film was performed in a different genre, for example, as a thriller, a game show, a fashion show, or a commercial.

The video films used renowned German theatre actors in improvised scenes with a pop art / trash kind of aesthetic, which is very typical for the Volksbuehne and avant-garde theatre. Ironic reinterpretations of well-known images and iconic symbols from other media constantly keep popping up, for example, a distorted test pattern for the television station named *Helsingoer TV*. The video film clips, which were often electronically post-edited, are only one level of the project.

There are plans to use another 111 games, comics, animations and 3D props. In addition, there will be animated segments of texts, ciphers and pictograms of various types, which, when you click on them, produce sounds or inter-activate screen pages with articles from encyclopaedias that explain terms such as love or murder:

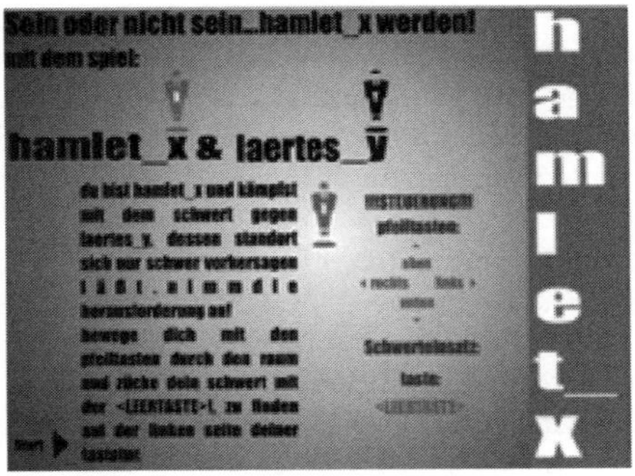

Figure 50
hamlet_X, screenshot from *Fight –*
an inter-active online game.

Figure 51
hamlet_X, screenshot from *Bloodhead: To be
or not to be* – an interactive online game.

Performing *hamlet_X*: Playing with different 'masks'

Fritsch was not interested in producing a new interpretation of *Hamlet* saying "There are already 69 *Hamlet* film interpretations". What he wanted to do was to put different film genres over the existing material – as in a *frame* or *filter* – within which the scene then has to function. Each and every film must stand on its own, but can also, in the overall rhizome structure of the project, be connected with the other elements.

This principle may best be explained here by using the example of *Tatort*, as in the 'Crime Scene' film. *Tatort* is a well-known German crime series that was filmed using the television actor detectives, Dominic Raacke and Boris Aljinovic. In the *hamlet_X* variant, the actors appeared in their detective roles as the Shakespearian characters of Rosencrantz and Guildenstern – but looking as they did in the television series, unshaven and with their leather jacket outfits. They request the File Polonius, interrogate the temporarily arrested Hamlet about where Polonius might be, and report to King Claudius using a telephone: "Where the dead body is bestow'd, my lord, we cannot get from him".

On the textual level, this *Tatort* uses a section of Shakespeare's text (Act IV. 2, 14; IV. 3, 15), and stays amazingly close to the original. However, on the image and action level of interpretation everything is alienated as it has been made to wholly serve the TV format of *Tatort*. It was filmed on the original TV set location with the directing instructions being: "Do what you always do!" A few cameramen with mini DVDs, usually a taboo for *Tatort*, filmed the scene and afterwards the material was edited using fast cuts. The idea of projecting the words of the old-fashioned language of the Schlegel/Tieck German translation onto the film screen is contrasted with a current television entertainment format, which created a friction amongst the audience, as well as curiosity to decode it all. Again, as in the Israeli actual/virtual project *Me-dea-Ex* we see the crucial role audience participation plays in intermedial projects.

Another instant of audience participation is the *chat* where the audience is invited to interact with the play but may only do so by using a theatrical mask. The *hamlet_X atomic chat* is probably the most advanced and interesting part of the project to date. Here, the lines of eleven characters from the play were split up into single words by a computer program, and then each word was transformed visually into numerous very short films:

> The analytical view of the text, its dissection into 'objects' (words) and its synthetic reorganization finds its pendant in object-oriented programming languages such as C++ or Java. The systematics of visual programming environments (MAXX/MSP, Visual Basic etc.) are also designed in the same way and remind one of children's toys such as Lego or Matador. This way of looking at things is due to our knowledge society. The methodology of dissecting and the claim that the individual parts are a complete building set of the 'whole' can be easily refuted by using the example of *hamlet_X*. The entire vocabulary of *Hamlet* is available; nevertheless, the probability that in the course of the chat even three lines of the original *Hamlet* text are recreated is quite low. The question is if Hamlet could possibly express himself clearly in such a chat (Rinnhofer 2003).[7]

In the chat, a user chooses a character and then can re-combine the *atomized* words from the play and build their own sentences with them. In addition, s/he appears behind the mask of a *virtual actor* and so, in a very real sense becomes a performer. One could say that chat works a bit like an interactive puppet theatre: by pulling electronic strings, the user can perform Laertes or Ophelia and create his or her own individual narrative by using their words.

Figure 52
Photo from the *hamlet_X* night at Prater, June 21, 2003 showing a user joining 'the chat'

Fritsch interprets the computer as a recombinant performer that allows the audience to interact with it[8] and the *chat* is a device to put this belief into place. When the *chat* was presented on the television night, it showed a few teething troubles: it was jerky and no chat to speak of took place so the audience was irritated. It may be that something, which is not immediately successful, has problems finding future funding and therefore cannot be completed. Nevertheless, it is in this part of the project that the theatricality of the internet and its far reaching artistic potentials is probably become most obvious. We should note that today, due to increasing technological competence *Hamlet_X* can already take further steps.

The theatrical framework

What is very clear is that in a carefully reflected dramaturgy, *hamlet_X* is not only directed towards the future, but also connects to theatre history. In Fritsch's project, the name of Hamlet was used as a sign of the seriousness of the artistic project through reference to the history of the play's performances and its theatrical-aesthetic discourse. Moreover, *Hamlet* is suitable for the project because of the non-linear elements of the original play text, with its multi-voiced, fragmentary and open nature, which at the time it was written—before it was polished by publishers and translators—was a working model for the actors. This comes close to the *materialwert* theory (material value), a concept coined by Bertolt Brecht, which was a driving force in Brecht's time and reappears again in the deconstructionist dramas of the so-called post-dramatic theatre of Hans-Thies Lehmann, and in productions of *Hamlet* by theatre directors such as Peter Brook, Robert Lepage or Robert Wilson (Lavender 2001). Clearly, *hamlet_X* is using similar techniques of post-dramatic theatre, but it tries to go beyond them. That the project has the prerequisites of a deconstructionist drama, as practised by Heiner Mueller, Einar Schleef and Frank Castorf is clear. In particular, Mueller's concept of theatre as a "dialogue with the dead" (Müller 1986: 138) and his *Hamletmachine* is an important reference point here. The approach is to view theatre as a medium of cultural memory – not in the sense of the restorative aspect of *Werktreue* (being loyal to the work) but rather to view it as the open process of a critical-dynamic memory function.[9] However, the new thing about *hamlet_X*, compared to Müller's *Hamletmaschine* is that Fritsch uses the new media of the Internet in order to hold a different dialogue with the ghosts and the dead.

From Shakespeare's *Hamlet* Fritsch uses as his motto: "O that this too too solid flesh would melt, Thaw and resolve itself into a dew". (Act I. 2, 129-130). He does this to remind everyone that he is attempting to free this canonical work from the ballast of the interpretations and images associated with it; and to keep the work, and the information we have about it, "fluid in the media". However, this is not always understood by the critical community:

> The accusation of dismantling classic texts, often made by cultural conservatives towards the Volksbuehne, definitely attains a new kind of quality here (Laudenbach in *Tip Berlin* 7/2001).

I suggest that Fritsch is not so much concerned with dismantling texts as with opening up a space for networked artistic performance, whose reference points are the cultural knowledge of *Hamlet*, the icon and paradigm of theatre. The variable '*X*' represents the multitude of valid or even rejected possibilities of interpretation.

It is necessary to talk briefly about the strong ironic perspective *hamlet_X* uses to achieve its aim of exhausting the possibilities of a hypertextual non-linear *Hamlet*. Through analogy, the final goal seems to be to comment playfully on the efficiency and profit-oriented communication strategies available via the internet. In particular, the quick search for information and the quick discovery of information. We can see this goal reflected in the fact that Fritsch wants the user to go astray: *hamlet_X* offers no legible information architecture, no navigation bars or buttons.

The key word here is *random navigation*, which leads the user into unforeseeable modules, fields and levels, or as Fritsch might put it, into the endless hypertext of a *digital Hamlet labyrinth*. By composing such a liquid, non-linear, rhizome-like structure, the project aims to inspire a never-ending process of playing with Hamlet. Just like a kaleidoscope, the chat, films, animations, and more are intended to provide new insights into the plot. Each person who moves through though the fragmented story takes their own pathway and makes the story their own:

> One can walk through it and lose oneself within it. Every possibility of finding an end to the story should be avoided at all costs (Fritsch ZKM 2003).

This project policy fits quite well to the project location within the Berlin Volksbuehne – a theatre that has a political-critical tradition and nowadays understands itself to be a type of research laboratory of experimental theatre. True, new approaches such as those of *hamlet_X* can cause friction with the acting taking place within the theatre complex, which has a core business that needs to be served, but its positioning within the Berlin Volksbuehne is appropriate.

The Volksbuehne and the future of *hamlet_X*

From its inception, *hamlet_X* was a local contextually driven phenomenon although it enters the global space. Fritsch has been for many years a member of the ensemble of the Volksbuehne, which is located at Rosa Luxemburg Platz in the former eastern part of Berlin. The house, which is still closely connected to the political theatre heritage of Erwin Piscator and Benno Besson, is open to new socio-cultural developments and this can be seen when looking at its program: www.volksbuehne.de.

In order to "save the theatre for the third millennium", Frank Castorf, the director of the theatre and Carl Hegemann, his chief dramaturge, proclaim their theatre to be a place for research on the "basic elements" of communication. In accordance with this artistic research policy, the theatre is pursuing the approach of having "different performance venues" which run parallel. There is the main stage (a theatre with 750 seats), the Red Lounge (a multi-purpose room where readings, concerts, discussions are held), the Green Lounge, the Starry Lobby and the Prater on Kastanienallee:

Figure 53
Photo of Prater exterior/Kastanienallee Berlin.

Additionally, they opened a digital film studio and a performance venue on the Internet. The Volksbuehne's "expanded conception of theatre" serves as an umbrella for the different activities of theatre, film, media performances, concerts and electronic music events and conferences. In this sense, the house defines itself as "a place of great events as well as small meetings". On these different levels, it is strongly connected to its audience: it understands itself as a community-raising institution, which invites the audience to share in their work and to interact with the theatre. As Hegemann puts it, the Volksbuehne is a "socio-cultural research establishment" [10]

The research done here is intermedial in nature in that it deals strongly with the dynamics and interplay between the different stages of the Volksbuehne and so is intermedial within the framework of an actual theatre location. Despite all the research, theatre remains the core business and reference point for each and every activity. The environs of the Volksbuehne and its community work as an interactive field, which takes into account "the increasing 'theatricalisation' of the entire society" (Hegemann ZKM 2003). It aims, according to its own self-definition, to systematically investigate the far-reaching effects of the media and changes in the media, in the sense of a culture's cognitive discursive convention.

The Volksbuehne has become very well known, and in a way, it is chic to belong to the Volksbuehne community. After reunification it was an important location and outlet for quite often loud communal reflection, aggression and irony. In short, the Volksbuehne attempts to find an attitude towards and take a stance on the social changes taking place in Germany. This is still the position nowadays in the era of business decline and radical economic change.

It is important to see *hamlet_X* as a long-term artistic research project in this context. It is easily recognizable as a Volksbuehne project through the foregrounding of its trash aesthetics and its subversive performance style and gesture, as well using many of the Volksbuehne actors. Completely in accordance with theatre policy, the research project playfully and critically enters the realms of the Internet, but always keeps theatre and performance as the central issue of the work. Although it exhausts all the conceivable possibilities of the hypertext, its strategy remains to be a theatre project, and it can only really be enjoyed and appropriately understood when one enjoys and understands theatre. One could say also that www.hamlet-x.de is one of the Volksbuehne's most fashionable additional performance venues, which has the effect of connecting its community with the house - and at the same time, it reaches an international audience. As *hamlet_X shows*, theatre has a lot to offer here as a reference point and model for artistic strategies in the third millennium. While it is true that *hamlet_X* is far from being realised as Fritsch originally conceived of it, it is to be hoped that it will gradually grow.

233

The problem of authorship: the artist as 'mastermind'

In this project, the name of Herbert Fritsch is present on all of the different levels of the project; he is an inventor, doer and marketing expert who wants to first realize his project – with the help and work of many – and who communicates his project intensively in many different directions. In accordance with the project description of the "interlinking of different talents for one theme" the project primarily addresses actors, as well as film people and media art creators, that are given an open anarchic space by Fritsch. It is Fritsch who creates a framework, which is a sort of adventure playground into which his numerous prominent and highly professional acting colleagues often enter into with a sense of longing, for here they can finally experiment and let off steam. The participants have created a sort of 'Who's who' of the current German acting profession, and they all agree to perform without a fee. The actors are not given any special directing instructions or limitations, but they are left to interpret things on an individual basis. Grounded in his own acting experience, it seems that Fritsch as director succeeds in releasing a lot of creative energy through improvisations that produce creative associations to *Hamlet*, and so he and the actors keep the project going. The connecting element therefore is not a thread running through all of the scenes; there is no such thing in this iridescent waxwork. Rather, it seems that "The joy of playing replaces the context" (Siemons 2003). We are dealing with the joy of playing that Fritsch, using his name and that of the project, is spreading like a virus.

However, Fritsch has been criticized for breaking one of the central premises of the media art scene because he proclaims a 'persistence of authorship'. His role of mastermind may be necessary in order to keep the project going but it is true that in the case of *hamlet_X* authorship – even though it understands conceptually itself as being communal and distributive – has not been wholly cast off. The process and aesthetics of the project show themselves, at a closer look, as being only partly open in spite of everything. At times, this results in the fact that the écriture of his intermedial dramaturgy shows the mark of the theatre upon it. What is being created here is not an endless line of delayed signifiers but rather a medial labyrinth, a rhizome, a calculated, complex structure that has an order and a central point. Fritsch might claim that "this central point is unknown to us as yet", (ZKM 2003), but possibly – please allow for this little unscientific pun – the central point is: himself.

Certainly, the project of *hamlet_X* is part of the consumerist model in that it sells itself with the aid of the DVD's of the video films, and other marketing tools, for example, merchandizing articles to do with the project. Thus, the position of the project and its creator is ambivalent: it is part of the system that it so colourfully criticizes. However, Herbert Fritsch does not gain financially in any personal way because all monies received from grants or selling consumables is immediately reinvested into the theatre and the project. What he wants is to offer a platform for intelligent play to all that want to use it. The user, on the other hand, is free to decide how to deal with the project and its different component, and to what extent. If s/he buys something or attends a performance then, as well as enjoying the performances they are contributing to the project, which continues to grow. On the *hamlet_X* website, with its several interactive games, the user is invited to "play forever": Other than in the theatre, performance time here is unlimited.

'Play forever'—Intermedial strategies as critical resistance

If 'language is virus' as New York multimedia artist Laurie Anderson has suggested (*Home of the Brave*, 1986), then this might be true for digital performance too. As I worked on Fritsch's project, I came to the conclusion that digital performance projects have the potential to deconstruct critically the hidden set of rules that govern the Internet. The rules call for profitability, flexibility, and optimization. In a critical resistance to market-orientated high-performance site based theatre, internet theatre might suggest alternative strategies. As John McKenzie (1997: 38) puts it:

> Resistance in electronic space is less about taking and maintaining a physical or logical position outside of power, and more about playing multiple language games in order to learn a variety of moves, to point out the different rules governing them, and to invent new ones when necessary.

Through subversive, doubtful gestures *hamlet_X* attempts to inhabit the internet like a virus. This playful virus transports an aesthetic criticism as well as a critique of the internet. The project is about reading and understanding the emerging rules of electronic societies, and it is about becoming active and defining new rules. Ultimately, this is what Fritsch's artistic research project is all about. *hamlet_X* explores the internet via intermedial acting. Moving through the different levels of various media, Fritsch provokes paradoxes, twists and surprising turns. Thus, the project addresses itself to an audience that is both interested in theatre as well as in media critique. *hamlet_X* offers intermedial strategies that have the potential of being an important corrective in the *l'art pour l'art* of the mainstream net art scene discussed earlier. However, it has also an influence, aesthetically as well as de facto, back on the theatrical performance onstage. Its virtual habitus connects a young audience with the 'old' medium of theatre and so, as Hegemann puts it, tries to help "to rescue the theatre into the third millennium".

Artistic projects like this confirm the definition of theatre as a *hypermedium*. Theatre has always been a medium that synthesises different systems of signs. Over the course of its long history, theatre has integrated new technologies constantly, as well as altered methods of communication and perception. Maybe this is the first time in its long history that theatre meets another hypermedium, which also synthesises a variety of signs—but in a very different way. However, theatre and the internet are not only different in their materiality (corporeality versus incorporeity), but also in the configuration and methods of functioning of their respective, different multimedia networks of signs. The elements of theatre are corporeality, space and sound and these elements are used to present a play, or at least a theme, within a certain period of time to a live audience that is also physically present. Contrary to this, the digital network of signs released from the limitations of space and time, consists of language, images and sound that receive new qualities in the realm of the internet. Within the non-linear flood of icons, images, text and sound, the limitation and interrelation between the different sign systems are becoming blurred. The audience, or 'users', of course, have to deal with that. The users have to find their own way through this flood of information and to retrace their steps, or, more to the point, they have to create their own individual stories.

There have been many attempts to bring theatre and the internet into direct interconnection during live events in so-called distributed performances. From what I have seen these artistic approaches do not feel satisfying mostly because of their technical problems, which in the near future might be solved. However, the question remains as to whether and how the two media can be directly connected with each other in meaningful ways. Too often, the debate is about confronting an 'old medium' with the 'new medium' and having to decide whether the old 'hypermedium' can survive. Fritsch's project moves beyond this either/or debate. Just as the attitude of

235

Shakespeare's *Hamlet* suggests, *hamlet_X* is as much about staging games, little tricks and possible strategies in between: it is about exploring the energy and interrelations between the different media and that is a project worth supporting.

Notes

1 Quoted from McKenzie (1997: 32).

2 Carl Hegemann: "Dino-Parc versus Cyberspace", lecture held on 18th January 2003, at the conference *FUTURE THEATRE* (curator Birgit Wiens), ZKM – Centre for Art and Media, Karlsruhe (transcribed from video recording of the conference).

3 Herbert Fritsch: hamlet_X – a (*theatre.film.internet*) project, lecture held at the conference *FUTURE THEATRE* at ZKM Zentrum für Kunst und Medientechnologie – Centre for Art and Media, Karlsruhe (transcribed from video recording of lecture).

4 See the press announcement for *Net condition. Art in the Online Universe*, curated by Peter Weibel. The exhibition, which started in Karlsruhe (1999-2000), toured internationally (Barcelona, Graz, Tokyo). http://www.zkm.de.

5 See Weibel, on his exhibition project. "This project about media in the media was not only about portraying the representation of reality in the media, it was rather about a new approach, namely to shed light on the different methods with which reality is constructed in various media"; unfortunately, this groundbreaking and programmatic exhibition "about media in the media" presented only one contribution done by theatre performance (Sergi Jordà, Toni Aguilar/La Fura dels Baus: "F@aust Music On Line).

6 "Designing human-computer experience [...] is about creating imaginary worlds that have a special relationship to reality—worlds in which we can extend, amplify, and enrich our own capabilities to think, feel, and act. [...] The theatrical domain can help us in this task" (Laurel 1993: 32).

7 Dominik Rinnhofer, programmer and artistic partner in this part of the project (2003, unpublished manuscript).

8 In this sense, he can refer to the fact, that the puppet concept—as a metaphor— is inherent to computer programs. Puppets can be found in MOOs and MUDs, and the programming language of Macromedia Director uses terms such as "events", "cast members" and "puppets". Laurie Anderson's interactive CD-ROM project *Puppet Motel* (New York/Voyager 1994) is one of the few who began to play with these interrelations between artistic and technological performance.

9 As he did with his *Hamlet* adaptation *Hamletmaschine*. See (Siegmund 1996).

10 Hegemann, Carl. *About the Artistic Conception of the Volksbuehne at Rosa-Luxemburg-Platz*; http://www.volksbuehne-berlin.de.

236 *I would like to thank Marc Heinitz, translator for the project hamlet_X, for proof-reading this article.*

REFERENCES

Abbott, H. Porter. 2002. *The Cambridge Introduction to Narrative*. Cambridge: Cambridge University Press.

Abel, Richard. 1994. *The Ciné Goes to Town: French Cinema 1896-1914*. Berkeley: University of California Press.

Adorno, Theodor W. 1963. 'Prolog zum Fernsehen' (1953) in *Eingriffe: Neun kritische Modelle*. Frankfurt am Main: Suhrkamp: 69-80.

Albersmeier, Franz-Josef and Volker Roloff (eds.). 1989. *Literaturverfilmungen*. Frankfurt am Main: Suhrkamp.

Albersmeier, Franz-Josef. 1992. *Theater, Film und Literatur in Frankreich. Medienwechsel und Intermedialität*. Darmstadt: Wissenschaftliche Buchgesellschaft.

Altenloh, Emilie. 1914. *Zur Soziologie des Kino. Die Kino-Unternehmung und die sozialen Schichten ihrer Besucher*. Jena (also online available: http://www.uni-oldenburg.de/kunst/mediengeschichte/allg/altenloh/ – consulted: 18-02-2005).

Altman, Rick. 1987. *The American Film Musical*. London: British Film Institute.

Amerongen, Martin van. 1983. *Wagner: A Case History*. London: Dent.

Anderson, Laurie. 1994. *Stories from the Nerve Bible: A Retrospective, 1972-1992*. New York: Harper Collins.

Cameron, Andrew. 1995. 'Dissimulations: The Illusion of Interactivity' in *Millennium Film Journal* 28, 33-47 (also available online: http://mfj-online.org/journalPages/MFJ28/Dissimulations.html - consulted 29 March 2005).

Anonymous. 1912. 'Bernhardt and Rejane' in *Moving Picture World*. (10 February 1912): 468.

Arden, Edwin. 1915. 'Stage and Screen Acting' in *Moving Picture World*. (18 December 1915): 2164.

Arnheim, Rudolf. 1974. *Film als Kunst* (1932). *Mit einem Vorwort zur Neuausgabe*. München: Hanser.

Aronson, Arnold. 1999. 'Technology and Dramaturgical Development: Five Observations' in *Theatre Research International* 24 (3): 188-197.

Atkinson, Michael. 2000. 'Shadow of the Vampire' in *Filmcomment* 36 (6): 27-29.

Auerbach, Nina. 1995. *Our Vampires, Ourselves*. Chicago: Chicago University Press.

Auslander, Philip. 1997. *From Acting to Performance. Essays in Modernism and Postmodernism*. London and New York: Routledge.

Auslander, Philip. 1999. *Liveness. Performance in a Mediatized Culture*. London and New York: Routledge.

Auslander, Philip. 2001. 'Cyberspace as a Performance Art Venue' in *Performance Research* 6 (2): 123-127.

Auslander, Philip. 2002. 'Ping Chong' in Bertens, Hans and Joseph Natoli (eds.). *Postmodernism: The Key Figures*. Oxford: Blackwell Publishers: 82-87.

Axjonow, Iwan. 1997. *Sergej Eisenstein. Ein Portrait* (1933). Berlin: Henschel/arte.

Balázs, Béla. 1924. *Der sichtbare Mensch oder die Kultur des Films*. Vienna and Leipzig: Deutsch-Österreichischer Verlag.

Balázs, Béla. 1970. *Theory of the Film: Character and Growth of a New Art*. New York: Dover.

Balázs, Béla. 1973 (1938). 'Zur Kunstphilosophie des Films' in Witte, Karsten (ed.) *Theorie des Kinos*. Frankfurt am Main: Suhrkamp: 149-170.

Baldassari, Anne. 2000. *Picasso working on paper*. London: Merrell.

Balme, Christopher B. 2001. 'Robert Lepage und die Zukunft des Theaters im Medienzeitalter' in Leeker, Martina (ed.) *Maschinen, Medien, Performances: Theater an der Schnittstelle zu digitalen Welten*. Berlin: Alexander Verlag: 668-683.

Balme, Christopher. 1999, 2001². *Einführung in die Theaterwissenschaft*. Berlin: Erich Schmidt.

Banes, Sally. 1998. *Subversive Expectations: Performance Art and Paratheater in New York 1976-85*. Ann Arbor: Michigan University Press.

Barrymore, Lionel. 1998. 'The Actor' (1916) in Cardullo, Bert et al. (eds.). *Playing to the Camera: Film Actors Discuss Their Craft*. New Haven: Yale University Press: 79-82.

Barthes, Roland. 1977. 'From Work to Text' in *Image – Music – Text* (essays selected and translated by Stephen Heath). London: Fontana Paperbacks: 155-164.

Barthes, Roland. 1977. 'The Third Meaning' in *Image – Music – Text* (essays selected and translated by Stephen Heath). London: Fontana Paperbacks: 52-68.

Barthes, Roland. 1977. *Image, Music, Text* (essays selected and translated by Stephen Heath). London: Fontana Paperbacks.

Barthes, Roland. 1982. 'L'esprit de la lettre' in *L'obvie et l'obtus. Essais critiques III*. Paris: Seuil, p. 95-98.

Bassnett, Susan. 1988. 'Eleonora Duse' in Bernhardt, Terry, *Duse: The Actress in Her Time*. Cambridge: Cambridge University Press: 119-170.

Baudrillard, Jean, Hannes Böjringer, Vilém Flusser, Heinz von Förster, Friedrich Kittler and Peter Weibel. 1989. *Ars electronica. Philosophien der neuen Technologie*. Berlin: Merve.

Baudrillard, Jean. 1985. *De fatale strategieën*. Amsterdam: Uitgeverij Duizend & Een.

Baudrillard, Jean. 1986. *In de schaduw van de zwijgende meerderheden*. Amsterdam: Uitgeverij SUA.

Baumgartel, Tilman. 2001. [net.art 2.0.] *Neue Materialien zur Netzkunst / New Materials on Net Art*. Nuremberg: Modern Art Edition.

Bazin, André. 1967. *What Is Cinema? (Vol.I)*. (translated by H. Gray). Berkeley: University of California Press.

Bazin, André. 1975. *Was ist Kino? Bausteine zur Theorie des Films. Mit einem Vorwort von Eric Rohmer, und einem Nachwort von François Truffault*. Edited by Hartmut Bitomsky, Harun Farocki and Ekkard Kämmerling. Köln: Du Mont.

Benjamin, Walter. 1972. *Das Kunstwerk im Zeitalter seiner technischen Reproduzier-barkeit. (1936) Drei Studien zur Kunstsoziologie*. Frankfurt am Main: Suhrkamp.

Benjamin, Walter. 1968. 'The World of Art in the Age of Mechanical Reproduction' in Illuminations. Essays and Reflections. Ed. and introd. Hannah Arendt. New York: Schocken: 217-252.

Benjamin, Walter. 1989 (1936). 'Das Kunstwerk im Zeitalter seiner technischen Reproduzierbarkeit' in Tiedemann, Rolf and Herbert Schweppenhäuser (eds.). *Gesammelte Schrifte. Vol. VII*. Frankfurt: Suhrkamp: 350-384.

Benjamin, Walter. 1996. *Selected Writings, Vol. 1*. Cambridge, Ma.: Harvard Univ. Press.

Bergson. Henri. 1965 (1896). *Matière et mémoire. Essai sur la relation du corps à l'esprit*. Paris: Presses Universitaires de France.

Birringer, Johannes. 1998. *Media & Performance: Along the Border*. Baltimore and London: Johns Hopkins University Press.

Bleeker, Maaike. 2002. *The Locus of Looking: Dissecting Visuality in the theatre*. Amsterdam: University of Amsterdam (PhD thesis).

Boenisch, Peter. 2003. "coMEDIA electrONica: performing Intermediality in Contemporary Theatre" in Theatre Research International 28/1: 34-45.

Bogatyrev, Pjotr. 1971. 'Les signes du théâtre' (1938) in *Poétique* 8: 517-530.

Bolter, Jay David and Richard Grusin. 1999, 2000, 2002. *Remediation: Understanding New Media*. Cambridge, Massachusetts: MIT Press.

Bondebjerg, Ib and Helle Kanik Haastrup (eds.). 1999. *Sekwens 99: Intertextuality & Visual Media*. Copenhagen: University of Copenhagen / Department of Film & Media Studies.

Bordwell, David. 1992. 'Kognition und Verstehen. Sehen und Vergessen in 'Mildred Pierce' in *Montage AV* 1/1: 5-24.

Borgmann, Albert. 1984. *Technology and the Character of Contemporary Life: A Philosophical Inquiry*. Chicago and London: The University of Chicago Press.

Brandstetter, Gabriele, Helga Finter and Markus Weßendorf (eds.). 1998. *Grenzgänge. Das Theater und die anderen Künste*. Tübingen: Gunter Narr Verlag.

Brandstetter, Gabriele (ed.). 2000. *ReMembering The Body*. Ostfildern: HatjeCantz.

Brecht, Bertolt. 1967. *Gesammelte Werke in 20 Bänden. Werkausgabe. Bd. 15: Schriften zum Theater*. Frankfurt am Main: Suhrkamp.

Brecht, Bertolt. 1991. *Werke. Berliner und Frankfurter Ausgabe, Vol. 24*. Berlin und Weimar / Frankfurt a. M.: Aufbau/Suhrkamp.

Brewster, Ben and Lea Jacobs. 1997. *Theatre to Cinema: Stage Pictorialism and the Early Feature Film*. Oxford and New York: Oxford University Press, 1997.

Brook, Peter. 1986 (1968). *The Empty Space*. Harmondsworth: Penguin Books.

Bürger, Peter. 1974. *Theorie der Avantgarde*. Frankfurt am Main: Suhrkamp.

Butor, Michel. 1969. *Les mots dans la peinture*. Genève: Skira.

Buxton, David. 1990. *From The Avengers to Miami Vice*. Manchester and New York: Manchester University Press.

Cameron, Andrew. 1995. 'Dissimulations: The Illusion of Interactivity' in *Millennium Film Journal* 28 (also available online: http://mfj-online.org/journalPages/MFJ28/Dissimulations.html - consulted 30 March 2005).

Certeau, Michel de. 1984. *The Practice of Everyday Life*. Berkeley: University of California Press.

Chalamov, Varlam. 1997. *Les années 20*. Paris: Verdier.

Chambers, Iain. 1993. 'The Aural Walk', in: Chambers, Iain (ed.) *Migrancy, Culture, Identity*. London: Routledge: 49-53.

Channel 4. 2000. *The Making of Big Brother*. London: World of Wonder.

Chomsky, Noam. 1965. *Aspects of theory of syntax*. Cambridge Mass: MIT Press.

Chong, Ping, Roger Babb, Jeannie Hutchins, Larry Malvern, John Fleming, and Louise Smith. 1994. *Nosferatu: A Symphony of Darkness*. Unpublished typescript.

Citron, Marcia, J. 2000. *Opera on Screen*. London: Yale University Press.

Claudy, C.H. 1911. 'Too Much Acting' in *Moving Picture World*. (11 February 1911): 288.

Cohen, David S. 2001. 'Script to Screen: Shadow of the Vampire.' Interview with Steven Katz. *Scr (i) pt* Jan./Feb. 2001: 30-33, 60-61.

Colebrook, Claire. 2002. *Gilles Deleuze*. London: Routledge.

Collier, Leslie Jo. 1988. *From Wagner to Murnau: The Transposition of Romanticism from Stage to Screen*. Ann Arbor: University of Michigan Press.

Cook, Nicholas. 1990. *Music, Imagination and Culture*. Oxford: Oxford University Press.

Crary, Jonathan. 1992. *Techniques of the Observer. On Vision and Modernity in the Nineteenth Century*. Cambridge, Mass. and London: MIT Press.

Creeber, Glen. (ed.). 2000. *The Television Genre Book*. London: British Film Institute.

Creed, Barbara. 2000. 'The Cyberstar: Digital Pleasures and the End of the Unconscious' in *Screen* 41 (1): 79-86.

Daverio, John. 1993. *Nineteenth Century Music and the German Romantic Ideology*. Oxford: Macmillan.

Davis, Erik. 1998. *TechGnosis. Myth, Magic, and Mysticism in the Age of Information*. New York: Harmony.

De Kerckhove, Derrick. 1982. 'Theatre as Information Processing' in *Western Culture in Modern Drama* XXV/1: 143-53.

Degli-Esposti Reinert, Cristina. 2001. 'Neo-Baroque Imaging in Peter Greenaway's Cinema' in Paula Willoquet-Miracondi, Mary Alemany-Galway *Peter Greenaway's postmodern/poststructuralist cinema*. London: Scarecrow Press.

Deleuze, Gilles. 1964. *Proust et les signes*. Paris: Presses Universitaires de France.

Deleuze, Gilles and Felix Guattari. 1987 [1980]. *A Thousand Plateaus: Capitalism and Schizophrenia* 2. Minneapolis: University of Minnesota Press.

Deleuze, Gilles. 1983. *Cinema 1. L'Image mouvement*. Paris: Minuit.

Deleuze, Gilles. 1985. *Cinéma 2 – L'image temps*. Paris: Minuit.

Deleuze, Gilles. 1989. *Cinema 2: The time-image*. London: The Athlone Press.

Dermot Moran. 2000. *Introduction to Phenomenology*. London and New York: Routledge.

Derrida, Jacques. 1981. 'Economimesis' in *Diacritics* 11: 3-25.

Derrida, Jacques. 1978. *Writing and Difference* (translated by A. Bass). London: Routledge and Kegan Paul.

Derrida, Jacques. 1990. 'Semiologie und Grammatologie: Gespräch mit Julia Kristeva' in Engelmann, Peter (ed.) *Postmoderne und Dekonstruktion. Texte französischer Philosophen der Gegenwart*. Stuttgart: Reclam: 140-164.

Dika, Vera. 1996. 'From Dracula - with Love' in Grant, Barry Keith (ed.) *The Dread of Difference: Gender and the Horror Film*. Austin, Texas: Texas University Press: 388-400.

Dowmunt, Tony. 1993. *Channels of Resistance*. London: British Film Institute.

Drucker, Johanna. 1997. 'The Art of the Written Image' in *The Dual Muse: The Writer As Artist, The Artist As Writer*. St Louis: Washington University Gallery of Art.

Dübgen. Veronika. 1977. *Theater im Fernsehen. Medientechnische Arbeitstechniken der Fernsehadaption von Theaterinszenierungen*. Berlin: Volker Spiess.

Dunbar, Brian. 2000. *Dracula*. Harlow: Longman.

Duynslaegher, Patrick. 2000. 'Camera Obscura'. Interview with Willem Dafoe. *Focus Knack* 15 Nov. 2000: 12-14.

Dyer, Richard. 1998. *Stars* (revised edition). London: British Film Institute.

Eco, Umberto. 1971. 'Die Gliederung des filmischen Kode' in Knilli, Friedrich (ed.) *Semiotik de Films. Mit Analysen kommerzieller Pornos und revolutionärer Agitationsfilme*. München: Hanser.

Eco, Umberto. 1977. 'Semiotics of Theatrical Performance' in *The Drama Review* T73: 107-117.

Eco, Umberto. 1985. *De alledaagse onwerkelijkheid*. Amsterdam: Uitgeverij Bert Bakker.

Eco, Umberto. 1987. *Travels in Hyperreality* (translated by W. Weaver) London, Pan.

Eco, Umberto. 1988. 'Postmodernismus, Ironie und Vergnügen' in Welsch, Wolfgang (ed.): *Wege aus der Moderne. Schlüsseltexte der Postmoderne-Diskussion*. Weinheim: VCH.

Einstein, Carl. 1981. 'Gerettete Malerei, enttäuschte Pompiers' (1923), in *Werke*, Vol. 2, Berlin: Medusa. 233-238.

Eisenstein, Sergej M. 1971. 'Dialektische Theorie des Films' in Prokop, Dieter (ed.) *Materialien zur Theorie des Films. Ästhetik, Soziologie, Politik*. München: Hanser: 53-68.

Elsaesser, Thomas. 2000. *Weimar Cinema and After: Germany's Historical Imaginary*. London: Routledge.

Elsaesser, Thomas. 2001. 'Six Degrees of *Nosferatu*' in *Sight and Sound*. Feb. 2001: 12-15.

Engelmann, Peter. 1990. *Philosophie und Totalitarismus: zur Kritik dialektischer Diskursivität: eine Hegellektüre*. Wien: Passagen Verlag.

Eshun, Kodwo. 1998. *More Brilliant than the Sun. Adventures in Sonic Fiction*. London: Quartet.

Everett, William, A., and Paul R. Laird. (eds.). 2002. *The Cambridge Companion to the Musical*. Cambridge: Cambridge University Press.

Fagiolo dell'Arco, Maurizio. 1990. *Futur-Balla. La vita e le opere*, Milano: Electa.

Festinger, Leon. 1962. *A Theory of Cognitive Dissonance* (1957). London: Tavistock Publications

Fiebach, Joachim. 2001. 'Avancierte Künste und Medien im 20. Jahrhundert' in Leeker, Martina (ed.) *Machinen, Medien, Performances: Theater an der Schnittstelle zu digitalen Welten*. Berlin: Alexander Verlag: 588–603.

Fiedler, Leslie A. 1988. 'Überquert die Grenzen, schließt die Graben. Über die Postmoderne' in Welsch, Wolfgang (ed.): *Wege aus der Moderne. Schlüsseltexte der Postmoderne-Diskussion*. Weinheim: VCH.

Fischer-Lichte, Erika. 2001. 'Wahnehmung und Medialität' in Fischer-Lichte, Erika, Christian Horn, Sandra Umathum and Matthias Warstat (eds.). *Wahrnehmung und Medialität*. Tübingen: Francke Verlag: 11-28.

Fischer-Lichte, Erika. 2004. *Ästhetik des Performativen*. Frankfurt am Main: Suhrkamp.

Forsythe, William. 1999. *Improvisation Technologies. A Tool for the Analytical Dance Eye*. Karlsruhe/Köln: Zentrum für Kunst- und Medientechnologie, Deutsches Tanzarchiv.

Frank, Manfred. 1977. *Einleitung zu Schleiermachers Hermeneutik und Kritik*. Frankfurt am Main: Suhrkamp.

Freud, Sigmund. 1953. 'The Interpretation of Dreams' in Strachey, James (ed.) *The Standard Edition of the Complete Psychological Works of Sigmund Freud*. Vol. IV. London: The Hogart Press.

Früchtl, Josef and Jörg Zimmermann (eds.). 2001. *Ästhetik der Inszenierung: Dimensionen eines künstlerischen, kulturellen und gesellschafgtlichen Phänomens*. Frankfurt am Main: Suhrkamp.

Fuller, Mary. 1911. 'My Adventures as a Motion-Picture Heroine' in *Colliers* 48 (15): 16-17.

Fuller, Mary. 1914. 'Photoplay Acting is Mental Radiation' in *Moving Picture World*. 11 July: 227.

Furtwängler, Frank, Kay Kirchmann, Andreas Schreitmüller and Jan Siebert (eds.). 2002. *Zwischen-Bilanz: Eine Festschrift zum 60. Geburtstag von Joachim Paech*. Online publication: http://www.uni-konstanz.de/paech2002/ - consulted 03-03-2005.

Garner, Stanton B Jr. 1994. *Bodied Spaces: Phenomenology and Performance in Contemporary Drama*. Ithaca: Cornell University Press.

Gaßner, Hubertus. 1982. *Rodchenko Fotografien*. München: Schirmer/Mosel.

Geertz, Clifford. 1993. *The Interpretation of Cultures*. London: Fontana.

Giannachi, Gabriella. 2004. *Virtual Theatres: An introduction*. London and New York: Routledge.

Gibbs, Christopher, H. (ed.). 1997. *The Cambridge Companion to Schubert*. Cambridge: Cambridge University Press.

Gillespie, Gerald (tr. and ed.). 1976. *Ludwig Tieck, Der Gestiefelte Kater*. Edinburgh: University Press.

Gilmore, Michael T. 1998. *Differences in the Dark: American Movies and English Theater*. New York: Columbia University Press.

Gledhill, Christine. 2000. 'Taking it forward: theatricality and British cinema style in the 1920s' in Fitzsimmons, Linda and Sarah Street (eds.). *Moving Performance: British Stage and Screen, 1890s-1920s*. Wiltshire: Flick Books: 5-25.

Goettlich, Udo et.al. (eds.). 1998. *Kommunikation im Wandel. Zur Theatralität der Medien.* (Communication in Change. On the Theatricality of Media.) Cologne: Herbert von Halem.

Gold, Arthur and Robert Fizdale. 1991. *The Divine Sarah: A Life of Sarah Bernhardt*. New York: Knopf.

Gould, Stephen Jay. 2001. 'Restoration and the Woolworth Building', in *Natural History* 110, 10A, Winter: 96-97.

Grimm, Gunter. 1977. *Rezeptionsgeschichte. Grundlegung einer Theorie. Mit Analysen und Biographie*. München: UTB Fink.

Grohmann, Will. 1954. *Paul Klee*. London: Lund Humphries.

Groot Nibbelink, Liesbeth. 2000. 'Verhevigde werkelijkheid' in *E-view 99* (1). On-line at http://comcom.kub.nl/e-view/99-1/groot.html (consulted 14-10-2004).

Gruber, Klemens and Aki Beckmann (eds.). 2004. *Der kreiselnde Kurbler. Dziga Vertov zum 100. Geburtstag*, Vol. 2: *Vorträge und Gespräche, Maske und Kothurn 1*, 2004. Wien: Böhlau.

Gunning, Tom. 1977. 'An Aesthetic of Astonishment: Early Film and the (In) Credulous Spectator' in: Williams, Linda (ed.) *Viewing Positions. Ways of Seeing Film*. New Brunswick, New Jersey: Rutgers University Press: 114-133.

Gussow, Mel. 1998. *Theatre on the Edge: New Visions, New Voices*. New York: Applause Books.

Haffner, Nik. 2000. 'Forsythe und die Medien. Ein Bericht' in *Tanzdrama 51* (2): 30-35.

Halazs, Frank and Mayer Schwartz. 1994. 'The Dexter Hypertext Reference Model' in *Communication of the ACM 37*(2), 30-39.

Hansen-Löve, Aage. 1992. 'Wörter und/oder Bilder. Probleme der Intermedialität mit Beispielen aus der russischen Avantgarde' in *Eikon 4*, 32-41.

Harding, Bertita. 1947. *Age Cannot Wither: The Story of Duse and D'Annunzio*. Philadelphia: Lippincott.

Harrison, Louis Reeves. 1915. 'Acting That Is Not' in *Motion Picture World*. 4 December: 1800.

Hefling, Stephen. E. 2001. *Mahler: Das Lied von der Erde*. Cambridge: Cambridge University Press.

Hegemann, Carl. 'About the Artistic Conception of the Volksbühne at Rosa-Luxemburg-Platz'. On line at http://www.volksbuehne-berlin.de (consulted 7 April 2005).

Heim, Michael. 1993. *The Metaphysics of Virtual Reality*. New York and Oxford: Oxford University Press.

Helbig, Jörg (ed.). 1998. *Intermedialität: Theorie und Praxis eines interdisziplinären Forschungsgebiets*. Berlin: Schmidt (also online available: http://www.uni-koeln.de/phil-fak/englisch/helbig/inhalt.htm - consulted 08-03-2005).

Hickethier, Knut. 1980. *Das Fernsehspiel der Bundesrepublik. Themen, Form, Struktur, Theorie und Geschichte 1951-1977*. Stuttgart: Metzler.

Hickethier, Knut. 1986. *Grenzgänger zwischen Theater und Kino. Schauspielerportraits aus dem Berlin der Zwanziger Jahre*. Berlin: Ästhetik und Kommunikation.

Hocke, Gustav René. 1991. *Die Welt als Labyrinth. Manierismus in der europäischen Kunst und Literatur* (1957). Reinbek bei Hamburg: Rowohlt.

Hosokawa, Shuhei. 1983. 'The Walkman as urban strategy' in *International Society for Music Education Yearbook* 10: 129-134.

Hosokawa, Shuhei. 1984. 'The Walkman Effect' in *Popular Music* 4: 165-180.

Hughes, William. 2000. *Beyond Dracula: Bram Stoker's Fiction and its Cultural Context*. London: Macmillan.

Huhtamo, Erkki. 2004. 'From Kaleidoscomaniac to Cybernerd: Towards an Archeology of the Media' in *dedigitalebalie* (an online archive of De Balie Amsterdam: http://www.debalie.nl/artikel.jsp?articleid=10104 - consulted 7 April 2005).

Hulton, Pontus et al. 1987. *The Arcimboldo Effect. Transformations of the face from the sixteenth to the twentieth century*. London: Thames and Hudson.

Iser, Wolfgan. 1976. *Der Akt des Lesens. Theorie ästhetischer Wirkung*. München: UTB Fink.

Jakobson, Roman. 1976. 'Message sur Malévitch', in *Change* 26/27: 293-294.

Jans, Erwin (et al). 2003. *Op zoek naar de verloren tijd. Proust 1: De kant van Swann. Script en werkboek*. Amsterdam: International Theatre and Film Books.

Jarratt, Vernon. 1972. *The Italian Cinema*. New York: Arno Press.

Jensen, Eric Frederick. 2001. *Schumann*. Oxford: Oxford University Press.

Johnson, Stephen. 1992. 'Evaluating Early Film as a Document of Theatre History: The 1896 Footage of Joseph Jefferson's 'Rip van Winkle' in *Nineteenth Century Theatre* 20 (2): 101-22.

Jones, Ernest. 1922. 'The Island of Ireland: A Psychoanalytical Contribution to Political Psychology' in Jones, E. (ed.) *Essays in Applied Psychoanalysis. Vol. 1: Miscellaneous Essays*. (International Psychoanalytical Library 40 vols). London: Hogarth Press. 1951: 95-112.

Jordan, Stephanie. 2000. *Moving Music: Dialogues with Music in Twentieth-Century Ballet*. Oxford: Oxford University Press.

Kaes, Anton (ed.). 1978. *1909-1929 Kinodebatte. Texte zum Verhältnis von Literatur und Film*. Tübingen: DTV Niemeyer.

Kafka, Franz. 1973. *Letters to Felice* (edited by Erich Heller and Jürgen Born; translated

243

by James Stern and Elisabeth Duckworth). New York: Schocken.

Kahnweiler, Daniel-Henry. 1958. *Der Weg zum Kubismus* (1920), Stuttgart: Hatje.

Kandinsky, Wassily. 1973a (1912). *Über das Geistige in der Kunst*. Bern: Benteli Verlag.

Kandinsky, Wassily. 1973b. 'Über Bühnenkomposition' (1912) and 'Über die abstrakte Bühnensynthese' (1923) in Bill, Max (ed.) *Kandinsky: Essays über Kunst und Künstler*. Bern: Benteli Verlag: 49-61 and 79-83.

Kant, Immanuel. 1986 (1790). *Kritik der Urteilskraft* (edited by Gerhard Lehmann). Stuttgart: Philipp Reclam.

Kaplan, E Anne. 1987. *Rocking Around the Clock*. London: Methuen.

Kattenbelt, Chiel. 1991. *Theater en film: Aanzet tot een systematische vergelijking vanuit een rationaliteitstheoretisch perspectief*. PhD thesis. Utrecht University.

Kattenbelt, Chiel. 1994. 'The triad of emotion, action and reflection: A sign-pragmatic approach to aesthetic communication' in *Kodikas/Code: Ars Semiotica* 17 (1/2): 123-139.

Kattenbelt, Chiel. 1997. 'Theater als Artefakt, ästhetisches Objekt und szenische Kunst' in *Forum modernes Theater* 12: 132-159.

Kehr, Dave. 2003. 'In a Digitally Animated World, Oscar Stands Rigid' in *New York Times* (9 March 2003).

Kern, Stephen. 1983. *The culture of time and space 1880-1918*. Cambridge, Massachusetts: Harvard University Press.

Khlebnikov, Velemir. 1987. *Collected Works, Vol. 1: Letters and Theoretical Writings*, edited by Charlotte Douglas. Cambridge, Mass: Harvard University Press.

Kirby, Lynne. 1997. *Parallel Tracks: The Railroad and Silent Cinema*. Exeter: Exeter University Press.

Kislan, Richard. 1995. *The Musical: A Look at the American Musical Theater*. Tonbridge: revised and expanded edition: Applause Books.

Kistler, Mark O. 1969. *Drama of the Storm and Stress*. New York: Twayne Publishers.

Kittler, Friedrich. 1982. 'Dracula's Legacy' (translated by William Stephen Davis) in *Stanford Humanities Review* 1 (1): 143-173.

Kittler, Friedrich. 1992. *Discourse Networks 1800/1900*. (translated by M. Metteer). Stanford, California. Stanford University Press.

Klapper, Joseph T. 1960. *The Effects of Mass Communication*. Glencoe, Ill: The Free Press of Glencoe.

Klawans, Stuart. 2000. 'Dead Stars, Alive Again: Yes Marilyn May Fall in Love with Viggo' in *New York Times* (1 August 2004).

Klibansky, Raymond, Erwin Panofsky and Fritz Saxl. 1964. *Saturn and Melancholy. Studies in the History of Natural Philosophy, Religion and Art*. London: Nelson.

Klotz, Heinrich / Centre for Art and Media Karlsruhe (ed.) 1997. *Kunst der Gegenwart (Contemporary Art)*. Munich, New York: Prestel.

Klumph, Inez and Helen Klumph. 1922. *Screen Acting: Its Requirements and Rewards*. New York: Falk Publishing.

Knilli, Friedrich, Knut Hickethier and Wolfdieter Lützen (eds.). 1976.*Literatur in den Massenmedien*. München: Hanser.

Kozintsev, Grigori. 1996. *Shakespeare, Time and Conscience* (translated by Joyce Vining). London: Dennis Dobson.

Kracauer, Siegfried. 1973. *Theorie des Films. Die Errettung der äußeren Wirklichkeit*. Frankfurt am Main: Suhrkamp.

Kracauer, Siegfried. 1947. *From Caligari to Hitler: A Psychological History of the German Film*. Princeton: Princeton University Press.

Kramer, Lawrence. 1990. *Music as Cultural Practice 1800-1900*. London: University of California Press.

Krämer, Sybille (ed.). 2004. *Performativität und Medialität*. München: Fink.

Krauss, Rosalind. 1985. 'In the Name of Picasso' in Krauss, Rosalind *The Originality of the Avant-Garde and Other Modernist Myths*, Cambridge, Mass.: MIT Press: 32.

Kreuzer, Helmut and Karl Prümm. (eds.). 1979. *Fernsehsendungen und ihre Formen. Typologie, Geschichte und Kritik des Programms in der Bundesrepublik Deutschland*. Stuttgart: Reclam.

Kristeva, Julia. 1977. *Tel-Quel. Die Demaskierung der bürgerlichen Kulturideologie*. München: Kindler.

Laban, Rudolf. 1992. *The Mastery of Movement*. Plymouth: Northcote House (4th edition revised by Lisa Ullmann).

Landow, George and Paul Delany. 1991. 'Hypertext, Hypermedia and Literary Studies: The State of the Art' in Packer, Randall, and Ken Jordan (eds.). 2001. *Multimedia: From Wagner to Virtual Reality*. New York: W.W. Norton.

Lasswell, Harold D. 1950. 'Propaganda and Mass Insecurity' in *Psychiatry* 13: 283-299.

Latham, Rob. 2002. *Consuming Youth: Vampires, Cyborgs, and the Culture of Consumption*. Chicago, Ill: Chicago University Press.

Laurel, Brenda. 1992. *Computers as Theatre*. Reading, Mass: Addison-Wesley (also expanded edition 2003).

Lavender, Andrew. 2001. *Hamlet in Pieces. Shakespeare Reworked by Peter Brook, Robert Lepage, Robert Wilson*. London: Nick Hern Books.

Lavender, Andrew. 2003. 'Pleasure, Performance and the Big Brother Experience' in *Contemporary Theatre Review*, Vol. 13 (2) 1-9. London and New York: Routledge.

Lavrentiev, Alexandr N. 1981. "The facture of graphics and words" in *Von der Malerei zum Design. From Painting to Design. Russische konstruktivistische Kunst der Zwanziger Jahre. Russian Constructivist Art of the Twenties*. Köln: Galerie Gmurzynska: 72-91.

Lea, Henry A. 1985. *Gustav Mahler: A Man on the Margins*. Bonn: Bouvier.

Leatherdale, Clive. 2001 [1985, 1993]. *Dracula: The Novel and The Legend*. Westcliff-on-Sea: Desert Island Books.

Leeker, Martina (ed.). 2001. *Machinen, Medien, Performances: Theater an der Schnittstelle zu digitalen Welten*. Berlin: Alexander Verlag.

Lehmann, Hans-Thies. 1999. *Postdramatisches Theater*. Frankfurt am Main: Verlag der Autoren.

Lehmann, Hans-Thies. 2000. 'Das neue Theater: Urbaner Raum, potentieller Raum', *Theaterwissenschaftliche Beiträge 2000 - Insert Theater der Zeit*. Berlin: Theater der Zeit.

Leighton, Patricia. 1992. *Re-Ordering the Universe: Picasso and Anarchism. 1897-1914* in Poggi, Christine *In Defiance of Painting. Cubism, Futurism and the Invention of Collage*. New Haven: Yale University Press.

Lenk, Sabine. 1989. *Theatre contre cinéma. Die Diskussion um Kino und Theater vor dem ersten Weltkrieg in Frankreich*. Münster: MAKS.

Lepecki, André. 1999. 'Skin, Body, and Presence in Contemporary European Choreography' in *The Drama Review* 164. 129-40.

Lessing, Gotthold Ephraim. 1974. 'Laokoon oder über die Grenzen der Malerei und

Poesie' in Gotthold Ephraim Lessing: *Werke. Vol. 6*. Darmstadt: Wissenschaftliche Buchgesellschaft (also available online via: http://gutenberg.spiegel.de/lessing/laokoon/laokoon.htm - consulted 26 July 2005).

Levin, Gail. 1995. 'The Ballets Suédois and American Culture' in Nancy Van Norman Baer, in *Paris Modern. The Swedish Ballet 1920 – 1925*. San Francisco: Fine Arts Museums of San Francisco: 118-127.

Levinson, Paul. 1997. *The soft edge. A natural history and future of the information revolution*. London: Routledge.

Levinson, Paul. 1999. *Digital McLuhan: a guide to the information millennium*. London: Routledge.

Link-Heer, Ursula and Volker Roloff (eds.). 1994. *Luis Buñuel: Film – Literatur – Intermedialität*. Darmstadt: Wissenschaftliche Buchgesellschaft.

Lista, Giovanni. 1989. *La scène futuriste*. Paris: CNRS.

Lister, Martin et al. 2003. *New Media: A Critical Introduction*. London: Routledge.

Löb, Ladislaus. 1974. *From Lessing to Hauptmann: studies in German Drama*. London: University Tutorial Press.

Lodder, Christina. 1983. *Russian Constructivism*. New Haven and London: Yale University Press.

Longyear, Rey M.1988. *Nineteenth Century Romanticism in Music*. New Jersey: Prentice Hall (3rd edition).

Lukács, Georg. 1963. *Ästhetik. Teil I. Zweiter Halbband*. Neuwied and Berlin: Luchterhand.

Lukács, Georg. 1973. 'Gedanken zu einer Ästhetik des Kino' in Witte, Karsten (ed.) *Theorie des Kinos*. Frankfurt am Main: Suhrkamp: 142-148.

Lunenfeld, Peter. 1995. *The Digital Dialectic: New Essays on New Media*. Cambridge, Mass: The MIT Press.

Lyotard, Jean-Francois. 1984. *The Postmodern Condition: A Report on Knowledge* (translated by G. Bennington, and B. Massumi). Manchester: Manchester University Press.

Magid, Ron. 2000. 'Dark Shadows' in *American Cinematographer* 81 (11): 68-75.

Manovich, Lev. 2001. *The Language of New Media*. Cambridge, Mass. and London: MIT Press.

Manvell, Arnold Roger. 1971. *Shakespeare and the Film*. London: Dent.

Marcadé, Jean-Claude. 1979. *Malévitch*. Lausanne: l'Age d'homme.

Marlowe, Christopher. 1965. *Doctor Faustus* (edited by Roma Gill). London: Ernest Benn.

Mayer, David. 1988. 'The Victorian Stage on Film: A Descriptive and Selective List of Holdings in the Library of Congress Paper Print Collection' in *Nineteenth Century Theatre* 16 (2): 111-122.

Mayer, David. 1999. 'Acting in Silent Film: Which Legacy of the Theatre?' in Lovell, Alan, and Peter Krämer (eds.). *Screen Acting*. London: Routledge: 10-30.

Maynard, Richard A. (ed.). 1975. *Propaganda on film. A nation at war*. Rochelle Park, New Jersey: Hayden.

McAuley, Gay. 1999. *Space in Performance: Making Meaning in the Theatre*. Ann Arbor: University of Michigan Press.

McKenzie, Jon. 1994. 'Virtual Reality: Performance, Immersion, and the Thaw' in *The*

Drama Review 38, 4. 83-106.

McKenzie, Jon. 1997. "Laurie Anderson for Dummies", in: *The Drama Review* 41, 2 (T154). New York University / MIT. 30-50.

McKenzie, Jon. 2001. *Perform or Else. From Discipline to Performance.* London and New York: Routledge.

McLuhan, Marshall and Quentin Fiore. 1967. *The Medium is the Massage.* Harmondsworth: Penguin Books.

McLuhan, Marshall. 1994/2001/2002 (1964). *Understanding Media: the extensions of man.* London: Routledge Classics.

Menhennet, Alan. 1981. *The Romantic Movement.* London: Croom-Helme.

Merleau-Ponty, Maurice. 1962. *Phenomenology of Perception* (translated by Colin Smith). London: Routledge and Kegan Paul.

Merleau-Ponty, Maurice. 1964a. 'Eye and Mind' (translated by Carleton Dallery) in Edie, James M. (ed.) *The Primacy of Perception and Other Essays on Phenomenological Psychology, the Philosophy of Art, History and Politics.* Evanston: Northwestern University Press.

Merleau-Ponty, Maurice. 1964b. 'The Primacy of Perception and Its Philosophical Consequences' (translated by James M. Edie) in Edie, James M. (ed.) *The Primacy of Perception and Other Essays on Phenomenological Psychology, the Philosophy of Art, History and Politics.* Evanston: Northwestern University Press.

Merleau-Ponty, Maurice. 1986. *Das Sichtbare und das Unsichtbare.* München: Fink.

Mersch, Dieter. 2002. *Ereignis und Aura: Untersuchungen zu einer Ästhetik des Performativen.* Frankfurt am Main: Suhrkamp.

Metz, Christian. 1986 (1976). *The Imaginary Signifier: Psychoanalysis & the Cinema.* Indiana University Press.

Michelson, Annette (ed.). 1984. *Kino-Eye. The Writings of Dziga Vertov.* Berkeley: University of California Press.

Michelson, Annette. 2004. 'Round Table: From DV to TV' in Gruber, Klemens and Aki Beckmann (eds.). *Der kreiselnde Kurbler. Dziga Vertov zum 100. Geburtstag, Vol. 2: Vorträge und Gespräche, Maske und Kothurn* 1, 2004: 115-123.

Miller, Jonathan. 1986. *Subsequent Performances.* London and Boston: Faber and Faber.

Mills, Sara. 2003. *Michel Foucault.* London. Routledge.

Moebius, Hanno, 2000. *Montage und Collage. Literatur, bildende Kunst, Film, Fotografie, Musik, Theater bis 1933.* München: Fink.

Moog-Grünewald, Maria and Christoph Rodiek. 1989. *Dialog der Künste: Intermediale Fallstudien zur Literatur des 19. und 20. Jahrhunderts. Festschrift für Erwin Koppen.* Bern, Frankfurt am Main and New York: Peter Lang.

Moore, Rachel O. 2000. *Savage Theory: Cinema as Modern Magic.* Durham: Duke University Press.

Moran, Dermot. 2000. *Introduction to Phenomenology.* London and New York: Routledge.

Morley, David. 1992. *Television Audiences and Cultural Studies.* London and New York: Routledge.

Morse, Margaret. 1998. *Virtualities, Television, Media Art and Cyberculture.* Bloomington and Indianapolis: Indiana University Press.

Mottram, James. 2000. *Interview with Elias Merhige.* On line at: http://www.bbc.co.uk/films/2000/11/08/e_elias_merhige_shadow_of_a_vampire_071100_interview.shtml – consulted 7 April 2005.

Mukarovsky, Jan. 1974. 'Zur Ästhetik des Films' (1934) in Beilenhoff, Wolfgang (ed.) *Poetik des Films. Deutsche Erstausgabe der filmtheoretischen Texte der russischen Formalisten mit einem Nachwort und Anmerkungen*. München: Fink: 119-130.

Mukarovsky, Jan. 1974. 'Die Zeit im Film' (193?) in Beilenhoff, Wolfgang (ed.) *Poetik des Films Deutsche Erstausgabe der filmtheoretischen Texte der russischen Formalisten mit einem Nachwort und Anmerkungen*. München: Fink: 131-138.

Mukarovsky, Jan. 1975. 'Zum heutigen Stand einer Theorie des Theaters' (1966) in Kesteren, Aloysius and Herta Schmidt (erds.) *Moderne Dramentheorie*. Kronberg Ts.: Scriptor Verlag: 163-171.

Mukarovsky, Jan. 1982. *Kapitel aus der Ästhetik* (1966). Frankfurt am Main: Suhrkamp.

Mul, J. de. 1997. 'De digitalisering van de cultuur' in Extra, Guus (ed.) *Lustrumbundel Faculteit der Letteren*. Tilburg: Katholieke Universiteit Brabant, 26-49.

Müller, Heiner. 1986. *Gesammelte Irrtümer. Interviews und Gespräche*. Frankfurt am Main: Verlag der Autoren.

Müller, Heiner. 1995. 'Hamletmachine' in *Theatremachine* (translated and edited by M. von Henning). London: Faber and Faber.

Müller, Jürgen E. 1998. 'Intermedialität als poetologisches und medientheoretisches Konzept: Einige Reflexionen zu dessen Geschichte' in Helbig, Jörg (ed.). 1998. 1998. Intermedialität: Theorie und Praxis eines interdisziplinären Forschungsgebiets. Berlin: Schmidt: 31-40 (also online available: http://www.uni-koeln.de/phil-fak/englisch/helbig/inhalt.htm - consulted 3 April 2005).

Müller, Jürgen E. 1996. *Intermedialität. Formen moderner kultureller Kommunikation*. Münster, Nodus Publikationen.

Mulvey, Laura. 1989. *Visual and Other Pleasures*. London: Macmillan.

Münsterberg, Hugo. 1970. *The film. A psychological study*. (*The silent photoplay in 1916*). New York: Dover Publications.

Murray, Janet H. (1997). *Hamlet on the Holodeck: The Future of Narrative in Cyberspace*. New York, London, etc.: The Free Press.

Murray, Janet H. 1998. *Hamlet on the Holodeck: The Future of Narrative in Cyberspace*. Cambridge Mass: MIT Press.

Musser, Charles. 1991. *Before the Nickelodeon: Edwin S. Porter and the Edison Manufacturing Company*. Berkeley: University of California Press.

Naremore, James. 1988. *Acting in the Cinema*. Berkeley: University of California Press.

Neely, Kent. 1992. 'Ping Chong's Theatre of Simultaneous Consciousness' in *Journal of Dramatic Theory and Criticism* 6 (2): 121-135.

Nelson, Robin. 2000. 'TV Drama: "Flexi-narrative Form" and "A New Affective Order"' in Voigts-Virchow, Eckart (ed.) *Mediatized Drama - Dramatized Media* (*Contemporary Drama in English*). Vol 7. Trier: Wissenschaftlicher Verlag.

Nelson, Robin. 1997. *TV Drama in Transition: Forms, Values and Cultural Change*. Basingstoke and New York: Macmillan / St Martin's Press.

Nussbaum, Martha, C. 1977. *Cultivating Humanity. A Classical Defense of Reform in Liberal Education*. Cambridge Massachusetts: Harvard University Press.

Oosterling, Henk. 2003. 'Sens(a)ble Intermediality and Interesse. Towards an Ontology of the In-Between' in *Intermedialités* No 1/ Printemps: 29-46 (also available online: http://cri.histart.umontreal.ca/cri/fr/intermedialites/Oosterling.pdf consulted 3 March 2005).

Owen, Rob. 1997. *Gen X TV: from the Brady Bunch to Melrose Place*. Syracuse, New York: Syracuse University Press.

Packer, Randall, and Ken Jordan (eds.). 2001. *Multimedia: From Wagner to Virtual Reality*. New York: W.W. Norton.

Paech, Joachim. 1998. 'Intermedialität: Mediales Differenzial und transformative Figurationen' in Helbig, Jörg (ed.). 1998. *Intermedialität: Theorie und Praxis eines interdisziplinären Forschungsgebiets*. Berlin: Schmidt: 14-30 (also online available: http://www.uni-koeln.de/phil-fak/englisch/helbig/inhalt.htm - consulted 3 April 2005).

Panofsky, Erwin. 1985 (1934; revised 1947). 'Style and Medium in the Motion Pictures' in Mast, Gerald and Marshall Cohen (eds.). *Film Theory and Critcism*. New York: Oxford University Press: 215-233.

Pasolini, Pier Paolo. 1994. "La mancanza di ogni perplessità" in Sergio Tuffetti, Giovanni Spagnoletti, *Alexander Kluge*. Torino: Museo Nazionale del Cinema / Lindau. 33-34.

Patrice. 1996. *L'Analyse des Spectacles*. Paris: Nathan.

Pavis, Patrice. 1987. 'Le theatre et les médias: spécificité et interférences" in Helbo, André et al. *Théâtre: Modes d'approche*. Bruxelles: Éditions Labor: 33-63.

Pavis, Patrice. 2000. 'Avignon 1999 (Nine Photo-Texts)' in *Performance Research* 5 (1), 62-69.

Pearsall, Judy (ed.). 1998. *The New Oxford Dictionary of English*. Oxford: Oxford University Press.

Pearson, Roberta A. 1992. *Eloquent Gestures: The Transformation of Performance Style in the Griffith Biograph Films*. Berkeley: University of California Press.

Petrucci, Armando. 1993. *Public Lettering. Script, Power and Culture*. Chicago: University of Chicago Press.

Phelan, Peggy. 1993. *Unmarked. The Politics of Performance*. London and New York: Routledge.

Pine, B. Joseph and James H. Gilmore. 1999. *The Experience Economy: Work Is Theatre & Every Business a Stage*. Boston: Harvard Business School Press.

Ploebst, Helmut. 2001. *No Wind No Word. New Choreography in the Society of the Spectacle*. München: K. Kieser.

Poggi, Christine. 1992. *In Defiance of Painting. Cubism, Futurism and the Invention of Collage*. Princeton NJ: Princeton University Press.

Pontiero, Giovanni. 1986. *Eleonora Duse: In Life and Art*. Frankfurt: Peter Lang.

Porter, Roy and Mikulá Teich (eds.). 1988. *Romanticism in National Context*. Oxford: Oxford University Press.

Poster, Mark (ed.). 1988. *Jean Baudrillard: Selected Writings*. Cambridge. Polity Press.

Prokop, Dieter (ed.). 1971. *Materialien zur Theorie des Films. Asthetik, Soziologie, Politik*. München: Carl Hanser Verlag.

Prümm, Karl. 1988. 'Intermedialität und Multimedialität' in *Theaterzeitschrift* 22 (4): 95-103.

Pudowkin, Wsewolod. 1973. 'Über die Montage' (194?) in Witte, Karsten (ed.). *Theorie des Kinos*. Frankfurt am Main: Suhrkamp. 113-127.

Raessens, Joost. 2001. 'Cinema and beyond: film en het proces van digitalisering' in *E-view*, 01 (online journal: http://comcom.uvt.nl/e-view/01-1/raes.htm - consulted 29 March 2005).

Rainer, Yvonne. 1999. *A woman who ---. Essays, Interviews, Scripts.* Baltimore: Johns Hopkins University Press.

Rajewsky, Irina O. 2002. *Intermedialität.* Stuttgart: W. Fink (UTB).

Ramsaye, Terry. 1926. *A Million and One Nights: A History of the Motion Picture Through 1925.* New York: Simon and Schuster.

Rieser, Martin and Andrea Zapp (eds.). 2001. *New Screen Media: Cinema/Art/ Narrative.* London: British Film Institute Publishing.

Sadoul, Georges. 1982. *Geschichte der Filmkunst.* Frankfurt am Main: Fischer-Taschenbuch-Verlag.

Sagarra, Eda and Skrine, Peter. 1997. *A Companion to German Literature.* Oxford: Blackwell.

Sarabianov, Dimitri V. and Natalia L. Adaskina. 1990. *Liubov Popova,* New York: Abrams.

Savio, Francesco. 1956. 'Didascalia. Cinema', in *Enciclopedia dello Spettacolo.* Roma: Le Maschere: col. 660.

Savran, David. 1988. *Breaking the Rules: The Wooster Group.* New York: Theatre Communications Group.

Schechner, Richard. 2002. *Performance Studies: An Introduction.* London and New York: Routledge.

Schiller, Friedrich von. 1959. *Love and Intrigue or Lousia Miller* (1783) translated by Frederick Rolf. New York: Barrons Educational Series.

Schivelbusch, Wolfgang. 1986 (1977). *The Railway Journey: The Industrialization of Time and Space in the 19th Century.* Leamington Spa: Berg Publishers.

Schlüpmann, Heide. 1990. *Unheimlichkeit des Blicks: Das Drama des frühen deutschen Kinos.* Basel: Stroemfeld and Roter Stern.

Schneider, Irmela. 1981. *Der verwandelte Text. Wege zur Theorie der Literaturverfilmung.* Tübingen: Niemeyer.

Schnitzler, Günter and Edelgard Spaude (eds.). 2004. *Intermedialität: Studien zur Wechselwirkung zwischen den Künsten.* Freiburg: Rombach.

Schröter, Jens. n.y. 'Intermedialität' in *Theorie der Medien* (online journal: http://www.theorie-der-medien.de/text_detail.php?nr=12 - consulted 8 March 2005)

Sconce, Jeffrey. 2000. *Haunted Media: Electronic Presence from Telegraphy to Television.* Durham: Duke University Press.

Seldon, Raman, Peter Widdowson and Peter Brooker (eds.). 1997. *A Reader's Guide to Contemporary Literary Theory,* 4th. edition. Harvester Wheatsheaf, Hemel Hempstead: Prentice Hall.

Shakespeare, William. 1996. *Hamlet* (edited by T.J.B. Spencer, with an introduction by Anne Barton). London: Penguin Books.

Shani, Hadassa and Ahuva Belkin. 2002. 'Actual-fictive-virtual space: theatre interactivity within a "Liquid architecture"' in *ISEA 2002: proceedings of the 11th International Symposium on Electronic Art.* Japan: Nagoya.

Shani, Hadassa. 2004. 'The Theatrical event: from coordination to dynamic interactivity' in Cremona, V.A, P. Eversmann, H. van Maanen et al (eds.). *Theatrical events: Borders, Dynamics Frames.* Amsterdam: Rodopi.

Sharrett, Christopher. 1996. 'The Horror Film in Neoconservative Culture' in Grant, Barry Keith (ed.). *The Dread of Difference: Gender and the Horror Film.* Austin, Texas:

Texas University Press: 253-276.

Shepherd, John and Peter Wicke. 1997. *Music and Cultural Theory*. Cambridge: Polity Press.

Shklovsky, Viktor. 2001. *Zoo or Letters Not about Love* (Berlin 1923), Chicago, Ill: Dalkey Archive.

Shohat, Zipi. 2003. 'Me Dea Ex is confined to her computer chair' on line at http://medeaex.org/haaretz_eng.html (consulted 8 March 2005).

Siegmund, Gerald. 1996. *Theater und Gedächtnis. Semiotische and psychoanalytische Untersuchungen zur Funktion des Dramas.* (Theatre and Memory. Semiotic and Psychoanalytical Examinations on the Function of Drama.) Tübingen: Narr.

Signorelli, Olga [Resnevic-Signorelli]. 1942. *Eleonora Duse: Leben und Leiden der großen Schauspielerin* (translated by Hanna Kiel). Berlin: Deutscher Verlag.

Silverman, Kenneth. 1991. *Edgar A. Poe: Mournful and Never-ending Remembrance*. New York: Harper Collins Publishers.

Siemons, Mark. 2003. 'Die Chance, sich im Labyrinth zu verlieren. Ein Spiel für fortgeschrittene Internetnutzer: Die Mitsommernachtsparty, hamlet_X – Die Welt ist aus den Fugen' in *Frankfurter Allgemeine Zeitung, Feuilleton*, 21/06/2003.

Smith, Emma. 2000. 'Sir J. and Lady Forbes-Robertson left for America on Saturday: marketing the 1912 "Hamlet" for stage and screen' in Fitzsimmons, Linda and Sarah Street (eds.). *Moving Performance: British Stage and Screen, 1890s-1920s*. Wiltshire: Flick Books: 44-55.

Smith, Paul. 1997. *Seurat and the Avante-Garde*. London: Yale University Press.

Sokolowski, Robert. 2000. *Introduction to Phenomenology*. Cambridge: Cambridge University Press.

Sothern, E.H. 1998 [1916]. 'The "New Art"' in Cardullo, Bert et al. (eds.). *Playing to the Camera: Film Actors Discuss Their Craft*. New Haven: Yale University Press: 28-32.

Spielmann, Yvonne. 1998. *Intermedialität. Das System Peter Greenaway*, München: Wilhelm Fink Verlag.

States, Bert O. 1985. *Great Reckonings in Little Rooms: On the Phenomenology of Theater*. Berkeley, Los Angeles, London: University of California Press.

Stephens, Chuck. 2000. 'Sunrise, Sunset'. Interview with Elias Merhige in *Filmmaker* 9 (1): 58-61, 101-104.

Sternberg, Josef von. 1974. 'Acting in Film and Theatre' in Hurt, James (ed.). *Focus on Film and Theatre*. Englewood Cliffs, N.J: Prentice Hall: 80-98.

Stewart, Garrett. 1999. *Between Film and Screen: Modernism's Photo Synthesis*. Chicago: University of Chicago Press.

Stoker, Bram. 1997. *Dracula: authoritative text, contexts, reviews and reactions, dramatic and film variations, criticism*. Auerbach, Nina and David J. Skal (eds.). New York: W.W. Norton and Company.

Sulcas, Roslyn. 1998. 'Eidos: Telos, Interview with William Forsythe, Paris 1998'. Included in the Ballett Frankfurt - press kit to the production.

Swales, Erika. 1988. *Schiller: Maria Stuart*. London: Grant and Cutler.

Szporer, Philip. 2002. 'Collecting Moments and Dancing on the Philosopher's Stone – Lynda Gaudreau: Encyclopoedia 3' in *Ballettanz* 7: 8-13.

Taranow, Gerda. 1972. *Sarah Bernhardt: The Art within the Legend*. Princeton: Princeton University Press.

Tholen, Georg Christoph. 1995. 'Der Verlust (in) der Wahrnehmung. Zur Topographie des Imaginären' in *Texte. Psychanalyse, Ästhetik, Kulturkritik* 3: 46-75.

Tholen, Georg Christoph. 1999. 'Überschneidungen. Konturen einer Theorie der Medialität' in Schade, Sigrid and Georg Christoph Tholen (eds.). *Konfigurationen. Zwischen Kunst und Medien*. München: Fink: 15-34.

Thomas, Ronald R. 2000. 'Dracula and the Cinematic Afterlife of the Victorian Novel' in J. Kucich, John and Dianne F. Sadoff (eds.). *Victorian Afterlife: Postmodern Culture Rewrites the Nineteenth Century*. Minneapolis: Minnesota University Press.

Tieck, Ludwig. 1974. *Der gestiefelte Kater. Puss-in-Boots* (translated and edited by Gerald Gillespie). Edinburgh: Edinburgh University Press.

Tieck, Ludwig. 1978. *The Land of Upside Down*. London: Associated Universities Presses.

Tretjakoff, Sergej. 1972 *Die Arbeit des Schritstellers. Aufsätze. Reportagen, Portraits* (edited by Heiner Böhncke). Reinbek bei Hamburg: Rowohlt.

Tuffetti, Sergio and Giovanni Spagnoletti. 1994. *Alexander Kluge*. Torino: Museo Nazionale del Cinema/Lindau.

Uricchio, William and Roberta E. Pearson 1993. *Reframing Culture: Vitagraph Quality Films*. Princeton, New Jersey: Princeton University Press.

Valente, Joseph. 2002. *Dracula's Crypt: Bram Stoker, Irishness, and the Question of Blood*. Urbana: Illinois University Press.

Vardac, A. Nicholas. 1987. *Stage to Screen: Theatrical Origins of Early Film: David Garrick to D.W.Griffith* (1949). New York: Da Capo Press.

Vaughn, William, Helmut Börsch-Supan, Hans Joachim Neidhardt. 1972. *Caspar David Friedrich, 1771-1840, Romantic Landscape Painting in Dresden*. London: The Tate Gallery, Catalogue.

Vaughn, William. 1980. *German Romantic Painting*. London: Yale University Press.

Vertov, Dziga. 1973. *Schriften zum Film* (edited by Wolfgang Beilenhoff). München: Hanser.

Vivian, Kim (ed.). 1992. *A Concise History of German Literature to 1900*. Columbia: Camden House.

Vliet, Harry van. 2002. 'Where Television and Internet meet … New experiences for rich media' in *E-view*, 02-1 (online journal: http://comcom.uvt.nl/e-view/02-1/vliet. htm - consulted 29 March 2005).

Wagner, Peter (ed.). 1996. *Icons – Texts – Iconotexts. Essays on Ekphrasis and Intermediality*. Berlin and New York: Walter de Gruyter.

Wagner, Richard. 1850. *Das Kunstwerk der Zukunft*. Leipzig: Otto Wigand.

Waldenfels, Bernhard. 1991. 'Das Rätsel der Sichtbarkeit. Kunstphänomenologische Betrachtungen im Hinblick auf den Status der modernen Malerei' in *Der Stachel des Fremden*. Frankfurt am Main: Suhrkamp: 204-224.

Waldenfels, Bernhard. 1998. *Topographie des Fremden* (Studien zur Phänomenologie des Fremden, Vol. 1), Frankfurt am Main: Suhrkamp.

Waldmann, Werner. 1977. *Das Deutsche Fernsehspiel. Ein systematischer Überblick*. Wiesbaden: Athenaion.

Watt, Ian. 1996. *Myths of Modern Individualism*. Cambridge: Cambridge University Press.

Weaver, William. 1984. *Duse: A Biography*. San Diego: Harcourt Brace Jovanovich.

Weibel, Peter and Timothy Druckery (eds.). 2001. *Net Condition: art and global media.* Cambridge, Mass: MIT Press.

Welsch, Wolfgang (ed.). 1988. *Wege aus der Moderne. Schlüsseltexte der Postmoderne-Diskussion.* Weinheim: VCH.

Wertow, Dsiga. 1967. *Aufsätze, Tagebücher, Skizzen.* Berlin: Filmwissenschaftliche Bibliothek.

Westfall, Suzanne R. 1992. 'Ping Chong Terra In/Cognita: Monsters on Stage' in Geoklin Lim, Shirley, Amy Ling, and Elaine H. Kim (eds.). *Reading the Literatures of Asian America.* Philadelphia: Temple University Press: 359-74.

Whittall, Arnold. 1987. *Romantic Music: A Concise History from Schubert to Sibelius.* London: Thames and Hudson.

Wicke, Jennifer. 1992. 'Vampiric Typewriting: *Dracula* and Its Media' in *English Literary History* 59 (2): 467-493.

Williams, Raymond. 1974. *Television, Technology and Cultural Form.* London: Fontana.

Williams, Raymond. 1975a. *Writing in Society.* Cambridge: Cambridge University Press.

Williams, Raymond. 1975b. *Television. Technology and Cultural Form.* New York: Schocken.

Williamson, John. 1993. *Strauss, Also Sprach Zarathustra.* Cambridge: University Press.

Wirth, Andrzej. 1985. 'Dekonstruktionseffekte auf dem Theater und das Problem der Notation' in Fischer-Lichte, Erika et.al. (eds.). *Das Drama und seine Inszenierung. Vorträge des internationalen literatur- und theatersemiotischen Kolloquiums.* Frankfurt am Main: Gunther Narr.

Wulff, Hans J. 1999. *Elemente der Pragmasemiotik des Films.* Tübingen: Gunther Narr

Wulff, Hans J. 1999. *Darstellen und Mitteilen. Elemente der Pragmasemiotik des Films.* Tübingen: Gunther Narr.

Youens, Susan. 1992. *Schubert, Die Schöne Müllerin.* Cambridge: Cambridge University Press.

Young, William C. (ed.). 1975. *Famous Actors and Actresses of the American Stage: Documents of American Theater History.* Vol. 2. New York and London: R.R. Bowker.

Zielinski, Siegfried. 1999. *Audiovisions. Cinema and Television as Entr'actes in History.* Amsterdam: Amsterdam University Press.

Zima, Peter (ed.). 1995. *Literatur intermedial. Musik, Malerei, Photographie, Film.* Darmstadt: Wissenschaftliche Buchgesellschaft.

Index of key concepts

acoustic 64, 91, 107,117, 118, 120, 148, 162, 163

adaptation 13, 14, 20, 41-53, 122, 167, 169-180, 195, 198, 199, 201, 204, 205, 207, 208, 211, 214, 216, 219, 221, 236

address 11, 14, 36, 58, 70, 80, 116, 122, 137, 143, 144, 146, 149, 152, 163, 233, 235

agency 56, 64, 105, 147, 149

AIDS 197-199, 202

aisthetic act 14, 17, 20, 103-116

alienation 45, 46, 115, 129, 132, 133

all-aboutness of film 71

analogue crisis 41-43, 51

apparatus 41-45, 58, 127, 128, 130, 137, 139, 171, 178

appropriation 5, 14, 41-53, 199, 204, 257

articulation 32, 33

audience 12, 17-19, 22, 23, 27, 30, 34, 36, 41, 43, 45-49, 51, 57-59, 61, 67, 70, 71-75, 77-79, 81-87, 90, 92, 94, 96-99, 101, 121, 128, 133, 134, 138-140, 144-147, 149, 152 154-158, 160, 161, 163-166, 171, 187-189, 202, 205, 207, 210, 212, 213, 215-217, 220, 226, 227, 229, 230, 232, 233, 235

authentic/authenticity 14, 15, 41, 44, 47, 58, 79, 103, 109, 110, 117, 126, 144, 155, 174, 187, 190, 220

authority 22, 79, 81, 146, 147, 214

Ballet Suédois 186

Beat Generation 190

bricolage 141, 201-203

Bühnenkomposition 31, 83

camera 23, 30, 34-36, 41, 44-48, 50, 51, 53, 57, 58, 61, 62, 67, 68, 71-73, 75, 76, 78, 79, 106, 108, 112-114, 144, 145, 147, 149, 150, 169-171, 174, 186, 188-190, 200, 201, 229

capitalism 19, 149, 172, 201, 204

choreography in the society of the spectacle 155, 166

cinematic 24, 27, 41, 42, 44-50, 83, 92-93, 97, 101, 104, 107, 167, 173, 174, 188, 195, 214

class 22, 87, 88, 116, 146, 197

close-up 36, 48, 61, 67, 68, 71, 73, 143

colonialism 196

comics 196, 225, 228

commodification 43, 152, 155

computer-generated 19, 41, 51-53

concentration 36, 119, 178

connectivity 138, 224

constructive thinking 172

constructivism 193

consumption 34, 65, 107,144, 161, 173, 197

contemporary dance performance 17, 151-166

corporeal intermediality 153-156

corporeal presence 126-127

corporeality 14, 37, 46, 127, 131, 153, 159, 235

cubism 186

cultivation of humanity 82-83

curriculum 83, 89

dance 17, 18, 24, 29-31, 33, 43, 60, 83, 85, 89, 90, 101, 151-166, 214, 221, 224, 232, 233

death scene 48, 49, 51

deconstruction 35, 116, 169, 177, 230, 231

delusion 217, 228

democracy 115

demonstration 44, 78, 226

device paradigm 29, 33, 34, 38

dialectic theory of film 172

digital crisis 41, 52

digital opera 14, 81-100

discourse 13, 20, 22, 41, 43, 82, 104-106, 109, 113, 117, 125, 126, 128, 136, 138, 139, 146, 155, 169, 172, 176, 177, 179, 196, 230

discrimination 198

documentary 109, 145, 147, 149, 196, 200, 201, 205

doubling 59, 136, 197

dramatic 123, 128, 133, 139-142, 153, 162, 169, 172, 174, 176, 188, 189, 225, 231

dramaturgy 30, 36, 72, 161, 223, 225, 227, 230, 234

education 14, 25, 81-100, 140

electronic 71, 104, 107, 112, 115, 151, 152, 175-178, 215, 223, 225, 226-228, 230, 232, 235

epic 29, 37, 43, 76, 78, 80, 83, 87, 88, 91, 93, 96, 97, 171, 172, 192, 193, 197,

epistemological euphoria 182

expressive immobility 48

extension of man 96, 106

filmic analogy 174, 175

flesh 59, 60, 86, 126-128, 131, 133, 135, 154, 155, 204, 208, 231

formalists/formalistic 224

frame 130, 134, 137, 139, 141, 142, 145, 148, 157-159, 176, 188, 195, 197, 200, 203, 205, 209, 229

framing 57, 60, 71, 77, 80, 95, 96, 131, 195, 204, 216

gender 22, 146

generative grammar 174

genotype 174

Gesamtkunstwerk 30, 31, 70, 83, 127, 151, 181

gesticulation 32, 33

gesture 32, 43-45, 49, 50, 59, 61, 97, 129, 135, 163, 185, 233, 235

Gutenberg Galaxy 107

hidden emotion 51

hierarchy 70, 80, 81, 109, 110, 156, 204, 208

histrionic codes 42

hyperfiction 91, 97, 99

hyperlinks 18, 97, 207-209, 213-216, 219, 221

hypermediacy 14, 22, 38, 49, 55-57, 59, 61-65, 84, 85, 90, 91, 95, 96, 99, 137, 138, 140-145, 178, 195, 220

hypermediality 11, 55, 56, 167

hypermedium 19, 20, 24, 29, 32, 37, 39, 127, 223, 235

hyperreality 38

hypertext 141, 178, 210, 221, 224, 231, 233

iconography 145, 195

identification 34, 116, 153, 159, 196, 198

illusion 83, 92, 130, 139, 144, 171, 176, 178, 179, 188, 189, 211, 217,

illusionism 195

illustration 186

imagination 11, 29, 35, 36, 46, 67, 77, 81, 82, 90, 91, 93, 95-98, 111, 134-135, 165,

immediacy 84, 85, 95, 129, 137, 138, 140-142, 144, 145, 147, 173, 178, 179, 188, 195, 205

immersion 30, 34, 37, 38, 133, 139

immersive 42, 139, 158, 207

imperialism 198, 201, 203

in-between realities 11, 12, 24, 85, 93

inner kothurn 175

intention of the author 175

interactive theatre 207

interactivity/inter-activity 19, 20, 109, 116, 138, 139, 146, 147, 150, 167, 178, 220, 224, 227

inter-corporeality 131

interculturalism 89

inter-subjectivity 128

intertextuality 11, 13, 83, 91, 99, 116, 204, 209

intertitles 50, 76, 188, 189, 191, 203

laokoon project 172

Lied(er) 88, 94, 98

linear/linearity 21, 23, 36, 75, 97-99, 107, 108, 115, 153, 165, 167, 184, 190, 191, 207-209, 214, 216, 219, 220, 223, 226, 227, 230, 231, 235

literature 13-15, 29, 32, 33, 42, 81-83, 89, 90, 92, 97, 115, 117, 161, 174, 181, 182, 190, 193, 199, 205

live performance 37, 52, 64, 67, 71, 78-81, 86, 103, 112, 116, 125-127,

liveness 15, 33, 42, 52, 64, 78, 79, 104, 139, 147

look/gaze 131

lyric(al) 29, 31, 37, 49, 67, 72, 73, 78, 80, 81, 83, 84, 91, 95, 191

magic 96, 110, 115, 169, 197

mask 197, 198, 204, 223, 229, 230

materialism 197, 218

materiality 16, 22, 37, 59, 64, 71, 113, 125, 128, 131, 132, 135, 136, 153, 188, 224, 235

mechanical reproduction 105, 108, 112

media consciousness 188, 190

media studies 13, 103, 104-106, 113

medial boundaries 82, 83, 87, 216-218
medial perception 126
medial specificity 103, 106
mediation 17, 35, 38, 55, 60, 63, 65, 84, 86, 106, 108, 110, 113-115, 151-166, 178,
mediatization 16, 17, 42, 52, 79, 104, 110, 112, 117-124, 127
memory/memories 35, 52, 67-70, 72, 74, 77, 78, 80, 151, 177, 226, 231
mesmerism 197
mise en scène 14, 22, 39, 42, 55-66, 81, 125, 135
modern dance 155-156
modularity 18, 20, 207-221
modulation 32, 33
monologue 76, 77, 133, 164, 197
multimedia(l) 19, 27, 69, 82, 87, 97, 115, 116, 139, 217, 221, 223-225, 234, 235
multiplication 77, 80, 115
narrator 62, 67-70, 77, 78, 92, 200
negative space 67
neologism 207, 208, 227
net art 137, 224, 225, 235
normative implications 172
numerical (representation) 17, 18, 112
object body 125-127, 129, 131
observer 109-115, 151-158, 161-166, 171, 173
ontology 13, 18-20, 77, 94, 126, 128
painting 14, 30, 52, 89, 91, 106, 107, 109, 178, 179, 181, 182-184, 204, 214, 215
Parole in Libertà 183
past 38, 49, 62, 72, 78, 104, 107, 112, 122, 147, 149, 171, 177, 210
perception 129, 132, 134, 136, 139, 144, 157, 171, 176, 182, 188, 190, 208, 217, 221, 235
performance art 14, 205, 224
performance space 11, 22, 37, 71, 159
performance theory 14, 15, 17, 22, 169, 177
performativity 12, 104, 144, 148, 190
perspective 11, 14, 20, 34, 36, 59, 61, 62, 64, 67, 69-72, 77, 80, 84, 90, 92, 94, 99, 101, 103, 105, 108, 111, 114, 115, 127, 130, 131, 149, 152, 157, 158, 163, 165, 169, 171, 174, 175, 177, 178, 181, 195, 199, 208, 215, 219, 231
phenomenology 64, 66, 125, 128-131

phenotype 174
photography 105, 106, 132, 173, 178, 179, 197, 201
pictorial reflection 171
pleasure 14, 55, 56, 64, 65, 86, 141, 145, 146, 162, 190, 203
pluri-focal networks 115
point of view 70, 73, 80, 147, 157, 170, 179
post-dramatic theatre 19, 21, 22, 80, 112, 231
postmodern dance 155, 156
postmodern discourse 126
post-structuralist 22, 147, 149
present 17, 20, 23, 33-35, 52, 56, 59, 62, 64, 65, 67, 68, 71-73, 75, 78-80, 89, 97, 107, 114, 125-127, 130, 132, 138, 139, 154, 155,159, 161, 171, 177, 179, 181, 183, 189, 191, 207, 210, 216, 226, 233, 235
presentation 45, 55, 59, 65, 75, 84, 91, 96, 98, 99, 110, 111, 114, 115, 137, 138, 142, 143, 153, 156, 161, 182, 201, 219
projection 37, 46, 57-60, 62, 64, 67, 68, 73, 74, 76-79, 92-94, 96, 108, 112, 153, 154, 157, 201, 202, 207
psychoanalysis 129, 184, 200, 203
puppet/puppetry 22, 97, 98, 101, 125-136, 202, 230, 236
race 22, 58
realism 42, 69, 176, 178, 179, 195, 204
reception theory 169, 175
reflexivity 11, 37, 80, 199
reincarnation 198
remediation 14, 15, 41-53, 55, 63, 100, 104, 106-109, 113, 137, 138, 140, 144, 145, 155, 169, 177-179, 204, 209, 217, 220
remembering 67-70, 72, 74, 78, 80
repetition 35, 42, 51, 74, 77
representation 11, 13, 14, 17-19, 22, 30, 31, 35-38, 41, 42, 45, 51, 55, 65, 67-80, 81, 83-85, 90, 94, 108, 109, 114-116, 125, 127, 134, 137, 138, 143, 151-153, 155-158, 176, 179, 216, 217, 236
repression 214
resistance 15, 43, 44, 52, 115, 133, 147, 149, 234, 235
rhetoric 196, 224

rhizome 19, 100, 226, 229, 231, 234
role-playing 139, 198
romanticism 81, 82, 84, 91, 94, 196, 197, 201
Russian Formalists 80, 172, 190
screen 17, 22, 44, 46, 47, 51, 52, 56-63, 65, 67-69, 72-75, 79, 91-94, 96-98, 103, 112, 114, 115, 137-150, 158, 160, 169, 170, 178, 189, 190, 192, 193, 196, 202, 211, 228, 229
selection 36, 120, 145, 159, 210, 213
self-referential(ity) 176, 197, 199
semiotic fundamentalism 39, 182, 190
senses 64, 65, 70, 80, 83, 84, 105-107, 118, 120, 142
silent cinema 14, 91, 95, 169
simulacrum 16, 44, 147
simulation 139
simultaneity 35, 55, 56, 64, 67, 72
sonic intermediality 152, 161, 162, 165
spatial intermediality 156-158, 160
spectacularity 201
spell of personality 45
spirit photography 197
stardom 46, 47
structuralist 203
surveillance 47, 48, 144, 147, 149
synthesis 29, 55, 61, 63, 219
synthespian 52
technology 21, 23, 25, 29, 33-35, 37, 38, 55, 67, 82, 88, 89, 97, 100, 104-108, 110-113, 116, 117, 119, 120, 125, 127, 130, 139, 142, 143, 146, 149, 150, 152, 156, 159, 161, 163, 176, 178, 179, 181, 182, 190, 195, 200, 201, 207, 218
testing ground 41, 45, 47
text-image 76
textual practice 162
the invisible / the other 129
the real 63, 65, 85, 106, 109, 122, 130, 137, 142, 147, 170
theatre as medium 217
theatre/theatrical performance 18, 22, 23, 29, 31, 32, 35, 36, 42, 43, 77, 94, 104, 112-115, 126, 135, 167, 207, 216, 225, 234-236
theatricalisation 32, 233

theatricality 41, 47, 50, 65, 103, 104, 113, 195, 225, 230
time-image 80
Totalkunstwerk 30, 83
train travel 196
transcoding 17, 18, 112, 114, 151, 152, 160, 161, 163, 164
translation theory 174
transparency/transparent 14, 34, 35, 37, 38, 41, 49, 76, 84, 92, 112, 114, 115, 130, 137, 153, 158, 159, 177, 178, 195
vampirism 198, 200, 203
variability 17, 18
Verfremdung 39, 82, 88
virtual/virtuality 14, 18, 34, 37, 52, 55, 56, 60, 61, 64, 65, 104, 109, 111, 115, 117, 121, 122, 139, 142, 143, 145, 146, 148, 176, 178, 179, 207-221, 223-236
walkman 117-124

Index of key names

Adorno, Theodor W. 38
Anderson, Laurie 223, 234, 236
Aronson, Arnold 207, 221
Auslander, Philip 15-17, 42, 78, 79, 104, 112, 138, 139, 149, 159, 166, 202
Baez, Joan 191
Balázs, Béla 35, 36, 43, 80, 171, 172
Balcombe, Florence 204
Balderston, John L. 197, 199
Balla, Giacomo 185, 193
Barthes, Roland 65, 110, 161, 181
Baudelaire, Charles 105, 191
Baudrillard, Jean 16, 38, 147, 176
Bazin, André 44, 173, 174, 179
Bel, Jérôme 153, 162, 163
Benjamin, Walter 41-47, 53, 103-112, 145, 173, 178, 179,183, 191
Bergson, Henri 80
Bernhardt, Sarah 41-43, 47-51, 169
Bogatyrev, Pjotr 37
Bolter, Jay David 14, 15, 35-42, 55, 56, 63, 65, 84, 85, 103, 106-109, 137-145, 169, 176-179, 217, 220
Borgmann, Albert 33, 34
Bowie, David 197
Brecht, Bertolt 36, 81-88, 99, 104, 172, 180, 187, 188, 190-192, 230
Brook, Peter 35, 103, 173, 231
Browning, Tod 197, 199
Builders Association, The 55, 57, 66
Cage, Nicolas 196, 198
Cassiers, Guy 19, 23, 67-80
Castorf, Frank 231, 232
Certeau, Michel de 118
Chong, Ping 195, 201-204
Coleridge, Samuel Taylor 199
Cooper, Merian C. 200, 201, 205
Coppola, Francis Ford 195, 196, 198-201, 205
Crary, Jonathan 103, 108, 109, 113
Creed, Barbara 52
Crommelynck, Ferdinand 186
Cunningham, Merce 151, 156-158, 162, 163
Curtis, Dan 199

Dafoe, Willem 166, 196-198
Dassin, Jules 214-216
Deane, Hamilton 196, 199
Deleuze, Gilles 19, 80, 100, 189, 193, 219
Deneuve, Catherine 197
Derrida, Jacques 116, 131, 147, 177
Diller + Scofidio 66
Duse, Eleonora 41-43, 47, 49-51
Dylan, Bob 190, 191
Eco, Umberto 22, 37, 38, 174, 176
Euripides 208, 210, 213-215
Fabre, Jan 35
Fleischer, Zipi 214, 215
Forsythe, William 151, 158-162, 165, 166
Foucault, Michel 90, 100, 106, 109, 148
Freud, Sigmund 193, 204
Friedrich, David Caspar 91, 196
Gaudreau, Lynda 151, 163, 164
Giannachi, Gabriella 56, 104, 209, 219, 221, 225
Ginsberg, Allen 190
Glover, Crispin 196
Goethe, Johann Wolfgang von 90, 92
Grau, Albin 197
Greco, Emio 89, 153
Gris, Juan 183
Grusin, Richard 14, 15, 35-42, 55, 56, 63, 65, 84, 85, 103, 106-109, 137-145, 169, 176-179, 217, 220
Hamann, Sigune 92
Haring, Chris 55, 58-60
Hegel, Georg 29, 30, 32
Hölderlin, Friedrich 193
Hopkins, Tim 82, 88, 90, 93, 95, 97, 98
Hosokawa, Shuhei 117-119, 123
Irving, Henry 198
Jakobson, Roman 181, 182
Jefferson III, Joseph 43
Jelinek, Elfriede 193
Jones, Dan 199
Jones, Ernest 202
Kandinsky, Wassily 29-31, 83, 84
Kant, Immanuel 29, 32
Kattenbelt, Chiel 72, 80, 84, 100, 142, 143
Katz, Steven 195, 196, 198, 200-202, 204
Kerckhove, Derrick de 104, 110, 111, 113

Khlebnikov, Velimir 184, 193
Kittler, Friedrich 86, 100, 106, 108, 200, 201
Kluge, Alexander 181, 191, 193
Kosintzev, Grigori 173
Kruchonykh, Alexei 184, 193
Lacan, Jacques 129
Lang, Fritz 91, 202
Lauwers, Jan 117, 120
Le Roy, Xavier 151, 153-156, 163
Lepecki, André 152, 154
Levine, Jeff 196
Lévi-Strauss, Claude 203
Lugosi, Bela 196, 197
Lukács, Georg 80, 170-172, 180
Lumière, Auguste 199
Lumière, Louis 199
Lyotard, Jean François 148
Malevich, Kazimir 181, 190
Malkovich, John 196, 197
Manovich, Lev 17-19, 25, 92, 97, 103, 107, 112, 116, 208, 209, 213, 221
Mari, Febo 50, 51
Markham, Pigmeat 198
Mayer, David 42, 43
McBurney, Simon 60
McKenzie, Jon 104, 148, 149, 159, 223, 225, 234, 236
McLuhan, Marshall 96, 103-107, 110, 113, 119, 179, 217
Merhige, Elias 195-205
Merleau-Ponty, Maurice 65, 66, 128-131
Metz, Christian 13, 39
Meyerhold, Vsevolod 83, 172, 186, 187
Michelson, Annette 182
Mukarovsky, Jan 29-32, 172, 175
Müller, Heiner 125, 132-136, 231
Münsterberg, Hugo 13, 43, 170-172
Murnau, Friedrich Wilhelm 195-204
Murphy, Gerald 186
Murray, Janet 34, 35
Muynck, Viviane de 117, 120
Needcompany 117, 120
Neora (.com) 208
Nussbaum, Martha C. 81, 82, 89, 100
Oakes, Meredith 90

Obermaier, Klaus 55, 58, 59
O'Brien, Willis 201
Oldman, Gary 196
Opera North 81, 82, 88-90, 100
Panofsky, Erwin 35
Pasolini, Pier Paolo 193, 214, 215
Pavis, Patrice 63, 116
Pearson, Roberta 42
Periférico de Objetos, El 125, 126, 128
Pirandello, Luigi 46
Piscator, Erwin 83, 104, 172, 187, 232
Platel, Alain 35
Ploebst, Helmut 155, 163, 166
Poe, Edgar Allan 204
Popova, Lyobov 186, 187, 193
Porter, Cole 186
Porter, Edwin 43
Proust, Marcel 67-80, 192
Reagan, Ronald 197
Reinhardt, Max 83, 196
Rijnders, Gerardjan 35
Rodchenko, Aleksandr 188, 189, 193
Ryder, Winona 198
Sarandon, Susan 197
Schechner, Richard 148
Schoedsack, Ernest B. 200, 201 ,205
Scholten, Pieter C. 89
Schopenhauer, Arthur 29, 30
Schreck, Max 195-198, 200, 201, 203
Schroeder, Greta 195, 197, 204
Schubert, Franz 88, 89, 92, 94
Scott, Tony 197, 202
Shakespeare, William 82, 126, 169, 173, 174, 204, 223-225, 228, 229, 231, 236
Shklovsky, Viktor 182
Sloane, Steven 82, 88, 90
Sothern, Edward Hugh 45, 46
Stanislavsky, Konstantin 195
Sternberg, Josef von 44-46
Stevenson, Robert Louis 196
Stoker, Bram 195-204
Tepes, Vlad 198, 199
Tholen, Georg Christoph 129-131
Tretjakof, Sergei 172, 180
Vardac, A. Nicholas 15, 42, 169, 197
Vertov, Dziga 172, 188-190, 193

Virilio, Paul 130
Wagner, Richard 30, 31, 83, 88, 91, 94, 195, 199
Waldenfels, Bernhard 132, 136
Weill, Kurt 81-84, 87, 88
Wilder, Thornton 198
Wilson, Robert 35, 104, 177, 231
Wooster Group, The 104, 159, 166, 196, 198
Zich, Otakar 31
Zielinski, Siegfried 108

Index of key titles

24 142-144
2001 - A Space Odyssey 176
A la recherche du temps perdu 67, 80
ALIE/NA(C)TION 159, 160
Ally McBeal 140-142
Also Sprach Zarathustra 91
Anaphase 151
Antichrist Superstar 197
Apocalypse 1:11 122
Big Brother 144, 145, 147
Black Square 181
Bohème 84
Bram Stoker's Dracula 195, 196, 198, 199
Broadcast News 138
Cave of the Heart 214
Cenere 49, 50
Citizen Kane 176
Cook, the Thief, His Wife and her Lover, The 176
Count of Monte Cristo, The 43
Crow, The 52
Crypt Orchid 197
D.A.V.E 58-60, 64
Death of Siegfried, The 91
Decreation 161, 162, 166
Der Januskopf 196
Document 3 163, 164
Dr. Jekyll and Mr. Hide 196
Dracula 195, 197-202
Draughtsman's Contract, The 176
Dream of Passion, A 214, 215
Dreigroschenoper, Die 188
Drums in the Night 188
Elephant Vanishes, The 60, 61
Erlkönig, Der 91, 92
Extra Ear 56
Falstaff 82
Fame Academy 144, 147
Fear and Loathing in Gotham 202
Fidelio 87, 91-95
Flucht 94
Flying Dutchman 199
Forest Murmurs: adventures in the German Romantic imagination, The 81, 82, 88, 90-96, 98-100

Four Quartets, The 120
German Requiem, A 88
Golden Windows 177
Great Reckonings in Little Rooms 64
Hamlet 126, 165, 169, 223-231, 236
hamlet_X 223-236
Hamletmaschine 231, 236
Hans Heiling 97
Hansel und Gretel 88
Happiest Day of My Life 151
Heartbeat 141
Home of the Brave 234
Hunger, The 195, 197, 202
Jet Lag: "Part One: Roger Dearborn" 57
Kammer/Kammer 166
Kanal Kirchner 117, 121-123
Kindertotenlieder 98
King Kong 195, 200, 201, 205
Kinopravda 189
Knaben Wunderhorn, Des 96
L.S.D. 166
La Double Inconstance 175
Le Cocu Magnifique 186
Les amours de la Reine Elisabeth 47, 48
Lieder: the Black, Black Earth 88
Lost Highway 176
Macbeth 82
Machina Typografica 185
Mailied 94
Making of Big Brother, The 150
Man with the Movie Camera 189, 190
Máquina Hamlet 125, 126, 132, 134, 135
Mary Reilly 196
Medea 208-216, 218
Medea about to kill her children 214, 215
Medea Furieuse 214
Me-Dea-Ex 207-209, 211, 213-218, 220, 221, 228, 229
Miami Vice 141, 149
Modern Medea 215, 216
Mother and Child in the Woods at Night Fall 91
Mystery Train 176
Needles and Opium 62
News & Stories 193
Nosferatu: A Symphony of Darkness 195, 201

Orestia 175, 177
Orfeo ed Euridice 89, 90
Othello 82
Prosperos's Books 176
Proust 1: Swann's way 67, 68, 73-76, 80
Proust 2: Albertine's Way 80
Proust 3: Charlus's Way 80
Proust 4: Proust's Way 80
Puppet Motel 236
Puss in Boots 91
Rambo 176
Rip van Winkle 43
Rise and Fall of the City of Mahagonny, The 81-85, 88
Rosenkavalier 84, 86
Route 1 & 9 195
Russian Ark 177
Scenes from Faust 95
Self Unfinished 153-155
Serpentia 197
Sex and the City 150
Shadow of the Vampire 13, 195, 197-201, 203-205
Shakespeare's Memory 177
Sky Captain and the World of Tomorrow 52
Sopranos, The 141
Sound of Time, The 117, 120, 122
Spider-Man 196
Split Sides 157
Subterranean Homesick Blues 191
Taboo 199
Tamboursg'sell, Der 96
Tatort 229
Teachers 141
Terminator 176
The Earth in Turmoil 187
Trial and Retribution 150
Tristan und Isolde 91
Troilus and Cressida 177
Trommeln in der Nacht 188
Upside Down 163
Winterreise 89
Within the Quota 186
World of Wonder 150
Wozzeck 91
X-Files, The 122, 147

NOTES ON THE CONTRIBUTORS

Christopher B. Balme
Christopher Balme is professor of Theatre Studies at the University of Amsterdam (The Netherlands). He is immediate past-president of the German Society for Theatre Research, a member of the executive committee of the International Federation for Theatre Research and editor of Theatre Research International. He has published widely on German theatre, intercultural theatre and theatre iconography. His most recent publications are: *Decolonizing the Stage: Theatrical Syncretism and Postcolonial Drama* (Oxford: Clarendon Press, 1999) and *Einführung in die Theaterwissenschaft* (Berlin: Erich Schmidt, 2003, 3rd edition). He is co-editor with Markus Moninger of *Crossing Media: Theater-Film-Fotografi* (München: epodium Verlag, 2003).

Peter M. Boenisch
Peter M. Boenisch is lecturer in Drama and Theatre Studies at the University of Kent at Canterbury (England). His principle research interests, on which he has published a number of essays, are dance and bodies on the stage, post-and early-modern theories of theatrical performance, and theatre in the 17th century. He is the author of *körPERformance 1.0* (München: epodium Verlag, 2002) and co-editor of *Theater ohne Grenzen* (München: Herbert Utz Verlag, 2003) and *Performance Research 8.2: Bodiescapes* (London: Taylor & Francis, 2003). He is book review editor for the journal *Theatre Research International* (Cambridge University Press).

Johan Callens
Johan Callens is professor of English, specializing in Theater Studies, at the Vrije Universiteit Brussel (Belgium). He is associate editor of *Documenta* and *The European Journal of American Culture* and former president of the Belgian Luxembourg American Studies Association and the Belgian Association of Anglicists in Higher Education, and former International Secretary of The American Theatre and Drama Society. He has published articles and reviews in national and international journals. He is the author of *Double Binds: Existentialist Inspiration and Generic Experimentation in the Early Work of Jack Richardson* (Amsterdam: Rodopi, 1993) *Acte(s) de Présence* (Brussel: VUB Press, 1996), and *From Middleton and Rowley's "Changeling" to Sam Shepard's "Bodyguard": A Contemporary Appropriation of a Renaissance Drama* (Lewiston, New York: Edwin Mellen, 1997). More recently, he has edited special issues of *Contemporary Theatre Review* on Sam Shepard (1998, 2 volumes) and of *Degrés* on intermediality (2000) besides a collection of essays, *The Wooster Group and Its Traditions* (Brussel & Bern: Presses Interuniversitaires Européennes - Peter Lang, 2004).

Freda Chapple

Freda Chapple trained as an actor and worked with Welsh National Opera, English National Opera, Australian Opera and Scottish Opera as a performer, stage manager and director. She is a lecturer at the University of Sheffield (England). She is the programme director of the English Studies and Performing Arts programme at the Institute for Lifelong Learning. She performs in and directs opera. Recent productions include: *Cavalleria Rusticana* and *Trial by Jury* (2004), *Façade* (2003); *The Rise and Fall of the City of Mahagonny* (2000), and *La Traviata* (2000). Recent publications: *Reading Digital technologies; the arts and Lifelong Learning* (SCUTREA, 2003), *Speaking out Loud: Narrative structures, Academic Literacy and Regenerative Influences* (SCUTREA, 2004) She is the holder of a Society for Theatre Research (UK) award, assessing the impact of digital technology on British Theatre practice and actor education.

Klemens Gruber

Klemens Gruber is professor at the Institute for Theatre, Film, and Media Studies at the University of Vienna (Austria). He is co-editor of *Maske und Kothurn. Internationale Beiträge zur Theater-, Film- und Medienwissenschaft*, author of *Die zerstreute Avantgarde* (Vienna: Boehlau, 1989) and editor of *daedalus-daedalus: Die Erfindung der Gegenwart* (Frankfurt: Stroemfeld / Roter Stern, 1990) and two special volumes of *Maske und Kothurn* on *Dziga Vertov zum 100. Geburtstag* (Vienna: Boehlau, 1996/2004). His book *2 oder 3 Dinge, die Sie von der historischen Avantgarde wissen sollten* is forthcoming.

Chiel Kattenbelt

Chiel Kattenbelt is associate professor in Media Comparison and Intermediality at Utrecht University (The Netherlands) where he teaches on the programmes of Theatre, Film and Television Studies, Communication and Information Studies, and New Media and Digital Culture. He is also associate professor at the Theatre Academy Maastricht (The Netherlands), where he is head of an interdisciplinary research programme on new theatricality, with respect to the public sphere, language and technology. He has published articles in several books and international journals on aesthetics, semiotics, theatre and media theory and intermediality.

264

Thomas Kuchenbuch

Thomas Kuchenbuch is professor of Media History and Theory at the Hochschule der Medien Stuttgart (Germany). He is the author of *Filmanalyse -Theorien, Modelle, Kritik*. Köln: Prometh, 1978), *Die Welt um 1900. Unterhaltungs- und Technikkultur* (Stuttgart: Metzler, 1992) and *Bild und Erzählung: Geschichten in Bildern. Vom frühen Comic Strip zum Fernsehfeature* (Münster: Maks, 1992). He has published many articles and reviews in national and international journals.

Andy Lavender

Andy Lavender is Head of Postgraduate Studies at the Central School of Speech and Drama, London (England). He is the artistic director of the theatre/performance company Lightwork, and has directed a number of devised and mixed media (theatre/video) performances. Publications include *Hamlet in Pieces: Shakespeare Reworked: Peter Brook, Robert Lepage, Robert Wilson* (London: Nick Hern Books, 2001) and articles on new theatre and performance in *Contemporary Theatre Review* (Vol. 13 (2), 2003), in Delgado, Maria & Caridad Svich (eds.), *Theatre in Crisis?: Performance Manifestos for a New Century* (Manchester: Manchester University Press, 2002) and in Gottlieb, Vera & Colin Chambers (eds.), *Theatre in a Cool Climate* (Charlbury: Amber Lane Press, 1999).

Sigrid Merx

Sigrid Merx is junior assistant professor in Theatre and Media studies at Utrecht University (The Netherlands). She is working on a PhD on Theatre and technology, specifically focussing on the influence of the use of video technology on the representation of time. She is also participating as in the research programme New Theatricality of the Theatre Academy Maastricht (The Netherlands). As a dramaturg and a playwright, she is active in theatre practice and teaching practical courses on Dramaturgy and Writing for theatre.

Robin Nelson

Robin Nelson is Professor of Theatre and TV Drama at Manchester Metropolitan University (England). His books on television are *Boys from the Blackstuff: the Making of TV Drama* (London: Comedia/Routledge, 1986) and *TV Drama in Transition* (London: Macmillan, 1997) and his essays are published widely in edited collections. He has published on media and contemporary performance topics in international journals such as *Performance Research*, *Modern Drama*, *Studies in Theatre & Performance* and *Media, Culture and Society*.

Ralf Remshardt

Ralf Remshardt is associate professor of Theatre History and Dramaturgy at the University of Florida (United States of America), where he is also resident dramaturg. His articles cover subjects as diverse as Eugene O'Neill, medieval carnival, contemporary American history plays, Nineteenth century melodrama, and modern productions of Greek plays. His publications in both English and German have appeared in *Comparative Drama*, *Theatre Survey*, *Theatre Journal*, *Essays in Theatre*, *Theater der Zeit*, *Western European Stages*, *Victorian Studies* and other journals, as well as in several edited collections. He is author of *Staging the Savage God: The Grotesque in Performance* (Carbondale: Southern Illinois University Press, 2004).

Hadassa Shani

Hadassa Shani is Faculty member of the Faculty of Arts at Tel-Aviv University (Israel). She specializes in the field of comparative studies of Theatre and Film, Theatre and the New Media, with special interest in modern adaptations of Ancient Greek Tragedies. Recent publications include: 'Ancient Greek Tragedy On Film: A Dream of Passion; A "Reference Book" of Adaptations from Stage to Screen' in Patsalidis, Savas. & Elizabeth Sakellaridou, *(Dis)placing Classical Greek Theater* (Thessaloniki: University Studio Press, 1999), 'The Use and Effect of a Theatrical Technique in a Different Domain of Meaning; the Soliloquy' in *Semiotica* (Berlin & New York: de Gruyter, 2001), 'Actual-fictive-virtual space: theatre interactivity within a Liquid architecture' (Nagoya: 2002), 'Observing the Act of Contemplation: Fantasy on Levin's Frame' (Hebrew) (Tel Aviv: 2003). Her book *Greek Tragedy goes to the Movies: a Media Perspective* is forthcoming (Hakibbutz Hameuchad, 2006). She is head of the Board of Directors, Bat-Sheva Dance Company, and a professional film editor.

Meike Wagner

Meike Wagner is coordinator of the international PhD programme 'Performance and Media Studies' at Mainz University (Germany). Her research interests are theatre and media, contemporary puppetry, the staging of the body, visuality and the spectator. Recent publications include: Christopher B. Balme & Meike Wagner (eds.), *Beyond Aesthetics. Performance, Media, and Cultural Studies* (Trier: Wissenschaftlicher Verlag, 2004), *Nähte am Puppenkörper. Der mediale Blick und die Körperentwürfe des Theaters.* (Bielefeld: transcript Verlag, 2003), "Muster auf Grund. Das Ornament als Strukturformel einer Medialität des Figurentheaterkörpers" in Balme, Christopher, Erika Fischer-Lichte & Stephan Grätzel (eds.), *Theater als Paradigma der Moderne? Positionen zwischen historischer Avantgarde und Medienzeitalter* (Tübingen and Basel: Francke Verlag, 2003).

Birgit Wiens

Birgit Wiens is professor for Theatre Studies at the Hochschule für Bildende Künste Dresden (Germany). She worked as a dramaturge, and as a curator and conference organizer for ZKM | center for art and media Karlsruhe (*Ghost Dances*, 2000/01; *Future Theatre*, 2003; *Mind the Gap. Between Theatre and Virtual Space: Research for new kinds of Scenography*, 2004). She is the author of *'Grammatik' der Schauspielkunst. Die Inszenierung der Geschlechter in Goethes klassischem Theater* (Tübingen: Niemeyer Verlag, 2000) and co-editor with Claudia Öhlschläger of *Körper-Gedächtnis-Schrift: Der Körper als Medium kultureller Erinnerung* (Berlin: Erich Schmidt Verlag, 1997). Her main fields of research are scenography and stage design in contemporary theatre, intermediality, the anthropology and dramaturgy of the image, and contemporary drama and dramaturgy.

several hours following the directions Haglund had given Wisting during their interview. It was too cramped to hold them all. The men in white suits left to make room for Wisting and Frank Robekk.

Where the fireplace had been, a pit had been dug. Gradually, the remains of the young woman buried there had been unearthed: brittle knuckle-bones, a cracked skull. Fragments of fabric and remnants of a shoe had been placed in a plastic bowl.

'How long . . .?' Robekk asked, clearing his throat. 'How long did he hold her prisoner?'

'Seven days,' Wisting said.

The muscles in Frank Robekk's face contracted. He picked the remains of what looked like a belt buckle out of the plastic bowl.

'He used a pillow,' Wisting explained quietly.

'It would have been better if he had thrown her into a ditch,' Robekk said, brushing earth from the buckle belonging to the young girl whose uncle he had been. 'Like Cecilia. Then we would at least have known where she was.'

'That was different for him,' Wisting said, using Haglund's own words. 'Letting us find Cecilia was a diversion to stop us looking for the hiding place.'

He stepped outside, giving Robekk time on his own. An unmarked police vehicle parked beside his own car at the farmhouse and Christine Thiis and Nils Hammer trudged down the grassy slope, Hammer carrying a folded newspaper. Wisting could see part of the front page where Audun Vetti's face was splashed.

'The investigators from the Bureau for the Investigation of Police Affairs picked him up for interview this morning,' Christine Thiis said. 'The public prosecutor has charged him.'

Hammer walked towards the crime scene technicians. Christine Thiis put her hand into her coat pocket. 'You should have this back,' she said.

He accepted his badge, turning it over in his hand, noticing how worn it was at the edges, how it had come unglued at one corner. For four days, he had not been a police officer. He had not only lacked his accustomed authority, he had also been accused of breaking the law. He had always thought what made him a good detective was his ability to see more than one side of a case. This was the first time he had actually been there. On the other side.

He ran his thumb over his picture, feeling the scratches on the little plastic cover. The photograph was old. He had looked better then. His hair had been thicker and darker, and his cheeks fuller, but he was a better policeman now. His hand closed tightly round it.